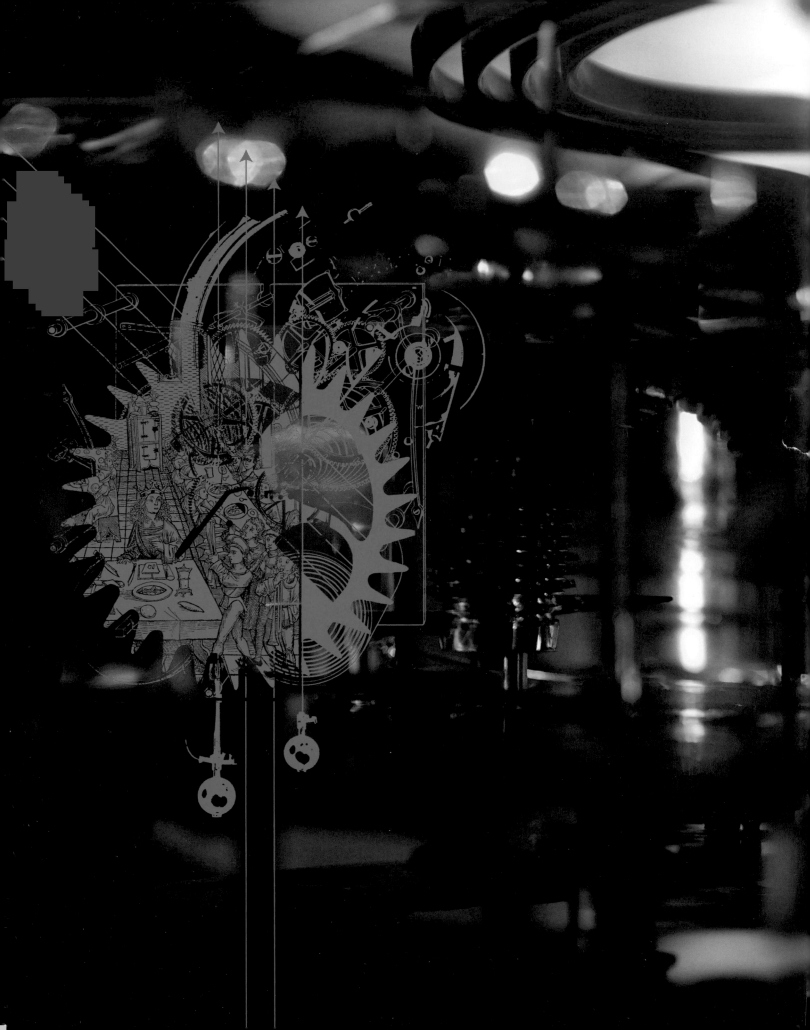

HISTORIC HESTON
BLUMENTHAL

ART BY DAVE McKEAN
PHOTOGRAPHY BY ROMAS FOORD

BLOOMSBURY

LONDON · NEW DELHI · NEW YORK · SYDNEY

CONTENTS

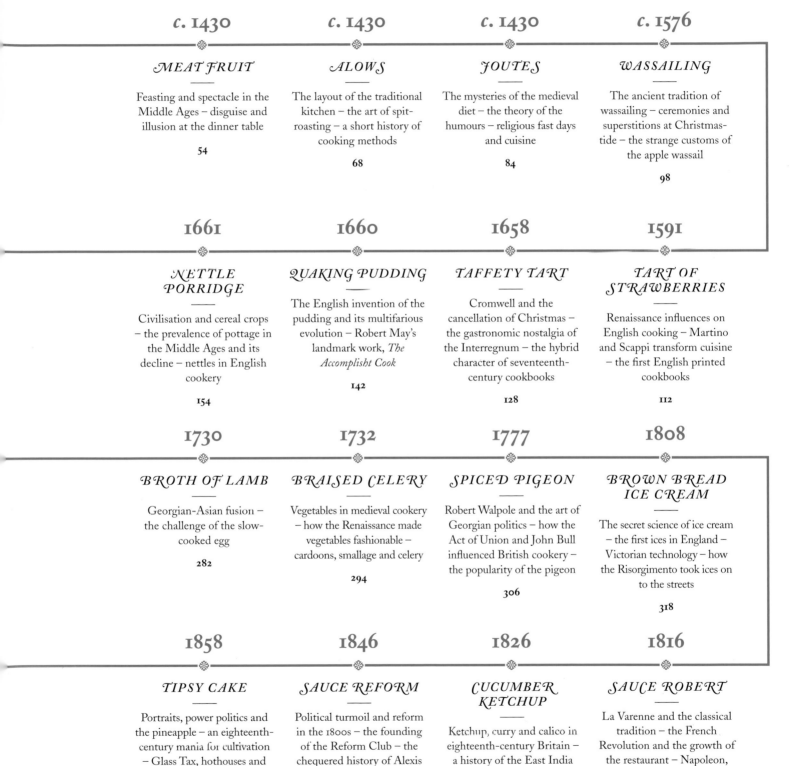

TO THE READER

[2013]

My eyes were opened to the potential of historical cuisine a decade ago, when I first delved into an extraordinary fifteenth-century manuscript known as *The Vivendier*. Among its pages was a recipe for a fish cooked three different ways—fried, roasted and boiled—that had flames coming out of its mouth. There was a recipe for making a roasted gosling, chicken or piglet appear to sing during service, and another for preparing a chicken that looked roasted but woke up just before carving and made off down the table, "upsetting jugs, goblets and whatnot". Reading this was a revelation. Up to that point, I'd had little idea that cooking of the past could be so playful, audacious and creative. With our sophisticated modern technology and centuries of accumulated culinary experience, it's easy to fall into the trap of thinking cooking is more creative now than in the past. *The Vivendier* was a salutary reminder that this is far from the case.

I had to find out more. I started poring over old books; I began attending lectures. But it was when I bumped into two amazing historians, Marc Meltonville and Richard Fitch, that my research took a big step forward. In the kitchens at Hampton Court, Marc and Richard undertake an unusual branch of culinary research, cooking the recipes of the past as precisely as possible, using the authentic utensils and ingredients of the time—even if that means travelling to the Canaries to obtain cochineal beetles for use as red food colouring. They gain from this a direct and practical understanding of food history, and the knowledge they have accrued in pursuit of their quest is encyclopaedic. I found it fascinating.

In the last few years, there has been a growth of interest in, and information on, British historical cuisine. Back at the start of the millennium, however, when I began looking into the subject, it hadn't really reached the mainstream, so I considered myself lucky to have happened upon two experts who could advise me. Soon after, I met another brilliant food historian, Ivan Day. Walking into Ivan's kitchen was like entering a time portal: bellows and salamanders hung from the whitewashed walls, a fire crackled in a cast-iron range rigged with a clockwork spit, and gleaming copper moulds were arrayed like sporting trophies on the heavy wooden dresser. It was a great place to get a truly hands-on appreciation of historical cookery. Between Ivan, Marc and Richard, I acquired as good an education in culinary history as anyone could wish for, some of which I hope to pass on to you in this book.

What started as an exercise in curiosity soon became something more. The originals of most of the cookbooks mentioned here are leather-bound volumes with mottled pages and library catalogue numbers as long as the one on your credit card. It was tempting to view them as museum pieces that simply shone a light on the past. But as I looked at *The Forme of Cury*, which was actually written by the cooks of Richard II, or browsed recipes with fanciful, dramatic and intriguing titles such as Salmagundy, Ragoo of Pigs' Ears, Cucumber Ketchup or Tipsy Cake, I came to see these books not just as historical documents. There are many people out there—both professionals like Ivan, Richard and Marc and dedicated amateurs—who spend their time faithfully reproducing recipes of the past. They have even been joined by television chefs and cookbook writers. But their emphasis is on historical re-creation, whereas I wanted to do something that, as far as I knew, hadn't really been done before. I wanted to approach this not as a historian but as a professional chef. Tradition is one of the mainsprings of innovation: we use the past as a springboard to leap towards the new. For as long as cooking has been documented, chefs of each generation have learned from their predecessors, picking up ideas and techniques and refashioning them to create exciting dishes of their own. And that's how I wanted to engage with these old cookbooks: as sources of inspiration.

So inspiration, not re-creation, was my watchword, but getting to grips with old recipes was undoubtedly challenging as well as fascinating. As you'll see, the language can be as obscure as a secret code. (Even now I'm not sure what a "coolio"—see page 286—is). And cookbooks of the past weren't designed to be reader-friendly. For a start, cooking tended to be regarded as a branch of medicine, a notion that makes sense once you read about the theory of the humours (see page 89), which dominated medieval ideas about health. Tracking down recipes thus meant ferreting among screeds of often bizarre remedies for Wind in the Stomach or Swooning-fits in Travel. Moreover, in many old volumes, sweet, savoury, small and substantial dishes are all mixed in together hugger-mugger, which certainly adds surprise and a sense of spontaneity to the experience of reading them. And in any case, before the rise of the domestic cook in the early eighteenth century, cookbooks were seen not as instruction

manuals but as *aides-mémoires* for professional chefs. Measurements tend to be imprecise and directions can be tantalisingly vague—but then part of the fun of exploring these dishes was using my chef's instincts and experience to find the way through such obstacles.

Gradually, a set of loose ground rules for what I was doing took shape. I aimed to build up a wide spread of recipes, taking as my starting point the end of the fourteenth century, when the first extant cookbook written in English, *The Forme of Cury*, appeared, and stopping on the cusp of the twentieth century, when cuisine became relatively well-documented and familiar. Within those parameters I explored whichever recipes caught my imagination. Sometimes I was inspired by the sheer showmanship of a dish, as with Meat Fruit; sometimes by a great set of ingredients, as with Nettle Porridge and Broth of Lamb. With Quaking Pudding I was drawn to the technical challenge of creating a delicately set mixture

that had the perfect wobble, while Mock Turtle Soup grew out of my abiding obsession with *Alice's Adventures in Wonderland*. Although some recipes in this book, such as Sambocade, mark the debut of a dish in this country, I didn't specifically hunt for things that were the first of their kind. The date, therefore, at the head of each chapter marks the year of publication of the cookbook I consulted, rather than the first appearance of a dish.

At the start I didn't generally have a fixed notion of which of my restaurants a recipe might be destined for, and waited until the dish acquired its unique character before making a final decision. Some, such as Eggs in Verjuice, are served at the Fat Duck; some, such as Hash of Snails and Wassailing, are on the menu at my pub the Hind's Head, but many come from my London restaurant, Dinner.

With wall-lights shaped like Victorian jelly moulds and chandeliers modelled on a Tudor rose in the windows of Westminster Abbey,

Dinner was designed to be a sympathetic, atmospheric setting in which to enjoy a menu based on historical British dishes. The restaurant's centrepiece is a giant clock mechanism, visible from the dining-room floor, that turns the kitchen's rotisserie. This clock already has a history: when Dinner first opened, I had a clock in place that worked only intermittently and I began searching for a replacement. I consulted Rolex, who put me in touch with a long-established British clock manufacturer. It turned out that one of the pieces they produce is a tribute to the Englishman who solved the problem of longitude, John Harrison (1693–1776). Harrison was a brilliant engineer who, despite much underhand opposition, was driven and obstinate enough to spend thirty years creating a timekeeper sufficiently accurate that sailors could establish precisely how long they had been travelling, and thus determine where exactly they were on the globe. Harrison's

original timepieces (which can be seen in the Old Royal Observatory in Greenwich) are not only historically significant, they're also beautiful, especially the earlier prototypes with their impossibly intricate mechanisms and spinning brass arms. So I commissioned the company to create a new mechanism for Dinner, modelled on Harrison's clocks.

The more you look into history, the more you stumble upon satisfying coincidences like this. One of the incidental pleasures of this book is the curious connections it reveals, such as the involvement of inventor of the *Rocket*, George Stephenson, in later life in the mania for growing pineapples that swept the country between 1750 and 1850. Or the fact that Richard Bradley, the first Professor of Botany at Cambridge and author of the first recipe for turtle soup, was also the first to bring a crocodile to Britain. Writing, research and recipe development took me down many unexpected pathways that are mapped out in these pages,

such as the cultivation of English saffron, our short-lived enthusiasm for snails, the popularity of the pudding cloth and the explosion of creativity that resulted from it. This is the story of our constantly changing and often surprising engagement with ingredients. The recipes in this book grow out of, and continue, that story.

Apart from scaling down the quantities and a handful of technical adaptations, the recipe instructions included here show how the dishes are prepared in my kitchens by a brigade of professional chefs, often using specialised technology and ingredients. For much of culinary history, chefs had to make do with limited equipment, cooking over an open fire, for example, until at least the 1700s. I was under no such constraints, so although these recipes involve many "traditional" techniques, such as searing and simmering, braising and roasting, clarifying and reducing, if development warranted use of a Thermomix, Pacojet or vacuum centrifuge, then that's what I chose. You'll

notice that at some point virtually every recipe employs a water bath and sous-vide machine. This may not seem very historical, but one day it will be. In the 1850s people were wary of gas technology and reluctant to cook with it, but by the end of the century one in four homes with a gas supply had a stove as well. Similarly, a few years from now almost every domestic kitchen will, I believe, have a sous-vide machine and water bath because they give cooks an unprecedented level of control, allowing them to cook many foodstuffs, particularly meat and fish, with exceptional precision and consistency.

So if you're interested in exactly what goes into making a recipe, here's where you'll get to know all the secrets. Some of them, such as Taffety Tart, are complex and demanding to prepare. Others, such as Spiced Pigeon and Powdered Duck, are more readily accessible. I hope that at least some of you will have a go at cooking the recipes; they will introduce you to some terrific dishes, often with exciting,

unusual or unexpected combinations of flavours, textures and aromas. If that seems too daunting, I hope you will nevertheless cherry-pick from among the many excellent techniques or elements within the recipes, such as the walnut vinaigrette on page 221 or the crab butter on page 206, and use them in your own dishes. The chapter on Lemon Salad alone has three reasonably simple techniques—curing and hay-smoking fish, and pickling lemons—that are extremely versatile.

It is very important to me that the recipes take inspiration from British history and cuisine. Ever since I can remember, British food has generally been dismissed worldwide as exceptionally bad. There was at one time some justification for this viewpoint. I grew up in the 1970s, when our cuisine was probably at its lowest ebb. Choice was limited and a bit provincial: virtually the only pasta you could get was spaghetti in long blue paper packets, and olive oil was generally sold in chemists as

a form of eardrop. I can still vividly recall the tasteless tomatoes, flabby sausages and tubs of strange-smelling, pre-grated Parmesan. Even now I can virtually taste the disappointment of biting into cakes that looked delicious but turned out to be bland confections of dense sponge and cheap cream.

There were historical catalysts for this culinary decline: the enclosures (the acquisition of public land during the sixteenth, seventeenth and eighteenth centuries) cut off a peasant tradition that would otherwise have stimulated our cuisine, much as it has done in Italy. A longstanding thraldom to French cooking, especially among the upper classes (the Whig aristocracy of the eighteenth century insisted on employing French chefs or, failing that, English ones who could cook French dishes), fostered an inferiority complex about our native tradition that led to its neglect. The rapid urbanisation of the nineteenth century compounded this, and the full-scale

industrialisation that went with it offered the means to produce food whose main virtues were volume, speed and convenience. Industrialisation also led to the rise of a Victorian middle class whose notions of conformity and correctness further undermined British cuisine. Food became prized for its appearance rather than flavour, and standards began to drop. The factor that sent them into free-fall, however, was probably the privations of World War II and its aftermath. Rationing continued in Britain for almost ten years after the war and, as an island with an urbanised population and highly industrialised food production, we had few alternative resources to augment our diet. A kind of culinary amnesia, to use Ivan Day's phrase, gradually overtook the country: we effectively forgot what good food was like, and became content with second best.

Yet this is a very small part of the picture of British cooking. If, as history encourages, you take the long view, our culinary heritage is in fact a glorious one. King Richard II was a noted gourmet who both gave and inspired magnificent feasts. Our invention of the pudding sent foreign visitors into raptures, and our skill at the spit was once the envy of the world. "The English men understand almost better than any other people the art of properly roasting a joint," observed the Swedish traveller Pehr Kalm in 1748. Among the pages that follow are dozens of other examples of a vibrant and refined tradition of British cuisine.

Somewhere along the line we seem to have forgotten that we once had an impressive culinary reputation. I want this book to provide a reminder of that fantastic heritage. Over the last decade or so, there has been revolution in British food. As a result, there is a new-found pride in this country's cooking that has led to us regaining our culinary identity. What you're about to read is a testament to that, and I hope it also shows how great cuisine comes from a sense of tradition mixed with the spirit of innovation.

RICE & FLESH

[1390]

RYSE OF FLESSH

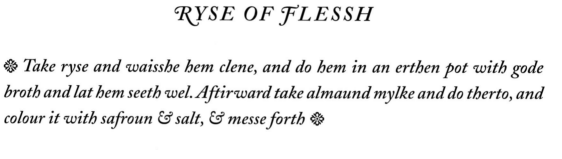

❊ *Take ryse and waisshe hem clene, and do hem in an erthen pot with gode broth and lat hem seeth wel. Aftirward take almaund mylke and do therto, and colour it with safroun & salt, & messe forth* ❊

The Forme of Cury (1390)

In the British Library there is a parchment scroll made of calfskin. Scratched upon it, in a spiky medieval hand full of curlicues and flourishes that make the script look almost like Arabic to the untrained eye, are just under 200 brief entries, from Grounden Benes to Payn Puf. Some look familiar—Chykens in Gravey, Spynoches Yfryed, Tartes of Fysshe— and some have their own strange poetry: Fylettes in Galantyne, Pesoun of Almayne. Many more are, frankly, quite mystifying: Bukkenade, Paynfoundew, Blank Desire, Balloc Broth. This is *The Forme of Cury*, the oldest extant cookbook in English. This is where the history of British cuisine really begins.

There is, naturally, evidence of cooking in England that pre-dates this. A cooking vessel from 800–600 BC was found in the Thames, for example, during dredging in the 1850s. In book IV of his *Geography*, the Greek historian Strabo (64 BC–AD 23) observed that the Britons exported corn and cattle but were often ignorant about how to make cheese. The Anglo-Saxon poem *Beowulf* mentions drinking mead, wine and beer, and *De Utensilibus*, the vocabulary book compiled by Alexander Neckam around the end of the twelfth century, contains descriptions of the kitchen, its utensils and practices. But these are fugitive, incomplete glimpses of what we ate and how we cooked. It's only when we reach *The Forme of Cury* ("cury" is the Middle English word for cookery, derived presumably from the French word *cuire*) that we actually get inside the head of a cook, and start to understand what was served.

It is, however, a highly specialised viewpoint. At this stage, and for a long time afterwards, nobody felt compelled to write down what ordinary people ate. Cuisine's early history is not a record of the everyday. Its documents are the menus, feasts and account books of the well-to-do—eating on a grand scale. Much of it, inevitably, centres on the monarchy, and *The Forme of Cury* is right up there. A whole subindustry of scholarly debate surrounds the text: eight versions exist, which appear to be fifteenth-century copies (of varying accuracy, legibility and completeness) of an original from around 1390, presumed lost. But none of the researchers dispute the manuscript's statement that it was "compiled of the chef Maister Cokes of kyng Richard the Secunde kyng of Englond aftir the Conquest. The which was accounted the best and ryallest vyaundier [provisioner] of alle cristen kynges." *The Forme of Cury* is an extraordinary piece of culinary history: a set of recipes from the chefs in the court of Richard II.

Richard acceded to the throne in 1377, when he was only ten years old. Inevitably, this destabilised the country, as the most prominent families took advantage of the king's youth to further their own ambitions and gain as much power as possible. He remained dependent on allies among the various court factions, and his reign was punctuated by putsches and political coups, like some high-stakes chess game. But in truth, England was already a troubled and volatile place. Richard's predecessor, Edward III, had achieved a string of military victories—Sluys, Crécy, Calais, Poitiers—but had bankrupted himself in the process. The Black Death, which first hit in 1348 and killed almost half the population over the next fifty years, further undermined the economy and shattered the social order. The brutal reduction in numbers of the population meant that the working man's services were suddenly at a premium, so he could name his own price, or move to a place where labour was better paid. The Plague was no respecter of class either

and, as it laid low the inhabitants of villages, no matter what their station in life, many people unexpectedly acquired or inherited wealth and property. Once they'd got all this, they were determined to hang on to it—by force if necessary. The Peasants' Revolt of 1381 was largely a protest against government measures aimed at containing these new-found freedoms, such as the statute that made it a crime to ask for higher wages or seek work elsewhere.

During Edward III's reign, much use had been made of ritual and pageantry to assert the court's authority, and Richard adopted similar tactics. His coronation was a deliberately magnificent affair, stage-managed to demonstrate the ascendency of the monarch. Richard reinforced the image of the king as mystically elevated above all others, instituting the forms of address "Your Majesty" and "Your Highness". He is also reputed to have invented the handkerchief, a sign of the formality and sophistication characteristic of his court and its concern with conduct and self-presentation.

Food offered an invaluable opportunity to show off generosity, wealth and power. The chronicler Adam of Murimuth describes a feast held by Edward III as "complete with richness of fare, variety of dishes, and overflowing abundance of drinks". According to the historian John Stow in *Annals* (1580), Richard II's kitchen fed a household of 10,000 people on a daily basis, hence his reputation as "the best and ryallest vyaundier". Dining became an incredibly ritualised affair, designed to reinforce social standing just as much as any courtly tournament. There was a high table upon which several special ornamental cloths would be laid. To one side, on a board set on trestles, the king's hand-basin and personal cup would be displayed (the origin of the term "cupboard"). Napkins and silver salt-cellars were placed at table; assays (the tasting of each ingredient to check it wasn't poisoned) were carried out; the washing of hands was performed, and eventually food was served, according to a rigid order of precedence. Richard extended this formality, insisting on use of the spoon at court; before this, people had used their fingers, and the fork reached England only in the 1600s. (Even then, the early adopters were laughed at.) It became his practice to sit enthroned in state from dinner until vespers (the evening prayers) observed by his courtiers, who were expected to drop on bended knee whenever his gaze fell on them.

It was the title that first caught my eye as I looked at *The Forme of Cury*. Rice of Flesh: it had a ring to it (although I had to tinker a little with the name before putting it on Dinner's menu, to avoid puzzling customers) and a disarming frankness, a bit like calling a dish Protein and Carbs.* But the ingredients also quickened my interest, especially the rice and saffron. I knew that the Arabs brought knowledge of rice cultivation to Spain when they invaded in 711, and from there it spread to Sicily and beyond, but I hadn't fully appreciated how early rice had become a part of the English diet. More than a hundred years before *The Forme of Cury* was written, rice was already an entry in the household accounts of Henry III.

Nowadays, rice is viewed as a staple, and we give little thought to its transportation from India, Italy, Spain or Thailand. In the Middle Ages, however, imported foodstuffs underwent an arduous journey by land and sea, and were unbelievably expensive as a result. The exotic spices that flavoured medieval cuisine really did cost a small fortune, and were carefully entered in household accounts, then kept under lock and key. Rice was brought in on the spice ships, and was often stored securely with the pepper, nutmeg, cloves, cinnamon, ginger, cardamom and mace. A host who served such ingredients was showing how much money and power he had as well as being generous. A recipe with rice and spices was indeed a dish fit for a king.

This is particularly true of saffron, which even today is the world's most expensive spice, mainly because harvesting it is a labour-intensive business that has gone virtually unchanged since medieval times. Saffron strands are the stigmas of one type of crocus (*Crocus sativus*), and are so fragile that they have to be picked by hand. It takes 70,000 flowers to produce 2.25 kilograms of stigmas which, once they've been carefully dried in the sun or over a fire, yield just 450 grams of saffron. In the Middle Ages, England's saffron was imported mainly from Spain (where the tradition of using saffron in cooking had come from Arab cuisine), or from Asia, via transportation by land to the Levantine ports, then on to Italy and the great

* *The term "protein" was actually first coined by the Swedish chemist Jöns Jacob Berzelius in 1838, and the structure of carbohydrates was first researched in the 1840s by the German chemist Justus von Liebig. Liebig was a great scientist—he identified the process we now know as photosynthesis—but in* Researches on the Chemistry of Food *(1847) he was the first to propagate the incorrect notion that searing meat seals in the juices.*

trading fairs in Flanders, Champagne and Basel. When it wasn't adulterated with other substances, the spice was as expensive as gold.

Although the stigmas of *Crocus sativus* are delicate and difficult to pick, the plant itself will grow readily in a range of climates. Given the astronomical cost and high demand for the spice (not only as a foodstuff, but also as a component of apothecaries' potions and as a dye for use in England's burgeoning textile industry), it made good business sense to grow it at home. During Edward III's reign there was a huge expansion in saffron production, making it the only spice to have been grown and exported from England. The crop was farmed in several counties on the east coast but, as its name suggests, Saffron Walden in Essex became the major area of cultivation. There's a story that saffron farming was established here because the first saffron corm, or plant stem, to be planted in England was brought by a pilgrim from the Holy Land to his native Chipping Walden, hidden in his hollowed-out staff, since the punishment for smuggling so valuable a commodity from its home country was death. Whether true or not, by the sixteenth century the spice was such a key feature of the town that its name was officially changed from Chipping Walden to Saffron Walden in 1514.

However, saffron and rice's one-time rarity wasn't the only reason I picked up on them. The combination called to mind one dish in particular. Rice of Flesh might have been more broth-like than its Italian counterpart, but it definitely looked like a relative of the classic risotto Milanese, and that association offered a new direction in which to take the recipe.

A few years back, I was researching risotto-making in northern Italy, visiting farmers, chefs and millers and exploring the basics—such as when to add stock to a risotto and in what quantities—as well as more cutting-edge techniques, such as using fragrant basmati rice instead of the usual Arborio or Carnaroli rice, or adding a little horseradish juice at the end in order to cut the richness. Crisscrossing Piedmont and Lombardy, I had made two discoveries I was especially excited about.

The first was the incredible flavour of aged rice. Amid the Renaissance magnificence of the Colombara estate, with its vast courtyard flanked on all sides by solid, high-walled buildings, Rinaldo Rondolino showed me how he lets Carnaroli rice mature in a temperature-controlled hangar for a year, allowing its sugars to develop and sweeten the grain and its lipids to oxidise, releasing fatty acids that acidify the

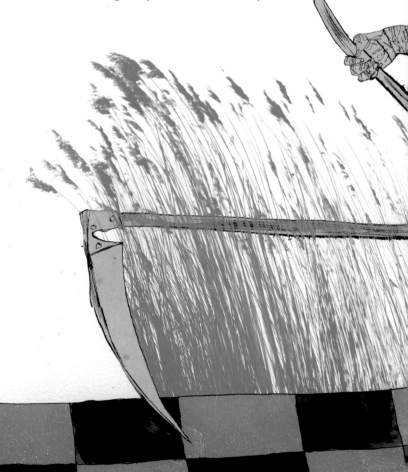

rice and harden it. Once rice has been harvested, most commercial companies grind it quickly and aggressively between stones, which damages the grains with little pits and fractures and causes them to cook unevenly. Rinaldo, on the other hand, has machines in which the grains are ground slowly so that the surface remains smooth and unblemished. Such care and attention to detail produces rice that cooks to a perfect consistency and has lots of flavour.

My second discovery was at the restaurant belonging to the father of modern Italian cuisine (and first non-French chef to gain three Michelin stars), Gualtiero Marchesi, who showed me his take on risotto Milanese. The dish was finished with a small square of gold leaf laid over the rice, which he did simply "to make it beautiful", but I liked the historical appropriateness of adding gold to saffron, an ingredient once worth its weight in gold.

What impressed me most, though, was his use of acidulated butter. Instead of putting finely diced onions in the pan at the start and letting them soften, Marchesi added what he called *burro acido* (butter flavoured with wine, onions and vinegar) at the end, during the *mantecatura* (the all-important addition of butter and resting of the dish at the end of cooking). This prevented the onion from dominating the other flavours. Moreover, since the wine and vinegar brought the necessary touch of acidity to the dish, the amount of Parmesan (which normally provides some of the acidic component of a risotto) could be reduced, making it much lighter. It was a clever, simple technique that had lots of potential, and I couldn't wait to start playing with it in my development kitchen. Marchesi's acidulated butter was essentially an adaptation of the classic *beurre blanc*, and I reckoned I could combine it with another mainstay of French cuisine, *beurre noisette*, to introduce a flavour that would complement the slight nuttiness risotto rice acquires when it fries in the oil before stock is added. Eventually I had something I was happy with: a butter emulsion that gave the risotto a great balance of complex flavours. But at the time, none of my restaurants served a dish in which I could use it.

It was at this point that I came across Rice of Flesh in *The Forme of Cury*. The dish's impressive historical origins made it a great candidate for the menu at Dinner, and a practical one, too. Risotto is user-friendly enough to be cooked on the large scale required in a restaurant with more than a hundred covers, and, since I've created a variety of risottos over the years (such as crab risotto with passion fruit and cauliflower risotto with cocoa), I'd already developed a set of techniques for making it that I was happy with. What's more, it was the perfect vehicle for both acidulated butter and aged Carnaroli rice. The foundations of the dish were already in place.

One niggle, however, was the "flesh" of the title. As careful readers of the original recipe will have noted, there's no mention of meat among the ingredients. A little digging in the British Library, however, revealed that another manuscript of the period contained a direct copy of the recipe called Ryse in Potage of Flesh. To me this seemed like confirmation that the flesh in Rice of Flesh must be in the "gode broth". Until about the eighteenth century, recipes weren't generally conceived as a set of foolproof instructions; they were more like sets of notes for professional chefs. In the Middle Ages, as now, a good saffron risotto called for a good chicken stock; there was no need to spell it out.

In a way, it was puzzling this out that gave me the idea for the final element of the dish. My head chef at Dinner, Ashley Palmer-Watts, regularly visits our butchers to check ingredients and scout for ideas. He brought back some calf tail from one trip, which looked delicate and had an attractive colour, paler than the deep brown of oxtail. I figured it would sit well with the other ingredients, enhancing their flavours without overpowering them. I also felt that, since flesh features so prominently in the title of the recipe, it would be a shame not to have some on the plate. So we developed a method for cooking jointed pieces of calf's tail, first putting them in a water bath at 82°C/180°F until soft and moist, then taking the meat off the bone and warming it in a sauce made from a red wine reduction and beef stock —another "gode broth". The rice is garnished with sprigs of earthy red amaranth and five pieces of calf's flesh, so the dish really lives up to its name.

RICE & FLESH

Makes 6 portions

Beef Stock

120g	Brandy
120g	Ruby port
600g	Red wine
1.6kg	Beef bones, chopped
1.2kg	Sectioned oxtail or calf's tail, in 2.5cm pieces
100g	Rendered beef fat
1.2kg	Lean beef shin, diced
900g	Peeled and finely sliced onions
10g	Star anise
900g	Peeled and finely sliced carrots
240g	Sliced cleaned button mushrooms
30g	Peeled and finely sliced garlic
15g	Thyme
2	Bay leaves
50g	Flatleaf parsley

Pour the brandy and ruby port into a saucepan on a moderate heat. Carefully flame the mixture with a blowtorch and simmer gently to reduce to 120g. In a separate saucepan, reduce the red wine to 300g using the same method. Set both aside to cool.

Preheat the oven to 180°C/350°F.

Spread the beef bones and the sectioned oxtail evenly on a roasting tray and roast them in the oven until golden brown, turning frequently.

In the meantime, heat a thin layer of rendered beef fat in a large pressure cooker and brown the lean diced shin in batches. Set aside.

Add the remaining beef fat to the pressure cooker and cook the onions and star anise until lightly caramelised. Add the carrots, mushrooms and garlic and cook for a further 5 minutes, stirring frequently.

Add the reduced alcohols to the pressure cooker, followed by all the roasted bones and meat. Pour 4.8 litres cold water into the pressure cooker and bring to the boil, skimming off all scum and impurities. Add the thyme and bay leaves and stir the mixture one last time before securing the lid. Cook for 2 hours.

Allow the pressure cooker to depressurise and the stock to cool slightly before opening the lid. Strain the stock through a fine-mesh sieve, add the parsley and leave to infuse for 10 minutes. Pass the stock through a fine-mesh filter bag and chill in the fridge overnight.

Remove and discard all the fat from the surface of the chilled stock. Heat the stock in a large saucepan and gently reduce to 15% of the original quantity, yielding approximately 725g reduced beef stock. It is important to continue skimming the stock as it reduces. Once the stock has reduced, pass it through a fine-mesh filter bag and refrigerate until needed.

Chicken Bouillon

2.9kg	Chickens (approximately 2 birds)
115g	Peeled and finely sliced carrots
115g	Peeled and finely sliced onions
45g	Finely sliced celery
40g	Trimmed and finely sliced leeks
5g	Peeled and finely diced garlic
2	Cloves
4g	Black peppercorns
15g	Thyme
20g	Flatleaf parsley
2	Bay leaves

Place the chickens in a large pot and cover with cold water. Bring to the boil. Carefully remove the chickens and rinse and refresh them under cold running water. Place the chickens in a large pressure cooker and add 2.3 litres cold water. Bring to a simmer, skimming off all scum and impurities. Secure the lid and cook for 1 hour 30 minutes.

Allow the pressure cooker to depressurise and the bouillon to cool slightly before opening the lid. Add the vegetables, cloves and peppercorns to the bouillon, secure the lid and cook for 30 more minutes. Allow the pressure cooker to depressurise and the bouillon to cool slightly before opening the lid. Add the herbs and let them infuse for 30 minutes.

Strain the bouillon through a fine-mesh sieve, then pass through a fine-mesh filter bag. Chill in the fridge overnight.

Remove and discard the fat from the surface of the chilled bouillon. Refrigerate the bouillon until needed. The recipe yields approximately 2.3 litres chicken bouillon, which can be frozen in batches for future use.

Red Wine Sauce

295g	Red wine
105g	Ruby port
65g	Peeled and finely sliced carrots
15g	Finely sliced cleaned button mushrooms
10g	Peeled and finely sliced garlic
280g	Reserved reduced beef stock
0.5g	Black peppercorns
2.5g	Thyme
1	Bay leaf

In a saucepan, combine the red wine, ruby port, carrots, mushrooms and garlic. Bring the mixture to the boil and carefully flame the alcohol using a blowtorch. On a gentle simmer, reduce the mixture to one-fifth of its original volume. Add the reduced beef stock and peppercorns, and simmer for a few minutes.

Remove the saucepan from the heat and add the thyme, allowing it to infuse for 5 minutes. Add the bay leaf and infuse for a further 5 minutes. Pass the sauce through a fine-mesh filter bag and refrigerate until needed.

(continued overleaf)

Acidulated Butter

265g Sliced onions
500g Ordinary dry white wine
500g Ordinary white wine vinegar
665g Unsalted butter, cubed and at
        room temperature

Combine the onions, wine and vinegar in a deep pan and place over a moderate heat. Stirring regularly, cook the onions until they are very soft, and until the entire mixture has reduced to approximately 230g.

Remove the pan from the heat and whisk in small amounts of butter at a time, until well emulsified. Leave the mixture to infuse for 15–20 minutes, then pass through a fine-mesh sieve. Refrigerate the butter until needed.

This recipe yields approximately 600g acidulated butter, which can be frozen in batches for future use.

Calf's Tail

1kg   Calf's tail
30g   Grapeseed oil

Preheat a water bath to 82°c/180°f.

Joint the calf's tail and place the pieces in separate sous-vide bags, keeping pieces of similar sizes grouped together. Ensure that the pieces are all lying flat in a single layer to allow for even cooking. Empty the grapeseed oil into the bags and seal under full pressure.

Place the sous-vide bags in the water bath for 8 hours, then cool them in a large bowl of iced water.

Once the temperature of the calf's tail reaches 10–15°c/50–59°f, open the sous-vide bags and remove the pieces. Carefully pick through the meat, keeping the small pieces of meat separate from the bones and cartilage. Discard the bones and cartilage and refrigerate the calf's tail pieces until needed.

Rice Base

485g Reserved chicken bouillon
        Saffron
30g   Extra virgin olive oil
250g Risotto rice
90g   White wine

In a small saucepan, bring the chicken bouillon to a simmer. Place a pinch of saffron in a small bowl and pour a small amount of heated bouillon over the saffron to infuse.

In the meantime, in another large saucepan, heat the olive oil and lightly toast the rice until nutty and light brown in colour. Add the white wine to the toasted rice, and once all the wine has been absorbed, add the warm chicken bouillon. Cook the rice over a moderate heat, stirring regularly.

Once most of the liquid has been absorbed, add the small bowl of saffron-infused liquid to the rice and stir well. Remove from the heat and place in the fridge until needed. It is best not to prepare the rice base more than a few hours in advance.

Finishing the Risotto

150g Reserved chicken bouillon,
        plus extra if necessary
600g Reserved rice base
90g   Mascarpone
35g   Finely grated Parmesan cheese
210g Reserved acidulated butter,
        cubed and at room
        temperature
30   Saffron strands
        Salt
30g   Lightly whipped whipping
        cream

Heat the chicken bouillon in a large saucepan and add the rice. Cook over a fairly high heat and stir in the mascarpone and grated Parmesan. Check the consistency of the rice— it should still have quite a bite to it. Add a little more stock, if necessary, to allow the rice to come together.

Remove the saucepan from the heat and add the acidulated butter, saffron and salt as needed. Combine well and cover the saucepan with foil to allow the rice to rest for 1 minute.

Return the saucepan to the heat and add the whipping cream. Adjust the seasoning before serving.

To Serve

210g Reserved red wine sauce
30   Pieces reserved calf's tail
        Finished risotto
        Red amaranth

Heat the red wine sauce gently in a small saucepan until reduced slightly— it should coat the back of a spoon. Add the calf's tail pieces to the saucepan to warm through gently.

When ready to serve, divide the finished risotto between 6 shallow plates, spooning it into the centre of the plate and allowing it to spread evenly by rotating the plate.

Place 5 calf's tail pieces in a ring on top of the risotto, followed by a very small spoonful of the red wine sauce over each piece. Finish with several sprigs of red amaranth on each calf's tail piece.

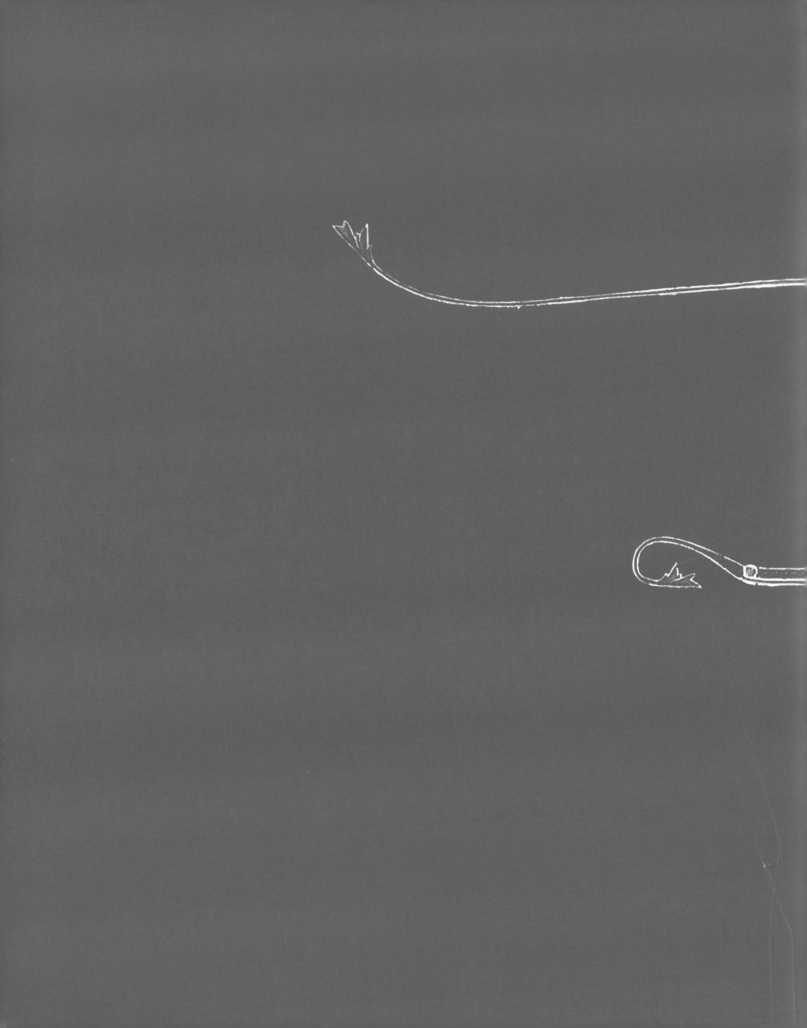

SAMBOCADE

[1390]

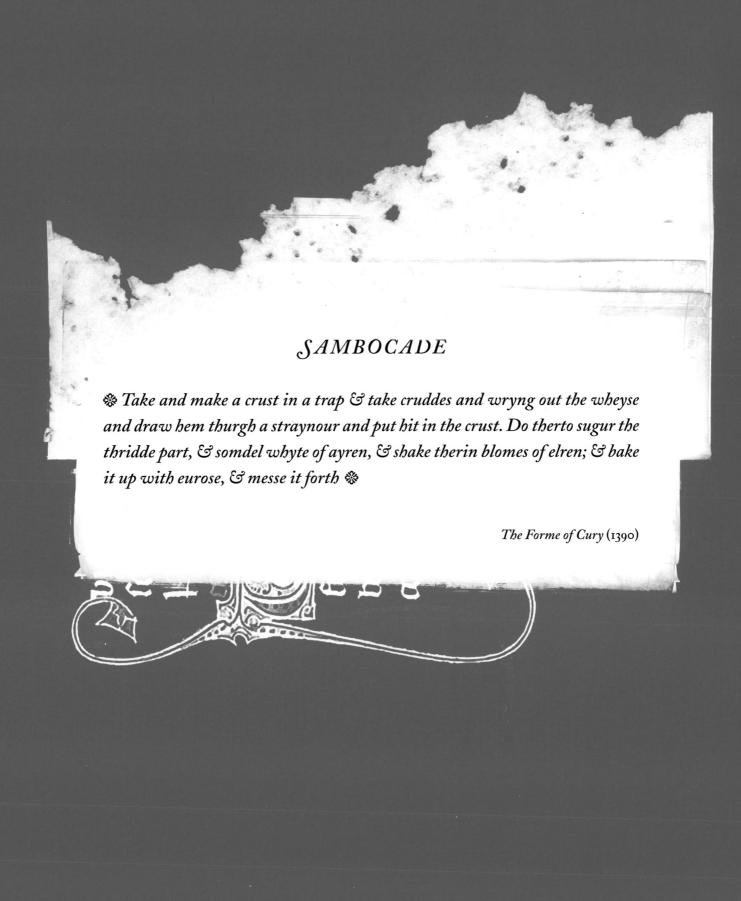

SAMBOCADE

❀ *Take and make a crust in a trap & take cruddes and wryng out the wheyse and draw hem thurgh a straynour and put hit in the crust. Do therto sugur the thridde part, & somdel whyte of ayren, & shake therin blomes of elren; & bake it up with eurose, & messe it forth* ❀

The Forme of Cury (1390)

Sambocade intrigued me from the start because it was, effectively, a baked cheesecake. I knew that cheese-making had been around in Britain since at least the Bronze Age, and that although the Greek historian Strabo thought the English somewhat ignorant on the subject before the arrival of the Romans, by the Middle Ages we were producing hard and soft cheeses, as well as "green" cheese made from curds, and sometimes flavoured with herbs. Nonetheless, I had imagined that cheesecake was a more modern dish, so the discovery that the Plantagenet court was tucking into a cheesecake flavoured with elderflower ("blomes of elren") in the late 1300s was surprising, and I decided to investigate further. It turned out that although there is a description of something resembling cheesecake in Cato the Elder's *De agri cultura* (*c*. 160 BC), *The Forme of Cury* has the earliest actual recipe for the dish. At the time it was probably a real innovation, and an English one at that. For me, this was a very seductive combination, and I began looking at ways to develop my own version, partly as a homage to this English first.

Development depended on solving two problems: first, how to incorporate the ingredients so that the flavour of elderflower, which seemed the key element of the original recipe, really shone through. Second, how to give it a bit of wonder. In restaurants and supermarkets, cheesecake usually appears in a familiar, highly processed form with an indeterminate flavour and claggy texture. It's generally reliably sweet, filling and vaguely fruity, and that's about it. In the Middle Ages, though, its novelty must have meant it was much talked about, and I wanted

to capture some of that excitement. Medieval chefs relished visual trickery and transformation —fruit that turns out to be meat, chessboards made from sweetmeats—and this gave me an idea that, if nothing else, shared that sense of humour: I could make a cheesecake that looked exactly like a roundel of goat's cheese.

There are two ways to make cheesecake: baked and unbaked. A baked cheesecake is essentially what chefs call a custard: an egg-liquid mixture that has set to a solid gel. (Quiche, crème caramel and crème brûlée are all examples of custards.) Every protein in an egg takes the form of a long chain of atoms folded into a tight mass. The proteins remain separate from one another until the heat of the oven begins to agitate them, causing them to unfold and bond together as a network, creating a relatively stable structure. In an unbaked cheesecake, the setting agent is not eggs but gelatine, a protein composed of long strands that kink and intertwine as they cool, creating a firm but fragile mesh. A baked cheesecake can be delightfully rich and creamy because of the eggs, but it also tends to be dense, and the application of heat inevitably gives the ingredients a slightly cooked flavour. For this dish I was looking to create something light that preserved as much of the fresh elderflower flavour as possible. If I used gelatine, a brief period in a bain-marie would be the only exposure to heat the filling would have. So the unbaked type was my best bet. I could introduce the elderflower flavour by adding a cordial to the filling once it had come off the heat. (In season, I could even add elderflowers to the cordial beforehand and let them infuse for a while to boost the freshness and fragrance.) That way, I'd be able to hold on to even the most delicate and volatile elderflower aromas.

I made a classic base with butter, sugar and *pâte sablée* (literally, "sandy pastry", so called because it contains a high proportion of sugar, giving it a nice crumbly texture). To maintain the goat's cheese illusion, the base would somehow have to be concealed, but I still wanted that welcome bit of crunch. For the filling, I planned to make a mousse by combining cream, sugar and cream cheese with gelatine and *pâte à bombe* (an airy, meringue-like preparation that helps create a light texture), but since my cheesecake was going to look like a goat's cheese, I wanted a hint of it among the flavours. I found, though, that simply adding goat's cheese to the basic mixture didn't work; it gave the dish a grainy texture and swamped every other flavour. Balancing this out by adding more elderflower cordial just gave me a different problem: more liquid meant I had to use more gelatine to set it, which made the cake denser. The solution, once we hit upon it, was elegant. By reducing the amount of whipping cream in the cheesecake mixture and replacing it with goat's cream we achieved a suitably subtle goat's cheese flavour. Since the amount of liquid was the same, there was no need to add more gelatine, and we could give the cake a nice, delicate set. And with goat's cream we no longer had the problem of graininess.

Cheesecake can easily end up bland and increasingly familiar and disappointing with each bite, and I was determined to confound such expectations. One way to do this, I decided, would be to give the cake a liquid centre, introducing a strong textural contrast and providing the diner with a delicious surprise at the same time. For the components of this, I took my cue once again from the goat's cheese idea, looking at ingredients that are often served with cheese. I settled on grapes and apples, two typical inclusions on the cheeseboard that might also suit a cheesecake. (I considered figs too, but decided that, roasted, they would make a great garnish for the dish instead.) First, I worked on using pectin to set grape juice to the consistency of a firm-ish *pâte-de-fruit* (a kind of refined fruit pastille). I then thinned it with elderflower cordial to make a sort of jam, which would also help reinforce the elderflower notes in the dish. This gave me a beautifully oozy, viscous liquid into which I could introduce another textural contrast: some crisp little cubes of apple that had been compacted in a chamber vacuum sealer to intensify their flavour.

Putting the components together was then just a process of assembling. I would prepare the crunchy base, pour the filling on top and put it in the freezer. Once firm, I'd scoop a cavity out of the top of the filling, add the *pâte-de-fruit* mix and cover it with more filling. The whole thing looked uncannily and gratifyingly like a roundel of goat's cheese, just as I had imagined. But then I thought of one final touch. Charcoal crackers are, like apples and grapes, a classic cheeseboard garnish. If I dusted the sides of the cheesecake with charcoal powder, it would appear to have the ash coating typical of French goat's cheeses such as Selles sur Cher—one last little piece of medieval trickery.

SAMBOCADE

Makes 8 portions

Pâte Sablée

250g	Plain flour
1g	Baking powder
	Salt
85g	Unsalted butter, cubed and at room temperature
85g	Icing sugar
48g	Whole egg

Place the flour, baking powder and a pinch of salt in a bowl and combine. Set aside.

Place the butter and sugar in a mixer bowl and cream at high speed until light and creamy, using the paddle attachment. Reduce the mixer to a moderate speed and gradually add the egg until well emulsified.

Add the flour mixture and mix until it comes together to form a dough. Remove the dough from the mixing bowl and place between 2 sheets of baking parchment. Roll the dough to a thickness of 5mm.

Place in the freezer while preheating the oven to 170°C/340°F.

Peel off the parchment and bake the dough until golden. Allow to cool, then store in a sealed container until needed.

Biscuit Base

350g	Reserved baked pâte sablée
80g	Unsalted butter, cubed and at room temperature
70g	Muscovado sugar

Place the pâte sablée in a Thermomix and blitz to fine crumbs. Set aside.

Place the butter and muscovado sugar in a mixer bowl and cream at high speed until light and creamy, using the paddle attachment. Reduce the mixer to a moderate speed and add the crumbs; mix until fully combined.

Line a baking tray with baking parchment and transfer the biscuit mixture on to it. Place another sheet of parchment on top and flatten the biscuit mixture with a rolling pin, ensuring it is compressed well. Place the tray in the freezer for 1 hour.

Using a 4.5cm-diameter cutter, cut 8 rounds out of the biscuit mixture. Gently place the biscuit bases on a clean tray. Place in the fridge until needed.

Compressed Apples

2	Granny Smith apples, peeled, cored and cut into 5mm slices
500g	Apple juice

Place the apple slices in a sous-vide bag, ensuring they are all lying flat and in a single layer. Seal under full pressure. Pierce the bag several times and repeat the process to compress the apples.

Place the compressed apple slices in a second sous-vide bag, followed by the apple juice. Seal under full pressure and place in the fridge for 24 hours. Dice them into 5mm cubes.

Elderflower Jam

200g	Elderflower cordial
1	Small handful fresh elderflowers (optional)
235g	White caster sugar
10g	Pectin jaune
5g	Tartaric acid
135g	White grape juice
65g	Glucose
	Reserved compressed apples

If desired, the flavour of the elderflower cordial can be intensified by infusing the fresh elderflowers in it for 30 minutes. Strain the cordial and set aside.

Combine the sugar and pectin in a bowl, mixing very well using a small whisk, and set aside.

Mix the tartaric acid and 5g water in a small bowl until fully dissolved. Set aside.

Place the grape juice and glucose in a saucepan and bring to the boil. Add the sugar and pectin mixture to the saucepan and reduce over a moderate heat, whisking continuously. Once the mixture has cooked to 67° Brix, remove from the heat and whisk in the tartaric acid mixture and the elderflower cordial. Allow to cool.

Place the mixture in a Thermomix and blitz for 2 minutes before passing through a muslin cloth. Combine 140g of the jam with 140g diced compressed apple and refrigerate until needed. It is best if they are combined shortly before filling the cheesecakes.

Goat's Cheese Cream

400g	Goat's cheese, rind removed
100g	Double goat's cream

Place the goat's cheese in a mixer bowl and beat at moderate speed using the paddle attachment. Add the cream and combine well. Spoon the goat's cheese cream into a piping bag and store in the fridge until needed.

Pâte à Bombe

265g	White caster sugar
150g	Egg yolk

Heat the sugar and 85g water in a small saucepan.

Meanwhile, whisk the egg yolk in a mixer at medium speed. Just before the sugar syrup reaches 121°C/250°F, increase the speed of the mixer.

(continued overleaf)

Once the sugar syrup has reached 121°c/250°F, remove from the heat and reduce the speed of the mixer to medium. Slowly add the sugar syrup to the whisked egg yolk mixture and whisk until the entire mixture has cooled.

Cheesecake Mousse

10.5g	**Bronze leaf gelatine**
25g	**Icing sugar**
400g	**Plain cream cheese**
335g	**Double goat's cream**
185g	**Reserved pâte à bombe**
85g	**Whipping cream**
15g	**Elderflower cordial**

Place the gelatine leaves in enough cold water to cover them. After 5 minutes, once the gelatine has softened, strain the leaves and ensure all the water has been squeezed out.

Place the icing sugar, cream cheese and goat's cream in a round-bottomed bowl and place over a pot of boiling water, mixing well until fully combined. Add the bloomed gelatine and continue to combine until all the gelatine has dissolved.

Remove the bowl from the boiling water and place over a bowl of iced water. Allow the cream cheese to cool to 45°c/113°F. Fold the pâte à bombe into the cream cheese.

In a separate bowl, whip the whipping cream until soft peaks have formed and add, along with the elderflower cordial, to the cream-cheese mixture. Place in a piping bag and store in the fridge until needed.

Cheesecakes

Biscuit bases
Reserved goat's cheese cream
Reserved cheesecake mousse
Reserved elderflower jam
Charcoal powder

Pipe a layer of the goat's cheese cream on the top of each biscuit, the same thickness as the biscuit.

Place a 6.5cm-diameter cookie cutter over each biscuit, and, using it as a mould, pipe the cheesecake mousse around the biscuit, concealing the sides, then fill the mould seven-eighths full with mousse, allowing some room for an additional layer later on. Repeat with the other 7 bases.

Keeping the cutters in place, put the tray in the freezer and reserve the remaining mousse.

Once the cheesecakes have frozen solid, remove them from the freezer and scoop out a small amount from the centre of each one. Fill the hollowed-out cheesecakes with elderflower jam.

Hide the elderflower jam pocket by piping additional cheesecake mousse to the top of the mould, and smooth over. Return the cheesecakes to the freezer.

Once they have frozen solid, remove them from the freezer and allow to stand for 5–10 minutes before gently lifting off the moulds.

Place a small piece of clingfilm over the top of each cheesecake to protect the top, then brush a small amount of charcoal powder on to the sides to resemble a round of goat's cheese. Remove the clingfilm and allow the cheesecakes to defrost completely in the fridge before serving.

Cinnamon Sugar

1.5g	**Ground cinnamon**
150g	**White caster sugar**

Mix the cinnamon and sugar together in a small bowl until well combined.

Roasted Figs

2	**Figs**
	Reserved cinnamon sugar

Quarter the figs and dip the flat sides into the cinnamon sugar. Heat a pan over a high heat and lightly griddle the flat sides of the figs until lightly golden.

The figs should be griddled just before serving.

Red Wine Fluid Gel

1	**Bottle Maury red wine**
2.5g	**Gellan F (low-acyl gellan)**
0.8g	**Sodium citrate**

Pour the wine into a saucepan over a moderate heat. Flame, bring to the boil and simmer to reduce the wine to 300g. Set aside.

Place the reduced wine in a Thermomix and bring to 90°c/194°F on a medium setting. Add the gellan F and sodium citrate and blitz for 1 more minute. Lift the lid and scrape down the sides of the jug halfway through.

Pour the mixture into a bowl and place the bowl in iced water. Using a hand blender, blend the mixture as it cools to achieve a smooth consistency.

Pass the red wine fluid gel through a fine-mesh sieve and store in a piping bag until needed.

To Serve

Defrosted cheesecakes
Reserved red wine fluid gel
Reserved roasted figs

Gently place each cheesecake on a serving plate.

Pipe a thin strip of red wine fluid gel alongside the cheesecake. Top with pieces of roasted fig.

COMPOST

[1390]

COMPOST

 *Take rote of persel, of pasternak, of rafens, scrape hem and waische hem clene. Take rapes & caboches, ypared and icorue. Take an erthen panne with clene water & set it on the fire; cast alle thise therinne. Whan they buth boiled cast therto peeres, & perboile hem wel. Take alle thise thynges up & lat it kele on a faire cloth. Do therto salt; whan it is colde, do hit in a vessel; take vyneger & powdour & safroun & do therto, & lat alle thise thynges lye therin al nyght, other al day. Take wyne greke & hony, clarified togider; take lumbarde mustard & raisouns coraunce, al hoole, & grynde powdour of canel, powdour douce & aneys hole, & fenell seed. Take alle thise thynges & cast togyder in a pot of erthe, & take therof whan thou wilt & serve forth* ❋

The Forme of Cury (1390)

A few years ago I created a miniature edible garden with borders of cress; gravel paths made of tapioca, waffle cones and fried baby eels; and a variety of baby vegetables—such as carrots, asparagus, broccoli and bok choi—poking their way out of soil made from chopped dried olives, crushed Grape-Nuts and chopped pumpkin seeds. So, as you can imagine, I was intrigued to see a recipe for Compost in *The Forme of Cury*. Given medieval chefs' predilection for culinary tomfoolery, it seemed entirely possible to me that they'd thought up a dish that looked like a kitchen waste dump, but tasted delicious. As I read it, of course, it became clear that this wasn't the case, but by then I'd become interested in the recipe.

Compost was a sort of fruit and vegetable preserve—a valuable standby to supplement the meagre, monotonous diet of the winter months. It's not that far from a relish or chutney, although its closest relative must be *mostarda*, the Italian condiment made from candied fruit flavoured with mustard seeds. Linguistically, it's linked to the modern French word *compote*, which is now generally used to describe preparations of stewed fruit, though it can also refer to a vegetable cooked until it softens and thickens to a pulp, and to various game dishes, such as rabbit, pigeon or partridge, in which the meat is cooked gently until it falls off the bone. Both *compote* and compost derive from the Latin verb *componere*, which means "to compose, arrange or bring together". In Old French, *composte* signified a mixture of fruit and vegetables flavoured with spices and preserved in vinegar and honey, and the English were happily using the Anglicised version of the word, compost, until the 1600s. By then, however, the term had also acquired its modern meaning, which made it problematic as a food

term, so "compote", also borrowed from French, took its place. For me, the fact that compost has a linguistic split personality offered an exciting culinary challenge: to create a recipe that captured both meanings of the word, ancient and modern—a pickled dish that had a little of the compost heap's earthiness.

My starting point was to try to reproduce the original as faithfully as possible, to find out what worked and what didn't. I ended up with a pickled salad in which carrots (called "pasternak" in *The Forme of Cury* after the botanical name *pastinaca*, which at this time was used to denote both carrots and parsnips) were the vegetable that really shone, particularly in conjunction with fennel seeds, but the pears didn't really work for me. I would have to find another way of introducing pears to the dish—perhaps in the form of a mostarda as a nod to the dish's Italian counterpart—but in the meantime I needed to supplement the carrots with another fruit or vegetable. Beetroot seemed the natural choice for its distinctive earthy flavour, which comes from a compound it contains called geosmin.[*] This is also present in soil, and causes that heady, humus-like smell that pervades the air after a summer rainstorm. I prepared the beetroots by simmering them in vinegar and then finishing them with a vinegar glaze, so that I could allude to the fermented nature of the compost heap.

---

[*] *Human taste buds are extremely sensitive to geosmin; the average person can detect 0.7 parts per billion (in other words, in concentrations of just 0.00000007 per cent). As well as beetroot, it's present in spinach, snails and sweetcorn. It's one of the compounds responsible for the characteristic smell of corked wine, and also causes the muddy aroma you sometimes get from freshwater fish.*

Compost is created by micro-organisms such as bacteria and fungi breaking down organic waste. Virtually the same process is at work in fermentation, during which benign microbes break down the sugars present in a foodstuff and convert them into various substances, notably acids and alcohol. Vinegar is a classic product of fermentation: it's created by airborne bacteria that are able to tolerate alcohol. They break it down into acetic acid and water, the two basic components of vinegar. So by using vinegar in several components of the dish, I could introduce a distinct fermented flavour that would add to its compost-like character.

At this stage, what I'd developed was essentially a plate of pickled vegetables, which was undoubtedly close to the spirit of the original, but hardly something I could serve at one of my restaurants. It needed more variety,

body and textural contrast. Looking for something with a smooth texture and a robust enough flavour to stand up to the pickle, I decided on goat's curd, which has a yoghurt-like acidity that fitted with the dish, and also gave me an idea for adding further complexity to the fermented aspect of the recipe. If I took goat's milk and separated out the curds and whey, I could mix the whey with a starter, leave it in a warm environment to ferment, then serve it as a foam. The light, frothy, airy structure would ensure that the sourness of the whey didn't overpower the other flavours, while allowing it to reinforce the fermented notes in the dish.

To pick up on the vegetal nature of the compost heap, I wanted to include a fresh, herbal note. We began looking at greenery that was grown in medieval kitchen gardens but has

since fallen out of favour, and among these it was lovage that most impressed. The plant itself looks like wild celery, and medieval chefs tended to use both as a flavouring or seasoning. As a result, the two became inextricably associated, and when wild celery was superseded in the kitchen by the milder, cultivated version, lovage too was set aside. But lovage has a distinctive flavour: sharp, citrusy, green and aromatic with a trace of anise, which was one of the ingredients in the original recipe. I wanted to use lovage as a sort of seasoning for the dish, much as chefs had used it in the past, and thought the best vehicle for this was an emulsion; in other words, a sort of eggless mayonnaise. It took a while to find the exact percentages of ingredients that let the lovage flavour come through while providing the right texture, but the process itself was a standard one at my restaurants for

making what I call a fluid gel (see page 289). The leaves were blanched a couple of times, then drained, after which oil was added and the mixture was frozen so I could put it in the Pacojet. Basically a powerful grinder that shaves a frozen block to a fine powder, the Pacojet is a great way to achieve a super-smooth texture, as it breaks down a substance very efficiently. Moreover, it does so in a cold environment, which ensures the ingredients don't acquire a cooked flavour (the whirring blades of a blender can generate a surprising amount of heat). After three stints in the Pacojet, followed by a final straining through a fine-mesh filter bag, the liquid is ready for combining with a setting agent to give it a purée-like consistency. Lovage responded extremely well to this technique, producing a flavourful, vibrant green emulsion with which to dress the goat's curd. Although

I didn't realise it until the recipe was more fully developed, this emulsion formed the backbone for the whole dish, making the mouth water and giving a lovely, smooth mouthfeel, while also providing the vital fresh, green top notes.

There was another technique I was keen to use because it seemed thematically appropriate for this dish. In Catalonia, the locals hold a festival called the Calçotada. The *calçot* is a large, mild spring onion and in the early spring they are harvested, flung on to giant barbecue grills set over fires in the street and charred until they're black. Strip off the outer layer, however, and you have a sweet, succulent vegetable that has been steamed in its own juices, with a lovely smoky note. There was an earth-bound naturalness about the whole process that seemed to fit with the integrity of my dish, and it offered a way of introducing a non-pickled vegetable element to the recipe. I chose to use leeks, which, since they looked much like *calçots* and were from the same family, would probably respond well to the process, and also cabbage, to bring in another vegetable from the original recipe. Through trial and error we found the optimal time that cooked them perfectly while adding a little smokiness: seven minutes for leeks, twenty-five minutes for cabbage. The final vegetables for the dish were in place.

There was just one thing missing. The dish was full of flavours that captured, albeit in a refined way, something of the character of the compost heap. But the plate still didn't look enough like one; it needed a bit of dirt. So I went back to the edible soil I'd created for my miniature garden and made a new version with roasted onion oil mixed with tapioca maltodextrin (a type of starch that can absorb oil while still remaining granular). I added to this a crumb and a crumble flavoured with mushrooms and truffle, both of which have a distinct from-the-earth characteristic. To finish it off and make it elegantly messy, I added matchstick-shaped stalks of minuscule enoki mushrooms, which I shredded to fine fibres and dried so that they resembled strands of straw. And then it was complete: my composition in decomposition.

COMPOST

Makes 6 portions

Soured Whey Foam

2kg	Goat's milk
1g	Rennet
3g	Live keffir grains
½ head	Garlic
3g	Soy lecithin
2g	Sodium caseinate
	Salt

Preheat a water bath to 30°C/86°F.

Bring the goat's milk to the boil, then reduce the heat until the temperature reaches 50°C/122°F. Add the rennet and maintain this temperature for 30 minutes.

Gently lift the curds out of the whey and hang them in muslin suspended over a container. Pass the remaining whey through a fine-mesh filter bag and set aside. Discard the curds.

Collect 1kg of the whey and combine with the keffir. Place the mixture in a conical beaker. Cover the opening of the beaker with a small piece of muslin secured with an elastic band, and place the beaker in the water bath for 18 hours.

In the meantime, preheat an oven to 180°C/350°F, and roast the garlic until golden and fragrant. Wrap it in kitchen foil and set aside.

Remove the whey from the water bath and add 5g of the roasted garlic. Season with salt.

Just before serving, heat the mixture to 50°C/122°F and add the soy lecithin and sodium caseinate. Use a hand blender to create a foam.

Burnt Leek and Cabbage

1	Medium head hispi cabbage
2	Large leeks

Preheat a convection oven to 300°C/572°F.

Put the cabbage and leeks on a baking tray and place in the oven. Remove the leeks after 7 minutes, but keep the cabbage in for 25 minutes. Allow the vegetables to cool, then peel away the burnt leaves.

Cut the cabbage in half and divide each half into 8 wedges. Trim the core carefully so that the cabbage will stand upright.

Using only the white part, cut the leek into 5cm lengths. Divide each length into 4 wedges. Set aside to keep warm.

Pickled Baby Carrots

9–12	Baby carrots, with leaves
10g	Fennel seeds
150g	White caster sugar
150g	White wine vinegar

Carefully peel and wash the baby carrots, keeping the leaves intact. Snip the leaves so they are equal in length. Bring a pan of water to the boil and blanch the carrots for approximately 20 seconds. Remove immediately and plunge into a bowl of iced water.

In a dry, hot pan, toast the fennel seeds until fragrant. Set aside to cool.

In a clean saucepan, bring the sugar, white wine vinegar and 300g water to the boil. Remove from the heat and add the toasted fennel seeds and carrots. Pour into a sous-vide bag, seal and allow to pickle for 4 hours.

Glazed Beetroot

20g	Peeled garlic
500g	Red wine vinegar
10g	Thyme
6–9	Baby beetroots, rinsed
5g	Grapeseed oil
75g	Cabernet Sauvignon vinegar
20g	Unsalted butter, cubed and at room temperature

Partly crush the garlic cloves with the back of a knife. Add to a pan with 1.5kg water and the red wine vinegar. Add the thyme and baby beetroots and simmer for 20–30 minutes, depending on their size. The beetroots should not be completely soft, as they will be cooked again later. They should still be slightly firm.

Remove from the heat and drain the beetroots, discarding the liquid. Carefully peel them by rubbing them gently with kitchen paper, and cut them in half or quarters, depending on their size.

Heat the grapeseed oil in a clean pan. Sear the beetroot pieces, then deglaze with vinegar. Add the butter and shake the beetroots in the mixture to melt the butter and create a glossy glaze. Set aside and keep warm.

Crispy Grelot Onions

5	Grelot onions, peeled, trimmed and quartered
	Saffron
100g	Chardonnay vinegar
500g	Grapeseed oil
50g	Cornflour
1g	Salt

Carefully separate the grelot onion quarters into individual leaves.

Soak a pinch of saffron in the vinegar and 300g water and place in a sous-vide bag. Add the onion leaves and seal. Allow to soak for 24 hours.

Drain the onion leaves on a tray lined with kitchen paper and heat the grapeseed oil in a pan to 140°C/280°F. Toss the onion leaves in a small bowl with the cornflour and salt. Shake off the excess flour and lightly fry the onion leaves until just starting to crisp. Remove with a slotted spoon and drain on a tray lined with kitchen paper.

Place the leaves on a dehydrator tray. Place in the dehydrator at 40°C/104°F for 4 hours.

Lovage Emulsion

200g   Lovage leaves
400g   Grapeseed oil
100g   Chardonnay vinegar
0.5g   Bronze leaf gelatine
        Salt

Blanch the lovage leaves in boiling water for 10 seconds, then remove and refresh immediately in a bowl of iced water. Return to the boiling water and boil for 1 minute, until tender. Remove and repeat the refreshing process.

Wrap the leaves in muslin and squeeze out the excess water. Reserve 50g of this water. Place the leaves, along with the grapeseed oil, in a Pacojet container and place in the freezer until frozen. Place the frozen contents in a Pacojet and blitz 3 times. Pass the resulting lovage oil through a fine-mesh filter bag and set aside.

Place the vinegar in a small saucepan and reduce to 30g over a moderate heat. Add 35g of the reserved lovage water, combine and set aside.

Soak the gelatine in a little water for 5 minutes, then squeeze out the excess water. At the same time, in a separate small saucepan, gently warm the remaining reserved lovage water. Add the bloomed gelatine. Stir to dissolve and cool to room temperature.

Ensuring all the elements are at room temperature, combine the gelatine and the vinegar mixtures well. Emulsify with 150g of the lovage oil using a hand blender. Season with salt. This should be made no more than a few hours in advance, as it tends to lose its vibrant colour.

Enoki Mushroom Strands

25g   Enoki mushrooms

Trim the enoki mushrooms off their base and remove the caps. With a pair of fine tweezers, strip the stalks into fine fibres and place each strand on a dehydrator tray.

Place the tray in a dehydrator at 60°C/140°F for 12 hours. Set aside.

Truffle Rye Crumble

100g   Unsalted butter, cubed and
          at room temperature
200g   Truffle juice
210g   Rye flour
40g   Granular maltodextrin, DE=19

Melt the butter in a small saucepan and heat to 180°C/350°F, whisking continuously. Strain the brown butter and set aside to cool to room temperature.

In a separate small saucepan, heat the truffle juice very gently until the liquid has reduced to 75g. Set aside to cool. In the meantime, preheat the oven to 100°C/212°F.

In a small bowl, combine 25g of the brown butter, 75g reduced truffle juice, the rye flour and the maltodextrin. Rub the ingredients together using your hands and spread it out on a tray. Bake in the oven for 2 hours.

Transfer the crumble to a dehydrator tray and place in a dehydrator at 60°C/140°F for a minimum of 12 hours.

Place the crumble in a Thermomix and blitz for 2 seconds. Set aside.

Mushroom Crumb

5g   Extra virgin olive oil
5g   Unsalted butter
6   Portobello mushrooms, peeled
     and diced
1g   Peeled and finely diced garlic
     Lemon juice
2g   Flatleaf parsley

Heat the oil and butter in a very hot non-stick pan and add the mushrooms. Just before the mushrooms are completely cooked, add the garlic and a dash of lemon juice. Remove from the heat.

Finely chop the parsley and add to the mixture. Strain on to a small tray lined with kitchen paper, then spread out on a dehydrator tray. Place in a dehydrator set at 60°C/140°F for a minimum of 12 hours.

Transfer the dried mushrooms to a Thermomix and blitz for 5–10 seconds. Set aside.

Roasted Onion Mixture

3   Peeled Spanish onions
500g   Grapeseed oil
165g   Tapioca maltodextrin

Preheat the oven to 180°C/350°F.

Cut the onions lengthways and place in a deep roasting tray. Cover with the grapeseed oil. Roast in the oven for 2 hours, then remove and allow the entire tray and its contents to cool.

Once cooled, gently strain the oil. Combine 75g of the roasted onion oil with the maltodextrin and set aside.

Truffle Syrup

100g   Truffle juice
100g   Granular maltodextrin, DE=19

Whisk the truffle juice and maltodextrin together and place in a small saucepan. Bring the mixture to the boil and allow to reduce by half. Set aside.

"Dirt"

10g   Finely diced truffle
65g   Truffle rye crumble
60g   Mushroom crumb
10g   Reserved roasted onion mixture
10g   Truffle syrup

Combine the ingredients to create the "dirt". Set aside until ready to serve.

To Serve

300g   Fresh goat's curd
6   Wedges reserved burnt leek
6   Wedges reserved burnt cabbage
9   Reserved pickled baby carrots
120g   Pear mostarda, finely sliced
6   Glazed beetroots
     Reserved lovage emulsion
     Reserved "dirt"
     Reserved enoki mushroom
      strands
     Reserved crispy grelot onions
     Reserved soured whey foam

Divide the components between 6 plates, arranging them attractively on a plate to resemble a compost heap.

MEAT FRUIT

[*c.* 1430]

POME DORRES

❊ *Take Fylettys of Raw porke, & grynd hem wyl; do Salt [and] pouder Pepir ther-to; than take the Whyte of the Eyroun [and] throw therto, & make hem so hard that they mow ben Rosted on a Spete; make hem round as an Appil: make fyre with-owte smoke; then take Almaunde mylke, & y-bontyd flour, do hem to-gederys; take Sugre, & putte in thin bature; then dore hem with sum grene thing, percely or yolkys of Eyroun to-geder that they ben grene; & be wyl war that they ben nowt Browne; & sum men boyle hem in freysshe broth or they ben spetid; and whan they ben so boylid, then they must ben sette an kelid; & than Spete hem, & dore hem with yolkys of Eyroun y-mengyd with the Ius of haselle leuys* ❊

Leche Vyaundez, Harley MS 279 (*c.* 1430)

I first came across Meat Fruit (or rather Pome Dorres, which roughly translates as "Apple of Gold") when the food historians at Hampton Court, Marc Meltonville and Richard Fitch, sent me a photograph of a recipe that they had tried out in the palace kitchens. It came, they explained, from the Harley Collection: an enormous set of manuscripts originally amassed by Robert Harley (who held the top government post, First Lord of the Treasury, from 1711 to 1714) and his son, Edward. The collection was bought by the government in 1753 as part of the foundation of the British Museum library, the forerunner of the British Library. Pome Dorres looked like an apple but, as Marc and Richard explained, it was in fact minced pork that had been fashioned into a ball, coated in a skin made from a paste of flour and green herbs, spit-roasted, then glazed with eggs and hazel-leaf juice towards the end of cooking. It was served to guests among all the other platters of food as a surprise to be sprung at a feast—and it was indeed served at one of the biggest feasts of the period: the meal celebrating the coronation of Henry IV in 1399. I took to the idea at once.

Much of what we know about eating in the Middle Ages comes, one way or another, from feasts. There are few extant written records, and what we do have are not cookery books as such, but household accounts or reminders for chefs about how to prepare the dishes for a feast. By the 1300s, these formal meals had developed into grand affairs consisting of several courses, during which the table would groan with an extravagant mixture of sweet and savoury dishes. The first course for a feast attended by Richard II in 1397 offered venison, capons, a boar's head, a couple of large tarts and roast swans, herons and pheasants. It was followed by roast pig, rabbits, curlews, venison, peacocks, teal, custard and fritters, with a final course of dates in syrup, roast cranes and plovers, larks, more peacocks (this time gilded), apple fritters and cheese-and-quince dumplings. You might think this was simply the host, Lord Spenser, pushing the boat out because he was entertaining royalty, but the bills of fare from manorial households of the period show a similar abundance. At a New Year's feast at the Acton estate of Dame Alice de Bryene in the early 1400s, two pigs, two swans, twelve geese, two joints of mutton, twenty-four capons, seventeen rabbits, beef, veal, suckling pig and a variety of sweet dishes were served up to 300 people.

However, an elaborate series of dishes was only part of what was on offer. The gap between the courses would be filled by the presentation of a "subtlety", a sort of food sculpture—sometimes edible, sometimes not—designed to impress the guests. This might take the form of a cooked swan, peacock or bittern decorated with a gilded beak, its body slashed and striped with brilliant colours, or sugar moulded into wild animals or scenes from the Bible. Increasingly, these performance pieces were joined by other forms of entertainment: acrobats, perhaps, or jugglers, comedians, magicians or musicians. Like the subtleties, these became ever more complex and ritualised. Feasts in the later Middle Ages were punctuated by three structured diversions: the "disguising", in which characters, probably from the household itself, would appear disguised or dressed in outlandish costumes; the "mumming", in which some form of mime would take place; and the "interlude", in which a short play or story would be enacted. With all this going on, it's no wonder that observers had difficulty conveying what they had seen and eaten. Writing about one of Henry VIII's feasts, Cardinal Wolsey's gentleman-usher, George Cavendish, threw in the towel:

But to describe the dishes, subtleties, the many strange devices and order in the same, I do both lack wit in my gross old head and cunning in my bowels to declare the wonderful and curious imaginations in the same invented and devised.

At first glance, this style of dining might seem odd and obscure, but in fact the motives behind it are very familiar. Meals were opportunities to demonstrate status, power and wealth. Food expertly cooked using dramatic or out-of-season ingredients flavoured with expensive imported spices showed how refined the host was in comparison with the lowly peasant and his bowl of pottage. Inviting guests to a memorable dinner that was as dramatic as it was gastronomically advanced was a great way to win powerful friends and influence people. In this respect, the medieval feast was little different from the modern-day corporate freebie: the business lunch at a smart restaurant, catered box at a sporting competition, or private view with champagne reception.

It was also about sheer entertainment, of course. In a society in which only 15 per cent of the population were literate, and in which leisure options were limited, food was one of the most accessible and inclusive (at least for the rich) ways of passing the time. The food at the feast had to be delicious but, like the mummers and tumblers and jugglers, it was also expected to entertain. As well as gourmet dishes like stuffed piglet or pears poached in ginger and wine syrup, food designed to surprise, tantalise, amuse or even shock the guests would be served. Medieval cookery manuscripts contain recipes for turning white wine into red before the diners' eyes, or preparing a chicken so that it appears to spring from the serving platter. A taste for counterfeiting and deception seemed to run right through the feast, from the practice of "disguising" to the food on the table, and even the tableware itself. There are several recipes for puzzle jugs, in which a vessel riddled with holes appears miraculously to hold the liquid poured into it (but which in fact goes into the hollowed-out handle). Similarly, Tantalus cups with concealed hollows and tubes made sure that the drinker either found that the wine disappeared as they lifted the cup to their mouth, or that it all came out at once, soaking them completely.

Pome Dorres belonged to this tradition of disguise and illusion, and it worked on several levels. There was, of course, the sheer pleasure of the artistry of the dish, the chef's skill at transforming one thing into another. But the dish was also a tease. In the Middle Ages, people were often wary about eating raw fruit. Unwitting diners would approach Pome Dorres with caution, only to discover that, not only was the fruit not raw, it wasn't even fruit! And, since the customs of the feast drew heavily on religious imagery and practices, it seems likely that diners would have been reminded of the apple on the Tree of Knowledge. Just like Eve, they would get a surprise when they bit in.

I find this medieval taste for culinary games, allusions and illusions very exciting because it has always been a feature of my cooking, from Nitro-scrambled Egg and Bacon Ice Cream to Hot and Iced Tea, so it was something of a revelation when I discovered that chefs of the

Middle Ages had taken a similarly playful approach. I didn't feel I needed a precedent for cooking the way I did, but it was nonetheless inspiring to find that I was part of a longstanding culinary tradition.

Gradually, since I started exploring historical dishes, a *modus operandi* has developed: I begin by following the original recipe as closely as I can, in order get a clear idea of the chef's intentions, and the overall look, feel and taste of his dish. But with Pome Dorres it was already obvious that what the chef wanted above all was for the apple to be as convincing as possible. Naturally, he'd want it to have great flavour and texture, but the illusion was paramount. However, in the 1400s the most common method of cooking, spit-roasting, was still a relatively crude system that must have made the chef's ambitions difficult to realise. In terms of technology, I certainly had the edge. My job, it seemed to me, was to take advantage of the latest equipment to create a meat fruit that the medieval chef could only dream of. A dish that, were he transported to my kitchen in a time machine, would appeal to his wit and—who knows?—perhaps the cunning in his bowels as well.

Although meat fruit is an unusual concept, the components were familiar to me. Minced and cooked meat appears in any number of dishes, from meatballs, burgers and bangers to terrines and pâtés; and the French classical tradition includes all kinds of forcemeat stuffing (or *farce*) for things like *terrine en croûte* (terrine baked in pastry) and *petits farcis* (stuffed vegetables), so I had a broad range of techniques to choose from for the meat filling. I had even

already worked on a way of creating a skin. At the Fat Duck I serve asparagus with salmon that has been coated in liquorice gel. To achieve this, the salmon is briefly dipped into a liquorice stock containing a setting agent. Once the fish is removed, the coating cools and sets almost immediately, giving the fish a lovely, glossy black covering. There seemed no reason why I couldn't do something similar with stock made from something green—probably parsley or watercress—to create a nice, shiny apple skin. Clearly I had a fair amount of testing to do: I'd have to heat the finely minced meat delicately in a bain-marie, using a temperature probe to determine the exact point when it had cooked to a smooth, velvety texture, and I'd have to do dozens of trials with different temperatures and amounts of setting agents to get a firm but fine (and convincing) skin. At this point, though, it was basically a question of perfecting a couple of techniques.

However, as my development chefs will attest, I have a habit of turning a technical challenge into something altogether more complicated. *Why stop at an apple?* I asked myself. *Why not try out all kinds of fruit to see which works best?* The idea was irresistible, but there's no doubt that it hugely increased the workload. Each fruit had to have a filling with a texture and flavour that suited it. That meant mincing and cooking a variety of meats over and over, in different ways and at different temperatures, until we found the ones that ate the best and went well with each type of skin. And every skin would, of course, have its own set of ingredients to be refined and revised.

Patiently, we worked our way through the fruit bowl and found combinations that made sense, such as grapes made of Jabugo ham

minced with onion and a bread paste to bind it together, and a mandarin with foie gras parfait inside that seemed to me especially delicious. For each fruit I developed a coating made mainly from a mixture of fruit purée, fructose, natural colouring and an essential oil to intensify the flavour. Each one then had to go through the same laborious process of testing. I added a specific amount of gelatine, then warmed the mixture to a particular temperature, looking for the point at which it set to an even and delicate layer around the meat once it had been dipped in the mixture and left to cool. If the mixture was heated too far above the temperature at which the gelatine set, it solidified too slowly and the mixture either ran off or could only be built up in layers, which made the skin uneven and gave clues as to how it had been created. (I definitely didn't want my diners to divine the trick. Maintaining the illusion was as important to me as it must have been to the chefs who hoped to amaze with Pome Dorres.) If, on the other hand, the mixture wasn't warmed enough, so that it hovered around gelatine's setting point, it set almost immediately, producing a layer that was too thick, and made for a less satisfying eating experience.

Trial and error, and endless digital probing and tabulating of results, led to the establishment of the optimal temperature for creating the perfect skin, which was slightly different for each fruit. By this stage, I had already singled out the mandarin as the most likely candidate for Dinner's menu, but then something extraordinary tipped the balance completely in its favour. During one session of skin-dipping we were interrupted and decided to freeze the coated mandarins, reserving them for future experimentation. Later, when we re-dipped the mandarins, I discovered that a second dunking, provided it was done when the surface was still speckled with frost from the freezer, had an amazing effect on the fruit. All over the surface were tiny pockmarks, exactly like the skin of a real citrus fruit. It was so unexpected that I just stood there with a giant grin on my face. And I was pretty sure it would have the same effect on diners at the restaurant, too.

MEAT FRUIT

Makes 8 portions

Parfait Spheres

100g	Peeled and finely sliced shallots
5g	Peeled and finely diced garlic
15g	Thyme, tied together with string
150g	Dry Madeira
150g	Ruby port
75g	White port
50g	Brandy
250g	Foie gras, veins removed
150g	Chicken livers, veins removed
18g	Salt
2g	Curing salt
240g	Whole egg
300g	Unsalted butter, cubed and at room temperature

Begin by placing the shallots, garlic and thyme in a container, along with the Madeira, ruby port, white port and brandy. Cover and allow to marinate in the fridge overnight.

Remove the marinated mixture from the fridge and place in a saucepan. Gently and slowly heat the mixture until nearly all the liquid has evaporated, stirring regularly to prevent the shallots and garlic from catching. Remove the pan from the heat, discard the thyme and allow the mixture to cool.

Preheat the oven to 100°c/212°F.

In the meantime, fill a deep roasting tray two-thirds full with water. Ensure that it is large and deep enough to hold a terrine dish measuring 26cm wide, 10cm long and 9cm high. Place the tray in the oven. Place the terrine dish in the oven to warm through while the parfait is prepared.

Preheat a water bath to 50°c/122°F.

To prepare the parfait, cut the foie gras into pieces roughly the same size as the chicken livers. In a bowl, combine the foie gras and chicken livers and sprinkle with the salt and curing salt.

Mix well to combine and place in a sous-vide bag. Put the alcohol reduction, along with the egg, in a second sous-vide bag, and the butter in a third bag. Seal all 3 bags under full pressure and place them in the preheated water bath for 20 minutes.

Carefully remove the bags from the water bath, and place the livers and the egg-alcohol reduction in a deep dish. Using a hand blender, blitz the mixture well, then slowly incorporate the melted butter. Blend until smooth. It is important to remember that all three elements should be at the same temperature when combined, to avoid splitting the mixture.

Transfer the mixture to a Thermomix, set the temperature to 50°c/122°F and blend on full power for 3 minutes. Pass the mixture through a fine-mesh sieve lined with a double layer of muslin.

Carefully remove the terrine from the oven, pour in the smooth parfait mixture and place the terrine in the bain-marie. Check that the water level is the same height as the top of the parfait. Cover the bain-marie with aluminium foil.

After 35 minutes, check the temperature of the centre of the parfait using a probe thermometer. The parfait will be perfectly cooked when the centre reaches 64°c/147°F. This can take up to an hour.

Remove the terrine from the oven and allow to cool to room temperature. Cover with clingfilm and place in the fridge for 24 hours.

Remove the terrine from the fridge and take off the clingfilm. To remove the oxidised layer on top of the parfait, scrape the discoloured part off the surface. Spoon the parfait into a disposable piping bag. Holding the piping bag vertically, spin it gently to ensure all air bubbles are removed.

Place 2 silicone dome-mould trays, each containing 8 hemispheres 5cm in diameter, on a tray. Piping in a slow, tight, circular fashion, fill the hemispheres with the parfait, ensuring they are slightly overfilled. Using a palette knife, scrape the surface of the moulds flat, then cover with clingfilm. Gently press the clingfilm on to the surface of the parfait and place the moulds in the freezer until frozen solid.

Taking one tray at a time from the freezer, remove the clingfilm and lightly torch the flat side of the parfait, being careful to only melt the surface. Join the two halves together by folding one half of the silicone mould on to the other half and press gently, ensuring the hemispheres are lined up properly.

Remove the folded half of the mould to reveal a joined-up parfait sphere, and push a cocktail skewer down into it. Place the moulds back in the freezer for 2 hours (the spheres are easier to handle once frozen solid).

Remove them from the mould completely, and smooth any obvious lines with a paring knife. Wrap the perfectly smooth spheres individually in clingfilm and store in the freezer. They should be placed in the freezer for at least 2 hours before dipping in the mandarin jelly.

Mandarin Jelly

80g	Glucose
2kg	Mandarin purée
180g	Bronze leaf gelatine
1.6g	Mandarin essential oil
7g	Paprika extract

Place the glucose and 1kg mandarin purée in a saucepan and gently heat to 50°C/122°F, stirring to dissolve the glucose completely. Bloom the gelatine by placing it in a container and covering it with cold water.

Allow to stand for 5 minutes. Place the softened gelatine in a fine-mesh sieve and squeeze out all excess water, then add it to the warm mandarin purée. Stir well until fully dissolved.

Take 250g of the warm purée mixture and add the mandarin essential oil and paprika extract. Stir gently to combine and add it back to the mandarin mixture. Add the remaining mandarin purée and stir again to fully combine, before passing the mixture through a fine-mesh sieve.

Allow the mandarin jelly to stand in the fridge for a minimum of 24 hours before using.

Herb Oil

180g	Extra virgin olive oil
15g	Rosemary
15g	Thyme
10g	Peeled and halved garlic

Place the olive oil, herbs and garlic in a sous-vide bag. Seal under full pressure and refrigerate.

Keep in the fridge for 48 hours before using.

To Serve

Reserved frozen parfait spheres
Reserved mandarin jelly
Mandarin stalks with leaves
Sourdough bread
Reserved herb oil

To make the fruits, preheat a water bath to 30°C/86°F.

Place the mandarin jelly in a saucepan over a low-to-medium heat and gently melt, ensuring the temperature does not rise above 40°C/104°F. Place the melted jelly in a tall container and place the container in the preheated water bath. Allow the jelly to cool to 27°C/81°F.

In the meantime, line a tray with kitchen paper covered with a layer of pierced clingfilm. This will make an ideal base for the parfait balls when they defrost. A block of polystyrene is useful for standing up the parfait spheres once dipped.

Once the jelly has reached the optimal dipping temperature, remove the parfait balls from the freezer. Remove the clingfilm and carefully plunge each ball into the jelly twice, before allowing excess jelly to run off.

Stand them vertically in the polystyrene and place immediately in the fridge for 1 minute. Repeat the process a second time. Depending on the colour and thickness of the jelly on the parfait ball, the process may need to be repeated a third time.

Soon after the final dip, the jelly will have set sufficiently to permit handling. Gently remove the skewers and place the balls on the lined tray, with the hole hidden underneath. Cover the tray with a lid and allow to defrost in the fridge for approximately 6 hours.

To serve, gently push the top of the spheres with your thumb to create the shape of a mandarin. Place a stalk in the top centre of the indent to complete the "fruit".

Serve each meat fruit with a slice of sourdough bread that has been brushed with herb oil and toasted under the grill.

ALOWS

[c. 1430]

ALOWS DE BEEF OR DE MOUTON

❊ *Take fayre Bef of the quyschons, & motoun of the bottes, & kytte in the maner of Stekys; than take raw Percely, & Oynonys smal y-scredde, & yolkys of Eyroun sothe hard, & Marow or swette, & hew alle thes to-geder smal; than caste ther-on poudere of Gyngere & Saffroun, and tolle hem to-gederys with thin hond, & lay hem on the Stekys al a-brode, & caste Salt ther-to; then rolle to-gederys, & putte hem on a round spete, & roste hem til they ben y-now; than lay hem in a dysshe, & pore ther-on Vynegre and a lityl verious, & pouder Pepir ther-on y-now, & Gyngere, & Canelle, & a fewe yolkys of hard Eyroun y-kremyd ther-on; & serve forth ❊*

Leche Vyaundez, Harley MS 279 (*c.*1430)

Alows—or allows or allowes—are essentially stuffed meat rolls. Once cooked, they apparently resembled little roasted birds, and it's this effect that gave them their name, which derives from *aloe*, the Old French word for lark. (The French term for sirloin, *aloyau*, comes from the same root.) Roasting posed a challenge for chefs at the time because cooking, even in the grandest houses, was done over an open fire. Closed Aga-style ranges started to appear only in the late 1700s (Thomas Robinson took out the first patent for one in 1780) and, despite the enthusiasm of celebrity chef Alexis Soyer, who had gas cookers installed in the Reform Club in 1841 (see page 374), gas didn't really take off until the end of the nineteenth century.

At first, cooking fires were set up over a hearth in the middle of the floor, but by the 1100s wide, shallow fireplaces were being built into walls, sometimes in a building separate from the main house to minimise the risk of fire. Since they were required to cook virtually every dish, these fireplaces were often constructed on a massive scale. The kitchens that King John had built at Clarendon Palace in 1206 had hearths big enough to roast several large cuts of meat at the same time. These hearths could also accommodate large cauldrons suspended on a tripod or bracket and filled with boiling water, in which several pots containing different dishes might be placed. Pots and pans with very long handles, like the paddle of a pizza chef, were available for frying and stewing, and gridirons of metal bars could be held over the flames for grilling. Dishes such as Alows and Pome Dorres, which called for small cuts of meat, would be cooked on a spit called a "broche" or "flesh-pike" laid upon on a pair of metal supports (andirons) or on a rack with pairs of hooks at various levels, which leaned against the back of the chimney breast.

Turning the spit was a hot and horrible job. It was given to one of the scullions (the most junior members of the kitchen) who was known as the turnspit or "child for the broches", and often lived and slept in the kitchen. As protection from the fierce heat of the fire, a guard was sometimes constructed from wood lagged with wet straw and pierced with a small hole at the centre so that the spits could still be viewed. Nonetheless, many turnspits stripped off when tending the flames—the original naked chefs! It was a sufficiently widespread habit that a King's Ordinance was issued in 1526 to put a stop to the practice:

> It is ordeyned by the Kings Highnesse [that] scolyons… shall not goe naked or in garments of such vilenesse as they now doe… nor lye in the nights and dayes in the kitchens or ground by the fireside.

Scullions could handle the mind-numbing grind of turning the spit, but a chef still had to oversee the cooking because, as anyone who has grilled on a barbecue will know, it takes skill and experience to manage an open fire well. The chef had to understand exactly how different woods burned, when to move food nearer to or further from the flames, how best to baste it, and at what moment. Over time, a valuable body of knowledge about the art of spit-roasting accrued, which could be passed on from one cook to another. Thus, in *The English Huswife* (1615), Gervase Markham gave detailed information about the requirements for successful spit-roasting, and finished with advice on how "To know when meat is enough".

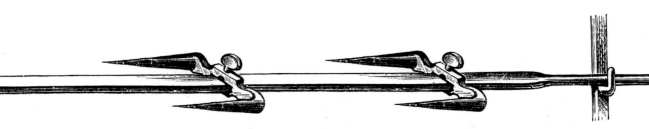

…as too much rawness is unwholsom, so too much dryness is not nourishing. Therefore to know when it is in the perfect height, and is neither too moist nor too dry, you shall observe these signs: First, in your large Joynts of meat, when the steam or smoak of the meat ascendeth either upright, or else goeth from the fire, when it beginneth a little to shrink from the spit, or when the gravy which droppeth from it is clear without bloodiness, then is the meat enough. If it be a Pigge, when the eyes are fallen out, and the body leaveth Piping: for the first is when it is half roasted, and would be sindged, to make the coat rise, and crackle, and the later when it is full enough, and would be drawn; or if it be any kind of Fowl you roast, when the thighs are tender, or the hinder parts of the pinions at the setting on of the wings, are without blood, then be sure that your meat is fully enough roasted.

By Markham's time, however, the whole process was being transformed. In 1570, the physician to Elizabeth I, Dr John Caius, had noted in *De Canibus Britannicus* that dogs made excellent turnspits: "for when any meat is to be roasted they go into a wheel, which they, turning about with the weight of their bodies, so diligently look to their business that no drudge or scullion can do the feat more cunningly". Some historians have suggested that, over the course of the seventeenth century, dogs and even geese were used in place of their human counterparts, on a treadmill positioned high up on a wall near the fireplace and connected to the spit by a pulley, though it has yet to be made clear how they were induced to do this for a useful length of time.

However, other more sophisticated technological advances were already under way. The spit was the first kitchen process to be fully mechanised. By the early 1600s, the counterweight jack had been devised: a cord or chain with a heavy weight at one end that was wound around a cylinder, then the weight would be left gradually to descend by means of gravity, rotating the cylinder as it did so, which in turn would rotate the spit through a series of cogwheels and pulleys. Alongside this development was another: the smoke jack, which harnessed the updraught from the fire by means of a sort of horizontal fan placed in the chimney flue, from which extended a vertical arm that was linked to the spit by a pinion and cogwheels. As hot air rose, pushing against the blades and causing them to revolve, the spit also turned as a result. It was an ingenious system, but an uneconomical one—keeping the vane turning required about as much fuel as a small steam engine.

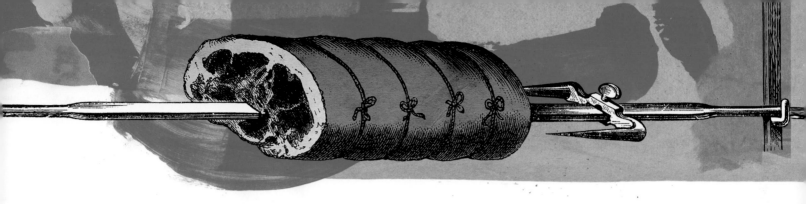

The kitchen set-up, especially in modest households, continued in much this form until at least the 1700s. For all the technological improvements, if you look at an illustration of the kitchen in an eighteenth-century cookbook, it still closely resembles the kitchen pictured in Bartolomeo Scappi's influential 1570 cookbook *Opera dell'arte del cucinare*, with the cook turning meat and tending to a number of pots over open flames. By the eighteenth century, however, the main source of fuel was not wood but coal, which needed an updraught to burn efficiently, so the flat hearth had been replaced by a brazier or firebasket, and the process of enclosing fire had begun. The benefits of doing so were significant. For the unskilled, cooking over an open fire could be smoky, messy and dangerous, and neither particularly efficient nor easy to control. Enclosure of the fire promised a solution to these problems, and over the course of the century a number of strategies were tried. People started building an oven into one side of the grate (although this tended to heat unevenly), and by 1750 manufacturers had created a stand-alone oven that would be positioned close to the fire so it could use the chimney flue. Out of these initiatives evolved the concept of a solid metal structure in which the fire could be housed and controlled. Within

thirty years, the first kitchen ranges had been developed and, although take-up was gradual, spit-roasting eventually lost its central role in the kitchen.

The Alows recipe from the Harley Collection presented me with three main issues to consider. First, I had to choose the best method for cooking the meat so as to really do it justice. Second, I had to find a way to enhance its flavour, because although fillet of beef has a beautifully tender texture, which is why we prize it so much, it can be a little bland because it doesn't have much fat to give it flavour. And somehow I had to achieve both of these tasks without straying too far from the spirit of the original dish.

The first of these decisions was easily made. Just as early-seventeenth-century chefs had access to radical new technology in the form of the counterweight jack, so in the last decade modern chefs have been able to take advantage of a revolutionary method of cooking: the *sous-vide* system. Sous-vide, which is the French term for "under vacuum", was first conceived as a means of preservation for the food industry. Food was placed in a bag in a chamber vacuum sealer, whereupon the air was removed and the

bag sealed shut. The absence of oxygen (which provides a benign environment for microbes, thereby causing spoilage) gave the food a longer shelf life, and the neatly sealed packages were easy to handle and store. But a handful of chefs, including me, started experimenting with cooking in a temperature-controlled water bath, and sous-vide turned out to be the perfect piece of complementary technology for it. Together, they offered a whole new approach to cooking.

Since a water bath can be set to a precise temperature that will be maintained without fluctuation, the chef has unprecedented control over the source of heat. And since the food is sealed in a bag from which air, an inefficient conductor of heat, has been removed, it cooks through evenly and efficiently while holding on to all the juices, volatile flavours and nutrients that tend to be lost when more aggressive forms of cooking are used. There are, though, a few things that sous-vide can't do. Most importantly, it doesn't generate Maillard reactions. These are complex chemical changes that occur when protein-rich foods are exposed to heat (generally above 120°c/250°f) and cause their amino acids to react with other compounds (mainly sugars) to create all sorts of new, intense flavours. With sous-vide, if browning is necessary it has to be done as a separate process, but this is a small

price to pay for food that's tender, succulent and supremely flavourful. So I chose to cook the beef fillet not on a spit but in a water bath, an approach that resembles the medieval cauldron bubbling away on its tripod, but gives the chef a degree of control that the fifteenth-century cook could only dream of.

As for enhancing the flavour of a lean cut of meat, it was another historical cookbook, Victorian rather than medieval, that helped shape my thinking. One of the advantages of delving into British cuisine's back catalogue is that you get to see how all sorts of professional chefs tackled traditional challenges. It's a great reminder of the sheer range of techniques available, including those that have been forgotten or superseded. I knew that, in his *Encyclopaedia of Practical Cookery* (see page 404), Theodore Francis Garrett had solved this very problem by "larding" a fillet of beef: in other words, taking strips of fat and actually sewing them into the surface of the meat. Needle and twine aren't a very elegant solution, but I could see a way of updating Garrett's technique with transglutaminase. This is a natural substance that causes a bond to form between two amino acids, lysine and glutamine. Since both of these are present in proteins, transglutaminase can act as a sort of glue, sticking proteins together.

Although common in Japanese cuisine (where it's employed principally to make the processed fish products known as *surimi*), transglutaminase was until recently almost unknown in the West. I was one of the first chefs to use it, as part of a method I developed for binding and cooking pigeon breasts so that they could be heated more briefly than usual, and thus avoid ending up overcooked. I had subsequently used it to create things like a ballotine of mackerel in which the fish appears to have no backbone running through it. This time, I began by dusting transglutaminase on to a trimmed rectangle of beef that had been dry-aged, which means that it had been stored for a period in an environment where the temperature, humidity and air circulation were carefully controlled, a process that encourages natural enzymes in the meat to tenderise the flesh and break down large proteins, making it much more flavoursome. On top of this I pressed a rectangle of beef fat so that it adhered to the beef, thereby creating the ideal piece of meat. As it cooked gently and precisely in the water bath, the flesh would become meltingly tender. But the presence of a layer of fat, which would gradually render and baste the meat, provided plenty of extra flavour. After a final quick sear in a frying pan, to finish rendering the fat and give it some colour, we had the ultimate steak.

The steak's accompaniments were inspired by an identity confusion of sorts. My chefs sometimes looked at old recipes and assumed that reference to marrow meant not the vegetable but bone marrow. It had led to some perplexing discussions in the development kitchen, but here I started thinking that replacing one with the other might be appropriate: bone marrow had a meaty richness that suited this dish. What's more, it offered me a way of incorporating a number of ingredients from the original recipe. Parsley, vinegar and eggs put me in mind of mayonnaise-based sauces such as tartare, its French cousin gribiche and celeriac remoulade, as well as creamed horseradish. The creamy sharpness of any of these would complement the texture of bone marrow and temper its richness, so I began structuring part of the dish around these elements.

We tried several milk and horseradish infusions until we had a liquid that held plenty of bone-marrow flavour, then experimented with setting agents until we arrived at a delicate, pale-coloured gel from which we could cut out bone-marrow discs to use as a garnish, along with ox tongue and sweetbreads to reinforce the meaty character, and a celeriac remoulade.

For the rest of the garnishes, it was that notion of the ultimate steak that guided me. Mushrooms are a typical, umami-rich accompaniment for steak, so I added nicely browned ceps to the plate. Another classic accompaniment is onion rings, and this is where I came full circle with the medieval recipe. To introduce that delightful crunch you get when you bite into perfectly deep-fried batter, I made shallot shards by dipping slices in a syrup and dehydrating them to a crisp brittleness. I also began developing a fluid gel (see page 289) that would deliver a very clean, intense, balanced onion flavour. As I worked, it occurred to me that this was the ideal vehicle for one of the defining characteristics of the original dish. By taking sliced onions and smoking them over wood chips before putting them in the gel mix, I could introduce a smoky note—a subtle reminder, from tongue to brain, of the fiery origins of the dish.

ALOWS OF BEEF

Makes 6 portions

Rendered Bone Marrow

750g   **Beef bone marrow, pushed out from the bones**

Preheat the oven to 160°C/320°F.

Spread the marrow out evenly on a large, deep tray and cook in the oven for about 35 minutes. Once fully melted, pass the rendered fat through a fine-mesh sieve lined with muslin and set aside in the fridge until needed.

This will be used in the smoked bone marrow garnish, the cooking of the beef, to finish the red wine sauce, and for the potato crisps. Any surplus can be frozen.

Smoked Bone Marrow

200g   **Reserved rendered bone marrow, liquid and at room temperature**
        Fine oak smoking chips

Place the rendered bone marrow in a container to make a layer no more than 5mm deep. Wrap the container in clingfilm and pierce 2 small holes in it. Keep the clingfilm nearby.

Put ½ teaspoon smoking chips in a smoking gun, insert the nozzle into one of the holes and light the gun, allowing the smoke to fill the container. After 15 seconds the container should be filled with smoke. Remove the nozzle and wrap the container completely with clingfilm. Leave to smoke for 5 minutes.

Remove the clingfilm, stir the bone marrow well and repeat the smoking process twice, with fresh smoking chips each time. Set aside in the fridge.

Smoked Bone Marrow Garnish

275g   **Semi-skimmed milk**
175g   **Whipping cream**
50g   **Creamed horseradish**
80g   **Reserved smoked bone marrow**
5g   **Salt**
0.2g   **Gellan F (low-acyl gellan)**
0.8g   **LT-100 (high-acyl gellan)**
0.5g   **Guar gum**

Place the milk and cream in a saucepan and heat to 80°C/176°F. Remove from the heat, add the creamed horseradish to the warm milk mixture and allow to infuse for 15–20 minutes.

Pass the infused mixture through a fine-mesh sieve, then place in a Thermomix with the smoked bone marrow and salt. Bring to 90°C/194°F at medium speed, then add the 3 gelling agents. Blitz for 2 more minutes at high speed, ensuring the gelling agents have dissolved. You may need to stop halfway through to scrape down the sides of the jug.

Pour the mixture on to a tray lined with clingfilm to a height of approximately 5mm. Allow to stand for at least 30 minutes, until set completely, then cover with clingfilm and store in the fridge until needed.

Before serving, take the tray out of the fridge and use a 3cm-diameter round cutter to cut out circles for the garnish.

Mayonnaise

45g   **Pasteurised egg yolk**
30g   **Dijon mustard**
350g   **Grapeseed oil**
35g   **Chardonnay vinegar**
3g   **Salt**

Whisk the egg yolk and Dijon mustard together in a small bowl. Slowly incorporate the grapeseed oil, whisking continuously until emulsified.

Fold in the vinegar and season with salt. Store in the fridge until needed.

Celeriac Remoulade

300g   **Peeled celeriac, cut into thin strips**
35g   **Wholegrain mustard**
18g   **Finely chopped Lilliput capers**
25g   **Finely diced gherkins**
150g   **Reserved mayonnaise**
1g   **Salt**
10g   **Flatleaf parsley**

Fold all the ingredients except the parsley together and season with salt.

Just before serving, finely chop the flatleaf parsley and add to the mixture. Combine well and store in the fridge until needed.

10% Herb Brine

100g   **Salt**
10g   **Rosemary**
10g   **Thyme**
1   **Bay leaf**
10g   **Peeled garlic**
2g   **Black peppercorns**

Place 1kg water and the salt in a saucepan and bring to the boil, ensuring all the salt has dissolved.

Allow the brine to cool to 40°C/104°F, then add the herbs and aromatics. Once the brine has cooled completely, place in the fridge until needed.

Veal Sweetbreads

150g   **Veal sweetbreads**
110g   **Reserved 10% herb brine**
10g   **Extra virgin olive oil**
50g   **Sherry vinegar**
50g   **Madeira**
10g   **Unsalted butter**

(continued overleaf)

Preheat the water bath to 65°c/149°f.

Trim off all visible fat from the sweetbreads and rinse under cold running water.

Place the sweetbreads in a sous-vide bag and add the brine. Seal under full pressure and allow the sweetbreads to brine for 2 hours.

Remove the sweetbreads from the sous-vide bags and rinse for 30 minutes under cold running water. Pat the sweetbreads dry and place them in a sous-vide bag, ensuring they are all lying flat and in a single layer. Seal under full pressure.

Cook the sweetbreads in the water bath for 2 hours, then place in iced water.

Once the sweetbreads are cool enough to handle, remove all sinew and dice into 1.5cm cubes.

Heat the oil in a non-stick pan and sauté the sweetbread cubes. Add the sherry vinegar and Madeira and shake the pan to coat the diced sweetbread fully. Allow the mixture to reduce slightly, then add the butter, creating a glaze. Remove the pan from the heat and allow to rest in the pan.

Brined Ox Tongue

145g	Salt
8g	Curing salt
1	Ox tongue

Preheat a water bath to 65°c/149°f.

Mix 1kg water, the salt and curing salt in a container and use a hand blender to combine it well. Store the brine in the fridge while preparing the tongue.

Wash the tongue well and scrape off any dirt. Trim off the front part of the tongue (it will not be used). Cut a rectangle from the centre of the tongue by trimming off the corners. Divide that piece again into quarters.

Place the 4 pieces of tongue along with 1kg of the brine in a sous-vide bag and seal. Cook the tongue pieces in the water bath for 48 hours.

Once the tongue pieces are cooked, plunge the bag in an ice bath. Allow to cool completely in the brine before removing.

Finishing the Ox Tongue

20g	Flatleaf parsley
50g	Japanese breadcrumbs
	Reserved brined ox tongue

Finely chop the flatleaf parsley and mix it with the Japanese breadcrumbs.

Dice the ox tongue into 1.5cm cubes (you will need a minimum of 6 cubes). Roll the diced ox tongue in the parsley-crumb mixture just before serving. There will probably be more than you need, but the ox tongue freezes well.

Shallot Crisps

50g	Granular maltodextrin, DE=19
150g	Peeled and finely sliced shallot rings (1–1.5cm diameter)

Place 50g water and the maltodextrin in a small saucepan and bring to the boil. Remove from the heat and set aside.

Dip the shallot rings in the syrup and place them on kitchen paper to remove any excess moisture. Place in a dehydrator for 12 hours.

Set aside in a sealed container until needed.

Smoked Onion Fluid Gel

5g	Fine oak smoking chips
250g	Peeled and finely sliced white onions
30g	Unsalted butter, cubed and at room temperature
1g	Thyme
200g	Semi-skimmed milk
95g	Whipping cream
150g	Chicken bouillon (see page 27)
1g	Salt
2.7g	Gellan F (low-acyl gellan)

Put ½ teaspoon smoking chips in a smoking gun. Place the sliced onions in a container and wrap tightly with clingfilm. Poke a small hole in the corner of the clingfilm and insert the tube of the smoking gun. Start the smoking gun and fill the container with smoke. Immediately remove the tube and cover the hole with clingfilm. Leave the container for 30 minutes.

Repeat this process twice more with fresh chips, shaking the container to smoke the onions evenly. Remove from the container and set aside.

Melt the butter in a saucepan and add the smoked onions and thyme. Gently sweat the onions over a medium heat until the onions leach their juices but still retain their acidity. Add the milk, cream, chicken bouillon and salt and simmer for 5 minutes.

Remove and discard the thyme and transfer the mixture to a deep-sided container. Partially blitz the onion mixture with a hand blender and pass this infused mixture through a fine-mesh sieve. Weigh 400g of the onion-flavoured milk and place it in a smaller, clean saucepan. Gently bring the onion milk to a boil.

Add the gellan F and blitz to incorporate fully, ensuring it has all been added.

Pour the mixture into a bowl, and place the bowl in iced water. Using a hand blender, blend the mixture as it cools to a smooth consistency.

Pass the smoked onion fluid gel through a fine-mesh sieve and store in the fridge until needed.

Potato Crisps

1	Large potato
50g	Three-cone wild garlic (also known as garlic grass)
100g	Reserved rendered bone marrow

Preheat the oven to 140°c/280°f.

Peel the potato and slice it as thinly as possible using a mandolin. The slices should be so thin they are transparent.

Place a wild garlic blade tip (which should be 3–4 cm long) between 2 thin potato slices and press gently together.

Trim the potato around the shape of the blade. Repeat with the remaining potato slices and wild garlic.

Brush a little melted bone marrow on the potato slices and place them on a baking tray. Cover the crisps with a heavy tray to ensure they remain flat during cooking.

Bake in the oven until cooked through and crisp. Gently remove them from the baking tray and set aside.

Preparing and Cooking the Beef

500g	Single piece of 28-day aged beef fat
3	Thick centre cuts from 3 x 28-day aged fillets
30g	Transglutaminase, EB
30g	Transglutaminase, GS
300g	Reserved rendered bone marrow

Place the beef fat in the freezer for 20 minutes. It should be firm, but not brittle.

Trim the top and bottom of one fillet to achieve a rectangular piece, approximately 7cm high. Slice the fillet in half across the grain and place the 2 halves next to each other so that the long sides touch, and the recently sliced meat is facing in the same direction. You will notice that the grains match.

Using a tea strainer, lightly dust a fine layer of transglutaminase EB between the long sides and press the pieces firmly together. Wrap tightly in clingfilm, place on a tray and store in the fridge for 1 hour.

Repeat this process with the other 2 fillets until you have 3 neat rectangles in the fridge.

To prepare the beef fat, place the large piece of fat on a clean dish cloth and place them on a steady chopping board. Using a very sharp knife and a rolling pin, trim and flatten the beef fat until it is 3mm thick.

Remove the 3 rectangles of beef from the fridge and use a tea strainer to lightly dust a fine layer of transglutaminase GS on the surface.

Cut 3 rectangles of fat the same size as the beef fillet pieces. Press the fat on to the top and bottom sides of the beef. Return to the fridge for 1 hour.

Score a 5mm cross-hatch pattern into the fat on each piece. Divide each piece in two to yield 6 rectangles measuring 12 x 4cm.

Place each piece of meat in a sous-vide bag along with 50g rendered bone marrow, and seal under full pressure. Set aside.

To cook the beef, preheat a water bath to 53°C/127°F.

Place the 6 beef portions in the water bath and cook until a core temperature of 52°C/126°F is reached. Remove the beef from the sous-vide bags and drain on a tray.

Place the beef pieces in a moderately hot pan, skin-side down, to render the fat. Turn each piece to colour the underside, but do not overcook it.

Red Wine Sauce

375g	Red wine
200g	Madeira
80g	Peeled and diced shallots
90g	Rinsed and diced celery
100g	Peeled and diced carrots
90g	Rinsed and finely sliced leeks
10g	Peeled and finely sliced garlic
280g	Reduced beef stock (see page 27)
0.5g	Black peppercorns
0.5g	Pink peppercorns
2.5g	Tarragon
1g	Thyme

In a saucepan, combine the red wine, Madeira, shallots, celery, carrots, leeks and garlic. Bring the mixture to the boil, then to a gentle simmer, reduce the mixture to one-fifth of its original volume.

Add the reduced beef stock and peppercorns, and simmer for a few minutes. Remove the saucepan from the heat, add the tarragon and thyme and allow them to infuse for 5 minutes.

Pass the sauce through a fine-mesh filter bag and refrigerate until needed.

Ceps

3	Medium-sized ceps, wiped clean
50g	Unsalted butter
5g	Grapeseed oil
	Salt

Cut the ceps into 2 equal pieces.

Add the butter and grapeseed oil to a non-stick frying pan and add the ceps. Sauté until a crust has formed, then turn the heat down to allow the ceps to cook through gently. Remove and drain on kitchen paper. Season with salt.

To Serve

200g	Red wine sauce
5g	Reserved rendered bone marrow
2g	Tarragon
2g	Peeled and finely diced shallot
	Reserved smoked bone marrow garnish
	Reserved smoked onion fluid gel
6	Reserved beef fillet pieces
	Reserved celeriac remoulade
6	Reserved cep halves
6	Pieces reserved diced ox tongue
6	Pieces reserved veal sweetbreads
	Reserved potato crisps
	Reserved shallot crisps

Gently heat the red wine sauce in a small saucepan and whisk in the bone marrow. Finely chop the tarragon and add it to the red wine sauce along with the diced shallot. Place the bone marrow garnish on a tray and cover with clingfilm. Warm through gently for a few minutes in the oven at 80°C/176°F.

Pipe or spoon some smoked onion fluid gel on to the plates. Divide the warm, cooked elements between them. Arrange the bone marrow garnish around the dish, with the celeriac remoulade, cep halves, coated ox tongue, diced sweetbreads and shallot crisps.

Spoon the red wine sauce around the elements and serve immediately.

JOUTES

[c. 1430]

JOUTES

❊ Take Borage, Vyolet, Malwys, Percely, Yong Wortys, Bete, Avence, Longebeff, wyth Orage an other, pyke hem clene, and caste hem on a vessel, and boyle hem a goode whyle; than take hem and presse hem on a fayre bord, an hew hem ryght smal, an put whyte brede ther-to, an grynd wyth-al; an than caste hem in-to a fayre potte, an gode freshe brothe y-now ther-to thorw a straynowr, [& caste] ther-to ii or iii Marybonys, or ellys fayre fresche brothe of beff, and let hem sethe to-gederys a whyl; an than caste ther-to Safron, and let hem sethe to-gederys a whyle, an than caste ther-to safron and salt; and serve it forth in a dysshe, an bakon y-boylyd in a-nother dysshe, as men servyth furmenty wyth venyson ❊

Potage Dyvers, Harley MS 279 (c. 1430)

When talk turns to historical British food, most of us picture rustic dishes such as pea and ham soup, steak and kidney pudding, fish pie, Eccles cakes and Sussex Pond Pudding. These are, of course, a valuable part of Britain's culinary heritage, but for much of its history the national cuisine was very different from this. If a keen foodie travelled back in time to the Middle Ages, they would be met with some strange fare. Much of it would be pounded and strained to a pulpy, gruel-like consistency, or turned bright red, yellow or green using sandalwood, saffron and parsley. It would be seasoned with cinnamon, mace, nutmeg, cloves, ginger, galangal, cardamom and other exotic-sounding spices that have since been forgotten, at least in Europe: cubeb, zedoary, grains of paradise, spikenard. There would be an unfamiliar mixture of sweet and savoury, of hot and sour—tastes we now associate more readily with the cuisine of Africa and Asia.

Historians offer various explanations for this. The range of ingredients was, of course, far more limited. The seasons and the difficulties of transportation made many now-common items, such as sugar and citrus fruits, rare. Chefs simply had fewer ingredients to play around with and use as inspiration, so perhaps colour and spice were needed to provide excitement and variety. It has also been suggested that the quality of the ingredients was poor and the spicing and pounding an attempt at disguise. However, while some ingredients may well have been different from their modern-day counterparts—the butter heavily salted, the milk perhaps slightly sour, the wine more oxidised—there's little evidence to support the notion that medieval cuisine was somehow inferior. Spicing was, of course, used to show

off wealth, but both this and colouring may also have been employed to help the food compete with the elaborate ceremony and decoration that took place at feasts.

However, the medieval mindset was radically different from our own, and the cuisine of the period was shaped as much by philosophy as gastronomy. Two major influences on early English food were the numerous fast days imposed by the Church and the theory of the humours. The notion that the body is governed by bile, blood and phlegm now seems like gobbledygook, but it underpinned medicine for more than a thousand years, and shaped dietary considerations as profoundly as the concept of a "balanced diet" of carbohydrates, protein and fibre does today.

The theory of the humours was based on the ideas of Aristotle and Hippocrates (which in turn derived from far older ideas, including Chinese medical philosophy), which the physician Galen (129 c. 200) extended and organised into a system. He argued that just as the cosmos is made up of four elements—earth, air, fire and water—so too is the human body, in which the characteristics of the elements—dry, cold, hot and wet, respectively—combine in various groupings and manifest as four bodily fluids or "humours": blood, phlegm, black bile and yellow bile. Each of these expresses itself as a personality trait; thus a detailed set of correspondences can be drawn (see overleaf).

A person's health depended on monitoring the humours and maintaining a delicate balance between them, and food naturally played a key role in this. Since food was made up of the same four elements, it too had particular characteristics. Fish, for example, was seen as cold and moist, while cabbage was hot and dry. By offsetting one type of food against

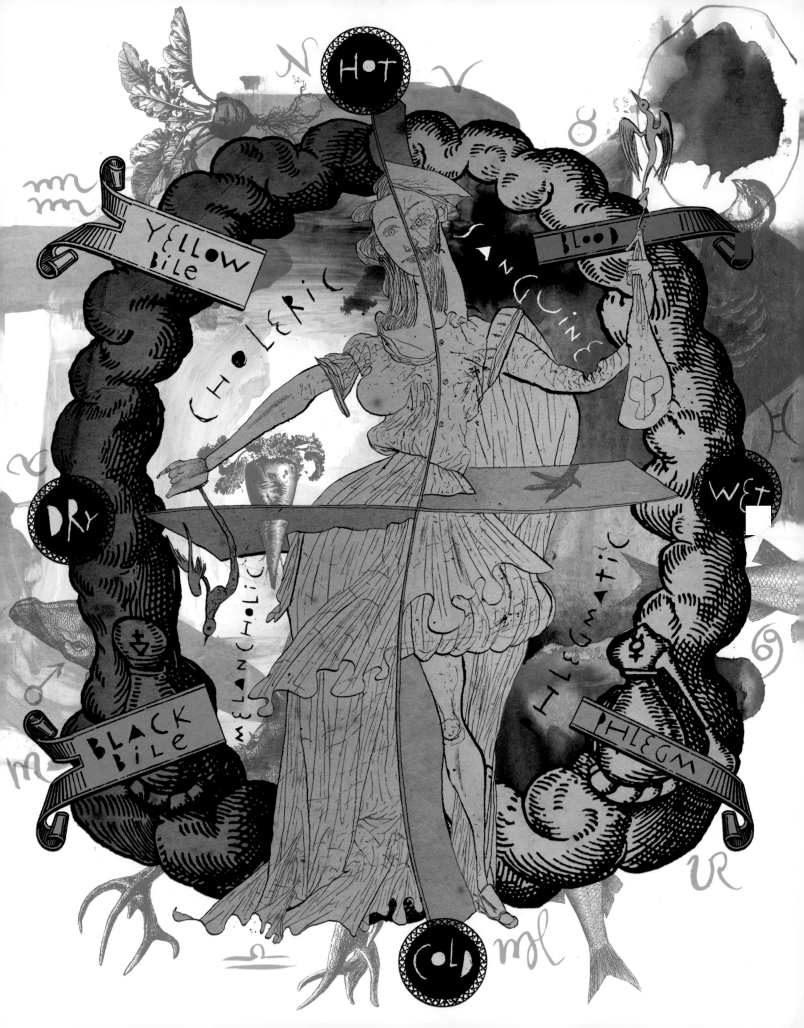

another, the careful diner could achieve a healthy equilibrium: a moderately moist, warm situation was considered ideal. If you suffered an excess of, say, melancholy—due to your personal physical make-up, or perhaps just as a consequence of overindulgence—the problem could be corrected by adjusting your diet to include food with the opposite humoral characteristics, in this case hot and wet ingredients. Thus old men and children, who were thought to be highly phlegmatic, were expected to avoid lamb, which was very moist and cold. A choleric person, on the other hand, had to forgo "hot" foods. The permutations are endless, and not necessarily self-evident. Venison was considered very dry, but small game birds were moist. Vegetables were dry because they came from the earth, while fruit was moist. Cucumbers were exceptionally moist and likely to generate fever, so best avoided—except in summer, which, being hot and dry, could counter the dangers of cucumber consumption. On top of this, each food had to be cooked by whichever method most complemented its humour. Beef (dry) was boiled, pork (moist) roasted, fish (cold and moist) fried. Vegetables were cut small and boiled, while fruit had to be baked or roasted.

Cooking with an eye to balancing the humours must have been as complicated as a game of three-dimensional chess, and it seems likely that the theory was a determining factor in how medieval cuisine developed. All that pounding, chopping, mashing, sieving and mixing was designed to combine hot, cold, dry and moist ingredients precisely and efficiently. The spicing, sugaring and seasoning with vinegar and verjuice (a medieval alternative to vinegar, made from fermented wine or crab apples) was a way of making minute final adjustments to the balance of humoral characteristics. (Vinegar was cold and dry; sugar, being warm and moist, was seen as a perfectly balanced ingredient.) Eventually, of course, resourceful chefs began to make a virtue out of necessity: it's thought that the development of sauces was largely inspired by the desire to find new ways to apply that final humoral seasoning. A green sauce made with parsley (warm and dry) was the ideal accompaniment for cold, moist pike or mackerel.

While the theory of the humours now seems mystifying and not a little mystical, at the time it was absolutely fundamental to people's view of how the world worked. It was certainly part of Shakespeare's outlook and vocabulary: "you are altogether govern'd by humours", Lady Percy says to Hotspur in *Henry IV Part 1*. Even at the end of the seventeenth century, John Evelyn—celebrated diarist, founder of the Royal Society and designer of greenhouses and hotbeds that took account of all the latest scientific advances—describes vegetables in terms of the humours in his 1699 book on salads, *Acetaria*. The theory was only finally dismissed at the close of the following century, when French scientist Antoine Lavoisier demonstrated in his *Elementary Treatise on Chemistry* (1789) how the body really worked, showing that animals were effectively combustion engines that used food for fuel. Fifty-one years later, in *Organic Chemistry and Its Applications to Agriculture and Physiology* (1840), German chemist Justus von Liebig outlined how living tissue is made up of fats, "albuminoids" (or, as we now call them, proteins) and carbohydrates, thereby paving the way for modern concepts of nutrition.

The intertwined concerns about moral and physical health were also at the heart of the medieval practice of fast days. By the tenth century, the Church had come to see food as a worldly temptation that led to gluttony and, by extension, all sorts of other ungovernable appetites. Meat in particular acquired an impressive list of negative connotations: it was symbolic of Cain's crime, violence, human weakness, cruelty and death, and its consumption heated the body, stoking sensuality and sexual longing. From this platform, the Church developed the idea that abstention from eating meat was an assertion of faith and a way of symbolically recovering one's innocence. Monks had to give up meat altogether, and the laity was expected to follow suit on a number of days and dates designated by the clergy. Wednesdays, Fridays and Saturdays were supposed to be meat-free (although this varied throughout Europe: in France, according to Taillevent's *Viandier*, the fast days were Sunday, Tuesday and Thursday), as were the forty days of Lent and the thirty days of Advent, during which people also had to give up animal products, such as milk, eggs and cheese. All in all, it meant that meat was off the menu for about half the year.

The effect this had on people varied. For the peasant, whose diet in any case had little meat and little excitement or variation, it can't have been much of a hardship, bar perhaps the restrictions on butter, cheese and eggs. Monasteries at first adhered strictly to the edict, but from the 1200s onwards such devotion began to lapse. Monks became as skilled at finding ways around the restrictions as they were at negotiating the subtleties of theological dispute. So, while one brother might be considering how many angels fit upon the point of a needle, another would be debating whether, since beavers use their tails to swim, they could technically be seen as fish and therefore eaten.

Fish, of course, became the mainstay of fast days. The less well-to-do and those without easy access to the coast were largely stuck with preserved fish that had been salted, pickled or smoked, or a form of salt cod called stockfish. It was hardly an inspiring diet. "Thou will not believe how weary I am of fish," runs a passage in one fifteenth-century schoolbook, "and how much I desire that flesh were come in again, for I have ate none other but salt fish this Lent, and it hath engendered so much phlegm within me that it stoppeth my pipes that I can neither speak nor breathe." For the rich, however, things were very different. Not only did their chefs cook with a variety of fish and seafood—including oysters, pike, porpoise, gurnard, salmon, eel, lampreys and turbot—they also made full use of substitutes for traditional dairy products such as butter, milk and cream made from almonds, to create an extremely refined and versatile alternative cuisine.

Joutes is a classic example of this adaptable fast-day cuisine. The recipe in the Harley manuscript calls for marrow bones or a "fair fresh broth of beef", but there's a version in *The Forme of Cury* that uses almond milk in place of meat broth, so it would have been a popular choice for meat-free days. Although I wasn't about to pass up the opportunity to include rich marrow bone in the dish, I was keen for the heart of this recipe to be a fresh, herby greenness. One of the most striking things about the Harley Joutes is that litany of plant life at the beginning—borage, violet, mallows, parsley, young greens, beet greens, avens, bugloss, orach—and I wanted my version to have a similar abundance of greenery.

Using green gazpacho as a rough template, I gathered handfuls of whatever green ingredients I could think of that went together well, and set about trying them out in various combinations and quantities, looking for a lively, vibrant colour and flavour, a sort of ultimate essence of greenness. To keep everything fresh-tasting, it was vital to expose the ingredients to as little heat as possible, so we took the approach of roughly slicing everything and letting it all macerate overnight in a mixture of vinegar and salt, which started the process of breaking down the ingredients, causing their flavours to meet and intermingle. After blending and straining, I had a liquid with an incredible lip-smacking, green-tasting zing: the ultimate pick-me-up. In the development kitchen, people started calling it the Tonic. Originally, I had conceived this as simply a foundation step in the recipe, a base preparation upon which to build the dish. Now I started thinking that, one way or another, I had to include this base in its freshest and most unadulterated form as well.

My first thought was to make beef consommé, cold-infuse it with fresh herbs such as borage and oyster leaf (which has an oyster-like flavour that works well with beef) and set it as a delicate jelly beneath the green joutes base. Dig in with a spoon and you'd have the experience of clean, fresh greenery and a deep, rich broth in a single mouthful. In the end, though, I decided this was too close to other dishes I had made. I relinquished the consommé and decided instead to look at one of its traditional accompaniments: the moulded savoury custard known as a royale. This offered a promising means of introducing marrow bone to the recipe: by infusing a mixture of milk and cream with marrow fat and roasted shin bones, then adding a heat-resistant setting agent, I could create a delicately textured, rich-flavoured, panna-cotta-shaped centrepiece for the dish. Since joutes was essentially a pottage-like broth, I developed a frothy velouté from the joutes base and vegetable stock, thickened with pea purée, to pour into the bowl around the bone marrow royale. With this and a little bottle of the Tonic on the side, I had the makings of a dish with a lovely gradation of flavour and texture, from the fresh, invigorating liquid of the Tonic, to the airy, flavourful velouté and the fragile firmness of the royale. There was a lot of richness in the dish, though, and not much body. It cried out for some contrast and a bit of acidity.

Texture can be introduced to soup in many ways—croutons, toasted nuts, diced vegetables—but one of the classics is a chargrilled slice of bread, rubbed with garlic and topped with cheese, and that seemed to me the perfect vehicle for the final touches for this dish. I've always held that any foodstuff, no matter how lowly, can be open to development, and I've spent some time over the years working on what amounts to a posh cheese slice for burgers, cheese toasties, onion soup and the like. For Joutes, I took another look at it and reworked it with beer, mushroom ketchup and Worcestershire sauce to give it more of a Welsh rarebit characteristic. I also added some rendered bone marrow so that my cheese-on-toast garnish reinforced the flavour of the bone marrow royale. On top of it I put little nuggets of marrow dusted with flour, along with pickled shallots and gelled cubes of verjuice to cut the richness. And to finish, of course, I had a scattering of flowers and fresh herbs to echo the list of plants at the start of the Harley recipe and reinforce the leafy character. So, for my dish, take borage, violet, chives, parsley, pea shoots, chervil, nasturtiums, red chard…

JOUTES

Makes 6 portions

Vegetable Stock

75g	Extra virgin olive oil
500g	Rinsed, trimmed and finely sliced leeks
375g	Peeled and grated carrots
340g	Peeled and finely sliced onions
325g	Grated cleaned button mushrooms
160g	Trimmed and grated fennel bulbs
160g	Trimmed and sliced celery
3	Bay leaves
2g	Thyme
45g	Flatleaf parsley

Heat the olive oil in a stockpot and add all the prepared vegetables. Sweat them, without colouring, for approximately 5 minutes. Add the bay leaves and thyme, followed by 3 litres cold water.

Slowly bring the stock to the boil, skimming off all scum and impurities, then reduce the heat and simmer very gently for 40 minutes.

Remove the pot from the heat and add the parsley. Allow the parsley to infuse for 20 minutes, then pass the stock through a fine-mesh filter bag. Chill in the fridge overnight.

Remove and discard the fat from the surface of the chilled stock. Refrigerate until needed.

The recipe yields approximately 3 litres vegetable stock, which can be frozen in batches for future use.

Bone Marrow Infusion

2kg	Beef shin bones
550g	Semi-skimmed milk
350g	Whipping cream

Preheat the oven to 180°C/350°F.

Spread the bones out on a roasting tray and roast until they are light brown and all the marrow fat has melted out. Do not discard any of the fat. Remove the bones from the oven and carefully scrape out all the marrow.

Pass the marrow and melted fat from the roasting tray through a fine-mesh sieve and set aside 80g for use in the royale. Reserve any additional rendered bone marrow for use in the cheese slice.

Place the roasted bones, milk and cream in a large sous-vide bag and seal. Allow the flavours to infuse overnight.

Pass the mixture through a fine-mesh sieve, followed by a double layer of muslin. Discard the bones.

Set 450g of the infused mixture aside to make the royale.

Bone Marrow Royale

450g	Reserved bone marrow infusion
80g	Reserved rendered bone marrow
	Salt
	Sherry vinegar
0.6g	LT-100 (high-acyl gellan)
0.15g	Gellan F (low-acyl gellan)
0.6g	Guar gum

Strain the bone marrow infusion into a Thermomix with the reserved bone marrow. Bring to 90°C/194°F at medium speed and season with salt and a few drops of sherry vinegar to taste.

Keeping it at the same temperature, add the LT-100, gellan F and guar gum and blitz for 2 more minutes at high speed. Ensure the gelling agents have dissolved completely, stopping halfway through to scrape down the sides of the jug if needed.

Pour the mixture immediately into 6 x 60ml timbale moulds. Do not move the moulds for 30 minutes to allow the royale to set fully.

Cover each mould with clingfilm and store in the fridge until needed.

Green Gazpacho Base

45g	Rinsed and roughly chopped celery
75g	Cored, de-seeded and roughly chopped green bell peppers
90g	Roughly chopped cucumber
175g	Cored and roughly chopped green tomatoes
100g	Roughly chopped spinach leaves
15g	Roughly sliced basil leaves
15g	Roughly sliced flatleaf parsley leaves
15g	Roughly sliced tarragon leaves
20g	Roughly sliced borage leaves
10g	Roughly sliced oyster leaves
15g	Roughly chopped dill
15g	Roughly chopped chervil
15g	Roughly chopped chives
75g	Garden peas
50g	Peeled and roughly chopped shallots
17g	Whole green chillies (optional)
100g	Rinsed and roughly chopped fennel bulb
10g	Salt
60g	Chardonnay vinegar
2.5	Slices white bread, crusts removed and chopped
50g	Roughly chopped green seedless grapes

Combine all the ingredients and place in large sous-vide bags. Allow to marinate overnight.

Blend in a Thermomix for 5 minutes at high speed. Pass the juice through a fine-mesh sieve, applying as much pressure as possible to obtain the maximum amount of juice.

Store in the fridge until needed to make the velouté and tonic. To ensure vibrancy of colour, do not prepare it too far in advance.

Pea Purée

500g	Peas

If using frozen peas, make sure they are fully defrosted. Place the peas in a deep container and roughly blitz using a hand blender. Pass the peas through a fine-mesh sieve, then place in a Thermomix. Blitz to a smooth purée. Reserve 120g of this purée for the velouté.

Velouté

100g	Reserved vegetable stock
30g	Unsalted butter, cubed and at room temperature
120g	Reserved pea purée
200g	Reserved green gazpacho base
2.5g	Salt

This velouté should be prepared moments before serving. Place the vegetable stock and butter in a saucepan and bring to the boil. Add the pea purée, green gazpacho base and salt.

Using a hand blender, foam the warm velouté and serve immediately.

Olive Oil Mayonnaise

12g	Pasteurised egg yolk
5g	Dijon mustard
5g	Chardonnay vinegar
10g	Chardonnay wine
60g	Extra virgin olive oil

Combine the egg yolk, mustard, vinegar and wine in a small bowl and mix well.

Gradually pour in the olive oil, whisking continuously until fully emulsified.

Tonic

300g	Reserved green gazpacho base
10g	Reserved olive oil mayonnaise

Place the green gazpacho base and olive oil mayonnaise in a container and blend for 30 seconds using a hand blender.

Pass the mixture through a fine-mesh filter bag and store in the fridge until needed. This tonic should be served as cold as possible, in a medicinal-style glass, alongside the bowl of warm velouté.

Pickled Shallots

115g	Chardonnay vinegar
4g	Salt
5g	White caster sugar
6–8	Small round shallots

Preheat the water bath to 85°c/185°F.

In a small saucepan, heat 60g water with the vinegar, salt and sugar until everything has dissolved. Remove from the heat and set aside to cool.

Before peeling the shallots, soak them in a small bowl of warm water for 5 minutes. Then, using a paring knife, carefully peel them, removing as little of the root as possible and retaining the point at the top of the shallot.

Place the peeled shallots and the cooled pickling liquid in a small sous-vide bag, ensuring that the shallots are lying flat and in a single layer. Seal under full pressure.

Place the sous-vide bag in the water bath to cook for approximately 1 hour, or until the shallots are soft all the way through. Plunge the bags in iced water to stop further cooking, then store them in the fridge until required.

Allow the shallots to pickle for 24 hours before using them.

(continued overleaf)

Verjus Jelly

180g	Verjus
200g	White grape juice
0.8g	Sodium citrate
1.7g	Gellan F (low-acyl gellan)

Line a tray with a double layer of clingfilm. Place the verjus, white grape juice and sodium citrate in the Thermomix and bring to 90°c/194°F. Add the gellan F and continue to blitz for 2 more minutes. Pour on to the prepared tray and allow the jelly to set.

Once set, cut the jelly into 5mm x 2cm rectangles and store in the fridge until needed.

Cheese Slice

25g	Unsalted butter
25g	Reserved rendered bone marrow
50g	Plain flour
125g	Strong beer
20g	Worcestershire sauce
20g	Mushroom ketchup
10g	English mustard
125g	Whole milk
125g	Finely grated Cheddar cheese
125g	Finely grated Gruyère cheese
2g	Cracked black pepper

Melt the butter and rendered bone marrow in a saucepan. Add the flour and whisk together. Cook this roux over a gentle heat for 2 minutes.

Add the beer and stir until well combined. Add the Worcestershire sauce, mushroom ketchup and mustard and combine well. Add the milk and heat gently. Slowly add the grated cheeses, followed by the black pepper, and whisk continuously until fully incorporated.

Line a baking tray with clingfilm and pour the mixture on to it. Spread it out evenly and cover with clingfilm. Set aside in the fridge until needed.

Cheese Toasts

20g	Extra virgin olive oil, plus 10g for frying
6	Slices sourdough bread, crusts removed
1	Peeled and halved garlic clove
	Reserved cheese slice
18–20	5mm cubes bone marrow
50g	Plain flour
18–20	Reserved verjus jelly rectangles
6	Reserved pickled shallots, cut into quarters
5g	Finely chopped chives
	Micro-red chard
	Micro-parsley
	Sea salt flakes
	Black pepper

Preheat the oven to the grill setting.

Heat the olive oil in a non-stick pan and fry the bread pieces on both sides until golden and crisp. Rub the garlic clove halves on each piece.

Cut the cheese slice into pieces the same size as the slices of bread. Top each with a slice of cheese and place them on a tray under the grill, until the cheese has melted and coloured.

Remove the cheese toasts from under the grill and trim each slice of bread into a 3.5 x 11cm rectangle. This segment should be taken from an area that contains no holes.

In the meantime, lightly dust the diced bone marrow pieces in the flour. Heat the remaining olive oil in a non-stick pan and fry the pieces. Set aside to drain on a small tray lined with kitchen paper.

Garnish the cheese toasts with the rectangles of verjus jelly, bone marrow pieces, pickled shallot quarters, chives, micro-herbs, sea salt flakes and cracked black pepper.

To Serve

Reserved bone marrow royales
Reserved velouté, warmed and frothed
Reserved cheese toasts
Reserved tonic
Violet flowers
Nasturtium flowers
Pea shoots
Borage leaves

Preheat the oven to 80°c/176°F. Carefully un-mould the bone marrow royales on to a tray and warm gently in the oven. Do not allow them to stay in the oven too long, as a skin may form.

Place a warm royale in the centre of each bowl and pour the warm, frothy velouté around it.

Garnish with violet flowers, nasturtiums, pea shoots and borage leaves. Serve with a slice of toast placed across the bowl and the chilled tonic served alongside.

WASSAILING

[*c.* 1576]

❋ *Wassail the trees, that they may bear*
You many a plum, and many a pear
For more or less fruits they will bring
As you do give them wassailing ❋

Robert Herrick, "Ceremonies for Christmas", *Hesperides* (1648)

It's 6 January: Twelfth Night. Wrap up warm—we're going for a walk in the West Country.

The air is keen, a cold blade touching the cheek. Ahead, people tramp through the dark. Some hold flaming torches; others carry shotguns or beat drums, like a ragtag militia. The scene is formal, processional, but the chatter is friendly and inconsequential. An orchard looms into view amid the flickering brands and the crowd gradually fans out into a circle around an apple tree and falls silent. A figure steps forward and addresses the tree with a long speech invoking gods and good spirits and fruitfulness, then takes a maple-wood bowl and pours the contents on the roots. A young woman approaches, dips some toast in the re-filled bowl and places it carefully among the boughs. A volley of shots rings out. Then another. A cheer goes up and all break into song:

O apple tree we wassail thee
And hoping thou will bear
For the lord doth know where we shall be
Till apples come another year.

This is the ritual of apple wassailing, which
has been practised in England since at least the
sixteenth century. The word itself is much older,
deriving from the Old English *waes*, which
means "be", and *hael*, which means "healthy"
(hence the word hale, as in "hale and hearty").
It's thought to have come over to England with
the Vikings in the invasions of the eighth and
ninth centuries, and a wassail was originally
simply a toast. "It is the custom in Saxland,"
explained the thirteenth-century poet and
priest Layamon in *Brut*, his chronicle of Britain,
"wheresoever any people make merry in drink,
that friend sayeth to his friend, with fair comely
looks, 'Dear friend, wassail!'" By extension,

wassailing came to denote the drinking session as well as the toast, and the Anglo-Saxons seem to have been enthusiastic upholders of the tradition. In *Gesta Regum Anglorum* (Deeds of the English Kings), William of Malmesbury, one of the foremost historians of the twelfth century, claimed that in preparation for the battle against the Normans at Hastings in 1066, "the English—so I have heard—spent a sleepless night in song and wassail". However, since William was of Norman descent, this may well have been just a piece of propaganda, giving the impression that the Anglo-Saxon soldiers were undisciplined revellers deserving of defeat.

Over time, the word slurred into a number of loosely interrelated meanings. By the late 1400s it had become strongly associated with Christmas and a tradition of communal drinking from a wassail bowl containing spiced, sweetened ale or cider and decorated with ribbons and rosemary or evergreens. (Henry VII's Household Ordinances for 31 December 1494 laid out guidelines for that night's wassail: the bowl was to be brought into the room accompanied by the chief officers of the household bearing staves). By the end of the following century, this custom already had two well-developed offshoots: visiting neighbourhood houses to wish people good health, offer a drink and sing songs in return for money or food (a forerunner of Christmas carolling), and visiting the fields on Twelfth Night to seek a blessing upon crops, animals or fruit trees for the coming year. Certainly by 1576, according to the *Records of Early English Drama: Kent—Diocese of Canterbury*, apple wassailing was sufficiently well established in Kent for ecclesiastical authorities in Fordwich to get in a lather about it and petition the mayor to end the "superstitious or old custom".

The manner and content of the apple wassail has varied over time and from county to county. I've seen old footage of a Somerset wassail where there was little frippery: a couple of accordions provide the music, the leader is dressed in a trilby and sheepskin coat, and the fusillades of firearms give the proceedings an air of serious intent. It feels more like supplication than celebration. In other wassails, many of the revellers wear clothes layered with hundreds of coloured strips of material, the leader's face is painted green and crowned with evergreen leaves, and the ceremony is leavened with wisecracks. There's disagreement as to whether it should be held on 6 or 17 January, the latter being when Twelfth Night fell until Britain formally adopted the Gregorian calendar in place of the Julian in 1752. Even the term "wassailing" isn't fixed; in Sussex it's often called "howling" instead.

For all this variety, the apple wassail has at its core a widely accepted set of rituals. A procession heads to the orchard where cider is poured round the base of a tree and toast dipped in cider is placed in the branches. Guns are fired or drums beaten, and wassailing songs are sung by the crowd. The percussion and gunshots are intended to frighten off evil spirits, while the toast in the branches attracts good spirits or, in some interpretations, robins, which are considered to be lucky birds.

When Kevin Love, my head chef at the Hind's Head, told me about the wassailing tradition and suggested we develop a dish based on it, I could see at once that this had potential. Here were ingredients that went together well and had a history. The seventeenth-century English poet Robert Herrick, who mentions wassailing often enough that he could be called the Bard of the Bowl, offers a list of wassailing essentials in "Twelfth Night: Or, King and Queen":

Add sugar, nutmeg, and ginger,
With store of ale too;
And thus ye must do
To make a wassail a swinger.

Then there was cider and the bread placed in the tree and, of course, the centre of all this attention: the apple itself. This was stuff we could definitely work with.

Our first thought was to combine the ingredients in a syllabub, a dish with a quintessentially English name that was popular in the sixteenth century, when references to apple wassailing first started to appear in print. And since some historians suggest that syllabubs and wassailing recipes provided inspiration for popular Victorian desserts such as Tipsy Cake (see page 380) and trifle, there was a satisfying aptness in combining the two. I pictured a cider syllabub with toast on the side, and I already had an idea for how to serve it.

The port sipper is an elegant contrivance with a barrel-shaped glass, from the base of which a slender drinking tube curves upwards in an S shape, giving it the appearance of an extravagant, transparent meerschaum pipe. It's undoubtedly beautiful and sculptural, and would make for an eye-catching piece of presentation. However, as I soon discovered, it was also far too brittle to survive the hustle of service at the Hind's Head. And without it, the dish was stillborn. It might strike you as odd to shelve a recipe because of the tableware, rather than, say, a technical impasse. But as far as I'm concerned, form and content are as intertwined

in cuisine as they are in any other creative discipline. Great food is about context: not just the ingredients on the plate (although this is of course a huge part of it) but the plate itself, the ambience, the associations triggered by the sights, sounds, smells and textures in the dish and surroundings, and so on. All of these contribute to the eating experience. The port sipper was as integral to the syllabub dish as any of the ingredients, and I couldn't find a substitute that matched it. It was time for a rethink.

Kevin and I decided to take the toast as our starting point instead. *Pain perdu* is one of my favourite dishes. Basically a sweet French version of eggy bread, it's a very good dish to make for Sunday morning breakfast. (Mix 3 eggs, 250ml milk and 20g unrefined caster sugar. Trim the crusts off 4 slices of bread, dip them in the mixture, cook quickly on both sides over a medium heat in clarified butter, sprinkle another 80g sugar on the slices and let them caramelise, and you've got pain perdu for four.) But take the techniques and ingredients up a notch—brioche, vanilla pods, a dark brown caramel—and you have a very refined and versatile preparation. This seemed like an excellent foundation for a wassailing dish, introducing plenty of rich caramelised flavour, as well as referencing the bread that's such a central part of the festivities. Upon this, I decided, we should present a celebration of the apple, combining it in a variety of forms and textures to produce a complex, intense apple flavour.

A spoonful of apple ice cream on top of the pain perdu seemed a natural choice, providing a nice smooth, icy contrast. Gradually, between these two, we structured other contrasts: a scattering of apple matchsticks for crunch and freshness, a sprinkling of dehydrated apple and crystallised brioche crumbs to add to the crunch and the complexity. To the pain perdu mixture I had added a little Calvados, the classic Normandy apple brandy, but the garnish offered an opportunity to introduce a more home-grown kick of alcohol. I had created a layer of caramelised apple to sit on top of the pain perdu by sealing Braeburn apples in a vacuum-packing bag with apple juice and fructose and cooking them sous-vide. Once cooked, the apples were removed from the bags and placed in a fridge to dry, leaving behind them all the delicious marinade. By combining this with an apple brandy liqueur from Somerset and reducing it to a syrup, I had the basis of an apple soup that could be poured into the dish around the pain perdu at the table.

I thought the recipe had a fantastic balance of flavours, and that we'd managed to capture something of the spirit of wassailing. But would Robert Herrick have agreed, and what would the diners at the Hind's Head think? We put it on the menu on 6 January as a seasonal dish, intending to serve it for a month. But it proved so popular that we had to keep it on until the end of the apple season forced us to take it off. So I guess we'd come up with a dish that would make a wassail a swinger.

Despite this, I found myself bothered by the presentation. Unlike the other recipes in this book, Wassailing was inspired by a custom, a narrative of sorts, and I didn't feel we had told the story well enough. The link between wassailing and the ingredients on the plate wasn't immediately apparent; the dish didn't provoke a moment of pleasurable recognition as the diner made the connections. Somehow I had to make it more visually explicit.

The centrepiece, then, had to be an apple. As I began thinking about the possibilities for this, I suddenly realised I'd already found the solution while researching another historical dish. For Meat Fruit we had made every effort to create an apple that looked exactly like the real thing, right down to the freckling on the skin. Now I could use those techniques to make what appeared to be an apple, but in fact had a surprise beneath its skin: a mousse that contained a number of different forms and flavours of apple. So into whipped cream and egg whites went apple juice, spray-dried apple, Calvados and malic acid. I included malic acid not only because it's a characteristic component of red apples (and other reddish fruit such as rhubarb and pink grapefruit), but also because using different types of acid as a seasoning has become a standard technique in my restaurants. The addition of a little malic acid is an incredibly effective way of enhancing the fresh notes in a dish. I decided to put some mead in there too, partly as a nod to the origins of wassailing in the mead halls of Viking England, and partly because there's a cider-like aspect to it.

For the skin I made a gel with similar ingredients to reinforce the flavours, but I also wanted to capture the apple's slightly floral characteristic, so I added bay leaves, cloves and rosemary (which also provided a nice olfactory allusion to the rosemary sprigs that traditionally garlanded the wassail bowl), plus some dried yeast to mimic the natural yeasts that are present on an apple's skin. (They're what cause apples to ferment and turn into cider.) A little milk to help create the speckled effect and some green tea powder to add a touch of bitterness, and I had a gel that both tasted and looked the part. The frozen mousse would be dipped into the gel, and the whole thing sprayed with a mixture of Calvados and red colouring to give it a convincing red sheen.

Even though the techniques for this had already been developed, isolating precisely the right combination and proportion of ingredients took a long time, during which we obsessed about apples to an unhealthy degree, endlessly scrutinising their appearance and considering every possible nuance of flavour. Such a close focus made me see lots of little details that I hadn't really noticed before, and that gave me an idea for a final touch of *trompe l'oeil* trickery to bolster the illusion of an apple. A pine nut is exactly the same size and shape as an apple pip; by toasting pine nuts to a dark golden brown, I could make credible edible pips. For service, I would place three apple wedges in a bowl, insert pips into them, lay a couple of triangles of pain perdu alongside and pour in some apple soup.

However, now that the recipe no longer contained apple ice cream, the pain perdu was slightly stranded and functionless, and I began playing around with the idea of toasting the brioche instead and using it as the base for a sort of *tarte fine*. A classic French *tarte fine aux pommes* is topped with thin-cut slices of apple that are closely overlapped, producing a pattern that looks like a turbine rotor or an elaborate pinwheel. As I put some of my tarts in the pan I noticed that, when the overlap was particularly tight, it looked like the rings in a cross-section of tree trunk. It was this happy accident that guided my thinking about the tart's appearance and its role in the dish. The crust on top of the brioche loaf had ridges across it where the dough had been slashed with a knife to help the rising. Now I noticed that, when you cut off a slice, the top edge had the gnarled, ridged look of bark, and I realised that, by leaving the slices untrimmed, we could create a tart that looked like a tree stump, as though it had just been sawn from the apple orchard. The dish had finally captured the full symbolism of the wassailing ceremony.

WASSAILING

Makes 9 portions

Apple Mousse Halves

220g	**Apple juice**
30g	**English mead**
1g	**Malic acid**
13g	**Bronze leaf gelatine**
50g	**Calvados**
50g	**Spray-dried apple**
100g	**Pasteurised egg white**
230g	**Whipping cream**

Place 9 x 8cm dome moulds inside silicone moulds that will hold them securely in place, and put them on a tray.

Combine the apple juice, mead, malic acid and bronze leaf gelatine in a saucepan off the heat, and allow the gelatine to soak. Once the gelatine has softened, gently heat the mixture, but do not allow the temperature to rise above 40°C/104°F. Stir to ensure all the gelatine has melted. Remove from the heat and set aside to cool to 20°C/68°F.

Place the Calvados and spray-dried apple in a second small saucepan and heat to 118°C/244°F.

In the meantime, whisk the egg white to soft peaks. In a separate bowl, do the same with the whipping cream.

Once the Calvados mixture has come to temperature, immediately and gradually pour the mixture into the beaten egg white, whisking continuously. Mix in the cooled gelatine mixture, followed by a quarter of the whipped cream, then the rest of the whipped cream. Pour this mixture into the dome moulds and level off the mousse with a palette knife.

Place the moulds in the freezer until frozen solid and ready to dip into the apple skin gel.

Pine-Nut Apple Pips

50g	**Pine nuts**
2g	**Salt**
10g	**Brown caster sugar**
	Icing sugar, to dust

Put the pine nuts and salt in a moderately hot pan and toast well, stirring continuously. Once they are dark golden in colour, sprinkle on the sugar and allow to caramelise.

Tip the contents on to a silicone mat and dust with icing sugar. Wearing gloves, use your fingers to ensure the pips have separated. Set aside to cool.

Just before serving, gently wipe the excess sugar off the pips.

Apple Soup

100g	**Apple juice**
200g	**Fructose**
6	**Braeburn apples**
50g	**Apple brandy liqueur**
15g	**Chardonnay vinegar**

Preheat a water bath to 90°C/194°F.

Place the apple juice and fructose in a saucepan and bring to the boil. Remove from the heat and allow to cool completely.

Peel, core and divide the apples into wedges. Place the apple wedges, along with the cooled syrup, in a large sous-vide bag and seal under full pressure. Cook in the water bath for 16 hours.

Allow the contents of the bag to cool before opening. Strain the apples, reserving the syrup. (You may want to reserve the apple compote for use in another dessert.)

Combine 480g of the apple syrup with the apple brandy liqueur and vinegar and set aside until ready to serve.

Brioche Slices

100g	**Hazelnut praline**
5	**Slices brioche (1.5cm thick)**
4–5	**Braeburn apples**
150g	**Brown caster sugar**
250g	**Melted clarified butter**

Spread the hazelnut praline on to each of the brioche slices.

Peel and core the apples. Cut them in half lengthways (through the core) and slice each side as thinly as possible using a mandolin, ensuring there are no visible areas where the pips were housed. The crescent shape should be smooth and all the pieces should be similar in size.

Layer the thin apple slices on to the brioche slices, allowing them to overlap, creating an attractive and uniform pattern lengthways. Follow this with a generous dusting of the brown sugar.

Use a pastry brush to brush the apple side of each slice with melted, clarified butter while you heat a large non-stick pan. Toast the brioche slices bread-side down first, then turn them over to caramelise the apple side.

To remove the slices from the pan, carefully turn them over so they are apple-side up, and place a layer of baking parchment over them. Gently flip the entire pan over, lowering the parchment on to a chopping board. The brioche slices will be ready for trimming, apple-side down.

Use a serrated knife to divide the brioche diagonally into 4 triangles, without slicing all the way through. Stop just before you reach the apple layer underneath. At this stage, switch to a sharp, un-serrated knife and slice through the apple layer. This ensures even, precise trimming.

There should be 2 triangles of caramelised apple brioche per person. If you like, you could trim off the crusts for a neater finish. These should be made just before serving.

Green Apple Skin Colouring

4.5g	Matcha green tea powder
150g	Whole milk
36	Drops green food colouring

Place the green tea powder in a small bowl and gradually whisk in the milk until well dissolved. Add the green food colouring and combine well. Set aside until needed.

Red Apple Skin Spray

15g	Calvados
1g	Red colouring powder

In a small bowl, combine the Calvados and red colouring powder and transfer to a small spray gun or pump bottle. Set aside until needed.

Apple Skin Gel

39g	Bronze leaf gelatine
300g	English mead
300g	Calvados
300g	Apple juice
150g	Spray-dried apple
60g	Honey
2	Bay leaves, finely sliced
45	Individual rosemary leaves
6	Cloves
2g	Malic acid
2g	Dried yeast
190g	Granny Smith apple peelings
	Reserved green apple skin colouring

Place the gelatine in a bowl and cover with cold water. Leave for 5 minutes.

In the meantime, bring all the remaining ingredients, apart from the green apple skin colouring, to the boil in a large saucepan, then remove from the heat and strain.

Squeeze out the excess water from the bloomed gelatine leaves and add the softened leaves to the mixture. It is important not to whisk this mixture, but to stir it gently until all the gelatine has dissolved.

Place the mixture in a bowl and put the bowl in an ice water bath until it has cooled to 20°C/68°F.

Stir in the green apple skin colouring mixture and allow to cool to 13–15°C/55–59°F, which is the ideal temperature for dipping the frozen apple halves. Unmould the apple mousse halves (see next step) just before it reaches that temperature.

Dipping the Apple Mousse Halves

9	Reserved apple mousse halves
	Reserved green apple skin gel
	Reserved red apple skin spray

While the apple skin gel is cooling, remove the 9 apple mousse halves from the freezer. Gently unmould each one by lowering them into a pan of boiling water for 1–2 seconds, then applying pressure to one side of the flat area of the mousse and quickly scooping the entire dome out.

When the green apple skin gel has reached the optimal dipping temperature of 13–15°C/55–59°F, dip the apple halves one at a time into the gel and place them flat-side down on a cake rack to allow the excess to drip off. It is important to work as quickly as possible. Dip each apple half twice.

To prevent bleeding of colour, as soon as the apples have been dipped, spray them with the red apple skin spray to mimic an apple skin.

Wrap a tray tightly in clingfilm and put the dipped and sprayed apple halves on it. Put them in the fridge to defrost. This takes approximately 3–4 hours.

To Serve

Reserved apple mousse halves
Reserved pine-nut apple pips
Reserved brioche slices
Reserved apple soup

Slice each defrosted apple half into 2 pieces, and divide one of those pieces into 2 wedges. This ensures each serving comprises 1 apple quarter and 2 wedges.

Arrange the apple pieces in each bowl and place the pine-nut pips into the appropriate area of the wedge. Place 2 triangles of brioche alongside the apple wedges.

Serve the apple soup in a small jug alongside the dish. A small amount should be poured into the bowl when serving.

TART OF
STRAWBERRIES

[1591]

TARTE OF STRAWBERIES

❀ Seson your Strawberyes with sugar, a very little Sinamon, a little ginger, and so cover them with a cover, and you must lay upon the cover a morsell of sweet Butter, Rosewater and Sugar, you may Ice the cover if you will, you must make your Ice with the white of an egge beaten, and Rosewater and Sugar ❀

A.W., *A Book of Cookrye* (1591)

The death in battle of Richard III in 1485, and subsequent marriage of the victor, Henry Tudor, to Elizabeth of York cleverly defused the York–Lancaster rivalry that had led to the Wars of the Roses. It also ushered in the Tudor dynasty, which was to rule England until Elizabeth I's death, without an heir, in 1603. Henry VII's shrewd union was, however, untypical of the Tudors, for whom marriage often proved problematic to say the least. Henry VIII married his brother's wife, Catherine of Aragon, then became convinced he was cursed by God to have no male heir as a result, and kick-started the Protestant Reformation of the English Church (which rejected the Pope's authority, dissolved the monasteries and declared the king to be the supreme head of the Church of England) in order to divorce her.

The Reformation became the defining act of the Tudor period, and each of Henry's children sought to influence the progress of the juggernaut he had started. After Henry's death in 1547, the country was subjected first to the Protestant extremism of Edward VI's reign, and then, after he died in 1553, to Mary's obstinate Catholicism. After Mary's death in 1558, her half-sister Elizabeth endeavoured to steer a middle course, pushing for the re-adoption of Henry VIII's form of Protestantism and trying to contain the Protestant extremists. Even so, some 250 Catholics were imprisoned or executed during her reign, which also saw the establishment of England's first official secret service under the leadership of the infamous spymaster Sir Francis Walsingham, a "most subtle searcher of hidden secrets", according to the historian William Camden's *Annals* (1615). In recent years there has been debate about whether the playwright Christopher Marlowe was murdered in a pub in Deptford because he was passing on information about possible Catholic plots as one of Walsingham's undercover agents. Certainly, there seems to have been a level of tension and paranoia in late Elizabethan England reminiscent of a police state.

However, the popular image of the Elizabethan period derives more from its exceptional artistic achievements: not only the plays of Marlowe and Shakespeare, but also Edmund Spenser's epic poem glorifying Elizabeth as *The Faerie Queene*, the choral works of Thomas Tallis and William Byrd, and the exquisite miniatures of Nicholas Hilliard. Political repression can, of course, be a seedbed for creativity, but other factors were also at work. The Reformation caused England to be isolated, in religious terms, from large parts of the rest of Europe, which reinforced the island-nation status of "this sceptred isle". This catalysed a strong sense of national identity that began to inform and shape theological, political and artistic debate. Protestantism became synonymous with patriotism, Elizabeth was apotheosised as the Virgin Queen—an image carefully stage-managed with the help of spectacular paintings such as *Queen Elizabeth Going in Procession to Blackfriars in 1601*—and the political and literary confidence fed off one another to develop a kind of national literature. The English had found their voice.

Meanwhile, the ideas of the Renaissance had gradually spread from Italy through Europe and on to England, particularly after the development of the printing press by Johannes Gutenberg in the mid-1400s. Renaissance thinking entailed a definitive shift away from medieval ideals, and the contemplation of man's life in this world in relation to the next gave way to a more humanist preoccupation with man's activities on earth and control of his own destiny: Shakespeare's seven ages of man, rather than Dante's nine circles of hell. Edward III's notion of the courtly knight—formal, pious and skilled with the lance—was replaced by the concept of what has since been termed the "Renaissance man": well-travelled, well-informed, urbane, witty and handy with the pen as well as the sword. By the time of Elizabeth's reign, these ideals held sway among her courtiers, who endeavoured to live up to them. Sir Philip Sidney was one of the foremost poets of the age, but also governor of Flushing in the Netherlands; between fighting against the Irish and leading expeditions to the New World, Sir Walter Ralegh wrote poetry and books on history, travel and politics.

Renaissance ideas were beginning to influence English cuisine, too, particularly through the recipes of Martino de' Rossi, who worked for the papal chamberlain in the 1460s, and Bartolomeo Scappi, who served various cardinals from the 1530s onwards, eventually becoming cook to Pope Pius V. Martino's work, *Liber de arte coquinaria* (The Art of Cooking), appeared in 1460, but his ideas reached a much wider audience fourteen years later, when the writer Platina (Bartolomeo Sacchi) reproduced the chef's 250 recipes more or less word for word in the second half of his 1474 work, *De honesta voluptate et valetudine* (Of Honest Indulgence and Good Health). This was one of the earliest printed cookery books, and became a bestseller, running to more than thirty editions over the next century, including translations into several languages. Martino's recipes are a major step forward in terms of presentation, giving detailed explanations and precise instructions. They show that Italian tastes were moving away from heavy spicing and disguise in favour of a style that emphasised the flavour of the key ingredients. Instead of the gruel-like pottages that were a mainstay of medieval cuisine, Martino prized dishes that had textural variety, forerunners of the stews and ragouts that would become typical of seventeenth-century cooking. He was also one of the first chefs to make specifically sweet dishes, rather than using sugar simply as a seasoning. These innovations were developed and refined over the next century, finding their fullest expression in Scappi's 1570 *Opera dell'arte del cucinare* (A Work on the Art of Cooking). In terms of size and influence, this was a monumental work, with 900 pages exploring meat, fish, eggs, pasta and sauces with greater detail and clarity than ever before. His book was the first to treat cooking as a science, and to treat taste as the guiding principle for recipe development.

This new thinking about food was given an added boost in England by the arrival of brand-new ingredients from the New World and elsewhere, as a result of exploration, improved communications and horticultural advances. Turkeys, pumpkins, vanilla, chocolate, olives, anchovies, globe artichokes, asparagus, apricots, quinces, raspberries, melons, red beetroot, red and green peppers, French beans, kidney beans and potatoes all made their earliest appearance in England during the Tudor period. It must have been very exciting for anyone interested in food, not least because the new printing technology meant it was possible to learn about and disseminate these developments far more quickly. Not surprisingly, this excitement was channelled into cookbooks, which appeared with increasing regularity during the sixteenth century. The very first cookbook printed in England, *This Is the Boke of Cokery*, was published in 1500 and started to become well known from about 1530. By the 1580s there was a steady stream of new titles, such as Thomas Dawson's *The Good Huswife's Jewell* (1585) and *The Good House-wives Treasurie* (1588). The original source of my Tart of Strawberries, *A Book of Cookrye*, was published three years later, followed quickly by *The Good Housewife's Handmaid for the Kitchen* (1594).

However, the most significant change to the English diet in the 1500s (for the wealthy, at least) was sugar consumption, which rocketed and caused impressive dental deterioration. Queen Elizabeth's teeth were, apparently, black: "a defect the English seem subject to, from their too great use of sugar", noted the German lawyer Paul Hentzner in an account of his travels around Europe between 1597 and 1600. Sugar had once been a relatively rare commodity, used sparingly like salt and pepper. That all changed from the mid-1400s onwards, when the Spanish and Portuguese set up sugar plantations on their colonies in Madeira, the Azores and the Canary Islands. The amount of sugar flowing into Europe increased to such an extent that by the 1540s, London had a refinery to turn the coarse product into large white crystalline cones, or sugar loaves.

In the Middle Ages, sugar had been considered medically beneficial. As part of the medieval theory of the humours (see page 89), it was the equivalent of a superfood—moist, warm and perfectly balanced—and a final course known as the *voidée* had developed around it. The most important guests at a medieval feast would be invited to drink a spiced wine called hippocras and eat crisp wafers and marmalades, which were supposed to aid digestion, sweeten the breath and warm the body. As sugar became more plentiful and the Elizabethans acquired a taste for it, the end of the meal evolved into a course called the "banquet", in which a diverse array of sweet treats would be presented: preserved and crystallised fruits, candied vegetables, comfits, fruit jellies (rendered beautifully clear by means of the classic technique of egg-white clarification, which had made its very first appearance in *Liber de arte coquinaria*), biscuits, spiced fruitbreads, marzipan, gingerbread, syllabubs, fruit tarts and other pastries.

In England, before the Tudors got to grips with pastry, it had generally been viewed solely as a handy container that could be made from typical kitchen staples. Chefs would take a stiff paste of flour and water and fashion it into a pot or "coffin", into which they would put a filling. Once cooked, it could be sealed with butter to prevent it going off and kept for several months. After reheating, the contents would be spooned out ready for service and the casing simply discarded. The banquet course, however, clearly stimulated the imaginations of Elizabethan chefs, and pastry techniques became increasingly sophisticated. Although there are almost no European recipes for making pastry before the publication of Scappi's *Opera* in 1570, by the early 1600s detailed, technically accurate accounts of how to make many different types of edible pastry, including puff and short, were appearing in books including Sir Hugh Platt's *Delightes for Ladies* (1602) and Gervase Markham's *The English Huswife*, which ran to thirteen editions between 1615 and 1683. The pastry cooks' time had come. From now on, their extravagant creations would be a prominent feature of cuisine.

We tend to think of the strawberry as quintessentially English, like fish and chips, afternoon tea and cucumber sandwiches, and it's true that it has a long and illustrious history in this country. It is mentioned as early as the tenth century in the *Glastonbury Herbal*, and the 1328–9 financial accounts of Edward III contain a reference to "*furcam de argento pro straubertis*" (payment of silver for strawberries). In 1530, according to the Privy Purse expenses, Henry VIII paid ten shillings for a "pottle of strawberries". He must have liked them because three years later the Hampton Court accounts show that strawberry runners had been bought for the king's garden. Shakespeare, too, has Richard III requesting a punnet or two from the Bishop of Ely:

> *My lord of Ely, when I was last in Holborn*
> *I saw good strawberries in your garden there.*
> *I do beseech you send for some of them.*

The fruit certainly seems to have been a royal favourite.

The strawberry, then, was appreciated by the sixteenth century—"much eaten at all men's tables in the summer time with wine and sugar," according to Thomas Hill in *The Gardener's Labyrinth* of 1577—and already capable of inspiring devotion. "Doubtless God could have made a better berry, but doubtless God never did," exclaimed the physician William Butler (1535–1618). But there wasn't yet any fol-de-rol about its Englishness. Elizabethan dramatists, poets and painters may have been busily forging symbols of national identity, but they weren't press-ganging the strawberry into service.

Even so, for me strawberries have always been strongly evocative of an English summer, conjuring up cricket whites, the buzz of wasps and the sharp scent of freshly cut grass. Those kinds of connections are very important because I believe that the deliciousness of a dish comes not only from what you taste, but also from the memories and associations it triggers and the emotions it stirs up, so my interest in A.W.'s recipe had as much to do with symbolism as with history. Naturally, I liked the idea of taking inspiration from a pastry recipe dating from when pastry-making first took off in England. In this case, though, I wasn't going to be too troubled by fidelity to the chef's directives: my aim was to showcase the strawberry. I saw the dish as a seasonal celebration, a welcoming-in of summer that would stay on the menu at Dinner only for as long as strawberries were in season—in fact I was already wondering whether I could do a companion piece with September's ingredients to herald the start of autumn. I wanted it to be very fresh and fragrant, with a sort of just-picked quality to it, probably involving very little application of heat, which can drive off the delicate top notes. I wanted to hold on to as much natural, unadulterated aroma and flavour as possible.

To that end, I decided that although pastry would form the foundation element of my recipe, I wouldn't be making a conventional tart, in which the amount of pastry might overpower the strawberries. Instead, I had in mind a series of layers, a light, delicate construction with a strip of pastry as its base. A.W.'s instructions for pastry-making are, as the recipe at the beginning of the chapter shows, extremely vague. (*Taste*, Kate Colquhoun's entertaining history of British cooking, singles out A.W.— about whom we know very little—as particularly confusing and imprecise on the subject.) I chose to interpret the references to butter and sugar as indicating that a short pastry was required.

(Later editions suggest a biscuit-like texture.) In late-Tudor kitchens, shortcrust pastry must have been about as cutting-edge as it gets, given that the technique only started to appear in print in Italy in 1570. Since then, though, we've gained a much greater understanding of the science involved, and I'd be making full use of that knowledge to produce a beautifully delicate and crumbly pastry.

Pastry has three main ingredients: flour, fat and some form of liquid (usually water or dairy products), plus perhaps salt or sugar. All these ingredients have important roles to play, but the one that probably most defines the character of a pastry is gluten, which is a kind of superprotein made from two proteins present in flour: gliadin and glutenin. When flour is mixed with water, the gliadin and glutenin molecules change shape as they react with the water molecules. No longer inert, they begin to spread out and develop bonds with one another, intertwining to form the gluten that gives dough its elasticity. This is great for bread, but if you're after a looser, crumblier texture, you need to control how much that gluten develops. One way to do this is to use a low-protein flour, such as plain flour (which has 9–11 per cent protein, while strong flour can have as much as 15 per cent). Another is to limit the amount of liquid used. This can have a surprisingly big impact. Adding 3 grams too much or too little water to 120 grams of flour can be the difference between a firm texture and a crumbly one. The drier the dough, the crumblier it will be. However, the most effective way to control the gluten is to add the ingredients in a particular order. Combining the flour and fat before adding any liquid allows the fat to coat the flour particles and act as a barrier to water, retarding the development of gluten.

On top of the pastry base I began to assemble layers that would complement or reinforce the strawberries, which, lightly caramelised with chamomile sugar, would be the centrepiece of the dish. First, a flat strip of strawberry gel, to give textural and visual contrast while underpinning the strawberry flavour. Above this I decided to have a yoghurt cream. Yoghurt would introduce a necessary touch of acidity to help temper the richness of the dish, and would be the perfect vehicle for a few grams of orange blossom water. This was a nod to the rosewater used in the original recipe, and would also add a wild-strawberry characteristic that I wanted in the dish; in the wild the fruit has a pronounced orange-blossom note, a flavour the Tudors would have recognised and appreciated.

Summarised like this, the recipe development seems straightforward, but it was, of course, more complicated than that. Before settling for a strawberry gel, we tried out various jellies, and experimented with a strawberry syrup before deciding that, since it was cooked for a while to reduce it, it took away from the freshness. Originally, the layer of cream was beneath the strawberries, but eventually I realised that if I piped it on top I could give the dish a nice bit of visual interest. The garnish offered an opportunity to add to the decorative aspect, and to further emphasise freshness: I dispensed with A.W.'s cinnamon and ginger, which to me had too autumnal a character, in favour of lighter, cleaner flavours, such as chamomile, which has a hay-like aroma that really complements strawberries. For a bit of crunch, I sprinkled some crystallised mint, crystallised violet and biscuit crumbs on the cream, plus some freeze-dried yoghurt pieces to reinforce the acidity. Among these I put honey cress and shards of strawberry tuile, and I placed biscuit crumbs and a spoonful of strawberry sorbet alongside for a nice contrast of texture and temperature. The final touch was a little Earl Grey salt. This seasoned the dish (salt is just as good at drawing out the flavours of sweet dishes as savoury ones, and is worth adding to most desserts), and the bergamot—which is what gives Earl Grey its distinctive fragrance—provided a refreshing wash of citrus. And there it was: summer on a plate, a celebration of the season's transience.

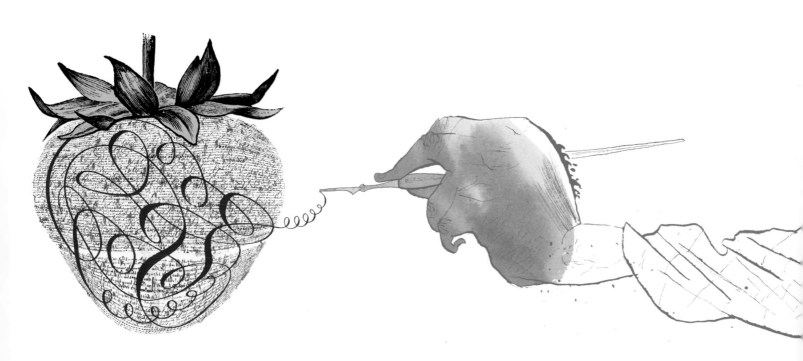

TART OF STRAWBERRIES

Makes 6 portions

Strawberry Sorbet

400g	**Fructose**
2kg	**Rinsed and hulled strawberries**

Place the fructose and 400g water in a saucepan and bring to the boil. Once the fructose has fully dissolved, pour the syrup into a container and chill immediately.

Place the strawberries in a Thermomix in 2 batches and blitz on full power for 3 minutes. Pass the strawberry purée through a fine-mesh sieve. Combine the smooth strawberry purée with the chilled syrup and stir to emulsify fully.

Churn the mixture and store the sorbet in the freezer until needed.

Almond Biscuits

250g	**Unsalted butter, cubed and at room temperature**
130g	**Icing sugar**
180g	**Plain flour**
115g	**Ground almonds**
1g	**Salt**
60g	**Egg yolk**

Preheat the oven to 170°C/340°F.

Make a template by cutting out a 12 x 3cm rectangular shape from a suitable material such as plastic or silicone.

Place the butter and sugar in a mixer bowl and cream until light and creamy, using the paddle attachment.

In a separate bowl, combine the flour, ground almonds and salt, and then gradually add the flour to the mixer.

Once the flour has fully incorporated, add the egg yolk and combine until the dough has come together. Take care not to overwork it.

Remove the dough from the mixer bowl and place between 2 sheets of baking parchment. Using a rolling pin, roll out to 2mm thick and rest in the freezer for 10 minutes.

Gently place the dough on a baking tray and peel off the top layer of parchment. Bake for 15 minutes, then remove. Using the template as a guide, cut into rectangular shapes. Return the biscuits to the oven and continue to bake until golden.

Allow to cool and set the biscuits aside in a sealed container. Reserve the biscuit off-cuts and blitz to make crumbs. Set aside in a sealed container.

Earl Grey Tea Salt

5g	**Loose-leaf Earl Grey tea**
20g	**Sea salt flakes**

Place the tea in a pestle and mortar and grind to a fine powder. Combine with the sea salt flakes and store in an airtight container.

Chamomile Sugar

6g	**Loose-leaf chamomile tea**
60g	**Fructose**

Place the chamomile and fructose in the Thermomix. Blitz at high speed for 2 minutes, then store in a sealed container.

Crystallised Mint

110g	**Pasteurised egg white**
55g	**Gum arabic powder**
18–24	**Mint leaves**
150g	**White caster sugar**

Place the egg white and gum arabic powder in a small, deep-sided container and blitz using a hand blender until fully combined.

Place 1 mint leaf in the palm of your hand and, using your finger, gently coat the leaf with the egg white mixture on both sides.

Gently cover the leaf with sugar and shake off any excess. Place on a tray lined with baking parchment.

Repeat this process until all the leaves have been coated. Allow the leaves to dry out overnight.

Yoghurt Cream

300g	**Fromage blanc**
11g	**Orange flower water**
25g	**Icing sugar**
100g	**Vanilla-flavoured yoghurt**

Place the fromage blanc in muslin cloth and suspend it over a bowl. Allow it to hang for 24 hours in the fridge.

Place 250g of the hung fromage blanc in a bowl and add the remaining ingredients. Whisk the mixture until well combined and firm. Transfer the yoghurt cream to a piping bag and store in the fridge until needed.

Strawberry Tuiles

130g	**Isomalt**
130g	**Glucose**
50g	**Freeze-dried strawberry powder**

Gently heat the isomalt and glucose in a small pan until fully dissolved. Increase the temperature and bring the syrup to 158°C/316°F.

Pour on to a silicone mat and place another one on top. Allow to cool.

Preheat the oven to 150°C/300°F and place a clean, dry silicone mat on a tray.

Break the cooled mixture into pieces and place in the Thermomix. Blitz to a fine powder and use a fine-mesh sieve to dust the powder on to the silicone mat. Ensure it is evenly covered.

Cover the dusted powder with a thin layer of freeze-dried strawberry powder through a fine-mesh sieve.

Place the tray in the oven for 2 minutes, or until the sugar becomes transparent. Remove from the oven and allow to cool.

Place the mat face down on to baking parchment and peel away the mat, leaving shards of tuile. Store the shards between baking parchment in a sealed container with silica gel.

Strawberry Fluid Gel

680g   **Strawberry purée**
55g   **White caster sugar**
4g   **Gellan F (low-acyl gellan)**

Place the strawberry purée and sugar in a Thermomix and bring to 90°C/194°F on a medium setting. Add the gellan F and blitz for 10 seconds at high speed. Lift the lid and scrape down the sides of the jug. Continue to blitz for 1 more minute to ensure the gellan has dissolved completely. Pour the mixture into a large bowl, and place the bowl in iced water. Allow to cool completely.

Once the mixture has cooled and set, return the set gel to a clean Thermomix jug and blitz at high speed for 4 minutes. Stop the Thermomix every minute to scrape down the sides of the jug.

To remove any air bubbles from the gel, scrape it into a shallow container and place in a chamber vacuum sealer. Under full pressure, close the lid and keep a close eye on the gel, stopping the vacuum as soon as the bubbles rise to the top. Repeat this process several more times until the gel no longer bubbles.

Pass the gel through a fine-mesh sieve and refrigerate until needed.

Strawberries

55g   **Reserved chamomile sugar**
18–20 **Strawberries**

Sprinkle a thin layer of chamomile sugar in a dry frying pan. Slice the strawberries in half, and place them flat-side down on to the sugar.

Heat the pan over a high heat and shake it slightly to allow the sugar to melt. Keep the strawberries in the pan for 1–2 minutes, depending on their firmness.

Remove the strawberries from the pan and allow to cool to room temperature before using.

To Serve

Reserved strawberry fluid gel
Reserved strawberries
Reserved almond biscuits
Toasted coriander seeds
Reserved yoghurt cream
Crystallised violet petals
Reserved crystallised mint
Freeze-dried yoghurt pieces
Reserved Earl Grey tea salt
Honey cress
Reserved strawberry tuiles
Reserved biscuit crumbs
Reserved strawberry sorbet

Spread the strawberry fluid gel on to each almond biscuit and place on one side of a plate.

Arrange the strawberries on the biscuit and place a coriander seed on each strawberry. Using a piping bag with a flat, decorative nozzle, pipe a layer of yoghurt cream over the strawberries.

Carefully arrange some crystallised violet petals, crystallised mint, freeze-dried yoghurt pieces, Earl Grey tea salt and honey cress on the piped yoghurt cream. Top with strawberry tuiles.

Place a small pile of biscuit crumbs and freeze-dried yoghurt pieces next to the biscuit and place a rocher of the strawberry sorbet on top of the crumbs and yoghurt pieces. Serve immediately.

TAFFETY TART

[1658]

TO MAKE TARTS CALLED TAFFATY TARTS

 *First wet your Past with Butter and cold Water, and rowle it very thin, also then lay them in layes, and between every lay of Apples strew some Sugar, and some Lemon Pill, cut very small, if you please put some Fennell-seed to them; then put them into a stoak hot Oven, and let them stand an hour in or more, then take them out, and take Rose-water and Butter beaten together, and wash them over with the same, and strew fine Sugar upon them; then put them into the Oven again, let them stand a little while and take them out* ❖

W.M., *The Queen's Closet Opened* (1658, 4th edition)

When *The Queen's Closet Opened* was first published in 1655, England was right in the middle of its brief experiment with republicanism. On 30 January 1649, Charles I had been beheaded in front of the Banqueting House in Whitehall. In 1660, parliament would invite his son to return from exile in France to become Charles II. For the time being, however, the country was ruled by Oliver Cromwell.

Cromwell hadn't started off in charge. Four months after Charles's death, England was declared to be "a commonwealth and free state", governed by a parliament known as the Rump (so called because it was composed of a small group of survivors from an earlier purge of the Commons). However, their initiatives for shaping this new, Puritan republic were clumsy and unpopular. For Cromwell and the army that he controlled, the religious reforms they'd gone to war for weren't happening fast enough. In April 1653 he dissolved the Rump, but its successor, Barebone's Parliament (named after the MP Praise-God Barebone), was so riven by infighting that in December the moderates declared that "the sitting of this Parliament any longer as constituted will not be for the good of the Commonwealth, and that therefore it is requisite to deliver up unto the Lord General Cromwell the powers they have received from him". Four days later, Cromwell became head of the country under the title Lord Protector.

Although it was the politicians who put Cromwell in charge, his relationship with parliament remained an uneasy one. If the government pursued policies he disapproved of—as it did in 1654, legislating to contain the army and clamp down on religious pluralism, and again in 1658—he simply dissolved

parliament. (Ironically, it was Charles I's cavalier use of this tactic that had led to the Civil War in the first place.) In the wake of that first dissolution, conscious that he had very little legal authority, Cromwell resorted to using the army to keep order, dividing the country into eleven regions, each ruled by a major-general. By the end of 1655, England was under military rule.

During the year it was in operation, the military regime tried to enforce a highly moral, Puritan way of life by banning Sunday sports, horse racing and cock fighting, closing alehouses and forbidding May Day celebrations. In the film *Robin Hood Prince of Thieves*, the sheriff of Nottingham (played by Alan Rickman) angrily recites a list of punishments to be exacted on the poor, finishing with a snarled "…and call off Christmas". This is so over-the-top it always gets a laugh in the cinema, but the major-generals did indeed try to prevent the traditional celebration of the Twelve Days of Christmas.

Against such a background, it's perhaps not surprising that there was a groundswell of nostalgia for the time before the Civil War. From 1653 onwards a number of cookbooks were published, such as *A Choice Manuall* by the Countess of Kent and a revised edition of Lord Ruthven's *The Ladies' Cabinet Opened*, which presented the culinary delights of the aristocratic table—a sort of gastro-porn for palates jaded by grim Puritanism.

One of the most popular of these was *The Queen's Closet Opened*, in which the queen in question was supposedly the exiled wife of Charles I. Henrietta Maria might have been unpromising to look at (van Dyck judiciously omitted her protruding teeth from his superb portraits of the royal family) and uncompromising in outlook (during the

Civil War she was among the Royalists who favoured the utter destruction of parliament), but by 1655, in comparison with the privations of the Protectorate, she seemed decidedly more attractive. This, of course, was the book's intention. W.M. is generally thought to be Walter Montagu, a servant and close confidant of Henrietta Maria, who aimed to rehabilitate the queen by presenting her as a sort of superior domestic goddess. The book consists of three parts: The Pearle of Practice, which describes hundreds of herbal remedies, A Queen's Delight, which concerns the art of confectionery, and The Compleat Cook, which contains a number of sweet and savoury recipes, including Taffety Tart.

Most of the medicinal advice now seems like voodoo or witchcraft (To Hold Urine directs that the claws of a goat should be burned to a powder and added to the sufferer's food) and is generally not for the fainthearted. The best cure for a sore throat is apparently to "mixe white Dog's turd and Honey, spread it on Sheep's leather, and apply it to the Throat". Fortunately, the recipes—dressed artichokes, pigeon pie, pickled cucumber, gooseberry fool, cheesecake—are a lot less extreme.

Among these remedies and recipes, W.M. artfully inserts entries with gossipy, name-dropping titles: "A Medicine for a Dropsie approved by the Lady Hobby, who was cured herself by it"; "A Medicine for the Plague that the Lord Mayor had from the Queen"; "To make a Posset, the Earl of Arundel's Way"; "To make a Cake the way of the Royal Princess, the Lady Elizabeth, daughter to King Charles the first"; "The Countesse of Rutland's Receipt of making the rare Banbury Cake which was so much praised at her Daughter's (the right Honourable the Lady Chawerth's) Wedding".

Shamelessly aspirational, they appear to grant the reader privileged access to the lifestyle of the rich and famous.

The name Taffety Tart carries a little bit of this sense of splendour. The word taffety derives from taffeta, a type of fabric that was traditionally made from silk. Taffeta is smooth to the touch and has a seductive shimmer to it, so it became a popular choice for formal dresses and ball gowns and was generally symbolic of luxury and sumptuous flamboyance. No-one seems to know how or why the material became associated with a tart, but taffeta has a certain stiffness to it, giving dresses that rustling sound you hear in period dramas, and I wonder whether the name is in fact a reference to the crisp, brittle surface of the tart. I certainly found the name appealing, with all those alliterative t's tripping tantalising off the tongue, but what really drew me in were the ingredients. Apples, sugar, lemon, rosewater and layers of thinly rolled pastry: here was a recipe that made sense to me because I already served something similar at the Fat Duck.

I really like tarte tatin. Rich, caramelised apple and buttery puff pastry are a fantastic pairing. So, when I first opened the Fat Duck as a simple bistro serving rustic French classics, I put one on the menu. Gradually, the restaurant moved away from the bistro concept, but the tart kept pace with the changes; I was able to adapt and refashion it so that it continued to fit with the other dishes on the menu. By 2007, however, it needed a rethink, and the inspiration I found took the dish in a whole new direction.

The Fat Duck menu at that time featured a galette of rhubarb, in which the fruit was gently poached and allowed to set, then placed on an olive-oil biscuit base and topped with yoghurt mousse, over which was laid a strip of *arlette* (an extremely thin, caramelised puff pastry). Now it occurred to me that an arlette could easily take the place of the more conventional puff pastry in a tarte tatin, giving a lovely crisp, delicate contrast of texture and a nice reinforcement of the caramelised flavour.

It still surprises me how changing a single ingredient can trigger a wholescale re-evaluation of a dish. The crispy arlette put me in mind of a millefeuille, which has several layers of pastry with cream in between them, and I saw that I could use that overall structure to create a new tarte tatin in which each ingredient was cooked separately, by whatever method and at whatever temperature suited it best, and then assembled layer by layer.

Over time I developed the contents of those layers: apples poached slowly in sugar syrup until intensely caramelised, then layered in slices and baked gently until firm enough to be cut into a wedge; the poaching syrup warmed and set with pectin to create a *pâte de fruit* (a sort of refined fruit pastille), and piped blobs of fromage blanc cream, all sandwiched by rectangles of crisp pastry and garnished with, among other things, dried apple pieces. A set of textures and flavours that, as I discovered when looking through *The Queen's Closet*, were also characteristic of Taffety Tart.

It's always exciting when a recipe from the past seems to chime with something you're working on. If nothing else, it's a reminder of how relevant and illuminating culinary history can be. Here, though, it also presented me with an opportunity to take my apple dish in a new direction. In W.M.'s recipe, the tart was given flavour complexity by sprinkling fennel seeds

and finely chopped lemon peel amid the layers, and adding rosewater to the buttercream. I decided to take this trio of flavourings and explore how I might use them in my dish.

Lemon was relatively easy to introduce. Candying the julienned zest created concentrated, sweet, firm strips that could be scattered on top of the tart, offering sudden bursts of citrus flavour and a welcome texture contrast. I wanted, though, to capture some of lemon's other characteristics as well—its freshness and sharpness—so I elected to have segments of it in the dish as part of a salad-style garnish that was taking shape in my mind.

Rosewater was trickier to incorporate. The delicate fragrance can be delightful, but if it's used with a heavy hand the scent is overpowering and can seem old-fashioned, summoning memories of the sort of perfume your gran might have worn. The best approach, I decided, was to let it mingle with the fromage blanc, and trial and error got me to an amount that made its presence felt without taking over. But I also had a bit of science up the sleeve of my chef's whites that I reckoned would help with the rosewater scent. There's a phenomenon that scientists call super-additivity, which has given rise to a valuable technique that I use in my restaurants. It's a process by which the brain combines a number of cues from the senses to produce a more intense or effective sensory experience. An example of this is how, in a noisy environment, we rely on lip-reading as well as listening in order to understand what someone is saying. It's the combination of sight and sound that creates full comprehension. At my restaurants I've explored super-additivity in a variety of ways, garnishing a lavender brûlée with lavender sprigs, for example, to enhance the flavour. Similarly, in the Fat Duck dish

"Sound of the Sea", diners eat while listening to a recording of the sounds of a seascape through earphones, which intensifies the maritime flavours of the dish. I reasoned, therefore, that if I crystallised rose petals and added them to the garnish, the sight of the petals would both prepare the diner for the rosewater flavour and subtly reinforce it.

Candying—coating ingredients in a sugar syrup—is a technique that has been practised since at least the Middle Ages, originally as a method of preservation, and it offered a good way of bringing fennel seeds into the dish. I first participated in the traditional method of making comfits when I visited food historian Ivan Day's house while I was researching the history of trifle. Comfits are seeds, nuts and spices, such as cardamom, caraway, aniseed, fennel seed, diced ginger or cinnamon strips, that have been coated in sugar. In the Tudor period they were served at the end of a meal with a glass of spiced wine to aid digestion, or as a garnish for sweet dishes like trifle. Comfits were still popular in the nineteenth century: in *Alice's Adventures in Wonderland*, Alice pulls out a box of them that she distributes as prizes in the Caucus Race. Since then, they've become less familiar, but the basic idea continues in the dessert decoration hundreds and thousands, which derive directly from comfits.

Making comfits the traditional way is a laboursome business. At Ivan's I crouched over a copper pan on the fire, continually massaging sugar syrup on to fennel seeds, then letting them dry, until they had acquired fifty coats of the stuff. A natural food colouring, such as spinach, saffron or mulberry juice, was added to the final few coatings to give the comfits a brilliant hue. The end result was worth the effort, however, providing not just a lovely crunchy texture, but also a little detonation of intense, fresh flavour. It was a great example of flavour encapsulation (see page 203), and I could see it would be invaluable for all kinds of dishes, so long as I could find a less cumbersome method for making them. At one point, my head of creative development, Jocky Petrie, was spinning seeds and syrup in a coffee can bolted on to a hand-drill while he trained a hairdryer on them, but eventually—as you'll see in the recipe—we came up with a simple technique that captured the flavour and texture I wanted.

Fennel seeds are strong, so they have to be managed carefully to prevent them dominating a dish. For Taffety Tart I again chose infusion as one way of introducing the flavour very gently, adding bagged seeds to the poaching caramel once it had come off the heat to let the aromas spread into the liquid. I also put crystallised fennel seeds in the crumble mixture that would top the tart and give it plenty of texture. But rather than leaving them whole, which means you get a real shot of fennel as the seed cracks open, I crushed them roughly to subdue the flavour-release effect a little. By now it was clear that fennel had become the main background flavour, present throughout the dish in a kind of supporting role, so I looked into bringing other forms of it into the recipe, settling on a final garnish of freshly sliced strips of fennel bulb and its delicate fronds. The resulting flavour combination is, I think, particularly unusual, even unexpected—a real flavour of the past.

TAFFETY TART

Makes 6 portions

Vanilla Ice Cream

1.2kg	Whole milk
5	Vanilla pods, seeds only
5	Coffee beans
195g	Light brown sugar
120g	Egg yolk
75g	Skimmed milk powder
300g	Whipping cream
110g	Vanilla-flavoured yoghurt

Place the whole milk, vanilla seeds and coffee beans in a saucepan and bring to 90°C/194°F. Remove from the heat and allow to cool to 52°C/126°F.

In the meantime, place the sugar in a separate bowl and add the egg yolk. Whisk well and gradually pour into the 52°C/126°F milk mixture, whisking continuously. Add the skimmed milk powder and whipping cream and return to the heat, continuing to whisk. Bring the mixture to exactly 70°C/158°F and hold it at this temperature for 10 minutes, stirring frequently.

Pour the ice cream base into a large sous-vide bag that has been placed carefully in iced water. Allow the ice cream base to chill to 5°C/41°F. Seal the sous-vide bag and store in the fridge overnight to allow infusion.

Using a fine-mesh sieve, strain the ice cream base into a container and add the yoghurt. Combine the mixture with a hand blender until fully emulsified.

Churn the ice cream and store in the freezer until needed.

Caramel

22g	Pectin NH
1.1kg	Golden caster sugar
30g	Fennel seeds
500g	Unsalted butter, cubed and at room temperature
1kg	Apple juice
100g	Verjus du Périgord

Combine the pectin NH with 100g of the sugar in a small bowl and set aside.

Wrap the fennel seeds in a muslin cloth and secure with string.

Place a large, deep pan over a medium heat and add a thin layer of sugar. As the sugar starts to melt and colour, swirl the pan gently and add another layer of sugar. Do not aggravate the melting sugar by stirring it, as it may seize and form crystals. Do so until all the sugar has melted and turned a dark golden copper colour.

Add the butter a little at a time, whisking it in well to emulsify after each addition. Remove from the heat and gradually add the apple juice, stirring regularly until the mixture is well combined.

Place the pan back on the heat and bring to the boil. Add the pectin mixture, the fennel parcel and the verjus. Remove from the heat and allow to cool.

Once cool, remove and discard the muslin parcel of fennel seeds.

Poached Apples

6	Braeburn apples
	Reserved caramel

Preheat the oven to 180°C/350°F.

Peel and core the apples and place them in a deep roasting tray. Pour enough caramel over the apples to cover them completely. You should use at least 750g, as you will need it again later. Cover the tray with baking parchment, allowing the paper to touch the surface of the caramel. Place a double layer of foil over the tray and carefully pierce 3 small holes in the foil.

Bake in the oven for 25 minutes, then remove the tray and turn the apples. Repeat this process every 15 minutes until the apples are caramel brown all the way through. Make sure the foil stays in place.

Remove the apples from the caramel and refrigerate, covered.

Pass the poaching caramel through a fine-mesh sieve and allow to cool. Store the poaching caramel in the fridge until needed.

Tatin

6	Reserved poached apples
200g	Reserved poaching caramel

Preheat the oven to 120°C/250°F. Line a tray with baking parchment.

Slice the apples into 4mm slices and place the slices, overlapping tightly, on the tray.

Remove the layer of fat from the chilled poaching caramel and discard it. Pour enough caramel into the tray to cover the apples and place in the oven.

After an hour, rotate the tray and return to the oven for 1 more hour. Continue to do this until most of the liquid has evaporated. Remove the tray from the oven and place it in the fridge.

Once the tatin has chilled, turn it out on to a work surface.

Make a template by cutting out a 10.5 x 11.5 x 5.2cm triangle from a suitable material. Plastic and silicone work well. Using the template, cut out 6 triangular shapes from the tatin and store in a sealed container in the fridge until needed, with layers of baking parchment separating the pieces.

Apple Caramel Gel

15g	Golden caster sugar
2.6g	Pectin jaune
250g	Reserved poaching caramel, fat removed
3.6g	Malic acid

Mix the sugar and pectin in a small bowl, combining it well using a small whisk. Set aside.

Place the poaching caramel and 85g water in a saucepan and bring to the boil. Add the sugar and pectin mixture and reduce the heat to medium. Whisk the caramel continuously until it reaches 66° Brix.

Mix the malic acid with 1.3g water and add to the caramel. Line a tray with baking parchment and pour the caramel on to the tray. Allow to cool and set completely.

Using the template as a guide, cut the set gel into triangular shapes. Store in the fridge until needed, with baking parchment separating the pieces.

Arlettes

150g   Puff pastry
75g   Icing sugar

Preheat the oven to 180°C/350°F.

Roll the puff pastry as thinly as possible between 2 sheets of baking parchment, dusting frequently with icing sugar to prevent it from sticking.

Roll the pastry until it is paper thin and place on a baking tray. It is not necessary to remove the parchment. Place a heavy tray on top and bake in the oven for 15 minutes.

Rotate the trays and bake for 10 more minutes. Carefully remove from the oven once the arlette is golden.

Lift the top tray off the arlette and peel off the baking parchment. Using the template as a guide, cut 12 arlettes and allow to cool. Store in an airtight container with silica gel.

Rose Cream

175g   Fromage blanc
35g   Icing sugar
50g   Whipping cream
1.8g   Rosewater

Place the fromage blanc in muslin and suspend it over a bowl. Allow it to hang for 48 hours in the fridge.

Place 125g of the hung fromage blanc in a bowl and add the remaining ingredients. Whisk until well combined and firm. Transfer to a piping bag and store in the fridge until needed.

Apple Fluid Gel

190g   Spray-dried apple
3g   Malic acid
7   Bay leaves
7.5g   Gellan F (low-acyl gellan)

Place 560g water, the spray-dried apple and malic acid in a saucepan and bring to the boil. Remove from the heat and add the bay leaves. Cover the saucepan with clingfilm and allow to infuse for 30 minutes.

Strain the liquid through a fine-mesh sieve and pour into a Thermomix. Bring the liquid to 90°C/194°F at medium speed.

Add the gellan F and blitz at high speed for 1 minute. Lift the lid and scrape down the sides of the jug. Continue to blitz for 1 more minute to incorporate fully. Pour the mixture into a large bowl and place the bowl in iced water. Allow to cool completely.

Place the gel in a clean Thermomix. Blitz for 1 minute, then lift the lid and scrape down the sides of the jug. Blitz for 1 more minute to incorporate fully.

To remove the air bubbles from the gel, scrape it into a shallow container and place in a chamber vacuum sealer. Under full pressure, close the lid and keep a close eye on the gel, stopping the process as soon as the bubbles rise to the top. Repeat several more times until the gel no longer bubbles. Transfer to a piping bag and store in the fridge until needed.

Vanilla Biscuits

250g   Unsalted butter
165g   Golden caster sugar
75g   Egg yolk
290g   Plain flour
4g   Salt
1g   Vanilla powder
2.5g   Baking powder

Place the butter and sugar in a mixer bowl and cream until light and creamy using the paddle attachment. Reduce the speed and add the egg yolk until combined.

In a separate bowl, combine the flour, salt, vanilla powder and baking powder, then gradually add the dry ingredients to the mixer. Taking care not to overwork it, mix until the dough starts to come together.

Remove the dough from the mixer bowl and wrap in clingfilm. Allow to rest in the fridge for 2–3 hours.

Preheat the oven to 170°C/340°F. Remove the dough from the fridge and place between 2 sheets of baking parchment. Using a rolling pin, roll to a thickness of 3mm and place in the freezer for 10 minutes.

Gently place the dough on a baking tray and peel off the top layer of baking parchment. Bake for 15 minutes, then remove. Using the template as a guide, cut the biscuit into triangular shapes. Return the biscuits and trimmings to the oven and bake until golden.

Allow to cool and set the biscuits aside in a sealed container. Reserve the biscuit trimmings and blitz them to crumbs. Set them aside in a sealed container.

Crumble Elements

250g   Almonds
60g   Unsalted butter, cubed and at room temperature
1.5g   Vanilla powder
15g   Sea salt flakes
35g   Fennel seeds
25g   Golden caster sugar

Preheat the oven to 160°C/320°F.

To make the almond praline, spread the almonds out evenly on a roasting tray and place in the oven for 10 minutes. Toss the almonds and return to the oven for 5 more minutes. Repeat this process until they have roasted to a dark golden colour. Remove from the oven and allow to cool.

(continued overleaf)

Place the almonds in the Thermomix and blitz to form a liquid paste. You may need to stop at intervals and scrape down the sides of the jug. Store in the fridge until needed.

To make the brown butter, place the butter cubes in a small saucepan and melt gently, whisking continuously. After several minutes, the butter will give off a nutty aroma and the solids will turn brown. Once the butter reaches 190°C/375°F, remove from the heat and pass through a fine-mesh filter bag. Refrigerate until needed.

To make the vanilla salt, combine the vanilla powder and sea salt flakes well. Store in a sealed container until needed.

To make the crystallised fennel seeds, toast them in a frying pan over a moderate to high heat until golden, stirring regularly. Remove the seeds from the pan and return the pan to the heat. Add the sugar and allow it to melt and caramelise. Add the toasted fennel seeds and stir to coat them in the caramel. Pour the coated seeds on to a silicone mat and quickly cover with a second mat. Roll it flat with a rolling pin and allow it to cool.

Store in a sealed container until needed.

Crumble Topping

200g	Reserved almond praline
40g	Reserved brown butter
60g	Reserved crystallised fennel seeds
8g	Reserved vanilla salt
300g	Feuilletine
50g	Spray-dried apple

Preheat a water bath to 50°C/122°F.

Place the almond praline in a sous-vide bag and seal. Place the brown butter in a second sous-vide bag and seal. Drop both bags in the water bath for 15 minutes.

In the meantime, put the crystallised fennel seeds in a bag and lightly crush using a rolling pin. Set aside.

Once the praline and butter have been removed from the water bath, put them in a round-bottomed bowl and add the vanilla salt. Stir well to combine. Add the feuilletine and crushed fennel seeds and stir.

Weigh out 140g of this crumble and add the spray-dried apple. Store in a sealed container until needed.

Crystallised Rose Petals

110g	Pasteurised egg white
55g	Gum arabic
9	Drops rosewater
	Rose petals from 3 edible roses
150g	White caster sugar

Place the egg white, gum arabic powder and rosewater in a deep-sided container and blitz using a hand blender until fully combined.

Place 1 rose petal in the palm of your hand and, using your finger, gently coat the petal on both sides with the egg white mixture. Gently cover the petal with sugar and shake off any excess. Place on a tray that has been lined with baking parchment. Repeat until all the petals have been coated. Allow the petals to dry out overnight.

Candied Lemon Zest

20g	Lemon zest peelings
50g	White caster sugar
25g	Glucose

Finely slice the lemon zest peelings into thin strips, julienne style. Ensure there is no visible pith.

Blanch the zest in boiling water for 1 minute. Pass the water through a sieve, reserving the zest and discarding the water. Repeat this process with fresh boiling water. Set the zest aside.

Place 600g water, the sugar and glucose in a saucepan and bring to a simmer, stirring until the sugar has dissolved.

Reduce the heat and add the blanched zest. Simmer until it is soft and almost transparent. Remove from the heat and allow the zest to cool in the syrup. Store in the fridge until needed.

To Serve

6	Reserved vanilla biscuits
6	Pieces reserved apple caramel gel
6	Pieces reserved tatin
12	Reserved arlettes
	Reserved rose cream
	Reserved apple fluid gel
	Reserved crumble topping
	Shaved fennel pieces
	Lemon segments, cut into small pieces
	Fennel fronds
	Reserved candied lemon zest
	Reserved crystallised rose petals, broken into pieces
	Reserved biscuit crumbs
	Reserved vanilla ice cream

Gently build up the tarts, using a vanilla biscuit as the base. Working from the bottom up, and ensuring the elements are lined up perfectly, place the apple caramel gel on top of the biscuit; the tatin on top of the apple caramel gel; the arlette on top of the tatin. Pipe several balls of the rose cream on top of the arlette.

Gently spread the apple fluid gel on a second arlette and scatter over the crumble topping. Place this gently on top of the rose cream to complete the tart. Transfer it to a plate, off centre.

To garnish, pipe a thin line of apple fluid gel along the open side of the plate and arrange the remaining elements on the gel strip. Twirl the shaved fennel into a spiral and place 2 on either end of the fluid gel strip. Place small lemon segments, fennel fronds and candied lemon zest pieces on the strip next to the fennel spiral. Top each end with a piece of crystallised rose petal.

Place a small pile of biscuit crumbs in the centre of the fluid gel strip and place a rocher of the vanilla ice cream on top of the biscuit pile. Serve immediately.

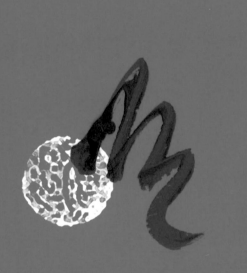

QUAKING PUDDING

[1660]

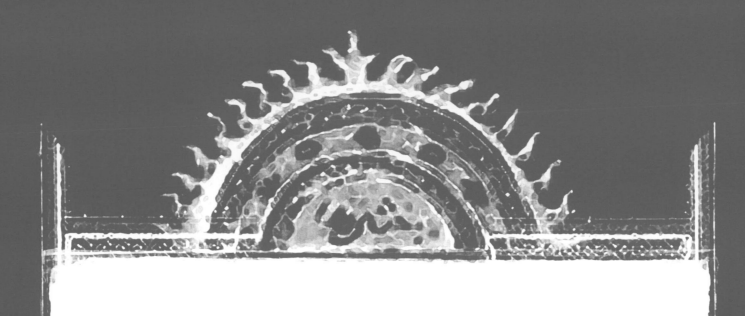

TO MAKE QUAKING PUDDING

❈ *Slice the crumbs of a penny manchet, and infuse it three or four hours in a pint of scalding hot cream, covering it close, then break the bread with a spoon very small, and put to it eight eggs, and but only four whites, beat them together very well, and season it with sugar, rosewater, and grated nutmeg: If you think it too stiff put in some cold cream, and beat them well together; then wet the bag or napkin and flour it, put in the pudding, tie it hard and boil it half an hour, then dish it, and put to it butter, rosewater and sugar, and serve it up to the table* ❈

Robert May, *The Accomplisht Cook* (1660)

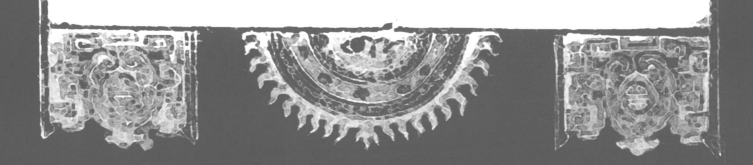

Nowadays, the term "pudding" has come to mean the sweet course at the end of a meal, and it has lingered on in the names of a perplexing variety of dishes, both sweet and savoury, which seem to have little connection with one another: rice pudding, sponge pudding, bread and butter pudding, black pudding, steak and kidney pudding. Go back a little, however, and it turns out that "pudding" once referred to a much more specific type of dish, and the diversity of the puddings we know today is evidence of the twists and turns in its evolution. What's more, the pudding is essentially an English invention. Although there are similar dishes in Greek, Roman and Norman cookery, the English took the basic idea and turned it into an art form. "They bake them in the oven, they boil them with meat, they make them fifty several ways; BLESSED BE HE THAT INVENTED THE PUDDING, for it is manna that hits the palates of all sorts of people… Ah, what an excellent thing is an English pudding!" exclaimed the French writer François Misson in *M. Misson's Memoirs and Observations in his Travels over England* (1719).

"Pudding" comes from the same root as the French word *boudin*, and it originally meant much the same thing: a type of sausage made from pigs' blood and fat, which were stuffed into a length of intestine. It must have looked and tasted rather like haggis or the black pudding you get with a full English breakfast. The dish grew out of a compelling seasonal logic. Since it wasn't economical to keep pigs through the winter, they were killed, and every part of the animal was turned into something to eat. Much of it was salted, smoked or pickled in order to have a reasonably long shelf life to help feed people through the exceedingly lean winter months.

Inventive medieval chefs began to realise that animal innards made a neat and convenient way of cooking all kinds of ingredients, so by the 1400s, white puddings had developed alongside the black. Instead of blood, the white version's basic ingredients were the paler fats, such as lard and suet, some form of starch to bind and thicken—often breadcrumbs, oatmeal or, later, rice (the starting point for modern-day rice pudding)—and perhaps bone marrow or cream to add some richness. Puddings became increasingly luxurious and indulgent, and there was even a trend for including ambergris and musk, two basic components for creating scents. Both would have been extremely costly (neither is easy to obtain: musk comes from the anal gland of the musk deer, while ambergris is a waxy deposit made in the sperm whale's intestine and then expelled into the ocean) and must have produced a pudding with an unusual perfumed character.

It seems likely to me that such a dish was appreciated more for its theatricality than its gastronomy, and the fact that it allowed for an ostentatious flaunting of wealth. (Charles II's favourite dish was, supposedly, ambergris and eggs.) Puddings became loosely associated with an element of theatre: there are blood pudding recipes using porpoise instead of pig, and in Swan-Neck Pudding the neck of the bird was stuffed and served. Quaking Pudding forms part of this tradition of spectacle, although Robert May's recipe benefited from the use of the pudding cloth (which became popular in England in the early seventeenth century and revolutionised pudding-making, inspiring chefs to make all kinds of new versions; see page 188). He didn't need to use innards or a swan neck—he could take his rudimentary batter, tie it tightly in a piece of floured linen and cook it until it had a gentle set. With Quaking Pudding, it's all about the wobble.

I've got a special affection for Quaking Pudding because it's the first historical recipe I worked on. I was introduced to May's book by the brilliant food historians at Hampton Court, Richard Fitch and Marc Meltonville, and as soon as I read the recipe for Quaking Pudding, I knew I wanted to do my own version of it. I was partly seduced by the fact that the pudding is a British invention, but, more than this, what really grabbed me about the recipe was that quake. A pudding that jiggled precariously, like a cartoon jelly, promised to be a lot of fun to make, and even more fun to eat: a great piece of showmanship that I found irresistible. My mind started playing with all kinds of possibilities for presentation: perhaps it could be served on a board sct on a spring, to really accentuate that wobble…

I've read a lot of historical cookbooks since I first developed an interest in the subject, but *The Accomplisht Cook* remains one of my favourites. Robert May's father, Edwarde, was chief cook for the noble Dormer family and so, as May himself put it, he was "bred up in this Art"—cuisine was in the blood. When he was ten, the family sent him to Paris for a five-year apprenticeship, after which he completed his training by spending seven years in London working as cook for the Star Chamber (the meeting room for the Lords of the Privy Council) before returning to the Dormers' Ascott House. He spent the rest of his career working for the Dormers and a number of lords—Castlehaven, Lumley, Montague,

Rivers—and other "Persons of great Honour", all of whom are listed in the highly detailed introduction to the book.

The Accomplisht Cook was published in 1660, when May was already seventy-two years old. In some ways it reads like the work of an old man. There are recipes for culinary special effects—a pastry stag that bleeds, pies containing live frogs or birds—that feel like a throwback to the tricks and subtleties of the medieval period, and there's a strong streak of nostalgia for the past, a hankering for "those Golden Days wherein were practised the Triumphs and Trophies of Cookery".

Nonetheless, *The Accomplisht Cook* is a landmark work. In his introduction, May complains that many cookbooks are "of as little use as some Niggards kitchens, which the Reader in respect of the confusion of the Method, or the barrenness of those authors experience, hath rather been puzzled then profited by". Behind these words you can hear the frustration of an exacting, precise, professional chef. (And I have to confess that, having struggled for years to persuade people of the value of scientific knowledge in cooking, it struck a chord with me when I read May's declaration that, in his quest for culinary clarity, "It hath been my task to denote some new Faculty, or Science, that others have not yet discovered.") In a compilation of more than 1,000 recipes, May set out to rectify this inexactitude, giving enough information to prevent the reader from being puzzled at how to cook his dishes. While the instructions might still seem vague to our eyes, the level of detail was a big advance for cookery writing. His was the first English cookbook to group recipes into logically themed sections, and the first to contain illustrations (woodcuts of lobsters and carp, various containers and moulds, and pastry designs as elaborate as snowflake fractals). Such accuracy, organisation and thoroughness meant it was indeed possible for an amateur seventeenth-century cook to attempt the recipes in *The Accomplisht Cook*. Unintentionally, it paved the way for a shift in emphasis in the cookbook, which over the next hundred years became aimed more at the domestic cook than the court chef.

May's recipe for Quaking Pudding centres on a technical challenge that any modern chef can relate to: using eggs to produce a gentle set. It's a technique that appears in many classic dishes: crème brûlée, crème caramel, savoury parfait, the filling for a lemon tart. In each case, what you're going for is an incredibly smooth, delicate, melt-in-the-mouth texture that depends largely on how you handle the cooking of the eggs.

As we all know from the variety of textures that can be coaxed out of an egg at breakfast time—from the delicate fluffiness of scrambled eggs to the firm white and oozy yolk of a perfectly boiled one—it has an extraordinary ability to set to a wide range of consistencies. An egg can do this because of the proteins it contains. A raw egg is runny because both the yolk and white are largely made up of water, in which the protein molecules are dispersed. In this raw state, each protein molecule is structured into a mass all folded in on itself—a bit like a car after it has been in the compactor—and floats separately from the others. However, when an egg is heated, this causes the molecules to move around increasingly quickly, bumping into one another as they do so, and their compact, folded shape begins to unravel into long chains that tangle together, creating an interlocked, three-dimensional network that traps the water among its interstices, preventing it from flowing freely. The egg has become a fragile solid. Take this too far, of course, and the proteins will bond together so thoroughly that they squeeze out all the water, turning the texture firm, dry and rubbery. The perfect set, therefore, depends of careful control of the cooking temperature.

The presence of other ingredients can affect the temperature at which an egg sets and its texture, and this can be used to the chef's advantage. A sprinkling of salt or few drops of an acid such as lemon juice or vinegar will speed up the bonding of the proteins, but also make them bond less closely. The eggs set at a lower temperature, and to a particularly tender texture. On the other hand, when eggs are diluted with milk, cream or sugar, this raises the temperature at which thickening begins: the egg's protein molecules are swamped by a huge number of water or sucrose molecules, so they require even more energy in the form of heat to get them moving at a rate that will allow them to collide frequently and combine together effectively. This still results in a tender texture: since the protein network spreads out to trap such a large volume of liquid, it's a fragile structure that produces a very delicate set.

As anyone who's been served a grainy brûlée or rubbery panna cotta will have discovered, chefs can find it difficult to get the right set. But Quaking Pudding presents an additional technical challenge: it has to be served warm. Most set desserts are served cold, which helps keep the shape, and often they have additional support from a ramekin, serving dish or pastry crust. Quaking Pudding has nothing to hide behind. It has to be set sufficiently to be brought, while still warm, quivering to the table.

I began exploring the effects of different combinations of the core ingredients (eggs, caster sugar, milk, whipping cream), looking for a set that wobbled beguilingly but was just robust enough to hold up under its own weight. It was a lengthy, painstaking process. If the set was too firm or was allowed to cool too much, the pudding didn't wobble at all, and the mouthfeel wasn't good. If the set was too delicate it wobbled a couple of times and then fell apart. Making minute adjustments, we cooked dozens that simply collapsed as soon as we turned them out of the moulds. Sometimes we produced one that jiggled back and forth without breaking, and I would think, *We've cracked it!* Then someone would say, "Hang on," and we'd watch as a fissure zigzagged its way up the side of the pudding, and *ploof!* it would splurge across the serving board. It took more than fifty attempts to come up with the right set.

Achieving this was a huge milestone in terms of development of the dish, but it still left me with some guesswork and interpretation to do. While May was very detailed about the essential ingredients, specifying precisely how many whole eggs and yolks or whites were needed, he was vaguer about how much of each flavouring and seasoning to use. Since the dish was unfamiliar to me, I had no idea of exactly how it was supposed to taste, so I set about exploring every possible combination of ingredients to see which one best captured the spirit of the original. At one point we invited Richard and Marc over from Hampton Court for a mammoth tasting session at which I served up about one hundred puddings for discussion.

Gradually, my thinking began to focus on the fact that the dish is, technically, a very delicate custard. *The Accomplisht Cook* had alternative versions of the recipe that included among their ingredients nutmeg and cinnamon, the classic spices for a custard tart, so I decided to try these in my pudding. The spices worked extremely well, producing a delicious dessert, but I found that they had solved the question of flavourings only to replace it with a problem concerning presentation. Occasionally the spices would sink to the bottom of the mixture during cooking. When the puddings were turned out, some would have a faint but unmistakeable spice ring around the top. It was exactly the kind of irritating little inconsistency that I tend to obsess over, and I tried all sorts of strategies for combating it, from passing the mixture through several layers of muslin to ensuring that the grade of spice from our suppliers was exactly the same every time. The spice ring, however, continued to appear with teasing irregularity. Working through whatever variables were left, I decided that, instead of whisking the spices into the eggs and sugar and then pouring hot milk and cream on top, I would add them to the milk mixture after it had boiled.

The effect was extraordinary. Not only did this approach eliminate the spice ring, but in side-by-side tastings puddings prepared using the new method also had a different colour and a far softer mouthfeel. I didn't know why a minor adjustment caused such a transformation; perhaps adding the spices to the milk lightened them and helped them disperse more evenly, and perhaps more effective dispersal helped improve the texture of the mixture—but that was a puzzle to be addressed in due course. For now, I was just happy that the pudding had found its perfect form, and to discover that, even after many years of testing and experimenting in the kitchen, food has not lost any of its capacity to challenge and surprise me.

QUAKING PUDDING

Makes 10 portions

Pudding Mixture

190g	Egg yolk
145g	Whole egg
150g	White caster sugar
250g	Whole milk
1kg	Whipping cream
3g	Ground nutmeg
3g	Ground cinnamon

Whisk the egg yolk, whole egg and sugar together in a large bowl until light and fluffy, and thoroughly combined.

Place the milk and whipping cream in a saucepan and bring to the boil, allowing the mixture to rise. Whisk in the nutmeg and cinnamon and allow it to rise one more time.

Slowly pour half the hot milk mixture into the egg mixture in a steady stream, whisking continuously. Take the saucepan off the heat and pour the egg and milk mixture back into the saucepan. Allow the mixture to stand for 2 minutes, stirring occasionally.

Pass the mixture through a double layer of muslin into a container. Cover with a layer of greaseproof paper to prevent a skin forming and chill in the fridge until needed.

Apple Garnish

320g	Sugar
2.5g	Salt
40g	Lemon juice
2	Granny Smith apples

Place 480g water, the sugar and salt in a saucepan and bring to the boil. Allow it to cool before adding the lemon juice. Set the mixture aside to cool completely.

Peel and core the apples, and thinly slice them using a mandolin. Place them in sous-vide bags, ensuring they are all lying flat and in a single layer, and seal under full pressure.

One hour before serving this dish, soak the compressed apple slices in the syrup.

To Cook and Serve

50g	Butter
	Reserved pudding mixture
	Reserved apple garnish

Preheat a steam-injected oven to 93°C/199°F and a water bath to 72°C/162°F.

Butter 10 quarter-pint (approximately 145ml) pudding moulds. Fill the moulds with the pudding mixture and place the lid on them.

Place the puddings in the oven and cook for 50 minutes, then transfer them to the water bath until ready to serve.

In the meantime, remove the apple slices from the syrup and fold them into decorative garnishes.

When you are ready to serve the puddings, remove the lids from the moulds and tip gently to drain out any butter. Unmould the pudding on to a serving board, and place the apple garnish alongside it. Serve warm.

NETTLE PORRIDGE

[1661]

TO MAKE A SPRING POTTAGE

❊ *Put on about a gallon of fair water, with a handful of great Oatmeal beaten small, and a piece of Ribb bacon; then take a handful of Brook-lime, as many Water-cresses and Nettle tops, Elder buds, Violet and Primrose-leaves, with young Alexander leaves; mince all these very small, put them to your broth, with a little large Mace; so season it with salt, and put in butter when you take it off; and so serve it to the table on fasting days, or eat it in the morning fasting. It is good to cleanse the blood* ❊

William Rabisha, *The Whole Body of Cookery Dissected* (1661)

Cereal crops have played an important role in mankind's development. Palaeoanthropologists cite the organised cultivation of emmer wheat and barley during the Neolithic period (*c.* 10,000–3500 BC) as a pivotal point in our progress towards civilisation, followed soon after by the use of earthenware pottery, which made it possible to cook food in boiling water. It was during this period that we became farmers rather than hunter-gatherers, and grains became a major source of nourishment. From then on, porridge of some sort or other was a normal part of the daily diet. Examination of pottery from Neolithic "Lake Dweller" sites around Neuchâtel, Zurich and other Swiss lakes has revealed traces of mixtures of wheat, corn, barley, dried apples, strawberries, blackberries and beechnuts. (It seems that the Swiss were eating a form of muesli long before Dr Maximilian Bircher-Benner invented it around 1900.) The final meal of the fourth-century-BC Tollund Man, famously preserved in the Bjaeldskovdal peat bog in Denmark, was a gruel made of barley and a variety of seeds including knotweed, linseed and chamomile.

Porridge—or pottage, as it was more commonly known (meaning "food cooked in a pot")—remained central to cuisine right through to the Middle Ages. In medieval England, everyone, rich or poor, ate pottage every day. By then the term encompassed not just dishes made with cereals, but also those thickened with pulses, bread, almonds, eggs, rice and so on. It had also split into two categories: "running" pottages, which were similar to a modern stew and would be served in a bowl over a "sop" (a piece of toasted bread); and "standing" pottages, which were more porridge-like in consistency, possibly even thick enough to eat with the fingers.

For the poor, pottage was basic and unenticing, consisting of boiled wheat, barley or oatmeal with, if they were lucky, a few herbs or bits of meat or fish to give it interest; or perhaps a thick pease pottage made from dried split yellow peas and garnished with raw onion relish. For the rich, however, it was a different story. By the late Middle Ages, chefs were making sophisticated versions using the best ingredients they could get their hands on. *The Forme of Cury* (see page 19) contains recipes for a number of traditional Anglo-Norman pottages, including Charlet (shredded pork with eggs, milk and saffron), Bukkenade (finely chopped meat with ground almonds, currants, sugar and powdered ginger), Civey (meat cooked with onions and stock and thickened with bread), Mawmenny (finely chopped chicken or rabbit, almond milk, beef broth, egg yolks, saffron and rice flour), Frumente (hulled wheat cooked with almond milk, eggs and saffron) and Blancmange, which is one of the few whose name has survived, though its modern-day incarnation as a moulded milk pudding bears little resemblance to the original mix of shredded chicken or capon, rice, sugar and almond milk.

Often, what separated the rich and poor versions of a pottage were ingredients that we now take for granted but were then costly luxuries. Pease pottage was eaten by all classes, but the wealthy enlivened it with white wine, garlic, butter and spices, or with ginger, butter and sorrel. The cherry pottage recipe in the fourteenth-century manuscript *The Goodman of Paris* (a manual of advice on various areas of conduct, including cooking and household management) is primped with white bread—rather than the more commonplace brown—wine and sugar. For feasts, chefs "flourished" pottages with scatterings of sugar, spice powder,

coloured comfits or even strips of silver or gold leaf. Colour played an important part in pottage's presentation. It might be turned red (using mulberries or sandalwood), yellow (saffron), green (parsley) or indigo (red wine and powdered cloves). Often it was also "departed", or served in a dish alongside another pottage of contrasting hue—white Blancmange, for example, with yellow Caudel Ferry or green Vert Desire.

Pottage remained a dominant feature of the English diet until the Tudor period. "Potage is not so much used in all Christendom as it is used in England," noted the physician and traveller Andrew Boorde in his *Dietary of Health* (1542). But by the time Boorde was writing, a shift in culinary taste was already under way. The ideas of the Renaissance had shaped a new approach to cuisine, with an emphasis on clean, distinct flavours and textural variety (see page 118). Pottage had little place in this way of cooking: the most influential text of Renaissance cuisine, Platina's *De honesta voluptate et valetudine*, has no recipes for pottage at all. When French chefs succeeded the Italians as the dominant force in cooking in the 1600s, they continued the culinary revolution. In place of exotically spiced pottages, they offered recipes for stews flavoured with garden herbs and native spices, and fricassées and hashes that became increasingly popular in England. The use of the pudding cloth from 1615 onwards (see page 188), which made puddings far simpler to make, pushed pottage further towards oblivion. Savoury puddings started to take over as the favoured method for making a meal both filling and substantial. William Rabisha's book has only five pottage recipes: alongside Spring Pottage there are Pottage of Broth, Capons in Pottage, Pottage Called Skinck and Red Pottage, in which he takes beetroot, which hadn't proved popular as

a pottage ingredient, and tries to rehabilitate it in a spicy venison-and-beetroot dish. "If the beet be good," he counsels, "it will be red enough; if not, you ought to colour it with Sanders; this is savoury red Pottage, and to be esteemed above the Venison."

Of course, culinary fashions can be slow to catch on, and were particularly so in the past, when means of communication were far more limited. Even in the early years of the next century, the last of the courtly cooks, Charles Carter (see page 273), offered more than a dozen pottages in *The Complete Practical Cook* (1730), including the endearingly named Pottage of Red Herrings. But the fate of Carter's book is perhaps the most persuasive sign that pottage really was on its way out. *The Complete Practical Cook* was aimed at professional chefs and, at 16 shillings, was by far the most expensive cookbook of the period. It didn't sell very well, and there followed a canny effort to commercialise it. When a revised version appeared two years later, under the title *The Compleat City and Country Cook*, every single pottage had been dropped.

Given pottage's importance in early English cuisine, Ash and I were keen to develop a form of the dish for Dinner's menu. Leafing through the pages of old recipe books, we found Rabisha's Spring Pottage. With its use of butter and fresh green herbs and leaves, it seemed a close companion to the parsley porridge I'd developed for the Fat Duck as a vegetarian alternative to Snail Porridge. So we decided to take another look at parsley porridge to see if we could reinvent it for Dinner, drawing on the history of pottage and Rabisha's recipe for additional inspiration.

A central component of my porridge is the butter flavoured with parsley that is added at the end of cooking (in much the same way as the Italians finish a risotto with butter and Parmesan), giving the dish a rich, liquid consistency and turning it a striking, vibrant green. This, we decided, would remain the foundation technique of the new dish, but we'd take the opportunity to add more garlic to make it bolder and more robust. At the Fat Duck, the porridge is part of a tasting menu, which imposes certain constraints on the chef. When you're serving a succession of, say, eighteen dishes, each of which has to have a distinct and distinctive effect on the palate, you need to achieve a very particular balance of ingredients. The strength and longevity of the flavour of garlic can easily upset that balance, so we use it sparingly. Dinner's menu, on the other hand, was à la carte—meaning we had to bring harmony to three courses rather than eighteen—and it featured a very different style of cooking, giving us the freedom to use ingredients like garlic to add depth and flavour. So we developed an intense garlic purée to be added to the butter as it's creamed.

One of the things that most excited me about Rabisha's recipe was the inclusion of nettles. Nettles were once a common ingredient in English cuisine, and were often used as a flavouring for pottages. But somehow, despite being nutritious and readily available for much for the year, they are no longer popular. You might come across the occasional recipe for nettle soup or tea, and some cheeses, such as Slipcote and Yarg, are wrapped in the leaves, but that's about it. To me this made no sense because nettles have a wonderfully fresh, green,

herbaceous flavour. I had already used baby stinging nettles as a garnish for Snail Porridge, but reading Rabisha's recipe made me realise I could go a lot further and make nettles a major part of the parsley butter. I replaced half the parsley with nettles, then followed the usual procedure: blitzing and freezing the leaves over and over until I had a super-smooth, jewel-green purée, which I then mixed with butter, mustard and garlic purée, plus almonds, sautéed mushrooms and cooked shallots for texture and fragrance. It worked fantastically well, giving the butter an even more interesting flavour profile.

The dish still needed, I felt, some form of protein, and we came up with the idea of using cod's head. Cod has been fished since at least Neolithic times, so it's not impossible that at some point prehistoric man settled down to a dinner of cod and porridge. Less speculatively,

cod's head was certainly a popular ingredient in Rabisha's time. On 23 January 1663, Pepys records "and so to dinner to Sir W. Batten's to a cod's head", and recipes such as William Salmon's Cods-Head to Dress in *The Family Dictionary; or Household Companion* (1695) offered plenty of appealing ingredients to play with:

Cut it fair and large, boil it in Water, and Salt, add a pint of Vinegar, so that all the Head and Appurtenances may be just covered, put into the mouth of it a quart of stewing Oisters, a bundle of sweet-Herbs, and an Onion quartered: and when it is sufficiently boiled, set it a drying over a Chafing-dish of Coals; then take Oister liquor, sliced Onion, and two or three Anchoves, a quarter of a pint of White-wine, and a pound of sweet Butter, shred the Herbs, mix them with the

Oisters, and garnish it with them, adding withal some slices of Lemon, grated Bread, and a little Parsley.

Dressed or baked cod's head featured in many cookbooks in the 1700s, including those of John Nott and Hannah Glasse; even into the nineteenth century, J.M. Sanderson could say with confidence in *The Complete Cook* (1864) that "the bones and glutinous parts of a cod's head are much liked by most people, and are very nourishing". Since then, for some reason, cod's head has fallen out of favour. Certainly we've become more squeamish about what we eat, and many people now baulk at fish served with the head on, even though it helps keep the fish succulent and flavourful; and admittedly, the words "cod's head" conjure a graphic image, all teeth, fins and eyeballs. But cod's head can be delicious: the cut includes not just the head, but also the "shoulders" and the palate, so there's plenty of flesh, and that "glutinous" or, rather, gelatinous quality makes it rich and moist, a texture that would complement beautifully the risotto-like character of the oats. Moreover, at Dinner, the kitchen set-up includes a *plancha* (flat-top grill), which meant we could cook the fish in a way that would bring out the best in it. We tried searing it on the plancha and it really added something to the dish.

There's one other unusual ingredient (at least in Britain) in the recipe that was inspired by an old cookbook, though not William Rabisha's. In Vincent La Chapelle's *The Modern Cook* (1733), I found a recipe-remedy with the eye-catching title of Broth with Snails and Frogs, Against a Dry Cough, which I wanted to develop into a dish. However, since there's not much call for frogs' legs in this country, it's difficult to get hold of them except in frozen form, which doesn't do much for the delicate flesh. So my first task was to establish whether I could find regular fresh supply. It turned out that there was someone who could provide me with legs twice weekly, delivered as little pairs on a stick. As we began taking consignments, it struck me that they'd work perfectly in nettle porridge, particularly since garlic and parsley are classic accompaniments for frogs' legs. We played around with ways of preparing the legs and eventually settled for coating them in Japanese breadcrumbs, deep-frying them and then injecting garlic butter to create a morsel with plenty of texture and flavour.

To counterbalance the unctuousness of the main ingredients, the garnishes needed to be fresh, sharp and fragrant, so I introduced fennel cress and shaved fennel dressed with a walnut vinaigrette. I also wanted to add some smoked and pickled flavours, which are great ways to cut richness and keep a dish from becoming too cloying. Nettle Porridge is therefore served with two types of beetroot: ruby beets vacuum-packed with a pickling liquor of vinegar, oil and salt, then cooked in a water bath; and golden beets cooked the same way with a smoked olive oil in the pickle. The beetroots bring balance to the dish, adding freshness and acidity. Beetroot is also, of course, the vegetable that Rabisha championed in vain for his venison pottage, and I like the idea that, 350 years later, I've brought aspects of two of his dishes together in a way he might have appreciated.

NETTLE PORRIDGE

Makes 6 portions

Parsley and Nettle Purée

90g	**Stinging nettle leaves**
90g	**Flatleaf parsley leaves, rinsed**

Be sure to wear protective gloves to pick the nettles. (If nettles are out of season, use 180g parsley.) Carefully remove the leaves from the stalks, discarding the stalks. Plunge the nettle leaves into rapidly boiling water for 10 seconds to neutralise the sting. Have a bowl of iced water to hand and refresh the nettle leaves in it. Drain them very well by placing the leaves in a fine-mesh sieve and squeezing out the excess water.

Place the parsley leaves in a Thermomix and blitz very well. Place the nettles and blitzed parsley in a Pacojet container, cover with a lid and place in the freezer immediately.

Run the frozen parsley and nettles through the Pacojet and return the container to the freezer to freeze again. Repeat this process 7 times. The purée should be completely smooth. Store in the fridge until needed.

Garlic Purée

120g	**Peeled and de-germed garlic**
45g	**Unsalted butter**
14g	**Lemon juice**

Dice the garlic cloves into 5mm pieces.

Heat a small pan and allow the butter to melt. Add the garlic and sauté until golden and caramelised. Deglaze the pan with the lemon juice and place the mixture aside to cool.

Once the mixture has cooled sufficiently, place the caramelised garlic in a Pacojet container, cover with a lid and place in the freezer immediately.

Run the frozen garlic through the Pacojet and return the container to the freezer

until frozen again. Repeat twice more. The purée should be completely smooth. You will need 60g.

Shallots

25g	**Unsalted butter**
50g	**Peeled and finely diced shallots**

Heat a pan, add the butter and allow it to melt. Add the shallots and ensure they are coated in the butter. Cover with a cartouche and allow the shallots to cook gently over a medium heat, stirring them regularly.

Remove from the heat when they are soft with a slight bite, and only slightly caramelised.

Store in the fridge until needed.

Mushrooms

35g	**Olive oil**
230g	**Large close-cap mushrooms, diced into 8mm cubes**

Heat the olive oil in a pan over a medium heat. Add the diced mushrooms and cook until soft and fragrant.

Remove the mushrooms and drain well. Store in the fridge until needed.

Parsley and Nettle Butter

200g	**Unsalted butter, cubed and at room temperature**
145g	**Reserved parsley and nettle purée**
60g	**Reserved garlic purée**
35g	**Reserved cooked shallots**
145g	**Reserved cooked mushrooms**
7g	**Salt**
30g	**Dijon mustard**
20g	**Ground almonds**

Cream the butter in a mixer at medium speed. Add the parsley and nettle purée

and garlic purée and mix well, scraping down the sides of the bowl regularly.

Reduce the speed and add the cooked shallots, cooked mushrooms, salt, Dijon mustard and ground almonds.

Scrape the butter into a shallow container and place in a chamber vacuum sealer. Under full pressure, close the lid and keep a close eye on the butter, stopping the process as soon as the butter rises to the top. Repeat 3 more times.

Roll the butter into a sausage shape, 3cm in diameter. Wrap in clingfilm and store in the fridge until needed.

Garlic Butter

250g	**Unsalted butter, cubed and at room temperature**
30g	**Peeled and finely diced garlic**

Melt 50g of the butter in a saucepan over a gentle heat and add the garlic, then cook until it starts to caramelise lightly. Add the remaining butter and allow it all to melt. Remove the pan from the heat, cover with clingfilm and set aside for 30 minutes.

Transfer the mixture to a deep-sided container and blitz using a hand blender. Blend until smooth.

Store in the fridge until needed.

Walnut Vinaigrette Base

65g	**Walnut vinegar**
5g	**Dijon mustard**
65g	**Grapeseed oil**

Place the walnut vinegar and Dijon mustard into a small bowl. Gradually whisk in the grapeseed oil to emulsify.

Store in the fridge until needed.

(continued overleaf)

Garlic-Walnut Vinaigrette

125g   **Reserved garlic butter**
125g   **Reserved walnut vinaigrette base**

In a pan, gently heat the garlic butter to 40°C/104°F. Add the walnut vinaigrette base and, using a hand blender, blitz to emulsify fully.

Smoked Olive Oil

200g   **Extra virgin olive oil**
        Fine oak smoking chips

Place the olive oil in a container to make a layer no more than 5mm deep. Wrap the container in clingfilm and pierce 2 small holes in it. Keep the clingfilm nearby.

Put ½ teaspoon smoking chips in a smoking gun, insert the nozzle into one of the holes and light the gun, allowing the smoke to fill the container. After 15 seconds the container should be filled with smoke. Remove the nozzle and wrap the container completely in clingfilm and leave to smoke for 10 minutes.

Remove the clingfilm, stir the olive oil well and repeat the smoking process with fresh chips. Set aside in the fridge.

Pickled Smoked Golden Beetroot

80g   **Reserved smoked olive oil**
3   **Golden beetroots**
70g   **Chardonnay vinegar**
4g   **Salt**

Preheat a water bath to 85°C/185°F.

Gently heat the vinegar in a small saucepan and add the salt, stirring until dissolved. Remove from the heat, add the smoked olive oil and set aside to cool.

Peel the beetroots, and depending on their size, quarter them or cut them into eighths. Place the beetroot wedges, along with the cooled pickling liquid, in a sous-vide bag and seal. Cook in the water bath until softened all the way through, checking regularly.

Plunge the bag in ice water and allow to pickle in the fridge for 24 hours before reheating to serve. Reserve the pickling liquid.

Pickled Ruby Beetroot

70g   **Chardonnay vinegar**
4g   **Salt**
80g   **Extra virgin olive oil**
3   **Ruby beetroots**

Preheat a water bath to 90°C/194°F.

Gently heat the vinegar in a small saucepan and add the salt, stirring until dissolved. Remove from the heat, add the olive oil and set aside to cool.

Peel the beetroots, and depending on their size, quarter them or cut them into eighths. Place the beetroot wedges along with the cooled pickling liquid in a sous-vide bag and seal. Cook the beetroot in the water bath until softened all the way through, checking regularly.

Plunge the bag into iced water and allow to pickle in the fridge for 24 hours before reheating to serve. Reserve the pickling liquid.

Finished Pickled Golden and Ruby Beetroot

140g   **Reserved golden beetroot pickling liquid**
140g   **Reserved ruby beetroot pickling liquid**
140g   **Vegetable braising liquid (see page 220)**
60g   **Extra virgin olive oil**
30g   **Chardonnay vinegar**
        Reserved pickled golden and ruby beetroot wedges
        Salt
        Cracked black pepper

Place the reserved golden beetroot pickling liquid, half the vegetable braising liquid, half the olive oil and half the vinegar in a saucepan over a medium heat. Add the golden beetroot wedges and gently heat through.

In a separate pan, do the same with the reserved red beetroot pickling liquid, the remaining vegetable braising liquid, olive oil and vinegar, and the ruby beetroot wedges.

Remove the beetroot wedges, drain them separately on kitchen paper and keep warm. Season them with salt and cracked black pepper.

5% Garlic Herb Brine

25g	Salt
10g	Peeled and sliced garlic
1g	Thyme
1g	Rosemary
2g	Lemon peel
1g	Black peppercorns

Bring a saucepan with 500g water and the salt to the boil, then remove from the heat. Allow the mixture to cool to 40°C/104°F, then add a secure muslin parcel containing the garlic, herbs and aromatics.

Remove and discard the muslin parcel once the brine has completely cooled. Store the brine in the fridge until needed.

Brined Frogs' Legs

3	Pairs frogs' legs
300g	Reserved 5% garlic herb brine

Split the frogs' legs into 6 single legs, then cut through the joint socket of each leg, ensuring the round ball of cartilage is left on the end of each bone.

Detach the larger muscle from the leg, ensuring it remains attached to the thigh. Remove the sinew from the end of the muscle. Cut through the joint socket of the thigh where it meets the mid-leg section. Discard the bone and webbed foot.

Using your fingers, strip the meat down the thigh bone and tuck the meat back on itself over the single muscle attached to the bottom of the thigh. Remove any visible veins.

Place the prepped frogs' legs in a sous-vide bag along with the garlic herb brine, and seal. Allow to brine for 40 minutes.

Remove the frogs' legs from the brine and rinse under cold running water for 5 minutes. Drain the frogs' legs on a tray lined with kitchen paper while prepping the ingredients to coat and cook them.

Cooked Frogs' Legs

70g	Cornflour
7g	Salt
120g	Egg white
30g	Egg yolk
400g	Japanese breadcrumbs
6	Reserved brined frogs' legs
500g	Oil
	Sea salt flakes
50g	Melted garlic butter

Sieve the cornflour into a bowl and add the salt. Mix well to combine. Whisk the egg white, yolk and 20g cold water in a second bowl.

Blitz 200g of the Japanese breadcrumbs in a Thermomix to make very fine crumbs. Place in a third bowl. Lightly crush the remaining 200g Japanese breadcrumbs in a pestle and mortar. Place in a fourth bowl.

Toss the frogs' legs in the flour and dust off the excess. Place them in the egg white and drain off the excess, then roll them in the fine breadcrumbs. Dip in egg again, then roll in the lightly crushed, coarser breadcrumbs. Wipe off any egg wash or breadcrumbs that have stuck to the bone.

In the meantime, heat the oil in a saucepan to 180°C/350°F. Gently lower the coated frogs' legs into the hot oil and fry until golden. Remove with a slotted spoon, but hold the legs over the hot oil, to allow them to drain adequately and for any residual heat to fully penetrate the legs. Drain on kitchen paper and season with sea salt flakes.

Using a pipette, inject a small amount of melted garlic butter into each frog's leg at the base of the bone.

Cooked Cods' Palate

15g	Extra virgin olive oil
6	Cods' palates
	Fine salt
	Reserved garlic butter, melted
	Lemon juice
	Cracked black pepper
	Sea salt flakes

Heat the olive oil in a non-stick pan and season the cods' palates on both sides with fine salt. Sear each side for 30 seconds, then remove the pan from the heat. Drain on a tray lined with kitchen paper and brush with melted garlic butter. Season with lemon juice, cracked black pepper and sea salt.

To Serve

210g	Chicken bouillon (see page 27)
45g	Porridge oats, sifted to remove any fine dust
150g	Reserved parsley and nettle butter
	Salt and pepper
	Reserved pickled golden beetroot wedges, warmed
	Reserved pickled ruby beetroot wedges, warmed
	Shaved fennel
	Reserved garlic-walnut vinaigrette
6	Reserved cooked cods' palates
6	Reserved cooked frogs' legs
	Fennel cress

Bring the chicken bouillon to the boil in a wide, shallow saucepan. Add the oats and cook for 3–4 seconds, stirring well, then remove the pan from the heat. Add the parsley and nettle butter and allow to melt. Mix well and season with salt and pepper.

Divide the porridge between 6 small warmed bowls and top with several beetroot pieces and shaved fennel. Add a few drops of garlic-walnut vinaigrette to each serving and complete the dish with a cods' palate and a fried frog's leg. Top with fennel cress.

POWDERED DUCK

[1670]

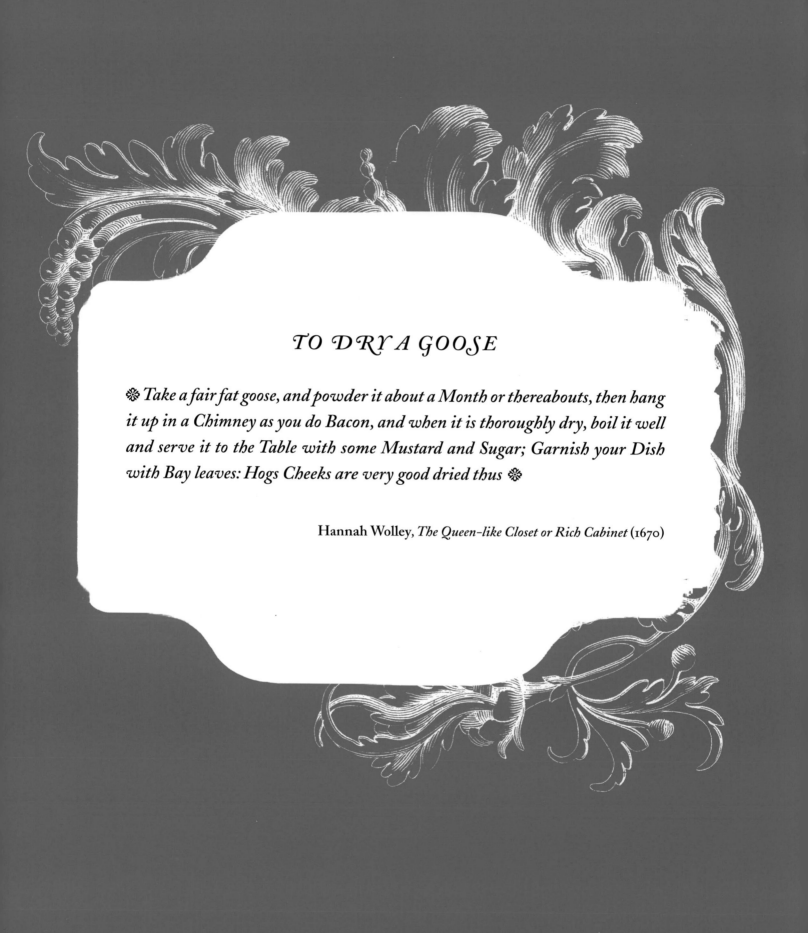

TO DRY A GOOSE

❧ Take a fair fat goose, and powder it about a Month or thereabouts, then hang it up in a Chimney as you do Bacon, and when it is thoroughly dry, boil it well and serve it to the Table with some Mustard and Sugar; Garnish your Dish with Bay leaves: Hogs Cheeks are very good dried thus ❧

Hannah Wolley, *The Queen-like Closet or Rich Cabinet* (1670)

In 1670, a casual observer might well have thought that England had managed to erase the chaos caused by the Civil War and turn the clock back to earlier, less troublesome times. A Stuart king named Charles was on the throne again. Religious extremism, which had spawned dozens of sects such as the Levellers, the Ranters, the Diggers, the Seekers and the Muggletonians, was virtually a spent force. The gentry once more controlled the Shires in the name of the king, running the local militia, administering justice, and being rewarded for these duties with titles and favours at court.

People certainly wanted to believe this rose-tinted view. The chef Robert May had idealised the time before the Civil War as "Golden Days wherein were practised the Triumphs and Trophies of Cookery", and many shared this view. But the idea that the Restoration had re-established the status quo was, of course, an illusion. During the Civil War things had been done which could not now be undone. Cessation of censorship in the 1640s had given ordinary people a voice and a taste for debate. (In 1640, twenty-two pamphlets were published. In 1642, 1,996 pamphlets appeared.) Parliament's opposition to the king and its decision to put him on trial had undermined the whole notion of monarchical authority and superiority. In February 1657, almost exactly eight years after Charles I was beheaded outside Whitehall, MPs actually offered the crown to Oliver Cromwell. After several months' agonised consideration, he refused, but the fact that a commoner could have become king shows how radically the social order had been shaken up. While the affable, unambitious Charles II was on the throne, this wasn't really put to the test. His successor James, on the other hand, was a Catholic convert and thus mistrusted by a populace convinced that England was in danger from an international Catholic conspiracy masterminded by the predatory French king, Louis XIV. Such fears were heightened when James's son, James Francis Edward, was born in June 1688, which opened up the possibility of a Catholic dynasty ruling England. Parliament was forced into direct action, and invited William of Orange—who, as ruler of the Protestant Netherlands and the husband of James's daughter Mary, was both a legitimate and politically acceptable candidate for the throne—to rule jointly with his wife.

In truth, even before the Glorious Revolution, there was already evidence that England was changing in ways that were bound to alter the established order. The role of women, for example, had become somewhat less circumscribed, allowing Hannah Wolley to become the first professional female English cookery writer and Aphra Behn the first professional female English playwright—this was in a country where, until 1660, women hadn't been allowed to play women's parts. At the Royal Society, Isaac Newton, Robert Hooke, Robert Boyle and their fellow scientists were busy remodelling the universe, and made breakthroughs in microbiology, chemistry and the laws of gravity. Meanwhile, the streets of London were being remodelled by Hooke and another member of the Royal Society, Christopher Wren, in the wake of the Great Fire of 1666.

But the capital was changing just as dramatically in other ways. By now it had over half a million inhabitants and was the biggest city in Europe by some distance. The vast metropolis offered plenty of opportunity for employment, trade and profit; the hundred wealthiest men in London were among the richest in the country. Wealth was no longer confined to landowners and the age of the upwardly mobile had arrived, giving rise to new social groups such as the urban gentry and a yeoman class content to colonise the professions and service industries and better themselves on the back of it.

Although no other place in the country could match London—it was bigger than the next fifty English towns combined—the population of large towns was also growing swiftly, and the country's economy was changing as a result. Shops were taking the place of market stalls, and offering a wide range of goods rather than just local produce. The enclosure of land and improved farming techniques had increased agricultural productivity to the point where England was for the first time a net exporter rather than importer of grain. Its merchant fleet was already one of the largest in Europe and would continue to grow in size and activity. Sugar, tobacco and other goods from newly acquired colonies in America, the West Indies and India bolstered the wealth of the upper echelons of society.

Inevitably, these major social developments had a knock-on effect in the home, too. Whereas most country houses had once had a communal great hall for meals and other activities, they now increasingly had "withdrawing" rooms and private dining rooms instead, with the servants sequestered in separate quarters. There had been a similar shift in the division of labour. The lady of the house had once played an active part in the endless domestic toil of the pre-technological age: the book-keeping and bee-keeping and candle-making and brewing and milking and distilling and salting and drying and pickling. Gradually,

however, she delegated most of these activities to servants and confined her role to that of overseer or administrator. The kitchen had changed, becoming both more specialised and more aspirational—even the middle-ranking gentry and yeomen now saw meals as an opportunity for showing off their social standing. Smart, sharp-eyed Hannah Wolley (or Woolley: both spellings appear in her books) spotted this, and in a series of publications—*The Ladies Directory*, *The Cooks Guide*, *The Queen-like Closet*, *The Ladies Delight* and *A Supplement to the Queen-like Closet*—she created a whole new genre of cookbook to cater for it: the comprehensive guide to household management.

The little we know of Wolley's background is largely conjecture, since the main source of information is a biography in *The Gentlewoman's Companion* (1673), which was falsely attributed to Wolley by a cynical publisher.[*] If the *Companion* is to be believed, from 1639 to 1646 Hannah worked as a servant in the house of an unnamed "noble lady" (generally assumed to be Lady Anne Maynard, whose daughter, Lady Anne Wroth, is one of the dedicatees of

---

[*] *Wolley herself dismissed the book in* A Supplement to the Queen-like Closet *a year later:*

> *Unto my self, who have been much abus'd*
> *By a late printed Book, my Name there us'd:*
> *I was far distant when they printed it,*
> *Therefore that Book to own I think not fit.*
> *To boast, to brag, tell stories in my praise,*
> *That's not the way (I know) my fame to raise...*

And this wasn't the only bogus title to be published under her name: The Accomplish'd Ladies Delight *appeared in 1675 and* The Compleat Servant Maid *a couple of years later. In an age when copyright restriction was in its infancy (the first copyright law—the Statute of Anne—came into being only in 1710), Wolley's success made her prey to unscrupulous writers and publishers, keen to cash in on her brand identity.*

Wolley's second book, *The Cooks Guide*), and may have risen to the position of stewardess.

In 1646 she married a schoolmaster, Benjamin Wolley, who ran Newport Grammar School in Essex. Six years later, amid the uncertainties of the Interregnum, they moved to Hackney in east London and opened another school with sixty boarders. In 1661, the year Benjamin Wolley died, Hannah's first book, *The Ladies Directory*, was entered in the Stationers' Register, so it's possible that financial necessity kick-started her writing career. With her husband dead, she had to find a way to make a living. She certainly appeared to have particular sympathy for the well-bred woman down on her luck, singling out "gentlewomen forced to serve, whose parents and friends have been impoverished by the late Calamities" as potential readers of *The Queen-like Closet*.

From Lady Maynard's house, Wolley would have gained the household management skills and medical and culinary knowledge that form the raw material of her books. From her time as a schoolmaster's wife she presumably gained an appreciation of the value of instruction; there's certainly a strong thread of betterment-through-education running through her books. From these experiences combined, she gained a sense of the skills and accomplishments women needed in post-war society, and that became the focus of her writing.

The Ladies Directory was firmly rooted in the traditional cookbook format, centring on remedies that smack of the witch's cauldron (a cure for consumption opens with "Take a red cock, pluck him alive, then slit him down the back and take out all his entrails" and calls for seven grains of unicorn horn). She followed the customary practice of talking up her credentials: the title page declares she "hath

had the Honour to perform such things for the Entertainment of His late Majesty, as well as for the Nobility". However, Wolley was a quick learner, and by the time of her second book, *The Cooks Guide* (1664), with its recipes for "Flesh, Fowls and Fish", the dedication to Lady Anne Wroth and her own daughter reveals a more contemporary-feeling modesty. The writing is already more self-effacing and better crafted, and the focus is on how women can best use their time. The book that sealed her success, though, was *The Queen-like Closet*, which ran to several editions and stayed in print for more than a hundred years. A large part of it is an adaptation of her first two books, but Wolley's scope has expanded to include virtually any area that might be considered the responsibility of the woman of the house or her servants, from cooking and market-shopping to needlework and letter-writing.

Not everything about *The Queen-like Closet* is groundbreaking. The structure has a medieval randomness to it, with sweet and savoury recipes side by side. (By contrast, Robert May, taking his cue from La Varenne's highly influential *Le Cuisinier françois*, organised *The Accomplisht Cook* in logically themed sections.) The liberal use of dried fruit and spices such as mace and nutmeg would have seemed old-fashioned to cutting-edge chefs who had picked up on the latest French culinary fashion for simple sauces and sharp flavourings, such as anchovy and lemon. Wolley's real strength is her recognition that the late seventeenth century was a time of great domestic uncertainty. As servants and professionals took on new responsibilities while the mistress jockeyed for position in an increasingly complex society, many people needed firm guidance in the kitchen. *The Queen-like Closet* makes this its priority, keeping

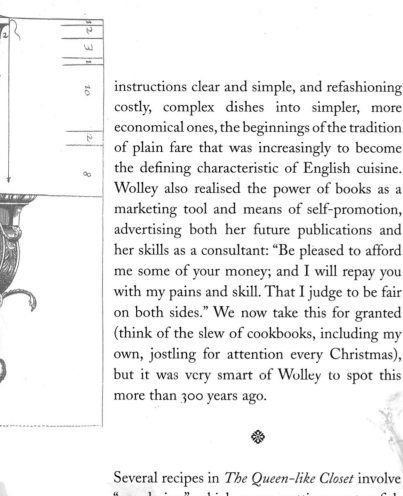

instructions clear and simple, and refashioning costly, complex dishes into simpler, more economical ones, the beginnings of the tradition of plain fare that was increasingly to become the defining characteristic of English cuisine. Wolley also realised the power of books as a marketing tool and means of self-promotion, advertising both her future publications and her skills as a consultant: "Be pleased to afford me some of your money; and I will repay you with my pains and skill. That I judge to be fair on both sides." We now take this for granted (think of the slew of cookbooks, including my own, jostling for attention every Christmas), but it was very smart of Wolley to spot this more than 300 years ago.

❧

Several recipes in *The Queen-like Closet* involve "powdering", which means putting meat or fish in salt (in the form of a cure or perhaps a brine) to alter the texture and flavour. Brining used to be a standard part of both the professional and the domestic cook's repertoire. But although we're still familiar with the technique for salting certain fish and turning beef into pastrami and pork into ham and bacon, in general it is no longer much practised.

To me, this makes little sense, because brining, particularly at lower salt concentrations of around 6–10 per cent, can have a very beneficial effect on food, especially meat. For a start, it's a great method of introducing flavour. Low-level brining is a very efficient way of adding seasoning, and if you include aromatics in the salt solution, they are drawn into the food along with the salt. Moreover, a low-level salt solution not only heightens the flavour of meat, it also makes it juicy (as opposed to the highly salted brine used to "ham" meats, which can dry them out a little). Salt breaks down the tough muscle filaments, tenderising the flesh and making it more receptive to whatever flavourings are added to the brining liquor. Salt also reacts with proteins to improve the water-holding capacity of muscle cells, allowing them to absorb water and flavourings from the brine. This is what helps the meat to stay moist.

As you can probably tell, I'm a big fan of brining, and have been for as long as I've been cooking professionally. When the Fat Duck first opened, the most popular main course on the menu was Petit Salé of Duck, for which I took the drumstick from the leg, placed it in a spicy brining liquor for day and a half, then pinned it up to look like a miniature leg of ham, simmered it, then glazed it and put it in the oven until brown.

Given my enthusiasm, you can imagine my excitement when, on one of my periodic visits to food historian Ivan Day's seventeenth-century Cumbrian farmhouse, with its antique kitchen artefacts and clockwork spit-jacks, he served me powdered goose, explaining how in the seventeenth century it was common to preserve meat, particularly goose, by putting it in a cure of salt, brown sugar, saltpetre and juniper berries for a time, then hanging it in a chimney and smoking it. Reading through *The Queen-like Closet*, I could see that Wolley had several recipes for salting meat, which employed a variety of techniques. So, while her recipe To Dry a Goose puts the meat in a dry salt cure—effectively "hamming" it—the recipe To Dry Tongues directs the cook to "Take some Pump water and Bay salt, or rather refined Salt-peter, which is better, make a strong Brine therewith, and when the Salt is well melted in it, put in your Tongues and let them lie one week." Despite the differences in technique, both the tongues and the goose are eventually served up in much the same manner, with mustard and sugar. I decided to bring together and adapt ideas from several of Wolley's drying and powdering recipes.

Wolley's use of a brining liquor to "dry" tongues pointed me towards using the kind of low-level brine I'd found so effective for giving meat flavour and juiciness. This also allowed me the opportunity to introduce still more flavour by adding aromatics to the salt solution. It was at this point that I realised I already had the perfect basis for a suitable brine, and I could use it to pull off a nice bit of historical symmetry. The brine in which my Petit Salé of Duck had been plunged contained many herbs and spices that also appeared frequently on the pages of Wolley's book, such as clove, nutmeg, cinnamon and juniper. Why not do a historical dish that took in a bit of my own history, substituting my duck for Wolley's goose and placing it in a brine with plenty of typically seventeenth-century aromatics?

As is often the way with recipe development, once the crystal of an idea had formed, it grew and took shape almost on its own. Reflecting on Ivan's powdered goose reminded me of another trip to his cottage, when I'd been served spit-roasted beef accompanied by smoked fennel, something I'd never had before, and which turned out to be absolutely delicious. Ever since, I had been keen to use it in a dish, and I could see that it would be an excellent garnish for the duck, and the flavours would marry very well. Even more satisfying was the fact that it would reinforce the dish's historical integrity. Introducing a delicate smoked flavour by cooking the fennel confit-style in a little smoked duck fat would be a further allusion to Hannah Wolley's original recipes, in which powdering was usually followed by a stint in the chimney. My recipe would be different from Wolley's, but it would nevertheless create a very seventeenth-century set of taste sensations.

POWDERED DUCK

Makes 6 portions

Duck Stock

300g	White port
5kg	Duck carcasses, chopped into pieces
190g	Duck fat
990g	Plum tomatoes, halved
710g	Peeled and finely sliced onions
10g	Star anise
710g	Peeled and finely sliced carrots
14g	Peeled and sliced garlic
10g	Coriander seeds
4g	Black peppercorns
15g	Thyme
3	Bay leaves
80g	Flatleaf parsley

Place the white port in a saucepan over a moderate heat. Carefully flame with a blowtorch and simmer gently to reduce to 150g.

Preheat the oven to 180°c/350°f.

Spread the duck carcasses out evenly on a roasting tray and roast them in the oven until they are golden brown, turning frequently. Once roasted, deglaze the trays and reserve the roasting juices.

Heat a large pressure cooker and melt half the duck fat. Place the tomatoes in the pressure cooker flat-side down and cook until they have caramelised. Remove the tomatoes and set aside.

Add the remaining duck fat and the onions and star anise. Cook until the onions have softened. Add the carrots, garlic, coriander seeds and black peppercorns and cook until the carrots have softened. Add the white port, roasted duck carcasses, caramelised tomatoes and 4.5 litres cold water.

Bring the stock to a simmer, skimming off any impurities. Add the thyme and bay leaves and stir one last time before securing the lid. Cook for 2 hours.

Allow the pressure cooker to depressurise and the stock to cool slightly before opening the lid. Add the parsley to the stock and allow to infuse for 10 minutes. Pass the stock through a fine-mesh sieve, followed by a fine-mesh filter bag. Chill in the fridge overnight.

Remove and discard all the fat from the surface of the chilled stock. Heat the stock in a large saucepan and gently reduce to 15% of the original quantity, to yield approximately 675g. It is important to continue skimming the stock as it reduces.

Once the stock has reduced, pass it through a fine-mesh filter bag and refrigerate until needed.

Duck Sauce

3g	Coriander seeds
1.5g	Allspice berries
1g	Juniper berries
1g	Cloves
75g	Honey
15g	Red wine vinegar
10g	Brandy
500g	Reserved reduced duck stock
10g	Peeled and sliced ginger
1g	Bay leaves

Toast the spices in a hot, dry pan. Once cooled, crush them roughly with a pestle and mortar and set aside.

In a separate pan, heat the honey over a moderate heat until it turns to a dark caramel. Be careful not to cook the caramel too far.

Carefully add the red wine vinegar and brandy and simmer for 1 minute to cook out the alcohol. Stir in the reduced duck stock.

Simmer gently until a slightly thicker consistency is reached, then remove from the heat. Add the spices and ginger and allow it to infuse for 15 minutes. Add the bay leaves and continue to infuse for 4 more minutes.

Pass the finished sauce through a fine-mesh filter bag and store in the fridge until needed.

15% Curing Brine

2g	Star anise
25g	Coriander seeds
1g	Cloves
5	Allspice berries
3	Juniper berries
10g	Peeled garlic cloves
2g	Peeled and finely sliced ginger
10g	Orange peel
5g	Lemon peel
1g	Rosemary
6g	Thyme
1	Bay leaf
225g	Salt

Toast the spices in a hot dry pan. Once cooled, crush them finely with a pestle and mortar. Make a secure muslin parcel of garlic cloves, ginger, citrus peel, herbs and the toasted spices, and place it in a saucepan with 1.5kg water and the salt.

Bring the saucepan of water to the boil, then remove from the heat. Allow the mixture to cool, then remove and discard the muslin parcel once it has cooled completely.

Store the brine in the fridge until needed.

(continued overleaf)

Smoked Duck Fat

| 200g | Rendered duck fat, liquid and at room temperature |
| | Fine oak smoking chips |

Place the rendered duck fat in a container to make a layer no more than 5mm deep. Wrap the container in clingfilm and pierce 2 small holes in it. Keep the clingfilm nearby.

Put ½ teaspoon smoking chips in a smoking gun, insert the nozzle into one of the holes and light the gun, allowing the smoke to fill the container. After 15 seconds the container should be filled with smoke. Remove the nozzle and wrap the container completely with clingfilm. Leave to smoke for 5 minutes.

Remove the clingfilm, stir the duck fat well and repeat the smoking process twice, with fresh chips each time. Set aside in the fridge.

Duck Hearts

9	Duck hearts
150g	Reserved 15% curing brine
75g	Reserved smoked duck fat

Preheat a water bath to 60°c/140°F.

Trim the duck hearts to remove any sinew. Rinse the hearts under cold running water for 10 minutes, then drain. Pour the 15% curing brine into a sous-vide bag and add the duck hearts. Seal the bag and allow to brine for 2 hours.

Rinse the duck hearts under cold water for 30 minutes, before draining and patting dry.

Place the duck hearts in a sous-vide bag along with the duck fat, ensuring the hearts are lying flat and in a single layer. Cook in the water bath for 5½ hours. Remove from the water bath and cool in iced water. Store in the fridge until needed.

Brining the Duck Breasts

| 6 | Duck breasts |
| 700g | Reserved 15% curing brine |

Remove any sinew from under the breasts, using tweezers to remove the vein. Using a sharp knife, make incisions halfway into the fat in a criss-cross fashion. Be careful not to cut into the flesh.

Pour the 15% curing brine into a large sous-vide bag and add the duck breasts. Seal the bag and allow to brine for 2 hours. Rinse the duck breasts under cold water for 30 minutes, before draining and patting dry.

Place the duck breasts in individual sous-vide bags and seal under full pressure.

Store in the fridge until needed.

Smoked Confit Fennel

| 3 | Fennel bulbs |
| 125g | Reserved smoked duck fat |

Preheat a water bath to 85°c/185°F.

Peel off the outer layer of the fennel bulbs and remove any discoloured, oxidised areas. Trim the tops of the bulbs. Cut the fennel bulbs into 4cm wedges. This should yield approximately 18 wedges. Trim the bottom of each wedge so that it will stand up.

Place the fennel wedges in a large sous-vide bag, ensuring they are lying in a single layer. Add the smoked duck fat and seal the bag under full pressure.

Cook the fennel wedges in the water bath until they have fully softened. This should take approximately 2 hours, depending on their size.

Cool the bags in iced water and store the fennel wedges in the fridge until needed.

To Serve

6	Reserved brined duck breasts
	Reserved duck sauce
	Extra virgin olive oil
	Spice salt (see page 316)
	Cracked black pepper
	Salt
18	Reserved smoked confit fennel wedges
9	Reserved duck hearts
	Fennel cress

Preheat a water bath to 63°c/145°F.

Cook the duck breasts in the water bath for 22 minutes. Allow them to rest for 10 minutes before removing from the sous-vide bag and patting dry. The ideal serving temperature is 56°c/133°F.

In the meantime, divide the duck sauce between 2 small saucepans. In the first saucepan, allow the sauce to gently warm through. In the second saucepan, over a moderate heat, allow the sauce to reduce to a glaze.

To finish the duck breasts, heat a little olive oil in a non-stick pan and sear the duck breast skin-side down. Remove from the pan, brush the crispy skin with the duck glaze and season with spice salt and cracked black pepper. Trim the breasts and slice into 2 pieces.

Sear the flat sides of the fennel wedges until caramelised. Transfer to a tray lined with kitchen paper to drain. Season with salt and pepper. Place 2 halves of duck breast and 3 seared fennel wedges on each plate, and season with salt and pepper.

Slice the duck hearts in half and add to the duck sauce to warm through. Season them with the spice salt and garnish with fennel cress.

Spoon the duck sauce on to the plate with 3 duck heart halves per serving.

BAKED LEMON SUET

[1670]

TO MAKE A SUSSEX PUDDING

❊ *Take a little cold Cream, Butter and Flower, with some beaten Spice, Eggs, and a little Salt, make them into a stiff Paste, then make it up in a round Ball, and as you mold it, put in a great piece of Butter in the middle; and so tye it hard up in a buttered Cloth, and put it into boiling water, and let it boil apace till it be enough, then serve it in, and garnish your dish with Barberries; when it is at the Table cut it open at the top, and there will be as it were a Pound of Butter, then put Rosewater and Sugar into it, and so eat it* ❊

Hannah Wolley, *The Queen-like Closet or Rich Cabinet* (1670)

In natural history there's a period known as the Cambrian Explosion, during which some unidentified circumstance triggered massive evolutionary diversification. Between 550 million and 530 million years ago (the merest blip in terms of geological or "deep" time), the fossil record suddenly fills with all manner of new and unusual creations. In English culinary history, the popularisation of the pudding cloth in the seventeenth century triggered something similar.

The pudding cloth was a large square of linen that would be generously coated in butter and/or flour. A mixture of batter or suet (the hard fat from around the kidneys and loins of cattle and sheep) could then be put into the cloth, the four corners knotted together or secured with twine, and the whole thing lowered into a bubbling pot. There had been vague references to such things in medieval recipes, and Italian chefs had been using rudimentary pudding bags since the late sixteenth century. But the first written record in an English cookbook appears in a recipe for a "good fryday pudding" in Gervase Markham's *The English Huswife* (1615), which directs the chef to mix oatmeal with "Egges, Milk, Suet, Penyryal; and boyl'd first in a linnen bag, and then stript and buttered with sweet butter."

To us, a piece of cloth might seem a rather simple innovation, but at the time its effect was revolutionary, and ushered in a wild diversity of sweet and savoury dishes: liver pudding, oatmeal pudding, marrow pudding, calf's foot pudding, Buckinghamshire bacon badger, steak and kidney pudding, whitepot, Sussex pond pudding, Prince Consort pudding, Rotherfield sweet-tooth, roly-poly, Welcome Guest, Uncle Toby, plum duff, apple bolster, figgy 'obbin, spotted dick... Seventeenth-century cookbooks show how quickly puddings grew in variety and popularity. Markham's book offers only a handful of puddings. Sixty years on, Hannah Wolley's book has recipes for more than forty.

In previous centuries, pudding-making was largely dependent on having a supply of animal intestines, which were not always available year-round, particularly for the poor. Moreover, as I found out during a research project on sausage-making, it takes delicacy and dexterity to stuff animal casings without tearing them or introducing air pockets. With the advent of the pudding cloth, pudding-making became easier and more accessible to all people at all times of year. For the poor, the pudding worked perfectly with their limited means. Most cooking was done in a big pot suspended over an open fire (a practice that continued right up to the 1800s): a pudding could be wrapped up and popped in the pot alongside a piece of mutton or beef, offering a simple and economical way of cooking two courses. As a result, puddings gradually took over from pottage as the favoured way to bulk up a meal; the standard practice was to serve up a good wodge of pudding first, followed by the meat course, in the hopes that people would fill up with the former and therefore not eat too much of the latter, which was more expensive. "Pudding is so natural to our Harvest men," William Ellis wrote in *The Country Housewife's Family Companion* (1750), "that without it they think they cannot make an agreeable Dinner".

At first, even after the introduction of the pudding cloth, the pudding was primarily a vehicle for savoury ingredients. But as it grew in popularity, so too did the taste for sweet puddings, which eventually eclipsed and edged out virtually all savoury versions of the dish. The sweet pudding wasn't by any means a new phenomenon: medieval cooking made no strict distinction between sweet and savoury, so a white pudding of hog's liver, suet and breadcrumbs often included ingredients we now associate with desserts, such as raisins, dates, mace, sugar and cream. And one of the distinguishing features of the new style of cookbook forged by Hannah Wolley, E. Smith and others in seventeenth and eighteenth centuries was the emphasis on tarts, puddings and cakes. However, it was only in the nineteenth century that the pudding became fashionable among the middle class and a star of the dessert menu. With its litany of puddings named after public figures such as Prince Albert and Edwin Landseer, and its fancy moulds—the great Victorian cook Mrs Marshall's *Book of Moulds* boasts 68 pages and over 400 engravings—the 1800s should probably be considered the pudding's golden age.

But inevitably, such enthusiasm and abundance couldn't be maintained. Within a couple of generations, fashion had moved on and the range on offer had shrunk considerably. Suet in particular came to be seen as stodgy, and was increasingly passed over in favour of sponges and boiled or baked batters. In any case, by the end of World War I, the social set-up had altered considerably. Households had to manage with fewer domestic servants and the lady of the house was nudged into a more active role in the kitchen, where her inexperience inevitably precipitated change. Ironically, the pudding cloth, which had originally been seen as such a step forward in terms of simplicity and ease of handling, was now considered hard to master. Housewives took to steaming puddings in a basin instead, and the cloth was shoved in the back of a drawer and forgotten.

❀

The pudding is such an iconic dessert that any restaurant serving historical or traditional British food probably has to have at least one on the menu. At Dinner I was keen to feature Sussex pond pudding, a delicious steamed suet concoction that springs a surprise: there's a whole lemon inside that flavours the juices that flood from the pudding as it's cut open, creating a "pond" on the plate.

It turns out, however, that this is not the only surprise the pudding springs. Although the lemon makes the dish, and is presented as an authentic part of it, it is in fact a very recent addition. Sussex pudding (Wolley's recipe had no "pond" in its title) might have been around since the seventeenth century, but it was lemon-less until about 1950. If I was trying to re-create historical dishes, therefore, I'd have to leave out the lemon. Fortunately, my approach of using old recipes simply as part of my inspiration for creating new dishes meant I wasn't confined to a particular set of techniques and ingredients. Wolley's recipe might have had no lemon among its ingredients, but it sought exactly the same effect as the modern pudding: "cut it open at the top, and there will be as it were a Pound of Butter". Lemon simply added to the theatre and flavour of the dish. If Wolley had thought of it, I reckoned, she would have put one in too.

That lemon, though, turned out to be a big headache. It works well enough in a big family-sized pudding at home, but back in 2005, when I first started developing a steamed-sponge version of the dish—for the Hind's Head rather than Dinner—we wanted to serve each customer with their own individual pudding. Having a whole lemon in there was just too much. Instead we prepared a lovely rich lemon filling made with pickled lemons, beurre noisette and cream, but this presented problems of its own: sometimes the sauce soaked into the sponge, sabotaging the pond effect. For me, the most important thing in a kitchen is consistency: a great restaurant's reputation depends on its ability to produce a dish to the same high standard every single time. The pudding was too hit-and-miss, so I took it off the menu.

And that's how things stayed until 2010 when, along with my head of creative development, Jocky Petrie, and the future head chef of Dinner, Ashley Palmer-Watts, I started thinking about the menu for Dinner. Since I wanted a pudding on the menu and felt I had unfinished business with Sussex pond pudding, we decided to take another look at it.

This re-examination benefited from some fortunate timing. I had recently acquired another beautiful old inn in Bray called The Crown (rumoured to be a stopping-off point for Charles II en route to assignations with Nell Gwyn in nearby Holyport). The menu I'd developed for it offered a lot of classic British pub grub, including a suet pudding of chicken, ham and mushrooms that was baked rather

than steamed. And this, I realised, might be the answer to my Sussex pond problems. Baking would be quicker than steaming, and meant the filling had less time to melt and soak into the suet. It would also crisp up the outside of the pudding, providing an interesting textural contrast. What's more, I had a good idea for the filling. In previous months, I had been looking into serving some form of high tea at Dinner. In the end the notion had proved too impractical, but one of the things we'd developed for it was a lemon tart made with a mixture of lemon curd and salted butter caramel. The combination seemed ideal for a pudding: soft, smooth, rich caramel tempered by the sharp citrus zing of the curd. Jocky and I made up a batch and began baking.

It still didn't work. Either the filling leaked or it drenched the suet casing. One time the consistency would be too thick, the next too thin. I wanted a pudding that really captured the pond effect—a lovely lava-like ooze on to the plate, of the sort you find with a perfectly made chocolate fondant—but instead what I got was, as Jocky memorably put it, "pissy lemon water". Clearly, we had to take the recipe apart and rebuild it some other way.

I had been trying to stay true to the pudding's original aesthetic and cook the whole thing in one. Reluctantly, I let go of this concept, hoping that, if I had more control over how each component of the dish was cooked, I could find a way through the technical issues. Gradually, my recipe evolved into something very different from the original. Using a form of tart pastry and replacing some of its butter content with suet, we got a pastry that was light but sufficiently impermeable that the filling stayed in place. The pastry was baked blind and the filling was prepared separately. Since both filling and casing were pre-cooked, the idea was that they could be brought together at the last minute, giving the filling little time to melt into the pastry.

All the same, I was taking no chances, and worked out a method of assemblage that gave the best chance of success. The warmed filling was decanted to a syringe. A sponge-cake disc was laid on top of a layer of lemon curd and the pastry case pressed in place over these two, creating a leak-proof seal. The filling could then be injected into the casing, ready to splurge perfectly on to the plate and create that lovely buttery lemony pond.

BAKED LEMON SUET

Makes 6 portions

Sponge-Cake Rounds

290g	Soft (T45) flour
12g	Baking powder
	Salt
250g	Unsalted butter, cubed and at room temperature
270g	Golden caster sugar
4	Eggs
60g	Double cream

Preheat the oven to 180°C/350°F.

Sieve the flour, baking powder and a pinch of salt into a bowl. Set aside.

Place the butter and sugar in a mixer bowl and cream together using the paddle attachment at medium-high speed until light and fluffy.

Reduce the speed to medium and add the eggs one at a time, ensuring each one is fully incorporated before adding the next.

Reduce the speed to low and add a third of the flour mixture. Once it is three-quarters incorporated, add a third of the cream. Do this with the remaining flour and cream in 2 additional stages until it has all been added.

Pour the mixture into a large square baking tin lined with baking parchment. Bake for 30–40 minutes, then remove and allow to cool.

Once cooled, trim the top and bottom crusts off the sponge cake and trim the height to 1.5cm. Use a 4.5cm circular cutter to cut 6 rounds from the cake. Store the cake rounds in a sealed container while you prepare the rest of the dish.

Salted Caramel

200g	Whipping cream
190g	Glucose
190g	White caster sugar
150g	Unsalted butter, cubed and at room temperature
6.5g	Salt
190g	Whole milk

Place the whipping cream in a small saucepan and set aside.

In a separate saucepan, allow the glucose, sugar, butter, salt and milk to melt, then bring to the boil, whisking continuously.

As soon as this caramel starts gaining some colour, place the saucepan of cream on the heat and gently bring to the boil. Remove from the heat, cover and set aside.

Continue whisking the caramel, allowing it to come to 147°C/297°F. Depending how long it takes, you may need to return the whipping cream to a gentle heat until it is needed.

Once the caramel has reached 147°C/297°F, remove it from the heat and gradually whisk in the warm whipping cream until the mixture is completely smooth and emulsified.

Pour the caramel into a container and cover the mixture with clingfilm, allowing the film to touch the surface of the caramel. Set aside to cool.

Lemon Curd

150g	Lemon juice
15g	Lemon zest
170g	Unsalted butter, cubed and at room temperature
240g	Whole egg
35g	Egg yolk
220g	White caster sugar

Place all the ingredients in a Thermomix and bring to 100°C/212°F. Allow to boil for 10 seconds, then strain immediately through a fine-mesh sieve.

Store the curd in a sealed container and refrigerate until needed. You will need 300g for the pond pudding filling, and the rest should be reserved in a piping bag for use in the presentation.

Pond Pudding Filling

300g	Reserved salted caramel
300g	Reserved lemon curd
10g	Lemon juice

Allow the salted caramel and lemon curd to come to room temperature.

Place the salted caramel in a deep-sided container and gradually add the lemon curd and lemon juice while blitzing with a hand blender.

Transfer the pond pudding filling into a sous-vide bag and seal. Store in the fridge until needed.

(continued overleaf)

Candied Lemon Zest

50g   Lemon zest pieces
125g   White caster sugar

Blanch the lemon zest in hot water twice, then slice them into thin julienne strips. Ensure there is no visible pith.

Place 100g water and the sugar in a saucepan and bring to 103°c/217°F.

Add the blanched lemon zest and simmer until al dente. Leave to cool in the syrup and store, in the syrup, in the fridge until needed.

Pond Pudding Pastry

80g   Suet
500g   Soft (T45) flour
170g   Unsalted butter, cubed
2g   Salt
1g   Vanilla powder
10g   Finely grated lemon zest
135g   Egg yolk
210g   White caster sugar

Gently melt the suet in a small saucepan and set aside to cool.

Place the flour, butter, salt, vanilla powder and lemon zest in a mixer and, using the paddle attachment, combine the mixture until it forms crumbs. Add the suet and rub in by hand until it is well combined and resembles coarser breadcrumbs.

In a separate bowl, whisk the egg yolk and sugar until fully combined. Add the yolk mixture to the flour mixture and mix until it just comes together.

Place the dough between 2 sheets of baking parchment and roll out to a thickness of 4mm.

Use your dariole moulds as a guide to the size you will need, then portion the dough into 6 rectangular pieces and 6 circular pieces. This will make it easier to line the dariole moulds. Place the sectioned pieces of dough on a tray, wrap in clingfilm and store in the fridge until ready to bake.

Spray 6 dariole moulds with non-stick baking spray and line the moulds using the pastry, pressing the pieces firmly together to ensure it is even. Rest the lined moulds in the fridge for 30 minutes. Preheat the oven to 180°c/350°F.

Fill each lined mould with rice that has been wrapped well in clingfilm. Bake for 25 minutes, then reduce the temperature to 170°c/340°F, and bake for 12 more minutes.

Remove the puddings from the oven and discard the bags of rice. Use a serrated knife to smooth the edges of the pastry and tip the baked casing out of each mould. Use a toothpick to make a hole in the centre of each pastry case. Gently ensure the hole is large enough to insert the tip of your syringe into it later; this is easier to do while the pastry cases are still warm. Set aside while getting all the elements ready to assemble.

To Assemble and Serve

      Reserved pond pudding filling
4–5   Finger limes
20g   Drained pickled lemon (see page 279), finely chopped
      Reserved candied lemon zest
25g   Limoncello
6   Reserved sponge-cake rounds
      Reserved lemon curd
6   Reserved baked pastry cases
      Apple blossom flowers

Preheat the oven to 100°c/212°F and a water bath to 65°c/149°F.

Place the sous-vide bag of pond pudding filling in the water bath to heat gently.

Obtain the caviar-like vesicles from the finger limes by cutting off the edges and running your finger along the length of them, scooping out the segments. Combine equal amounts of these vesicles and finely chopped pickled lemons. Set this finger lime and pickled lemon salad aside.

Drain the candied lemon zest on a small tray lined with kitchen paper, and reserve 25g of the syrup. Combine this syrup with the limoncello in a small bowl. Mix to combine well. Use a pastry brush to gently brush the limoncello syrup on to both sides of each of the 6 sponge-cake rounds.

Using a 6.5cm-diameter presentation ring as a guide, pipe a layer of lemon curd into the centre of 6 plates. Place the limoncello-soaked sponge cake disc in the centre of the lemon curd on all 6 plates.

Place the 6 baked pastry cases in the warm oven for 5–6 minutes, to warm through gently.

In the meantime, carefully remove the warm pond pudding filling from the water bath and transfer the contents to a syringe.

Remove the warm pastry cases and place open-side down on to the lemon curd on the plates, hiding the sponge cake. Gently press down to create a leak-proof suction. Insert the plastic tip of the syringe into the hole you made earlier and fill with the warm pond pudding filling. You may need to refill the syringe in stages until all 6 puddings have been filled.

Hide the hole at the top of the pastry with a spoonful of finger lime and pickled lemon salad, and arrange apple blossom flowers on and around the pudding. Place the drained candied lemon zest around the plate as well.

Serve immediately.

BUTTERED CRAB LOAF

[1714]

LOBSTER LOAVES

❁ Brown butter with flour, stir in onions and parsley shred very fine, pepper, anchovy liquor, gravy and egg yolks. Add the lobster. Take three small loaves, hollow out the crumb and fill with the mixture then put the top back on. Fry in dripping ❁

Mary Kettilby, *A Collection Of Above Three Hundred Receipts In Cookery, Physick And Surgery; For The Use Of All Good Wives, Tender Mothers, And Careful Nurses* (1714)

BUTTERED CRABS

❁ Boil your crabs, take the meat out of their bodies and strain it with the yolks of three or four hard eggs, claret wine, vinegar, sugar and beaten cinnamon; then put it into a pipkin with fresh butter and let it stew for a quarter of an hour; then serve them up as before ❁

John Nott, *The Cook's and Confectioner's Dictionary* (1723)

BUTTER'D CRAY-FISH & BUTTER'D CRABS

❁ Take your Cray-Fish, and pick the Tails out whole, and put what is in the Inside of the Body-shells in likewise, and put to them a little Wine; brown a Piece of Butter gold Colour; put in your Fish and Wine and a little good Gravy, and season them with a little Pepper, Salt, Nutmeg and Ginger, and stove them a while till tender; then toss them up with thick Butter and the Juice of an Orange; dish them on Sippets, and garnish with Orange or Lemon, and serve them hot ❁

Charles Carter, *The Complete Practical Cook* (1730)

Butter is now such an integral part of the Western diet that a foil-wrapped pack can be found in nearly every fridge, so it's easy to imagine that it has always been a feature of British cuisine. In the Middle Ages, however, things were very different. There was no refrigeration, so preventing dairy products from going off was a tricky business, particularly in summer, and butter was heavily salted to prevent it going rancid. (In the early fourteenth century, Overton Manor dairy was adding a pound of salt per ten pounds of butter; these days, butter usually contains around 1.5–2 per cent salt.) But there seem to have been other reasons for butter's limited appearance in recipes of the period. For a start, butter was seen as peasant food by the rich and therefore shunned. It was thought to linger on the stomach, "as the fatness doth swim above in a boiling pot", as the physician Andrew Boorde later put it. Religious practices also helped keep butter out of the kitchen. The Catholic Church had decreed that meat should not be consumed on certain days of the year (see page 91), and since it was an animal product, butter was also proscribed. Those who adhered strictly to the rules avoided butter entirely during the forty days of Lent. Some historians suggest that butter's eventual rise in popularity in England was directly connected to the Catholic Church's loss of authority during the Reformation.

Two other factors also encouraged a greater use of butter. The increase in population and prosperity in the Tudor period led to the emergence of a middle rank of people who weren't so concerned about which foods were beneath them and happily used butter in cooking. The expulsion of tenants by landowners and the appropriation of common land to maximise profits from animal grazing, known as enclosures, had led to a huge rise in cattle numbers. By the eighteenth century there were more cows in England than ever before, and farmers were making cheese and butter out of the milk and selling at local markets or in the fast-growing towns. Butter became an essential feature of all manner of dishes; it was added to boiled vegetables as they cooked, stirred into dishes just before they were taken to the table, or served on the side, melted and perhaps thickened with a little flour, as a sauce of sorts. This was the golden age of butter in English cookery.

Unsurprisingly, some seventeenth- and eighteenth-century chefs took their enthusiasm for the new ingredient too far. Now that they had recognised butter's potential, they put it in everything, and lots of it. The French diplomat Talleyrand's famous observation that "England has three sauces and 360 religions, whereas France has three religions and 360 sauces" was supposedly prompted by the ubiquity of butter sauce on English tables. However, it wasn't only foreigners who thought English cooks had gone overboard for butter. In his diary entry for 17 October 1756, Sussex shopkeeper Thomas Turner complained that dinner at his uncle's was "spoiled by almost swimming in butter … there was almost but enough in it to have drowned the pig, had it been alive". Although the fact that his uncle risked serving a butter pond pudding after roast pig and turnips dressed in butter suggests a fairly devil-may-care approach to menu planning in any case.

The crab and lobster recipes by Mary Kettilby, John Nott and Charles Carter show that eighteenth-century cooks were capable of using butter in a restrained and skilful manner,

however. It was Kettilby's lobster loaf that first caught my attention, not least because the name conjured up a surreal image—a sort of companion piece to Dali's *Lobster Telephone*, in which the animal is slumped across the handset. Talking it over with Ash, I reckoned we could do something for Dinner's menu with that loaf, perhaps developing a variant on pain perdu, which involves a classic French technique that has been the foundation of several of my dishes. I liked, too, the idea of combining this with some sort of crustacean, and as I read some the recipes of the early eighteenth century, I discovered there was quite a tradition for this at the time. Charles Carter gave instructions for buttered lobsters, buttered crayfish and buttered crabs, as well as his own version of lobster loaf. Ash and I pored over dozens of recipes, gaining a feeling for what the chefs had wanted to achieve—the spirit of the dish, if you like—and getting a sense of the direction we wanted to take. I was increasingly attracted to the idea of using crab because it's one of the great British ingredients, and counties such as Devon and Dorset offer crabs that rival those from anywhere else in the world.

Since pain perdu is essentially eggy bread, we took that basic concept a stage further and created a type of crab custard by combining a fairly conventional egg mixture with an intense crab stock, and then put slices of brioche in the custard overnight. To keep these soaked slices as moist and flavourful as possible, they were then heated very gently in a bain-marie, so that the egg set to a delicate consistency and didn't overcook or dominate the other flavours. The result was a set of little crab loaves with a wonderfully rich, fragrant crustacean flavour.

The dish needed some contrast, something cool, fresh and light to counterbalance the warmth and fragrance of the loaf, so we developed a crab-meat salad with cucumber dice, tiny cubes of celery, confit shallots, pickled lemon and delicate herbs such as coriander and chervil—plenty of flavours that complement crab beautifully, and give a nice bit of crunch and an all-important spritz of acidity to cut through the richness. Little spheres of smoked herring roe that burst on the tongue and a deep-flavoured cucumber fluid gel provided what I call flavour encapsulation: shots of flavour delivered in a concentrated form. It's a technique I often use to reinforce the flavours in a dish and offer contrast and stimulation to the palate; it can be as simple as garnishing a dish with two or three whole coriander seeds, rather than grinding them, so they give a hit of spice and citrus as you bite into them. Or it can be something more artful, such as methodically vacuum-packing and compressing cucumber to make dense, intense little cubes.

The dish is garnished with micro-herbs. These provide subsidiary notes rather than the main flavours and, as long as it's done sympathetically, they can be swapped for other ingredients that bring something different to the dish without compromising its overall character. For a number of years I've been taking advice from foragers on which wild herbs and plants are available, and based on this we decide which ones will suit particular dishes. As autumn shades into winter, for example, the crab loaf will be garnished with lemony, herby rock samphire, sorrel and stonecrop, which tastes a bit like grapeseeds and has lovely seaweed-like texture. At other times of year we'll use different herbs, depending on what the forager can find.

There's one last, essential detail of the recipe that not only brings it all together, but also recalls the recipe's origins in the golden age of butter. Seafood shells and meat bones are fantastic sources of flavour. At my restaurants they're often roasted and combined with other ingredients to add depth and complexity to, say, a stock. Here I saw an opportunity to use crab shells to create a crab butter that could be dotted over the loaf and around the plate. By crushing whole crabs and then gently colouring them in a pan (which gives a slightly more fried characteristic than oven-roasting them, although it's a more aggressive source of heat so you have to be careful not to overcook the shells and turn them bitter), I could draw out lots of crab flavour and an intense nuttiness as well. Adding butter over a low heat and letting it infuse for an hour meant that plenty of the flavour transferred to the butter. After straining and mixing in a little pickled lemon and bergamot juice to add fragrance and temper the richness, I had a delightfully fresh, light butter emulsion to finish the dish. I'm not sure what Thomas Turner's uncle would have made of it, but I believe it's in the spirit of Kettilby, Nott and Carter's work.

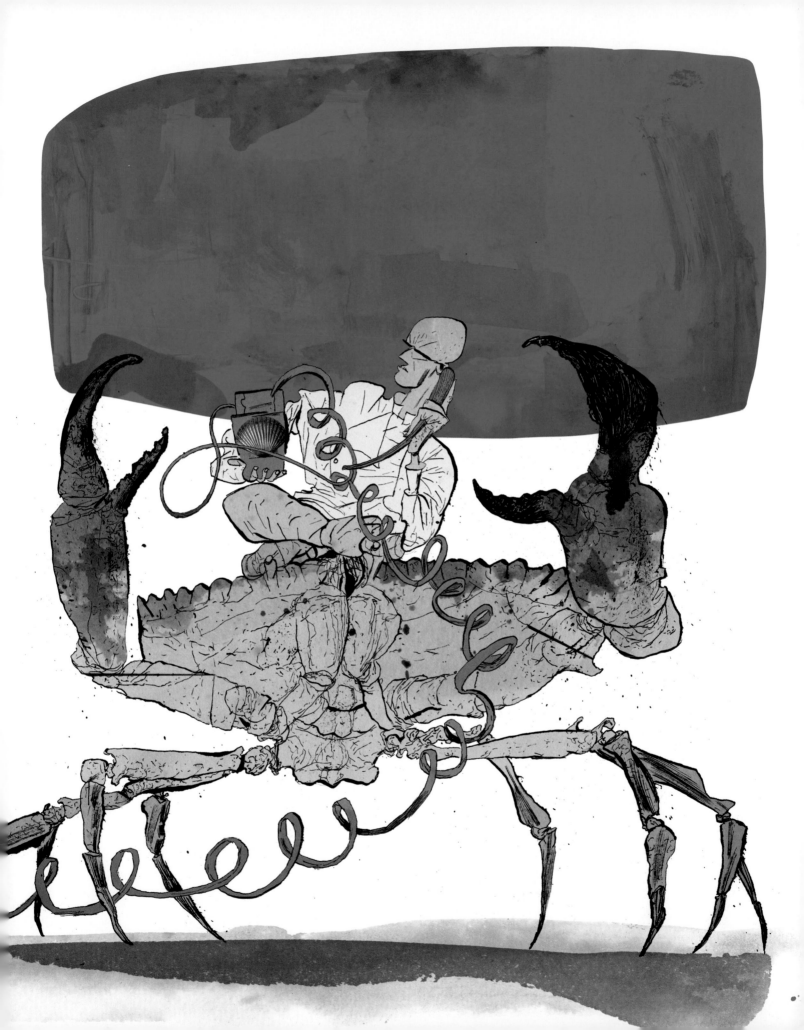

BUTTERED CRAB LOAF

Makes 6 portions

Crab Stock

250g	**White wine**
190g	**Brandy**
2.5kg	**Cock crabs**
200g	**Olive oil**
625g	**Peeled and finely sliced carrots**
410g	**Peeled and finely sliced onions**
190g	**Finely sliced cleaned button mushrooms**
135g	**Rinsed and finely sliced leeks**
65g	**Rinsed and finely sliced celery**
5g	**Peeled and finely sliced garlic**
225g	**Chopped ripe plum tomatoes**

Pour the white wine and brandy into separate saucepans and flame the mixtures with a blowtorch until all the alcohol has burnt off. Combine them in one saucepan and reduce the mixture by half over a moderate heat. Set aside to cool.

Using a heavy knife, cut the crabs in half. Remove and discard the gills. Crush the crabs well with a crab mallet. Place the crushed crabs in a colander and drain, reserving the juices.

Heat half the olive oil in a large pressure cooker and add the crushed crabs to the hot oil. Allow them to caramelise until golden in colour. You may need to do this in 2 batches. Remove the crab and add the remaining olive oil. Add the carrots, onions, mushrooms, leeks, celery and garlic, and cook until softened. Add the chopped tomatoes and cook for a further 5 minutes.

Add the reduced alcohols to the pressure cooker, followed by the crushed crab and the reserved juices. Pour 4 litres cold water into the pressure cooker and bring the stock up to the boil, skimming off all scum and impurities. Secure the lid and cook for 2 hours.

Allow the pressure cooker to depressurise and the stock to cool slightly before opening the lid. Strain the stock through a fine-mesh sieve, followed by a double layer of muslin. Chill in the fridge overnight.

Remove and discard all the fat from the surface of the chilled stock. Heat the stock in a large saucepan and gently reduce to 1.6kg. It is important to continue skimming the stock as it reduces.

Once the stock has reduced, pass it through a fine-mesh filter bag and store in the freezer until needed.

Crab Butter

750g	**Cock crabs**
95g	**Grapeseed oil**
750g	**Unsalted butter, diced and at room temperature**

Using a heavy knife, cut the crabs in half. Remove and discard the gills. Crush the crabs well with a crab mallet. Place in a colander to drain.

Heat the grapeseed oil in a pot and cook the crushed crab until golden in colour. Over a gentle heat, add the diced butter. Once the butter has melted and the temperature reaches 85°c/185°F, remove the pan from the heat and cover the pot, allowing the flavours to infuse for 1 hour.

Pass the crab butter through a fine-mesh sieve and discard the shells. Once cooled, store in the fridge until needed.

Crab Dressing

200g	**Reserved melted crab butter**
65g	**Pickled lemon juice, reserved from Pickled Lemons (see page 279)**
65g	**Bergamot juice**

Ensure the temperature of the crab butter is approximately 28°c/82°F. Whisk it well in a clean bowl, then slowly add the pickled lemon juice and bergamot juice. Whisk until fully emulsified.

Store in the fridge until needed.

Lemon Mayonnaise

100g	**Pasteurised egg yolk**
40g	**Dijon mustard**
7g	**Lemon juice**
40g	**Chardonnay vinegar**
7g	**Salt**
485g	**Grapeseed oil**

Place the egg yolk, mustard, lemon juice, vinegar and salt in a small bowl and combine well. Transfer to a Thermomix.

While the Thermomix is running, gradually add the oil until the mayonnaise is fully emulsified. You may need to stop halfway through, lift the lid and scrape down the sides of the jug.

Store in the fridge until needed.

Confit Shallots

50g   **Unsalted butter**
100g **Peeled and finely diced shallots**

Melt the butter in a small pan and add the diced shallots. Cook them over a gentle heat under a cartouche, until they have caramelised slightly. They should have softened, retaining only a slight bite.

Drain off the butter by placing the shallots in a sieve, and store them in the fridge until needed.

Crab and Egg Mixture

335g **Reserved crab stock**
135g **Whipping cream**
7g   **Coriander**
7g   **Chervil**
230g **Whole egg**
3g   **Salt**

Combine the crab stock and whipping cream in a pan and gently heat to 85°C/185°F.

While the mixture is heating, lightly chop the coriander and chervil. Once the mixture has reached temperature, remove from the heat, add the chopped herbs, cover with clingfilm and allow to infuse for 10 minutes.

Pass the stock mixture through a fine-mesh sieve into a deep-sided container and ensure all the moisture is squeezed from the herbs. Add the egg and salt and use a hand blender to emulsify the mixture fully.

Pass the mixture through a fine-mesh sieve and store in the fridge until needed.

Crab Toast

1   **Brioche loaf**
    Reserved crab and egg mixture

Trim the crusts off the brioche and cut the bread into 3cm-thick strips.

Line a large loaf tin with baking parchment and place the brioche strips in the tin, ensuring there are no gaps in between the pieces and they are all of equal depth.

Pierce the brioche with a fork and pour enough crab and egg mixture over the brioche to absorb completely. Place the tin in a chamber vacuum sealer. Set the machine on its gentlest setting and close the lid. Repeat this process 3 times. Allow the brioche to soak overnight in the fridge.

Preheat the oven to 100°C/212°F. Fill a deep tray with 4cm water and place in the oven.

Place a piece of baking parchment on top of the soaked bread and cover the tray with clingfilm. Carefully place the tin of soaked brioche inside the bain-marie in the oven. Bake until the core temperature has reached 68°C/154°F.

Remove the brioche from the oven and remove the clingfilm and baking parchment from the top. Place in the fridge for 10 minutes, then cover again with pierced clingfilm. Allow to chill completely.

When ready to serve, carefully remove the brioche from the tin, discarding the baking parchment from the bottom of the loaf. Trim the brioche strips to make 6 equal pieces measuring 8cm long, 3cm wide and 3cm deep.

Store in the fridge on a tray lined with baking parchment.

Cucumber Dice

5   **Large cucumbers**

Cut the cucumbers into 8cm lengths. Square off these cucumber pieces by trimming them into a perfect rectangle, reserving all offcuts in a large bowl.

Using a mandolin set to 4mm thick, slice the cucumber around the heart. Place the cucumber sheets in a sous-vide bag, ensuring that they are lying flat. Seal under full pressure. Pierce small holes in the bag and repeat the process once more.

Trim off any visible cucumber skin and dice the flesh into 4mm cubes. Store the diced compressed cucumbers in the fridge until needed.

Juice all the cucumber offcuts and pass through a fine-mesh filter bag. Store the cucumber juice in the fridge until needed.

(continued overleaf)

Cucumber Fluid Gel

135g	Chardonnay vinegar
35g	Sugar
850g	Reserved cucumber juice
8g	Salt
9g	Gellan F (low-acyl gellan)

Combine the vinegar and sugar in a small saucepan. Bring to the boil, then remove from the heat and set aside to cool.

Place the cucumber juice and salt in the Thermomix and bring to 90°C/194°F on a medium setting. Add the gellan F and blitz for 10 seconds at high speed. Lift the lid and scrape down the sides of the jug. Blitz for 1 more minute to ensure the gellan has completely dissolved. Pour into a large bowl and place in ice water. Allow to cool completely.

Place the set gel, along with cooled vinegar and sugar mixture, in a clean Thermomix. Blitz for 1 minute, lift the lid and scrape down the sides of the jug. Continue to blitz for 1 more minute to incorporate fully. Pass through a fine-mesh sieve.

Scrape the fluid gel into a shallow container and place in a chamber vacuum sealer. Under full pressure, close the lid and keep a close eye on the gel, stopping the process as soon as the bubbles rise to the top. Repeat several more times until the gel no longer bubbles.

The cucumber juice and fluid gel should be made on the day to retain their bright, vibrant colour.

Crab Salad

120g	Picked white crab meat
50g	Reserved cucumber dice
50g	Rinsed and finely diced celery
25g	Reserved confit shallots
25g	Finely chopped pickled lemon (see page 279)
12g	Coriander
10g	Chervil
2g	Tarragon
50g	Reserved lemon mayonnaise
3g	Salt

Spread out the picked crab meat on a tray lined with kitchen paper to absorb any excess moisture.

In a small bowl, combine the drained crab meat, compressed cucumber dice, celery, shallots and chopped pickled lemon.

Finely chop the coriander, chervil and tarragon and add to the mixture. Add the lemon mayonnaise and salt and stir well to combine. Store in the fridge until needed.

Crab Butter Emulsion

150g	Reserved crab butter, cut into cubes

Gently heat 60g water in a small saucepan and gradually whisk in the cubes of crab butter. Use a hand blender to emulsify it, then set aside until needed.

To Serve

30g	Reserved crab butter
6	Pieces reserved crab toast
	Reserved crab butter emulsion
30g	Sea purslane leaves, rinsed
30g	Picked stonecrop leaves, rinsed
	Reserved cucumber fluid gel
	Reserved crab salad
	Sheep's sorrel leaves, rinsed
	Reserved crab dressing
	Coriander cress
80g	Smoked herring roe
	Salt
	Cracked black pepper

Heat the crab butter in a non-stick pan and colour the crab toasts until golden on all sides. Set aside and keep warm.

Gently heat the crab butter emulsion in a small saucepan and add the sea purslane. After 1 minute, add the stonecrop and cook gently for 30 more seconds. Drain them on a tray lined with kitchen paper and season well with salt and pepper. Place a small amount of cucumber gel on a plate. Arrange the buttered crab toast partly on top of the cucumber gel and top with the crab salad. Arrange the warm sea purslane and stonecrop, and the sheep's sorrel, around the dish.

In the meantime, gently heat the crab dressing to no more than 28–30°C/82–86°F and generously drizzle it on and around the elements on the plate. Garnish with coriander cress and a small spoonful of herring roe.

SALMAGUNDY

[1723]

TO MAKE A SALAMONGUNDY, SALMINGONDIN, OR SALGUNDY

❁ *Mince a couple of Chickens, either boil'd or roasted very fine or Veal, if you please; also mince the Yolks of hard Eggs very small; and mince also the Whites of the Eggs very small by themselves; also shred the Pulp of Lemons very small; then lay in your Dish a Layer of your minced Meat, a Layer of Yolks of Eggs, a Layer of Whites, a Layer of Anchovies, a Layer of your shred Lemon Pulp; a Layer of Pickles, a Layer of Sorrel, a Layer of Spinage and Cloves, or else Shalots shred small: When you have fill'd your Dish with all these Ingredients, set an Orange or Lemon on the top; then garnish it with Horse-radish, scrap'd, Barberries, and slices of Lemon. Then for the Sauce, beat up some Oil with the Juice of Lemons, Salt, and Mustard thick, and serve them up for a second Course, Side-dish, or a Middle dish for Supper* ❁

John Nott, *The Cook's and Confectioner's Dictionary* (1723)

Given the medieval suspicion of raw ingredients, and the taste for flesh and spectacle (which brought swan, peacock and porpoise to the dining table), you might assume there was little interest in salad in the Middle Ages. But this is not the case; there's a recipe for Salat in the earliest extant cookbook in English, *The Forme of Cury*, which was compiled around 1390 (see page 19):

Take persel, sawge, grene garlic, chibolles, oynouns, leek, borage, myntes, porrettes, fenel, and toun cressis, rew, rosemarye, purslarye; lave and waische hem clene. Pike hem. Pluk hem small with thyn honde, and myng hem wel with rawe oile; lay on vynegar and salt, and serve it forth.

Clearly, salad composition was already relatively sophisticated by the fourteenth century. We shouldn't be surprised at this, as there was a well-developed tradition of horticulture in England, and most people grew vegetables such as onions, garlic, cabbage, and most of all leeks, to enliven their plain and basic fare, while manors and monasteries cultivated a range of plants and herbs as food and medicine. In *De Naturis rerum* (On the Nature of Things),* a compendium of twelfth-century scientific knowledge, Alexander Neckam gives a lengthy list of plants he'd expect to find in a garden, including some that are familiar, such as parsley, fennel, coriander, sage, savory, sorrel, mustard, and others that are not, such as smallage, dittany, pellitory, southernwood and orach. A fifteenth-century manuscript in the British Library (Sloane MS 1201) has an alphabetical list of more than a hundred herbs to be found in a well-stocked garden, from Alexanders and anise to verbena and wormseed.

From this wealth of plant life, mixed herb and flower salads were created that proved extremely popular throughout the Middle Ages and beyond. The inclusion of edible flowers provided the drama of colour that medieval diners took such delight in. And, since they were thought to have medicinal properties, salad leaves escaped the stigma attached to many raw fruits and vegetables (though not everyone agreed: in the *Boke of Kervynge*, written around 1500, Wynkyn de Worde warned: "beware of grene sallettes & raw fruytes for they wyll make your soverayne seke"). Besides, the composed nature of a salad made it easy for a chef to juggle ingredients so as to achieve the necessary balance of humours essential to health (see page 89), introducing "warm", "dry" aromatic herbs to counterbalance the presence of "cold" leaves of endive or purslane, and finishing it off with a "warm" oil-and-vinegar dressing.

By the end of the Tudor period, the salad had made an evolutionary leap. It was now important for it to smell as good as it looked, and scented flowers such as cowslip, elder and gillyflowers joined violets and primroses on the plate. The leaves and flowers would be garnished with hard-boiled eggs and all sorts of fruits: in *The Good Huswife's Jewell* (1596), Thomas Dawson advises pared and sliced lemons; in *A Newe Booke of Cookerie* (1617) John Murrell suggests pomegranates, currants and barberries. These concoctions had become known as compound salads, which Gervase Markham (author of *The English Huswife*, 1615) defines as "young buds and knots of all manner of wholesome hearbes

---

* *This, and his vocabulary* De Utensilibus, *are invaluable works for the culinary historian. They're also the source of Neckam's main claim to fame as the first person in Europe to refer to the practice of using a magnetic needle for navigation at sea.*

at their first springing; as red-sage, mints, lettice, violets, marigolds, spinage, and many others mixed together, and then served up to the table with vinegar, sallet oyle and sugar", before going on to outline a version including chopped almonds, shredded figs, currants, raisins, capers, olives and a variety of leaves, all generously garnished with slices of orange and lemon.

In part, this move towards something more formal and fancy was simply a reflection of the fashion of the times. The sacking of the monasteries and appropriation of their land begun by Henry VIII in 1536 had provided those who found favour at court with wealth and influence. Keen to show off their enhanced status, the Tudor gentry adopted an extravagant style of dress and built architecturally elaborate houses flanked by knot gardens: rectangular beds containing arrangements of plants and herbs into complex shapes such as ovals, mazes, fleur-de-lys, or even heraldic beasts. In some ways, therefore, the compound salad was simply a parallel opportunity to create a formal composition of greenery that flaunted their money and taste. There were other factors at work too, though. The Renaissance approach to cuisine was increasingly being taken up in England, and salads fitted in well with the new Italian emphasis on fresh, clean flavours and the plentiful use of lemon. Allied to this, the produce coming from the New World generated huge excitement about food and gave cooks an expanded set of ingredients to work with (see page 118). Not surprisingly, this inspired many innovative and ambitious dishes, and compound salads were among them.

Meticulously prepared using a plethora of ingredients, the compound salad provided a template for development over the next century or so. The seventeenth century is known as the age of the "grand salad", which required an even more diverse range of ingredients and a distinctly artful arrangement on the plate. These were salads for show, designed to be carried to the table with some ceremony. Robert May, whose beautiful woodcuts of intricate designs for tarts show a strong sense of presentation, was an expert practitioner of the grand salad, offering no fewer than fourteen recipes in *The Accomplisht Cook* (1660). May selected all sorts of leaves, fruit, flowers and vegetables—lettuce, endive, borage, olives, currants, pickled capers, pickled mushrooms, boiled beetroots, shredded cabbage—and neatly piled or laid them out either in a series of concentric rings or "in a cross partition-ways", like a heraldic device.

Towards the close of the century, this approach was taken to its logical extreme, with the cornucopia of ingredients now including cooked meats or seafood as well as vegetables, eggs, leaves, fruit and pickles, and the whole thing built up to give an impression of decorative magnificence. This was the salmagundy (as the heading to Nott's recipe shows, its spelling was open to wild variation), whose name is supposedly derived from the French word *salmigondis*, which means "hodgepodge", although the eighteenth-century dish was anything but. Patrick Lamb's recipe for Sallad-Magundy in *Royal Cookery* (1710) is several pages long, giving detailed instructions for the chopping and placement of each ingredient. First a bed is made of lettuce shredded "as fine as a Thread". Above this, in the centre of the plate, "like the Top of a Sugar-Loaf", is a mound of diced chicken leg meat, hard-boiled egg yolks and chopped parsley, anchovy and lemon. Surrounding the mound, and laid neatly from the plate rim towards the centre, are strips of cold roast chicken breast and wing "three inches long, as thin as a Knife, and a Quarter of an Inch broad", interleaved with anchovies. The dish is garnished with cooked small onions, with the largest placed on top of the diced meat, and the rest around the rim "as thick as they can lie one by another". For service, Lamb says: "beat up some Oil and Vinegar, Pepper, and Salt, and pour all over it. But this is commonly done at Table. You may garnish this Sallad with some Grapes, just scalded, or with *French* Beans blanch'd off, or Station-Flowers..."

This is a salad fit for a feast, and it was served at one of the most famous of all. As the king's master cook, Lamb presided over the spectacular coronation dinner for James II, which took place at Westminster Hall on 23 April 1685. Among the 144 dishes on offer, including puffin, pickled scallops, Beef à la Royal, venison pasty and gooseberry and apricot tarts, there was a salmagundy.

Like Patrick Lamb, Charles Carter and William Rabisha, John Nott is part of a group whose refined style of cooking, inspired by French cuisine, especially François Massialot's *Le cuisinier roïal et bourgeois*, is now known as court cookery. The term is a useful but loose one, encompassing a broad range of personalities in the late seventeenth and early eighteenth centuries. Some court cooks were skilled but not particularly innovative; others were more open to the radical ideas coming from France. Nott was one of these: like Massialot, he arranged *The Cook's and Confectioner's Dictionary* (1723) alphabetically, and many of his recipes are taken from *Le cuisinier roïal et bourgeois*, or from the 1716 expanded edition of Lamb's *Royal Cookery*, which drew heavily on Massialot's book. Nott's work isn't a straightforward steal, though. He picks and chooses from Lamb and Massialot with an eye both to culinary fashion and British tastes, adapting and simplifying where necessary.

Nott has two recipes for salmagundy in *The Cook's and Confectioner's Dictionary*. The first is obviously taken from *Royal Cookery*; the writing style is streamlined slightly, but otherwise the ingredients, techniques and terminology are identical. But the second was the one that captured my attention: I liked the way it had stripped the dish back a bit, emphasising that the key to composition was a series of layers, each with a separate and distinct flavour that complemented all the others. I also really liked Nott's use of horseradish, a feature I hadn't seen in other salmagundy recipes. Horseradish, particularly in the form of a cream, can be a fantastic addition to a dish, giving it a little kick of sharpness that brings it alive. I've used it to great effect with oysters and in a beetroot risotto, and I felt that here too it would help create a salad with true character.

Nott, then, was the starting point. But since there are at least as many recipes for salmagundy as there are ways to spell it, I didn't feel we had to be faithful to a specific approach or set of ingredients. In any case, most of the historic recipes I'd read were impressive rather than refined. There was a lot happening on the plate, which was fine for a royal blowout with hundreds of dishes and guests, but perhaps not appropriate in a restaurant setting. So I was determined to pare the dish back. The essence of a salmagundy, it seemed to me, was beautifully cooked chicken, fresh green leaves and a condiment-style garnish. We'd take that and build our own version to go on the menu at Dinner.

For the chicken, I already had in mind a favourite ingredient of mine that I was sure would be perfect for a salmagundy. Indeed, it was one of the reasons I'd wanted to develop the dish in the first place. The chicken's "oysters" are two round, thumb-sized pieces of meat that lie either side of the backbone where it meets the thighs. In France they're known as *sot-l'y-laisse*—or "the fool leaves it there"—because they're often overlooked during carving and left attached to the carcass. But if you do so, you're missing out on one of the best bits of the bird, which is firm, tender and full of flavour. And the neat oyster shape means they're ideal for presentation (Patrick Lamb, with his three-inch-long, thin-as-a-knife strips of chicken, would certainly have approved). Ash and I tried out all sorts of different approaches to cooking them—hot and fast, slow and low temperature—but it was only when we started playing around with smoked duck fat that things fell into place. The development of salmagundy was happening in the run-up to the opening of Dinner, and I wanted the menu to have light smoked notes running through it, partly because I really like that barbecued characteristic, but also to give a suggestion of the smell of the hearth, as a reminder of how central the fireplace has been to kitchens and cookery over the centuries. (That's also why I wanted a spit-roast in Dinner's kitchen that would be visible to diners in the restaurant; see page 389.) So we vacuum-packed the oysters with smoked duck fat and cooked them gently in a water bath.

This technique produced beautifully textured chicken with just the right subtle, smoky note, but we wanted the dish to have the rich, unctuous quality of a roast chicken as well. Ash and I tried out dozens of fast and slow cooking techniques aimed at capturing this, but we couldn't find a method that was consistent enough. The solution we came up with was to make an intense roast chicken stock by roasting carcasses, deglazing the pan, adding aromatics and cooking it all in a pressure cooker to maximise the flavour, and then to use the stock, once reduced, as a glaze. Going down this route meant that the dish's final preparation would be virtually one-pan cooking: the cooked oysters were browned in the pan, followed by salsify, which was also browned, after which a mixture of chicken stock and walnut vinaigrette was added and reduced to make a coating. Towards the end of cooking, slices of bone marrow were added to warm through.

With each element in place, the dish could be put together in the classic composed salad style: a horseradish and onion fluid gel (for sweetness and flavour release) spooned on to the plate, the oysters, salsify and bone marrow criss-crossed above it, garnished with a variety of green leaves, dressed with walnut vinaigrette and a little grated fresh horseradish. The leaves are partly foraged, so that at different times of year salmagundy might include chickweed, sheep's sorrel, or whatever is in season. This offers a range that gives some idea of the sheer variety and abundance of British plant life that has been inspiring chefs for centuries.

SALMAGUNDY

Makes 6 portions

Roast Chicken Stock

3.5kg	Chicken carcasses
10g	Thyme
2	Bay leaves
3g	Black peppercorns

Preheat the oven to 180°C/350°F.

Chop the carcasses into smaller, evenly sized pieces. Spread them out evenly on a roasting tray and roast in the oven until golden brown, turning frequently.

Deglaze the roasting trays with water, then place the roasted carcasses and roasting juices in a large pressure cooker, followed by 3.2 litres cold water. Bring to the boil, skimming off all scum and impurities.

Add the thyme, bay leaves and peppercorns, and stir the mixture one last time before securing the lid of the pressure cooker. Cook for 2 hours.

Allow the pressure cooker to depressurise and the stock to cool slightly before opening the lid. Strain through a fine-mesh sieve, followed by a fine-mesh filter bag. Chill the stock in the fridge overnight.

Remove and discard the fat from the surface of the chilled stock. Heat the stock in a large saucepan and gently reduce to 300g. It is important to continue skimming it as it reduces.

Once the stock has reduced, pass it through a fine-mesh filter bag. Set aside 190g stock in the fridge for this dish; the rest can be frozen.

Chicken Oysters

30	Chicken oysters, skin on
55g	Smoked duck fat (see page 182)

Preheat a water bath to 70°C/158°F.

Carefully check each chicken oyster for shards of bone, which should be trimmed off. Place them in a sous-vide bag along with the duck fat. Ensure they are all lying flat and in a single layer. Seal under full pressure.

Cook the chicken oysters in the water bath for 14 minutes. They should be cooked through. Place the sous-vide bag in iced water and refrigerate the chicken oysters until needed.

Vegetable Braising Liquid

4g	Coriander seeds
1g	Black peppercorns
25g	Extra virgin olive oil
155g	Peeled and chopped onions
155g	Peeled and chopped carrots
30g	Rinsed and chopped leeks
45g	Chopped fennel
10g	Peeled and sliced garlic
385g	Chardonnay wine
500g	Vegetable stock (see page 94)
60g	Chardonnay vinegar
15g	Lemon juice
15g	Flatleaf parsley
7g	Thyme
1g	Rosemary
1g	Tarragon
15g	Salt
95g	Extra virgin olive oil

Heat a dry pan and toast the coriander seeds and black peppercorns until fragrant. Set aside to cool, then lightly crush using a pestle and mortar.

Heat 25g olive oil in a stockpot, add the onions and carrots and sweat until softened. Add the leeks, fennel and garlic, as well as the toasted, crushed aromatics, and cook for 5 more minutes, stirring regularly. Add the white wine and gently reduce by half.

Add the vegetable stock, 500g water, the vinegar and lemon juice. Bring to a gentle simmer, then add the herbs. Simmer gently for 30 minutes, then remove the pot from the heat and allow to stand for 30 minutes.

Pass through a fine-mesh sieve. Once cooled, add the salt and 95g olive oil. Whisk well and refrigerate until needed.

Salsify

2	Lemons
200g	Salsify (approximately)
400g	Vegetable braising liquid

Preheat a water bath to 90°C/194°F.

Make a bowl of acidulated water: cut the lemons in half and squeeze the juice into a large bowl of cold water. Add the lemon halves and set aside.

Prepare the salsify one piece at a time, working as quickly as possible to prevent discolouring by oxidisation. Peel and cut it into 8cm pieces. Cut them lengthways into quarters (you need approximately 36 pieces in total). Plunge into the acidulated water, ensuring they are fully immersed by placing a cartouche on top of the water.

Once prepped, place the salsify in a single layer in a sous-vide bag, along with the vegetable braising liquid. Seal the bag under full pressure and place in the water bath to cook until soft all the way through. This should take about 2 hours.

Cool the sous-vide bag in iced water to prevent further cooking, and store in the fridge until needed.

Onion and Horseradish Milk

60g	Unsalted butter
500g	Peeled and finely sliced onions
400g	Semi-skimmed milk
190g	Whipping cream
300g	Vegetable stock (see page 94)
60g	Peeled and finely grated horseradish

Melt the butter in a saucepan, add the onions and sweat over a medium heat until softened and translucent.

Add the milk, whipping cream and vegetable stock and bring the mixture to 80°C/176°F. Remove from the heat and blitz using a hand blender.

Add the grated horseradish and cover the saucepan. Allow the mixture to infuse for 10 minutes. Strain through a fine-mesh sieve and store in the fridge until needed.

Onion and Horseradish Fluid Gel

800g   **Reserved onion and horseradish milk**
10g   **Salt**
5g   **Gellan F (low-acyl gellan)**
120g   **Creamed horseradish**

Pour the onion and horseradish milk into a Thermomix and add the salt. Bring to 90°C/194°F on a medium setting. Add the gellan F and blitz for 10 seconds at high speed. Lift the lid and scrape down the sides of the jug. Blitz for 1 more minute to ensure the gellan has completely dissolved.

Pour the mixture into a large bowl and place the bowl in iced water. Allow to cool to 40°C/104°F.

Place the gel in a clean Thermomix and blitz for 35 seconds, then add the creamed horseradish. Stir to incorporate fully (do not blitz again). Pass through a fine-mesh sieve and store in the fridge until needed.

Walnut Vinaigrette Base

245g   **Walnut vinegar**
15g   **Dijon mustard**
245g   **Grapeseed oil**

Place the walnut vinegar and Dijon mustard in a bowl. Gradually whisk in the grapeseed oil to emulsify. Store in the fridge until needed.

Walnut-Chicken Vinaigrette

190g   **Reserved reduced chicken stock**
60g   **Lemon juice**
450g   **Reserved walnut vinaigrette base**

If the chicken stock has been chilled, you may need to melt it first very gently in a small saucepan, then leave to cool slightly before making the vinaigrette. Place the stock and lemon juice in a bowl and gradually whisk in the walnut vinaigrette base to emulsify.

Fried Japanese Breadcrumbs

50g   **Japanese breadcrumbs**
500g   **Grapeseed oil**

Pass the breadcrumbs through a fine-mesh sieve and set aside. Line a small tray with kitchen paper and place the grapeseed oil in a small saucepan.

Heat the grapeseed oil to 170°C/340°F, then add the breadcrumbs. Stir the crumbs with a whisk and fry until golden.

Strain the crumbs and discard the oil. Spread out the strained crumbs on the lined tray and place kitchen paper on top of them to absorb all the excess oil. Allow to cool.

Store the cooled breadcrumbs in a sealed container and use within 1 day.

Bone Marrow Discs

6   **Beef bone marrow bones, sectioned into 6cm segments**
500g   **Grapeseed oil**

Rinse the bone marrow sections for 10 minutes under cold running water. Wearing protective gloves, push the marrow out of the bone and discard the bone. Slice the cylindrical marrow piece into 4mm discs (5g each) and set aside on a tray in the fridge until needed.

To Serve

   Reserved salsify pieces in vegetable braising liquid
   Extra virgin olive oil
   Reserved chicken oysters
400g   **Reserved walnut-chicken vinaigrette**
   Salt
   Cracked black pepper
24   **Reserved bone marrow discs**

   Reserved fried Japanese breadcrumbs
   Reserved onion and horseradish fluid gel
   Seasonal leaves
   Horseradish root, peeled

Remove the salsify pieces from the sous-vide bag and drain, reserving 290g of the liquid. Heat a little olive oil in a deep, non-stick pan and add the chicken oysters, skin-side down. Cook until golden and crispy. Set aside on kitchen paper.

In the same pan, sear the salsify pieces until caramelised. Set aside on kitchen paper.

Add the reserved vegetable braising liquid to the pan and reduce by a third over a moderate heat. Add the walnut-chicken vinaigrette and reduce it, whisking; you will notice the colour changing to a thickened, glossy golden sauce. It will yield about 270g.

Return the salsify to the pan to gently heat through, and set aside to keep warm.

Place the chicken oysters skin-side up in the walnut-chicken vinaigrette sauce, without fully submerging them, and allow them to heat though. Place the oysters on kitchen paper and season with salt and cracked black pepper.

Just before plating up, gently lower the bone marrow discs into the sauce to gently heat through, then remove. Sprinkle some fried breadcrumbs on to each disc.

To plate up, spread a thin layer of onion and horseradish fluid gel on to each plate, followed by 5 warm chicken oysters. Place 5–6 warm salsify pieces on to the plate and arrange the seasonal leaves on and around them. Gently add the bone marrow discs and spoon over the remaining walnut-chicken vinaigrette sauce. Season with salt and pepper and finish the dish with finely grated fresh horseradish.

HASH OF SNAILS

[1723]

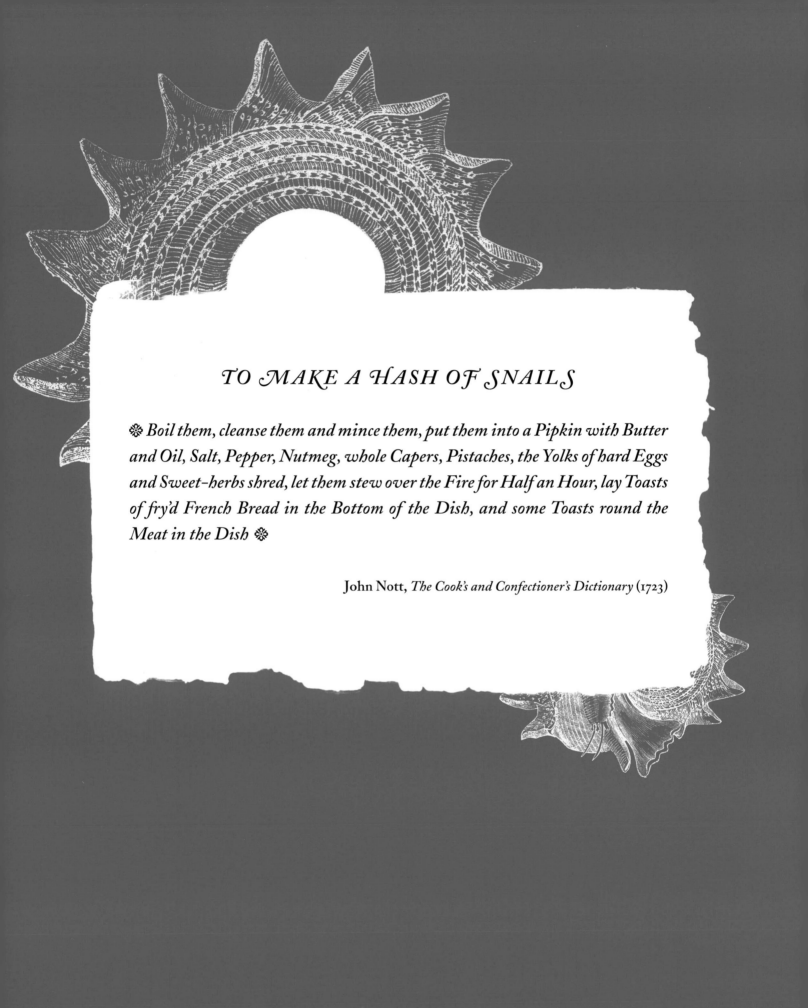

TO MAKE A HASH OF SNAILS

❈ *Boil them, cleanse them and mince them, put them into a Pipkin with Butter and Oil, Salt, Pepper, Nutmeg, whole Capers, Pistaches, the Yolks of hard Eggs and Sweet-herbs shred, let them stew over the Fire for Half an Hour, lay Toasts of fry'd French Bread in the Bottom of the Dish, and some Toasts round the Meat in the Dish* ❈

John Nott, *The Cook's and Confectioner's Dictionary* (1723)

Some food historians believe that the snail was one of the earliest animals to be bred for food—an activity that represents a significant step towards civilisation. From as far back as the Palaeolithic period (2.6 million–10,000 BC), there is evidence of mounds of discarded shells, and these often contained snails that were larger than modern-day varieties, which suggests that early man was already selecting for size. By the Mesolithic period (10,000–5000 BC) there are large shell middens (refuse heaps) of molluscs and gastropods from the Pacific shores of the Americas to Scandinavia, Spain and Scotland (at Kilmore and Lón Mór near Oban, for example). At Mesopotamian settlements inhabited by the Sumerians from around 4500 BC, snail shells are sufficiently plentiful to suggest that they were a major feature of their diet. The snail trail of archaeological evidence makes it possible that this little gastropod was one of the first farmed animals. After all, it's simple to cultivate—it comes neatly packaged in its own shell, feeds by grazing and is small and slow enough to be easily managed—and provides a nice piece of protein.

Despite these positive attributes, the snail has made surprisingly little impact on culinary history. For the Romans, they were a delicacy to be fattened on milk or wine-must and spelt until they no longer fitted in their shells, then fried in oil and served with *garum*, a sauce similar to the Thai condiment *nam pla*. But their enthusiasm has been shared by few others. Food historians have ferreted out early recipes for snails in sixteenth-century works by Diego Granado and Frantz de Rontzier, among others, but overall it's a thin legacy. Even in France, the gastropod's gastronomical success is a relatively recent phenomenon. There's a recipe called

Snails Known as Escargots in *The Goodman of Paris* (c. 1392–4), and they had a brief surge in popularity in the early sixteenth century, but they made few appearances in cookbooks over the following 400 years. There was a rustic tradition of cooking snails, particularly in areas such as Alsace and Lorraine that had no access to the coast and its bounty of seafood, but until the nineteenth century they remained a resolutely regional speciality. In 1815, no restaurant in Paris had snails on its menu.

Things started to change as brasserie culture developed in the French capital from the 1840s onwards. The word *brasserie* had been around since medieval times, originally meaning a place where beer was made, but in the mid-1800s it broadened to signify a restaurant where beer might be served. These places were often opened by Alsatians (since the area has a long beer-making tradition), who put their local cuisine, including snails, on the menu. French chefs turned this regional cookery into a series of extremely refined dishes, but even so, the attitude to snails was slow to change. It was rationing in World War II that finally prompted chefs to really explore the gastropod's potential, and turn it into a classic of French cuisine.

Although in Somerset snails are traditionally known as "wallfish" and served with butter and herbs, in general the British have been fiercely resistant to the idea of eating snails. In old English cookbooks, snails are more likely to be found among the remedies than the recipes, as they were considered a cure for consumption (W.M.'s *The Queen's Closet Opened* and E. Smith's *The Compleat Housewife* both have instructions for making snail water). So I was amazed to find a number of snail dishes in English cookbooks of the late seventeenth and early eighteenth centuries. Robert May's

The Accomplisht Cook contains nine recipes, including baked, fried and stewed snails. *The Country Housewife and Lady's Director* offers snails in white and in brown sauces. In *The Cook's and Confectioner's Dictionary*, as well as Hash of Snails, John Nott includes recipes for dressed and baked snails.

It's impossible now to determine exactly why English chefs dabbled briefly with such a recherché ingredient. Perhaps May worked alongside an Alsatian chef during his apprenticeship in France and they got talking about native dishes. Perhaps, since May and Nott were both exponents of court cookery, which was ambitious, creative and extravagant (see page 218), it was simply a case of professional chefs doing it because they could, and because they enjoyed pushing the boundaries. More prosaically, since eighteenth-century attitudes to plagiarism were very different from ours, and chefs shamelessly stole from one another, it may be that May's profusion of recipes caused a snowball effect, and that others adapted his ideas for their own books. Nott's instructions, for instance, are certainly very similar to May's. In the end, though, the reason didn't matter to me: I just found it exciting that there had been a tradition—albeit fleeting—of British chefs cooking with this now supposedly un-British ingredient. I wondered if they had met with the same sort of resistance that I did when I first put Snail Porridge on the menu at the Fat Duck.

One of the catalysts for Snail Porridge had been the discovery that, in a bunch of Nissen huts in Herefordshire, an ex-army photographer called Tony Vaughan was breeding snails of exceptional quality: large, succulent and beautifully textured. Over time I had worked out a method of braising them extremely slowly overnight, followed by a gentle herbal infusion. In short, I had access to a great product and I knew how to get the best from it, so when head chef Kevin Love and I began thinking about putting some new and slightly more unusual dishes on the Hind's Head menu, we decided to comb old cookbooks for snail recipes. Among them we found Nott's Hash of Snails, which stood out because it had an arresting title and a good list of ingredients to work with.

The cooking of the snails was already in the bag (quite literally: once the snails for this dish are cooked, they're placed in a water bath in a sous-vide bag for service). Like Nott, I normally cooked snails in butter, so I had already created a garlic butter that would suit this dish. And a little nifty word-shuffling of "toasts of fried *French* Bread" offered up the notion of using French toast, otherwise known as *pain perdu* or eggy bread, as the base for the dish. It needed, of course, to be savoury rather than sweet, and we tried out dozens of different breads before settling on a nicely acidic sourdough called a San Francisco, which was then brushed with an egg mixture that had the savoury tang of English mustard and malt vinegar. Grilling this until nicely striped with bar marks produced toast that was sharp, slightly eggy and had a lovely crust on it.

The foundations of the dish, then, were complete. It was now a question of building on top of this. Taking our cue from Nott's original instructions, we gradually isolated a set of ingredients that would complement my refined version of snails on toast. This dish needed a variety of contrasting textures, and I've learnt that snails benefit from quite high levels of acidity, so we put in caper berries, pickled walnuts, pickled pearl onions and crunchy deep-fried capers, along with thinly sliced fresh fennel (which goes beautifully with snails) in a walnut dressing. Nott included pistachios in his recipe, and I picked up on this because I once deliberately overcooked an egg-rich pistachio ice-cream mixture in order to demonstrate how important temperature control is to making ice cream. When I tasted the results, I discovered that, although what I'd done had completely the wrong texture for ice cream, the mixture was nonetheless delicious. So we spread pistachio paste on the eggy bread and added salt-and-vinegar pistachios to the garnish (these are whole shelled, peeled pistachios that are roasted, then seasoned with salt and pickled-walnut liquid while still in the pan) for a crunchy texture. Eventually, the preparation of the dish resolved itself into a neat production line, with each of the ingredients in its own little white pot. The chef simply works from one to the next, spreading pistachio paste on the toast, sprinkling on chives, placing the snails, and so on, finishing with a pinch of baby parsley and fennel leaves. It typifies the Hind's Head approach to cooking, which could be described as "technical simplicity": dishes that look simple on the plate, but in fact depend on many different ingredients and complex techniques.

HASH OF SNAILS

Makes 6 portions

Snails

30	Uncooked snails
15g	Peeled and diced carrot
15g	Rinsed and chopped leek
25g	Peeled and diced onion
10g	Rinsed and chopped celery
10g	Chopped fennel
2g	Peeled garlic
3g	Flatleaf parsley
2g	Thyme
2g	Rosemary
1	Bay leaf
2g	Black peppercorns

For the herb infusion

3g	Flatleaf parsley
2g	Thyme
2g	Rosemary

Preheat the oven to 120°c/250°f.

Rinse the snails under cold running water for 10 minutes. Place the snails, carrot, leek, onion, celery, fennel and garlic in a saucepan. Make a secure muslin parcel with the flatleaf parsley, thyme, rosemary, bay leaves and peppercorns, and place in the saucepan. Add enough cold water to cover the mixture and slowly bring to the boil, skimming off all scum and impurities.

Remove the saucepan from the heat and transfer the contents to an ovenproof dish. Make a cartouche and cover the mixture with it. Cover the dish with foil and carefully place it in the preheated oven for 8 hours to braise.

Once the snails are cooked, remove the dish from the oven and remove the foil, but leave on the cartouche. Allow the snails to cool to 80°c/176°f.

In the meantime, create a second secure muslin parcel with the infusion herbs.

Once the mixture has cooled to 80°c/176°f, add the infusion-herb parcel and allow to infuse for 30 minutes, with the cartouche still covering the mixture, then remove and discard both muslin parcels.

Once the mixture has cooled, strain it, reserving a small amount of liquid, and store the snails in a sealed container, along with the reserved liquid, in the fridge until needed.

Salt-and-Vinegar Pistachios

100g	Peeled pistachios
5g	Salt
15g	Pickled walnut juice (from a jar of pickled walnuts)

Preheat the oven to 170°c/340°f.

Spread the pistachios on a roasting tray and lightly toast them in the oven. Remove from the roasting tray and transfer to a large frying pan over a high heat, ensuring they are spread out evenly. Stir the nuts to allow them to release their oils. Add the salt and pickled walnut juice. Cook until all the juice has evaporated.

Remove from the heat and allow to cool on a tray lined with baking parchment.

Store in a sealed container until needed.

French Toast Mixture

125g	Whole milk
65g	Pasteurised egg white
30g	Pasteurised egg yolk
2g	Salt
15g	English mustard
10g	Undistilled malt vinegar

Combine all the ingredients and whisk until fully incorporated.

Store in the fridge until needed.

Garlic Butter

300g	Unsalted butter
30g	Peeled and roughly chopped garlic

Melt 50g of the butter in a saucepan over a gentle heat and add the garlic. Cook it, without allowing it to colour, until soft.

Transfer the garlic to a deep-sided container and blitz using a hand blender, adding the remaining butter gradually. Continue to blend until smooth.

Store in the fridge until needed.

Walnut Dressing

5g	Dijon mustard
75g	Grapeseed oil
40g	Walnut vinegar

Combine all the ingredients and whisk until fully incorporated.

Store in the fridge until needed.

Fried Capers

50g	Salted capers
250g	Grapeseed oil

Rinse the capers under cold running water to remove all traces of salt. Soak in a small bowl of cold water for 10 minutes, then drain. Heat the grapeseed oil in a small saucepan and fry the capers until they are crisp and have opened like a flower.

Drain the capers and reserve in a container. They should be prepared no more than 2 hours before using.

Garlic Snails

150g	Reserved garlic butter
30	Reserved snails
	Salt

Gently melt the garlic butter in a pan and add the snails. Keep the snails warm in the melted butter until ready to assemble. Season with salt.

To Serve

125g	Finely shaved fennel
	Reserved walnut dressing
150g	Reserved French toast mixture
6	Slices white sourdough bread, sliced 1cm thick
30g	Pistachio paste
6g	Chives, finely chopped
60g	Reserved salt-and-vinegar pistachios, roughly chopped
30	Reserved garlic snails
8	Pickled walnuts, cut into quarters
8	Pickled pearl onions, cut into quarters
8	Caper berries, cut into quarters
	Reserved fried capers
	Micro-parsley and micro-fennel fronds
	Cracked black pepper

Preheat the oven to the grill setting.

In a small bowl, combine the shaved fennel with a dash of walnut dressing. Set aside.

Spoon 25g French toast mixture on to each slice of bread, ensuring the crusts remain visible. Grill the bread on both sides until golden brown and crisp.

Remove the toasts from under the grill and spread 5g pistachio paste on to one side of each slice of toast. Sprinkle the chives on top of the pistachio paste, followed by 10g chopped salt-and-vinegar pistachios.

Remove the warm snails from the melted butter and arrange 5 snails on each dressed slice, followed by 5 each of the quartered walnuts, pickled onions and caper berries.

Top with the fried capers and arrange the shaved fennel on top of each toast.

Garnish with the micro-herbs and season with cracked black pepper.

EGGS IN VERJUICE

[1726]

EGGS IN VERJUICE

❀ *Beat them up well in a little Verjuice, season them with Salt and Nutmeg, and set them over the Fire with a little Butter: When they are come to the Thickness of Cream, serve them* ❀

Patrick Lamb, *Royal Cookery* (1726, 3rd edition)

The title of Patrick Lamb's book, *Royal Cookery*, is well justified. His father and grandfather had both been in service in the royal kitchens. Patrick himself took up a position as "younger child of the pastry" in 1662 and worked his way up the hierarchy to become first master cook of the king's kitchen in 1683, a position that he kept, bar a brief stint as second master cook during the reign of James II, until his death in 1709 (the first edition of his book was published posthumously a year later). Lamb, therefore, cooked at the top level for four English monarchs. "His Name and Character are so well known," declared the book's preface, "and establish'd in all the courts of *Christendom*, that I need observe no more of him, than that he liv'd and dy'd a very great Rarity, having maintained his Station at Court, and the Favour of his Prince, for about Fifty years together."

Lamb was, in effect, a brand name, and commercially minded publishers put out greatly altered and expanded versions of *Royal Cookery* in 1716 and 1726. Although these editions were still credited to Lamb, his contribution had been cut back and the bulk of the material was lifted from other sources, particularly the French chef François Massialot's *Le cuisinier roïal et bourgeois*, which came out in 1691 and was published in English as *The Court and Country Cook* in 1702. At the time, borrowing and butchery of recipes were common features of publishing, and the author's integrity was often compromised. Hannah Wolley was sufficiently incensed by a bogus work going out under her name that she composed a complaint in rhyming couplets (see page 176 footnote), and put it in her *Supplement to the Queen-like Closet* (1674). Lamb wasn't around to protect his interests, but in *Court Cookery* (1723) his colleague R. Smith (who's often thought to have been called Richard or Robert, but there's no definitive proof for either name) struck out: "several of those Receipts, as they are now printed in his *Royal Cookery*, were never made or practis'd by him; and others are extreme defective and imperfect, and made up of Ingredients unknown to him."

Nonetheless, it's still possible to get a feel for the kind of chef Lamb was, especially if you look at the 1710 edition. In contrast with the brevity of Eggs in Verjuice, his instructions are usually extremely detailed and his recipes extend to several pages. This is the work of a professional, for whom the appearance and presentation of dishes is extremely important. Interleaved among the recipes are fold-out sheets with diagrams of table settings for formal meals catered by Lamb, such as "King's Dinner at my Lord Ranelaugh's May 20, 1700" and "Queen's Dinner, February 6, 1704", which show that he thought of his cooking as a public performance and spectacle. His recipes are heavily indebted to the new French style of cuisine pioneered by La Varenne in *Le Cuisinier françois* (see page 338) and refined by Massialot. There's much less mixing of sweet and sour than in medieval, Tudor and even Stuart cookery, almost no use of sugar in savoury dishes, and the food is flavoured and garnished with fresh herbs rather than exotic spices such as cinnamon and nutmeg. Butter is used liberally, and lemons and capers often take the place of vinegar as the acidic component in a dish. Like Massialot, Lamb was particularly interested in spectacular dishes requiring a lot of luxury ingredients—especially meat—and complex processes that were only easily achievable in a professional kitchen. This style dominated cuisine and cookbooks from the mid-1600s to

the early 1700s and has since become known as court cookery; other practitioners included Charles Carter, Robert May, William Rabisha and R. Smith. It was unashamedly elitist: the preface to *Le cuisinier roïal et bourgeois* boasts that the meals it describes "have all been served not long ago at the Court, or at the tables of the Princes of persons of the first rank", and most of Massialot's British counterparts pushed their aristocratic connections just as hard; Charles Carter, for example, name-dropped a duke, an earl and a lord on the title page of *The Complete Practical Cook.*

The eighteenth century was, however, a period of rapid social change; court cookery, with its French bias and elitist slant, soon fell out of fashion. The wholesale "borrowing" that took place among cookbooks at the time meant that it continued to exert a significant influence on eighteenth-century cuisine, as chefs such as Vincent La Chapelle ransacked Massialot's work for their own. But from the 1730s onwards, popular taste was more inclined towards cookbooks with a practical domestic bent, and Lamb, Carter and R. Smith were eclipsed by Mary Kettilby, Hannah Glasse and E. Smith.

Patrick Lamb was far from my mind when I first began working on the recipe that eventually became Eggs in Verjuice. A number of Fat Duck dishes have their origins in unexpected or serendipitous situations; this one grew out of a dinner for which I was commissioned to devise a series of courses to accompany particular Italian wines. The dessert wine was a beautiful Moscadello di Montalcino, a version of white Muscat with apricot, honey and citrus characteristics, so we started working on a panna cotta flavoured with apple, honey, vanilla and citrus. Seeing the bright yellow of lemons alongside the bright white of a panna cotta mixture put me in mind of the yolk and white of an egg, and so that was the form the panna cotta took. We garnished the plate with shards of "eggshell" made from brown sugar and honey, and when the diner dug their spoon into the panna cotta, it revealed a yolk made from citrus fruits set with gelatine and thickened with a very small amount of guar gum. (Guar gum is sometimes the most viable option for creating a particular texture, but it has to be used sparingly, otherwise it can make the end result too gummy.) At this level, it was just a surreal bit of fun—after all, there was no good reason why a panna cotta should be made to look like an egg. The dish didn't have an internal logic. But by then the egg-as-dessert idea had taken hold of me, and I wanted to develop it further.

I've created fake fried eggs in the past with a mango purée yolk on top of a fromage blanc white, but this time I planned to go one better and serve what looked like an honest-to-goodness egg, still in its shell. What's more, I wanted the illusion to be sustained right up to the first mouthful, so the shell had to have just the right amount of brittleness as it was hit by the spoon, and the texture of the filling needed the viscosity of a perfectly cooked soft-boiled egg. That was the brief I outlined to my head chef at the Fat Duck, Jonny Lake, and the head pastry chef, Hideko Kawa, and we set about making it happen.

Perhaps the most difficult part of the development process was creating a shell that shattered exactly like the real thing. My first idea for this was mannitol, the sugar alcohol used to coat chewing gum pieces in a hard, shiny carapace. But although it looked the part,

it had a slight cooling effect, like menthol, that was too intrusive. Instead, I decided to try chocolate. Fashioning a shell out of chocolate is, of course, nothing new, but it's usually made thick enough to withstand a bit of handling. That was no good for this dish, because it would be too strong and pliable to break convincingly. For verisimilitude, we somehow had to make a shell that was robust enough to survive service, but also suitably fragile.

The solution we came up with was to create a shell with two layers to ensure structural integrity, one of which would be as thin as we could make it, so that overall the shell was still extremely fine. The outer layer was made simply by spraying a mould shaped like half an egg with a mixture of cocoa butter, milk chocolate and natural food colour to lighten it. Once this had set, a second, slightly thicker inner layer was created by pouring into the mould a blend of white chocolate, cocoa butter and natural food colour and turning it upside down to let the excess run off. This produced shells with the appropriate texture and density. All we had to do then was flash-freeze the eggs with a spray of liquid nitrogen to give them just the right degree of brittleness.

In order to maintain the illusion, it was essential to reproduce the pale brown of the outside of an egg shell and the pristine white of the inside, and we spent weeks working on different combinations of chocolate, cocoa and red, yellow and white food colours, mixing and remixing like an artist at their palette, until we'd achieved the precise shades. Close scrutiny of eggs, though, showed me there was another visual trick we had to pull off. The surface of an egg isn't a single, pure colour; it's speckled with little brown freckles, so we devised a first step of spraying the inside of the mould with a spritz of cocoa powder. This meant that, when we sprayed the first layer of chocolate into the moulds, it picked up little dark flecks on its outer surface, which gave it a realistic freckled appearance. This was an impression I intended to reinforce by placing the egg in a "nest" created either with some skilful sugarwork or with the kind of pastry used to make *kataifi*, the Greek sweetmeats that look a little like Shredded Wheat.

For the egg's yolk, we began experimenting with adding different percentages of gelatine to various mixtures of citrus juice, zest and purée, looking for the ideal viscosity. For the egg's white, I tried a creamy parfait, but it didn't end up sufficiently white-like, so I decided just to hide a little puck of it at the base of the egg, to provide a welcome texture and temperature contrast. I set about creating a white by refining my original vanilla panna cotta mixture, trying to make it as tremulously delicate as possible by reducing the amount of gelatine to the very smallest amount I could get away with. It was around this point, as I wrestled to perfect my egg, that I happened to read Lamb's recipe for Eggs in Verjuice.

Deriving from the French words *vert* (green) and *jus* (juice), verjuice is a condiment that dates back to the Middle Ages. It was originally developed as a way of using grapes that hadn't ripened by the end of the season, although crab apples soon came to be seen as a viable alternative. Either way, the fruit was allowed to ferment into a kind of mild vinegar and was used in much the same way: as a pickle, dressing or seasoning for all kinds of dishes. It was a common ingredient throughout the medieval, Tudor and Stuart periods, but by Lamb's time its role had largely been taken over by citrus fruits, and it had more or less disappeared from the British kitchen. Lamb's Eggs in Verjuice— essentially a kind of sour scrambled eggs—was therefore a curious anomaly.

The disappearance of verjuice is a shame, because it can play a useful role in the kitchen. Milder than vinegar, but more tart than lemon juice, it offers a particular sort of acidity that enhances certain dishes in ways that vinegar and lemon can't. I had been using a couple of varieties at the Fat Duck for years to bring balance to, for example, a grape marinade. But until Lamb's recipe flagged it up, I hadn't thought of verjuice for this dish. To the yolk I introduced an unusual verjuice with a distinctive sweetness; to the parfait, which was sweet enough already, I added a reduction of Verjus du Périgord, which has a sharper, more characteristically acidic profile. The effect was startlingly good. The dish had better balance, the texture was smoother and creamier, and the flavours had become richer and deeper. For most of the dishes in this book, the historical recipe provided a starting point of sorts for development. Lamb's recipe had performed a different function: it had helped my dish find its final form.

EGGS IN VERJUS (1726),
VERJUS IN EGG (2013)

Makes 6 portions

Chocolate Egg Shells

To create the freckle effect

10g	Cocoa powder
50g	Kirsch

Place the cocoa powder in a bowl, add the kirsch and mix well. Fill an atomiser with the mixture and spray it directly on to 12 silicone half-egg-shaped moulds. Reserve the mixture for use later when finishing the egg.

Set the moulds aside in a dry place and at room temperature to set completely.

To create the milk chocolate layer

200g	Milk chocolate
60g	Cocoa butter
0.6g	Red food colouring
0.8g	Yellow food colouring
2.2g	White food colouring

Preheat a water bath to 48°c/118°f.

Place the chocolate in a sous-vide bag and seal under full pressure. Place in a second sous-vide bag and seal again under full pressure. Place the chocolate bag in the water bath for 6 hours.

Preheat a second water bath to 55°c/131°f.

Place the cocoa butter in a sous-vide bag and seal under full pressure. Place in the second water bath and allow the cocoa butter to melt completely.

Remove the melted cocoa butter and place in a bowl. Add the 3 food colourings and use a hand blender to blend well. Remove the melted chocolate from the water bath and add to the bowl of coloured cocoa butter. Combine well.

To temper it, pour three-quarters of the warm, melted chocolate mixture on to a marble work surface. Agitate the mixture by scraping the chocolate back and forth along the surface until it thickens and reaches a temperature of 27°c/81°f. Return the mixture to the remaining chocolate and hold it at 32°c/90°f.

Pass through a fine-mesh sieve. Fill a spray gun with the chocolate mixture and spray it directly on to the freckle-marked egg moulds. Reserve the rest of the mixture for use later when finishing the egg.

Set the moulds aside in a dry place and at room temperature to set completely.

To create the white chocolate layer

600g	White chocolate
90g	Cocoa butter
6g	White food colouring

Preheat a water bath to 48°c/118°f.

Place the chocolate in a sous-vide bag and seal under full pressure. Place in a second sous-vide bag and seal again under full pressure. Place the chocolate bag in the water bath for 6 hours.

Preheat a second water bath to 55°c/131°f.

Place the cocoa butter in a sous-vide bag and seal under full pressure. Place in the second water bath and allow the cocoa butter to melt completely.

Remove the melted cocoa butter and place in a bowl. Add the white food colouring and use a hand blender to blend well. Remove the melted chocolate from the water bath and add to the cocoa butter. Combine well.

Temper the chocolate mixture, as before. Once the first layer has completely set, fill the egg moulds with the tempered white chocolate. Turn the moulds upside down and tap the sides to allow any excess chocolate to run off.

Turn the moulds back over and scrape off the excess chocolate by running a palette knife along the surface of the mould.

Turn the moulds upside down again and place on a tray lined with baking parchment. Scrape the moulds smooth and clean and place in the fridge for 10 minutes.

Carefully unmould the chocolate shells and place in a dry, sealed container at room temperature, not exceeding 20°c/68°f.

Citrus Reduction

50g	Orange juice
50g	Blood orange purée
50g	Mandarin purée
50g	Pink grapefruit purée
25g	Lemon purée

Place the juice and purées in a saucepan and heat gently to reduce to 45g.

Store in the fridge until needed.

Sterilised Egg Shells

1	Sterilising tablet
6	Small eggs

Prepare a bath with 2 litres water and the sterilising tablet. Set aside.

Using an egg cutter, gently trim the bottom of each egg and empty out the raw contents.

Under a gentle stream of running water, rinse out the shells, ensuring nothing remains inside. Be careful not to remove the membrane from inside the shell.

Carefully place each shell in the water for 30 minutes. Preheat the oven to 120°c/250°f.

Place the clean, sterilised egg shells on kitchen paper to drain well, then place them with the hole facing upwards on a tray and place in the oven for 5 minutes. Turn them upside down, with the hole facing downwards, and allow them to dry out completely in the oven for 35 more minutes.

Remove them from the oven and store in a dry, sealed container until needed.

Soaked Powdered Gelatine

10g   Powdered gelatine

Soak the powdered gelatine in a small bowl with 50g water. Set aside for use later.

Parfait for the Bottom of the Egg White

For the pâte à bombe

100g   Pasteurised egg yolk
100g   White caster sugar

Put the egg yolk in the bowl of a mixer and whisk it at medium speed. Place 25g water and the sugar in a small pan and cook until the temperature reaches 118°C/244°F.

Remove the syrup from the heat and gradually add it to the whisked yolk, continuing to whisk until the mixture has cooled, and is stiff in consistency.

For the parfait

20g   Reserved citrus reduction
90g   Verjus du Périgord
6g   Reserved soaked powdered gelatine
40g   Unsweetened Greek yoghurt
60g   Whipping cream
60g   Reserved pâte à bombe
10g   Curaçao triple sec

Warm the citrus reduction gently and set aside.

In a separate small saucepan, reduce the verjuice to 15g over a moderate heat. Add the warm citrus reduction and combine well. Remove from the heat and add the soaked powdered gelatine, ensuring it dissolves fully. Set aside.

Place the yoghurt and whipping cream in the bowl of a mixer and whip until soft peaks are formed. Place the pâte à bombe in a large, clean bowl and add the verjuice reduction mixture. Fold in the whipped yoghurt cream and the Curaçao triple sec. Spoon this mixture into a piping bag.

Place 3.7cm-diameter silicone hemisphere moulds on a tray. Pipe the parfait into the moulds, cover with clingfilm and place in the freezer.

Verjuice Egg Yolk

15g   Reserved citrus reduction
30g   Verjuice (preferably 8° Brix)
40g   Mandarin purée
4g   Fresh lemon juice
2g   Finely grated orange zest
2g   Finely grated lime zest
2g   Finely grated lemon zest
10g   Honey
0.7g   Guar gum
5g   Reserved soaked powdered gelatine
4g   Curaçao triple sec
3g   Campari
7g   Mead

In a small saucepan, warm the citrus reduction.

Place the verjuice, mandarin purée, lemon juice, all the zest and the honey into a bowl, along with the warm citrus reduction. Stir well to combine, then gradually whisk in the guar gum until well dissolved. Strain through a fine-mesh sieve.

Take a quarter of this mixture and heat gently in a small saucepan. Add the soaked powdered gelatine and mix gently until fully dissolved. Remove from the heat and return to the rest of the mixture. Add the Curaçao triple sec, Campari and mead, and stir well to combine fully.

Spoon into a piping bag and store in the fridge until needed.

Vanilla-Thyme Infusion

1   Vanilla pod
300g   Whipping cream
1   Coffee bean
3g   Lemon thyme

Preheat a water bath to 85°C/185°F.

Cut the vanilla pod in half and scrape out the seeds.

Bring the whipping cream to the boil in a saucepan and add the vanilla seeds and pod and coffee bean. Cover the pan with clingfilm, reduce the heat and simmer for 30 minutes over a very low heat.

After 30 minutes, twist the lemon thyme in your fingers to release the flavours and add to the saucepan. Allow to infuse for 30 more minutes.

Strain the mixture and place in a sous-vide bag. Seal and place in the fridge until needed.

Panna Cotta for the Top of the Egg White

250g   Reserved vanilla-thyme infusion
24g   Golden caster sugar
18g   Reserved soaked powdered gelatine
50g   Unsweetened Greek yoghurt
6   Reserved sterilised egg shells
        Reserved verjuice egg yolk

Place 125g of the vanilla-thyme infusion and the sugar in a saucepan and gently warm to 60°C/140°F. Stir in the soaked powdered gelatine and allow to dissolve completely. Remove from the heat.

Place the remaining vanilla-thyme infusion in a clean bowl along with the Greek yoghurt. Add the gelatine mixture and combine well.

Prop 6 empty sterilised egg shells, hole facing upwards, in empty silicone sphere moulds to keep them steady. Place the moulds on a tray.

Pour the panna cotta mixture into the egg shells and place in the fridge to set. Reserve the remaining mixture.

(continued overleaf)

Once the panna cotta in the eggs has set completely (approximately 2–3 hours), use a melon baller to scoop out a space in the white where the yolk will be added. Carefully pipe 8g of the verjuice egg yolk into each hollowed-out area.

Reheat the reserved panna cotta mixture to 24°C/75°F and spoon it into a piping bag. Pipe this on top of each egg to hide the yolk completely.

Place the tray of eggs in the fridge until ready to assemble.

Olive Oil Biscuits with Feuilletine

140g	Unsalted butter
125g	Golden caster sugar
220g	Plain flour
4g	Salt
1g	Vanilla powder
2g	Baking powder
60g	Egg yolk
50g	Extra virgin olive oil
90g	Feuilletine

Using the paddle attachment in a stand mixer, cream together the butter and sugar, then add the flour, salt, vanilla powder and baking powder. Add the egg yolk and olive oil and bring the dough together. Wrap in clingfilm and allow to rest in the fridge overnight.

Preheat the oven to 150°C/300°F.

Roll the dough to 2mm thick between 2 sheets of baking parchment and place in the freezer on a tray for 30 minutes. Place the dough on a baking sheet, peeling away the baking parchment at the same time. Sprinkle the feuilletine on it. Place in the oven and bake for 14 minutes, then remove.

Using a 6cm-diameter round cutter, cut out the biscuits, then return them to the oven to finish baking until golden in colour.

Allow to cool, then set aside in a sealed container until needed.

Kabosu Jelly

5.2g	Pectin jaune
120g	Fructose
240g	Kabosu juice
40g	Glucose
2.5g	Citric acid

Combine the pectin and fructose in a small bowl and set aside. Place 200g of the kabosu juice and the glucose into a saucepan. Add the pectin-fructose mixture and heat gently.

In the meantime, combine the citric acid and 20g kabosu juice in a small bowl and allow to dissolve.

Once the glucose mixture has reached 105°C/221°F, remove from the heat and whisk in the citric acid mixture. Combine well. Line a tray with baking parchment, pour the mixture on to the tray and place in the fridge.

Once the jelly has set, cut it into 1.5mm cubes and place in a small container. Add the remaining 20g kabosu juice to the cubes and mix well.

Store in the fridge until needed.

Kataifi Nests

15g	Icing sugar
15g	Honey
5g	Finely grated orange zest
15g	Fresh orange juice
5g	Lemon juice
1g	Orange blossom water
15g	Clarified butter, melted
25g	Kataifi pastry

Preheat a water bath to 70°C/158°F and the oven to 150°C/300°F.

Combine all the ingredients apart from the kataifi pastry in a bowl and stir well over the warm water bath. Add the kataifi and stir gently. Place the mixture in a sous-vide bag and seal. Place the bag in the water bath for 5 minutes.

In the meantime, line a baking tray with baking parchment.

Remove the contents of the bag. Break down the threads using your fingers, and shape the threads into round nest-like shapes, making a hole in the centre. The nests should be approximately 7.5cm in diameter. Place them on a baking tray.

Place the nests in the oven and bake for 10 minutes. Rotate the tray to ensure they are evenly baked and golden in colour. Allow to cool, then set aside in an airtight container until needed.

Honey Tuile Nests

30g	Golden caster sugar
27g	Golden syrup
30g	Honey
5g	Bicarbonate of soda
	Verjus du Périgord

Place the sugar, golden syrup, honey and 65g water in a saucepan and heat to 150°C/300°F. Add the bicarbonate of soda and a drop of verjuice, whisking continuously, and allow the mixture to foam.

Remove the saucepan from the heat and pour the foaming mixture on to a silicone mat. Use a palette knife to spread the mixture out evenly and remove any bubbles. It should be completely smooth.

Wearing gloves, stretch and fold this honey tuile mixture until it resembles a gold, shiny mass. Pull very small amounts into thin threads and make 6 nests.

Store in a sealed container with some silica gel until needed.

Candied Orange Zest

15g	Orange peel
50g	Golden caster sugar
15g	Honey

Ensure the orange peel contains no pith and finely slice it into 1mm julienne strips.

Bring a small saucepan of water to the boil and add the orange peel for 5 seconds. Refresh in iced water. Repeat with fresh boiling water.

In a separate saucepan, cook the sugar, 50g water, honey and blanched orange zest over a medium heat to 58° Brix.

Allow the zest to cool in the syrup and store in the fridge until needed.

Candied Lemon Zest

15g   **Lemon peel**
50g   **Golden caster sugar**
15g   **Honey**

Ensure the lemon peel contains no pith and finely slice it into 1mm julienne strips.

Bring a small saucepan with 50g water to the boil and add the lemon peel for 5 seconds. Refresh in iced water. Repeat this process with a fresh batch of boiling water.

In a separate saucepan, add the sugar, 50g water, honey and blanched lemon zest over a medium heat and cook to 58° Brix. Allow the zest to cool in this syrup and store in the fridge until needed.

Assembling the Eggs

12   **Reserved chocolate egg shell halves**
6   **Reserved filled sterilised egg shells**
6   **Reserved frozen parfait hemispheres**
100g   **Liquid nitrogen**
    Reserved coloured chocolate
    Reserved freckle effect spray

Place a metal baking tray in a warm oven and allow to warm gently, then remove.

Place the chocolate egg shell halves hollow-side down on to the warm tray to melt the edges slightly. Set aside. There should be 12 (to make 6).

Peel the real egg shells away from the set panna cotta and discard the shells. There should be at least 6.

Unmould the hemispheres of frozen parfait and carefully dip them briefly into a bowl of liquid nitrogen. Join them one at a time with the set panna cotta to create a whole egg shape. There should be at least 6. The frozen parfait will become the bottom element of the egg.

Place the newly created egg into one half of a chocolate egg shell and seal the shell with the other half, enclosing the egg completely.

Gently heat the reserved coloured chocolate mixture and carefully patch up the seal where the 2 halves of the egg shell joined. Use the reserved Kirsch-cocoa powder spray to finish the egg.

The eggs can be stored in silicone hemisphere moulds in the freezer while you are preparing them, and until ready to serve.

To Serve

6   **Reserved olive oil biscuits**
90g   **Reserved kabosu jelly cubes**
6   **Reserved kataifi nests**
18   **Reserved candied orange zest pieces**
18   **Reserved candied lemon zest pieces**
6   **Reserved honey tuile nests**
    Lemon thyme leaves
    Liquid nitrogen spray
6   **Reserved assembled eggs**

Place an olive oil biscuit in the centre of each dessert plate and arrange the kabosu jelly cubes around the biscuits.

Gently place a kataifi nest on top of each biscuit and position some pieces of candied orange and lemon zest within the nest so that they are still visible. Top with a honey tuile nest and garnish with lemon thyme leaves.

Just before serving, spray liquid nitrogen on to each egg and balance it very carefully on the nest.

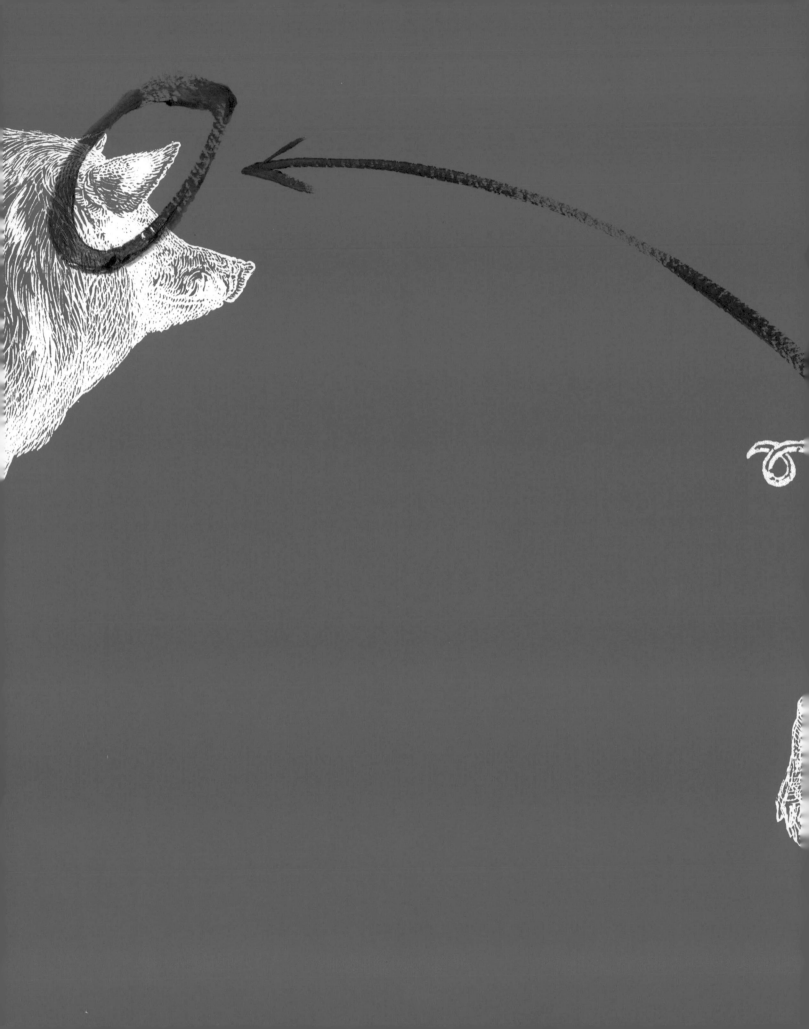

RAGOO OF PIGS' EARS

[1727]

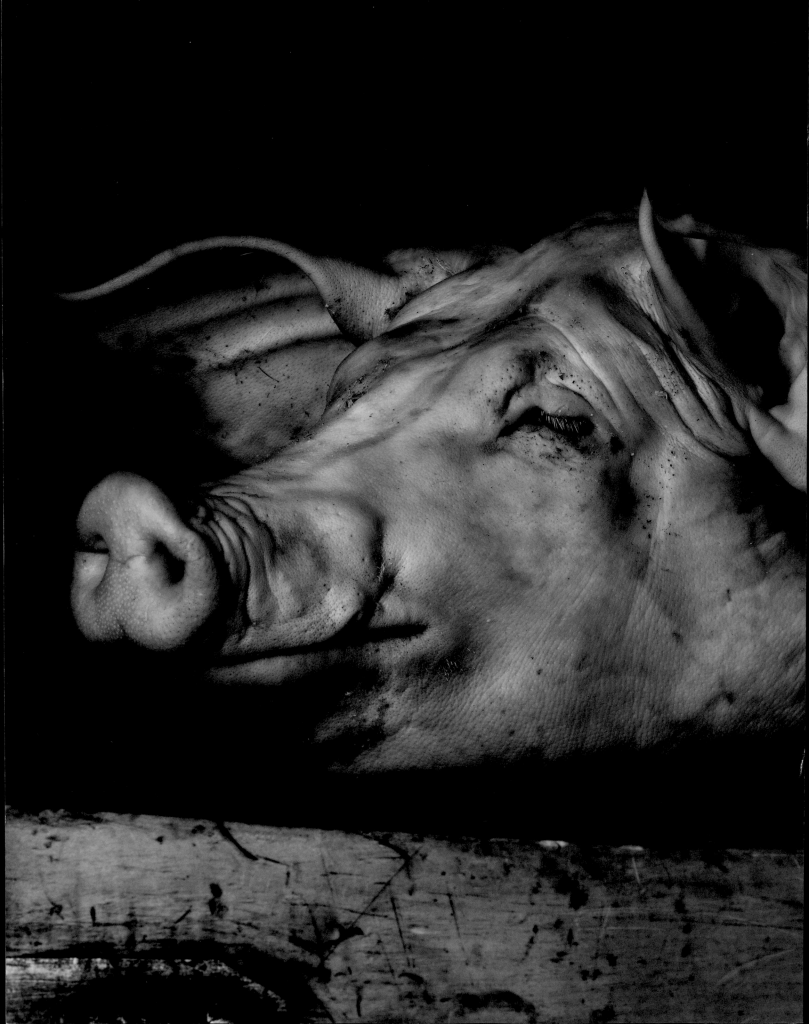

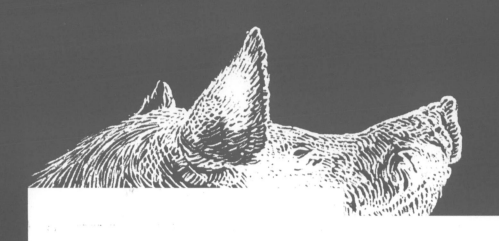

TO MAKE A RAGOO OF PIGS-EARS

❊ *Take a quantity of Pigs-Ears, and boil them in one half wine and the other water; cut them in small pieces, then brown a little butter and put them in, and a pretty deal of gravy, two anchovies, an eschalot or two, a little mustard, and some slices of lemon, some salt and nutmeg: stew all these together, and shake it up thick. Garnish the dish with barberries* ❊

E. Smith, *The Compleat Housewife* (1727)

In the Middle Ages, farming was a backbreaking scrabble for survival. Most peasants were serfs, bound to the lord of the manor and expected to devote much of their time to working his fields. Time free from this bondage was spent cultivating common land. Each villager would have a number of half-acre strips, situated in different parts of the village so that good and bad land was evenly distributed, from which to feed his family. There were fewer crops than nowadays, but barley, oats, rye and wheat were all grown, along with peas, beans and leeks. Some of this produce might go to the lord of the manor, and a tenth (the tithe) had to be handed over to the Church. A crude rotation system was in place to ensure the soil remained productive: somewhere between a third and half the land would at any one time lie fallow so that it could recover its fertility. During this period, England was still swathed in forest and roads were rudimentary. Each village was basically an enclosed community, largely dependent on its own resources. Little money changed hands; people bartered for what they needed and paid in kind.

In an environment like this, the pig was of immense value. Unlike other domestic animals, it needed neither a special diet nor special care. Hardy and well able to protect itself from predators, a pig could be left to roam the forest and forage for acorns and beechnuts. Come the winter months, when it was difficult and impractical to feed livestock, the pig was the ideal animal for slaughtering and preserving; its flesh responded better to salting than beef or mutton, which tended to become dry and tough. It was extremely economical, too, since almost all of the animal could be used—"everything but the squeal", as the saying goes. The meat was salted to make ham and bacon, the blood used in black puddings, the intestines turned into sausage casings. For many peasants, pork was the only fresh meat they ever got to eat, and once salted it was a vital part of the stored provender that would help them survive when food was scarce. The pig was such an intrinsic part of daily life in the Middle Ages that it crops up frequently in the art and literature of the period. *Piers Plowman* and *The Canterbury Tales* both make reference to pig-keeping (the poor widow of the Nun's Priest's Tale boasts of owning three large sows). Illustrated manuscripts, such as the Queen Mary Psalter and Luttrell Psalter, often feature the pig among their detailed observations of rural life, depicting swineherds swinging cudgels at oak trees to release a scatter of acorns for their charges snouting among roots; or standing, reaper-like, holding a vicious-looking axe that is poised to fall and fill the winter larder. One of the surprises of these pictures is how different the medieval pig is from the modern-day animal. Long-legged, razor-backed, bristly and prick-eared, it looks like a small wild boar.

The pig's importance reached its peak around the eleventh century and was on the wane by the 1300s. There are several reasons for this porcine decline. Many farmers had come to see pigs as a menace because if they found their way into the fields they could cause enormous damage to crops.* Pigs could also damage the surrounding forest and, as the market for wood and charcoal grew from the 1200s onwards, the amount of land available for animal foraging (known as pannage) shrank accordingly. The

The cute-looking nose ring beloved of children's book illustrators was in fact a restraining device: it had two sharp points that gripped the pig's nostrils, and if it shoved its snout into the earth, the points would cut into its nose.

pig's natural habitat was diminishing, and pig-keeping was no longer the cheap and easy practice it had once been. There was also perhaps a touch of snobbery involved in the pig's loss of popularity. Throughout history, food has been used as a mark of status, from the extravagant use of spices in the medieval period to the inevitable appearance of turtle soup on the menu at virtually any Victorian civic event (see page 403). Since pork was marked out as peasant food, it was largely eschewed by the well-to-do in favour of mutton or beef.

The single biggest reason for the fall from favour of the pig, however, was the rise of the sheep. Although it might not seem like much of an adversary, by the early sixteenth century Thomas More (who later became Lord Chancellor before being beheaded for his opposition to the Reformation and Henry VIII's divorce from Catherine of Aragon) was portraying the sheep as a symbolic monster in *Utopia* (1516): "Your sheep that were wont to be so meek and tame, and so small eaters, now, as I hear say, be become so great devourers and so wild, that they eat up and swallow down the very men themselves. They consume, destroy, and devour whole fields, houses and cities." Against such an opponent, the pig didn't stand a chance. Sheep eclipsed pigs in economic importance, and encroached on their habitat as, from the 1300s onwards, wool became big business.

Wool was the commodity that first brought significant wealth to England. It became the country's biggest export, and was transported across Europe, particularly to Flanders, where it was woven into fine cloth. Landowners weren't slow to spot the opportunity for profit, and many began to concentrate on keeping sheep, gradually transforming the country's approach to agriculture in the process. Estate owners started setting aside as much land as they could for sheep-grazing rather than cultivation, and once they'd reached the limit of their own lands, they simply took over other people's, forcing out tenants by raising rents, or fencing off common and waste land. These enclosures, as they became known, severely worsened the peasants' lot, shrinking the land where they could forage for or grow food, keep and feed pigs, geese and other animals, or collect firewood. (Fuel, essential for cooking and heating, was one of the biggest drains on a household budget.) The enclosures caused food shortages and unemployment, as sheep-herding required far fewer people than crop cultivation. In some cases, villages suffered economic collapse, dwindled and disappeared. Enclosures became a source of huge resentment and were a key issue in several of the most notorious uprisings in English history: the Peasants' Revolt in 1381, in which riots broke out in various parts of the country and mobs descended on London "like a pack of hungry wolves"; Jack Cade's Rebellion in 1450, in which 5,000 Kentish men stormed London, killing the Lord Treasurer and forcing King Henry VI to flee the city; Kett's Rebellion in 1549, in which some 16,000 protestors marched on Norwich and took it over; and the Captain Pouch Rebellion of 1607, in which several thousand protestors in Northamptonshire, Warwickshire and Leicestershire dug up hedges and filled in the moat-like ditches that enclosed the land.

Although wool prices had dropped by the 1650s, thus calming the zeal for sheep-grazing, by now the push by landowners and farmers to consolidate their land and farm it more efficiently had gained a momentum that proved impossible to stop. The process might have been socially divisive, but it also had a positive effect on growth and development. Before the 1700s, the English population had a critical mass of 5–6 million people; whenever it reached this figure, as had happened in the early fourteenth and the mid-seventeenth centuries, it stopped growing. In the mid-1700s it breached this barrier and thereafter continued to expand rapidly. In many ways, this population explosion marked the end of the medieval way of life and the beginnings of the modern age. The profits from farming had ushered in a wealthy class of entrepreneurs, and this, along with the task of feeding, housing and employing the masses, became one of the driving forces behind the agricultural and industrial revolutions of the eighteenth century. Certainly, in farming from the late 1600s onwards, there was what the agricultural historian Mark Overton calls an "ascending spiral of progress", most notably in farming methods.

One of the biggest influences on farm productivity was the development of the Norfolk Four-Course Rotation, which superseded the far less efficient two- and three-field crop-rotation systems that had been practised since Roman times. These outdated systems had required that a large part of the land lie fallow—an enormous waste of resources. With four-course rotation, the fields were sown with wheat, followed by turnips, barley and clover, and no fields lay bare. Turnips provided fodder for animals during the winter so they no longer had to be slaughtered in the autumn. Clover was not only an excellent grazing crop, but also "fixed" nitrogen in the soil, improving its fertility. In addition, the animals eating these crops produced a rich manure that could be used to improve the quality of farmland.

A similar process of appraisal was happening to livestock, too, through the efforts of men like Robert Bakewell (1725–95), who developed New Leicester sheep, Dishley Longhorn cattle and the forerunner of the Shire horse by careful breeding. Although pigs readily interbreed and have a high reproductive rate, Bakewell appears to have been less successful with them (in his 1805 *General Treatise on Cattle*, John Lawrence reported that locals didn't hold Bakewell's improvements in high esteem). Nevertheless, during the eighteenth century a number of farmers began cross-breeding British pigs with those from other countries, particularly Italy and China, hoping to come up with a more profitable porker. The problem with the native pig was that it took around two years to reach maturity and start putting on fat (which gives the meat flavour), making it costly to house and feed. Moreover, the long maturation led to a large-bodied pig with a high proportion of bone, so breeders geared their efforts towards producing a smaller, lighter-framed animal that matured quickly and fattened rapidly.

With the new pig shape came a new pig environment. The new breeds were less hardy than native pigs and their fattening-up had to be carefully managed, so they were put in sties and fed, rather than being allowed to forage freely for a naturally balanced diet. When large-scale commerce becomes involved, flavour often seems to drop down the list of priorities, and eighteenth-century pig-farming was no exception. In 1726, just a year before Smith's *Compleat Housewife* was published, the latest edition of the *Dictionarium Rusticum* (an encyclopaedic illustrated account of the tools and practices of rural life) declared that roaming pigs tasted superior. "Let them graze, and get what food they can," it advised. "Haws, Hips, Sloes, Crab, Mast, Acorns, etc, with which if you have plenty enough to fat them, their Flesh will prove much better than if fatten'd in a Stye."

Since England still had an agrarian economy, enclosures and the developments in farming methods had a gradual but decisive impact on the social order, too, and opened up opportunities for advancement. Land ownership, rather than nobility, became the key to success, wealth and status. Through careful investment and land management, even people of the middle rank could climb the ladder, and in the seventeenth century land purchases doubled and rents increased threefold as people scrambled for a foothold. The age of the country house had arrived, and it was now the landed gentry who, as a body, had the greatest influence on the country. Ambitious and socially competitive, this new group was in the market for cookbooks such as Hannah Wolley's *The Queen-like Closet* (see page 177), which showed them how to live and dine in appropriate style.

In the first half of the eighteenth century, this new style of cookbook grew into a recognisable genre through the works of E. Smith (about whom virtually nothing is known, including her first name—although many books give it as Eliza, there's no proof of this), Mary Kettilby, Elizabeth Moxon, Elizabeth Raffald and Hannah Glasse, whose *Art of Cookery Made Plain and Easy* of 1747 was the biggest seller of the period. The preface to Kettilby's *A Collection of Above Three Hundred Receipts in Cookery, Physick and Surgery* (1714) showed just how different these books were from their competitors, the cookbooks written by court-based professional male chefs such as Robert May, Charles Carter and William Rabisha. Unlike them, Kettilby saw her readership not as professionals, but:

Young and Unexperienc'd Dames, who may from hence be Instructed in the Polite Management of their Kitchins, and the Art of Adorning their Tables with a Splendid Frugality. Nor do I despair but the Use of it may descend into a Lower Form, and teach Cook-maids at Country Inns to serve us up a very agreeable Meal, from such Provisions as are the Plainest, and always at hand; instead of Spoiling those which are most Rare and Costly.

She cleverly anticipated the most significant developments in cooking during the eighteenth century: the middle class's interest in frugality and household economy; a growing respect for plain fare over fancy (i.e. French) food; and the move towards cooking being seen as a "below-stairs" occupation.

Although Kettilby and Smith assumed that the mistress of the house was still involved in culinary activities, albeit in a more advisory capacity than her Tudor counterpart, the shift away from the traditional model was already sufficiently advanced to provoke comment. "The great Fatigue, or rather Slavery, of House-keeping," wrote John Essex in *The Young Ladies Conduct* (1722) "is but too much neglected by Ladies of Fashion, as an Imployment … too mean and insignificant for Persons of their Quality; and rather fit for Women of inferior Rank and Condition." While Essex grumpily attributes this to laziness, other writers saw it more as a natural evolution of society, a view that suited a swelling and aspirational middle class keen to cement its status. Employing others to do menial work was an effective way of demonstrating wealth and breeding. The mistress of the house had abandoned the kitchen in favour of the parlour.

Cookbook writers noted the change and adapted accordingly. Hannah Glasse makes no reference to the country gentlewoman, dispenses with recipes for medicines, and her clear writing style and attention to detail—she gives specific weights and measures and explains culinary techniques—shows that *The Art of Cooking Made Plain and Easy* was intended above all as an instruction manual for servants. Her book was published only twenty years after Smith's *Compleat Housewife*, the other bestseller of the eighteenth century, but has a shift in emphasis that shows just how quickly and radically society was changing.

Ragoo of Pigs' Ears is a great name for a dish. It prompted an image of pigs' ears on toast, and I liked the idea. I also liked the fact that Smith's recipe was a perfect example of that eighteenth-century notion of "Splendid Frugality": making good use of a neglected part of the animal and teaming it with big flavours like anchovy, lemon, mustard and nutmeg. What's more, it felt like the right moment for such a dish to make a reappearance. Throughout my career as a chef, I've championed under-used cuts of meat such as calf's head, pig's cheek and onglet, otherwise known as beef skirt, which I think is one of the most flavourful parts of the animal. Until a few years ago, however, most people weren't up for it, especially the bits that reminded them of body parts, such as tongues, trotters and testicles. Now that has all started to change; the nose-to-tail philosophy is an aspect of traditional British cuisine that has been embraced enthusiastically by the restaurant-going public. I was pretty sure that pigs' ears would go down a treat.

Over the years, I have served pigs' ears in a number of ways. They first appeared on the Fat Duck menu some time ago, as a sauce to accompany a pork chop and little shepherd's pie made with andouillette sausage, potato, braised apples, Savora mustard and braised lettuce. For the sauce, I put carrots, onions and chopped pigs' ears in a tray, roasted them, deglazed the tray with white port and let that reduce, then filled the tray with water, let it all reduce once more and finished it off with some balsamic. The end result was wonderfully porky, jammy and sticky, and that's the route I wanted to go down with this new dish, too. The only question, really, was how to make sure the ears themselves had just the right texture.

It takes a long time to cook a pig's ear so that it breaks down and the flesh becomes soft, but I thought a pressure cooker could help me with that. The pressure cooker has become a standard feature at most of my restaurants because its ability to heat liquids to more than 100°C without allowing them to boil means it's a superb way to make stocks that are particularly clear and full of flavour (see page 342). This high temperature can also be used to cook an ingredient like pigs' ears significantly more quickly than in a pan, helping the flesh to soften up evenly. Ash and I started by putting a few ears in a pressure cooker with some carrots, onions and a little alcohol for 2½ hours. The results were slightly too soft for my liking but good enough to take a stage further. We spread them out to let the gelatine set, then sliced

them and browned them in a hot pan. It worked beautifully: the strips had acquired a lovely tagliatelle-like texture and had a fantastic savoury, meaty flavour. Now all we had to do was juggle the other flavourings to get the right balance.

Two of the main ingredients for achieving this were the same as Smith's—onions and lemon—but I had already developed both of these in particular ways. At Dinner we were pickling lemons by steeping them in a mixture of water, vinegar and caster sugar, and acidulating softened onions by adding white wine vinegar to them. We used both as seasonings to add touches of acidity and texture to a number of dishes. They contributed depth and complexity to this recipe, and introducing smoked onion as well would, I thought, take this even further. The end result was a dish with big, intense flavours that was nonetheless very simple to execute once the foundation elements had been prepared—it was barely more complicated than my original trial run. Get a pan hot, put the ears in to colour, add acidulated onions and sauce and reduce, then add anchovies, mustard and pickled lemons towards the end so that their fresh notes aren't destroyed by heat. Add parsley, check the seasoning and serve on lightly griddled bread.

The funny thing is that despite its simplicity, for some reason this is a dish that professional chefs love to eat when they come to Dinner— ironic when you consider that Smith's book represents a move away from the professional tradition towards a more domestic style of cuisine.

RAGOO OF PIGS' EARS

Makes 6 portions

Pigs' Ear Stock

1.4kg	Trimmed pigs' ears (approximately 13)
80g	Extra virgin olive oil
640g	Peeled and sliced onions
480g	Peeled and diced carrots
10g	Peeled and sliced garlic
320g	Madeira
480g	Red wine
5g	Rosemary
15g	Thyme

Using a blowtorch, carefully burn any fine hairs off the pigs' ears. Rinse the ears under cold running water for at least 15 minutes, and pat dry.

In a large pressure cooker, heat the olive oil, add the onions and carrots and cook them until they have softened and are just starting to caramelise. Add the sliced garlic and continue to cook for 5 more minutes.

Pour in the Madeira and red wine and reduce the liquid to a syrup. Add the pigs' ears, rosemary and thyme, as well as 5.6 litres cold water. Bring the stock up to a simmer while skimming off all scum and impurities. Secure the lid of the pressure cooker. Cook for 2 hours 30 minutes.

Allow the pressure cooker to depressurise before opening the lid. Let the stock cool to 30°C/86°F before removing the pigs' ears carefully and placing them on a flat tray. Cover the tray tightly with clingfilm and store the pigs' ears in the fridge until needed.

In the meantime, strain the stock through a fine-mesh sieve, followed by a fine-mesh filter bag. Chill the stock in the fridge overnight.

Remove and discard all the fat from the surface of the chilled stock. Heat the stock in a large saucepan and gently reduce to 10% of the original quantity, to yield approximately 540g reduced

pigs' ear stock. It is important to continue skimming the stock while it reduces.

Once the stock has reduced, pass it through a fine-mesh filter bag and refrigerate until needed.

Confit Cippolini Onions

9	Small cippolini onions
40g	Smoked duck fat (see page 182)

Preheat a water bath to 85°C/185°F.

Before peeling the onions, soak them in a small bowl of warm water for 5 minutes. Then, using a paring knife, carefully peel them, removing as little of the root as possible and retaining the point at the top of the onion.

Place the peeled onions, along with the smoked duck fat, in a small sous-vide bag, ensuring that the onions are lying flat and in a single layer. Seal under full pressure.

Place the sous-vide bag in the water bath for approximately 1 hour, or until the onions are completely soft.

Refrigerate until needed.

Low-Acid Onions

500g	Peeled onions
60g	Unsalted butter
15g	Chardonnay vinegar
1g	Salt

Slice the onions to a 4mm thickness in the root-to-tip direction.

In a large pan over a medium heat, melt the butter and add the sliced onions. Cover the onions with a cartouche. Check the onions every 5 minutes to make sure they are sweating, not browning.

After approximately 15–20 minutes, remove the cartouche and continue to cook the onions gently for 5 more

minutes. They are done when they still have a slight bite to them. It is important that they retain their shape.

Remove the pan from the heat and immediately add the vinegar and salt, stirring to combine.

Refrigerate until required.

Pigs' Ear Sauce

540g	Reserved pigs' ear stock
15g	Red wine vinegar
2g	Thyme
2g	Black peppercorns
1	Bay leaf

Heat the reduced pigs' ear stock to 80°C/176°F.

Immediately remove from the heat and add the red wine vinegar, thyme, peppercorns and bay leaf. Allow the ingredients to infuse for 10 minutes before passing through a fine-mesh filter bag.

Refrigerate until needed.

Crispy Pigs' Ear Strips

2	Eggs
7g	Dijon mustard
100g	Plain flour
200g	Japanese breadcrumbs
250g	Reserved cooked pigs' ears (from making the stock)
450g	Grapeseed oil
	Salt

Whisk the together the eggs and mustard in a small bowl. Place the flour in a second small bowl and the Japanese breadcrumbs in a third bowl.

Slice the pigs' ears into thin strips and toss them in the flour, dusting off any excess. Place them in the egg wash and shake off the excess egg. Finally, roll the strips of pigs' ear in the breadcrumbs and gently press the crumbs into the flesh. Shake off any excess crumbs.

In the meantime, heat the oil in a small saucepan. Once the oil has reached 180°c/350°f, gently lower the coated pigs' ears into the hot oil and fry until golden. Remove with a slotted spoon and drain on kitchen paper.

Season with salt and set aside.

To Serve

100g	**Herb oil (see page 65)**
6	**Slices sourdough bread**
9	**Reserved confit cippolini onions, sliced in half**
540g	**Reserved cooked pigs' ears (from making the stock)**
60g	**Extra virgin olive oil**
240g	**Reserved low-acid onions**
500g	**Reserved pigs' ear sauce**
25g	**Finely diced anchovy fillets**
45g	**Wholegrain mustard**
40g	**Strained pickled lemon (see page 279), finely chopped**
	Salt and pepper
	Reserved crispy pigs' ear strips
20g	**Flatleaf parsley**
30	**Rocket leaves**

Preheat the oven to 180°c/350°f.

Remove the herb oil from the fridge and allow it to come to room temperature. Strain before using.

Trim the 6 slices of bread into 12 x 4cm rectangles. Brush with the herb oil and char both sides on a hot griddle. Finish toasting the slices in the oven.

Heat a small non-stick pan and place the onions flat-side down. Grill to a golden colour. Set aside.

Slice the cooked pigs' ears into 5mm strips. Heat the olive oil in a large non-stick pan and add the strips of pigs' ears. Fry the strips, ensuring a golden crust is formed. Add the low-acid onions and continue to fry. Add 300g of the pigs' ear sauce and gently reduce to a thick consistency.

To this mixture, add 15g of the diced anchovies, 30g of the wholegrain mustard and 30g of the chopped pickled lemon. Season with salt and pepper.

In the meantime, in a separate small saucepan, gently heat the remaining 200g pigs' ear sauce. Add the remaining 10g diced anchovies, 15g wholegrain mustard and 10g chopped pickled lemon. Season with salt and pepper.

Just before serving, finely chop the flatleaf parsley and stir 15g of it into the ragoo, and the remaining 5g into the small pan of additional sauce.

Add the cippolini onions to the small pan of additional sauce to gently warm through.

To serve, spoon some ragoo on top of each piece of toast and place the toast in the centre of a plate. Remove the onion halves from the saucepan of additional sauce, and place 3 halves on each serving.

Finish the dish by spooning the additional sauce over and around the toast. Garnish each serving with several crispy pigs' ear strips and the rocket leaves.

LEMON SALAD

[1730]

LEMON SALLAD, OR LEMON COMPORT

❀ Take the clearest and thickest Rind Lemons, cut them in Halves, and with a sharp-pointed Knife cut out the Pulp, but not too close to the Rind; then slice it round in long Rings into fair Water, and let it lie an Hour or two; then boil it in fair Water till pretty tender and then make a Syrup of half white Wine and half White-wine Vinegar, and boil it up into a Syrup with double-refin'd Sugar; Send it with other Sallad, that in the Middle, after it has lain four or five Days in the Syrup ❀

Charles Carter, *The Complete Practical Cook* (1730)

Historic recipes have many virtues, but lightness isn't generally one of them; bent on impressing their masters, professional chefs have often been drawn to something spectacular and substantial. So when I came across Charles Carter's recipe for lemon salad, I was instantly drawn to it. Consisting of lemons cut into rings and lightly pickled, it promised to be simple, cleansing and refreshing. I could already picture several dishes in which that little burst of acidity would balance perfectly the richness of other ingredients.

The drive towards simpler cuisine was characteristic of eighteenth-century cooking, and was in sharp contrast to the culinary habits of the 1600s. The Stuart kings, taking their cue from the French court (Charles II had spent much of his exile there while Cromwell and the Puritans ruled England), had developed a taste for the flamboyant showmanship of the Baroque style, and patronised artists such as Rubens, Wren, Lely and van Dyck. Their meals were shaped by the same aesthetic, their tables piled high with fancy fricassées, fried meats, often served with a thick sauce called a "cullis" (a severely reduced stock that required dozens of ingredients and man-hours to prepare), and dense ragouts garnished with cockscombs and truffles. By the 1700s, however, chefs had started to move away from such profusion, choosing to use fewer ingredients and make lighter sauces.

Charles Carter's lemon salad, or compote, is such a confident and refined example of this approach that you might assume *The Complete Practical Cook* (1730) was at the cutting edge of the latest trend in cooking. In fact, Carter's book belongs to the end of the older tradition rather than the start of a new one. Like Robert May and Patrick Lamb, Carter was a professional cook with impressive credentials, including employment in embassies in Berlin, Hanover, the Hague and Spain. Having been "Latcly Cook to his Grace the Duke of Argylle, the Earl of Pontefract, and the Lord Cornwallis, &c.", his book is designed chiefly "for the more Grand and Sumptuous Manner of Entertainments". In other words, this is high-end stuff and a typical example of the court-cookery tradition—a serious cookbook by a serious chef, aimed largely at other professionals. Unfortunately *The Complete Practical Cook* wasn't a commercial success, probably because by the time it was published popular taste had moved towards a more domestic style of cookbook by authors like Mary Kettilby, Elizabeth Moxon, Elizabeth Raffald and Hannah Glasse (see page 261).

This shift in interest was the result of the fundamental changes taking place at the time in England (or rather Great Britain, since England and Scotland were joined together by the Act of Union in 1707). The fact that parliament had invited William of Orange to take the throne in place of King James II—that he was, in effect, its nominee—shows how the balance of power had tipped in its favour, and members set about consolidating their position, setting limits on the king's powers, formalising the rights of parliament and excluding Catholics from ascension to the throne. (Parliament had had to sort out two messy successions in thirty years, first Charles II and now William III, and it was determined not to have to do so again.) By the time of the Georges (George I acceded in 1714), the level of the king's influence was in part dependent on which politicians he sided with. Increasingly, the public perceived power to be in the hands of parliament as much as of the king. So, whereas in the 1640s the question was whether you were for the Roundheads or the Cavaliers, people now identified with a political grouping instead: either the Whigs (who were liberal, anti-Catholic advocates of a constitutional monarch) or the more reactionary Tories.

The accession of William III (formerly William of Orange) in 1689 had many repercussions for the country and, in unexpected but far-reaching ways, its cuisine. For the next twenty-five years, the country was almost continually at war with France, first in the Nine Years War (1689–97) and then the War of the Spanish Succession (1701–13). These wars led to the development of the biggest and strongest navy in Europe (which would be the foundation for Britain's trade supremacy in the eighteenth and nineteenth centuries) and the treaties that ended them increased Britain's colonial reach. The wars also fostered an anti-French sentiment that found expression in food and, once it had taken root, became a defining characteristic of the British attitude to cuisine. Plain food became somehow patriotic. By the 1730s, the opening paragraphs of a cookbook were almost bound to contain a dig at French cooking, even if many of its recipes were directly inspired by it. In *The Compleat City and Country Cook* (the 1732 revision of *The Complete Practical Cook*), Charles Carter is at pains to explain that he gives "not Directions so much for Foreign Dishes but those we have at home; and indeed we have no need of them" and goes on to declare that "Some of our Nobility and Gentry have been too much attach'd to French Customs and French Cookery." This may seem dismissive enough, but it's nothing compared to Hannah Glasse's rant in *The Art of Cookery Made Plain and Easy*: "if gentleman will have French Cooks, they must pay for French tricks," she warns. "So much is the blind folly of this age that they would rather be impos'd on by a French Booby than give encouragement to a

good English Cook!" Our national mistrust of funny, fussy, fancy French cooking, which has perhaps now diminished but was certainly still prevalent when I was growing up in the 1970s, has its origins in the early 1700s.

By the time George II became king in 1727, the Whigs, led by the skilfully manipulative Robert Walpole, had managed to make Britain's economy aggressively competitive and profit-conscious. The upsurge in wealth filled the pockets of the aristocracy, but there were now other social groups that stood to benefit, such as the gentry, whose income derived from their estates and investment in fledgling industries or overseas trading ventures. This energetic pursuit of business required a huge financial, military and administrative framework: in the thirty years after 1689, the Bank of England was created, the army increased from 20,000 to 120,000 men, and the civil service trebled in size, all of which made social and financial advancement possible for a much broader cross-section of society.

Naturally, meals offered a great opportunity for people to exhibit their sudden access to wealth. Dining tables were populated with ornate tableware, such as doilies, damask napkins, epergnes and glasses of the lead crystal recently invented by George Ravenscroft. There was also a craze for fine Meissen china (invented in 1708 and soon to acquire one of the very first trademarks: a pair of crossed swords). For an increasingly large part of society, eating was now a highly ritualised way to show off one's taste and elevated status, and, not surprisingly, many of the newly well-to-do needed advice on the right way to deal with culinary dilemmas (presumably such as whether to employ a French Booby or a good English cook). They wanted to know what food to serve, and how to cook and present it—hence the growing appetite for detailed, patiently explained books like those of Hannah Glasse and Elizabeth Raffald.

Food preservation is an ancient practice. People have been letting grapes ferment to make wine since at least 6000 BC, and packing meat in salt since the Iron Age. Because of its perishability, fish—especially those such as mackerel, whose oiliness makes them liable to spoil quickly—has long been subjected to air-drying, salting and smoking. The ancient Egyptians exported dried, salted fish to Syria and Palestine, and there is archaeological evidence of smokehouses in Sumeria from around the same time. Nowadays these techniques are seen simply as useful tools in the cook's arsenal, more a way of changing the essential character of a foodstuff than a method of preservation, but for centuries they were an essential culinary activity. During the Middle Ages in particular there was limited fresh food available in winter, and even the rich subsisted partly on what had been stored. In the absence of refrigeration, this meant a variety of salted, smoked and pickled meat, fish and vegetables. Despite advances in husbandry and cultivation by the 1600s, the need for food with a long shelf-life that would see people through the lean months of the year remained. Preservation was still a vital tool in cooks' repertoires, but by then they had made a virtue of necessity, and pickled not just vegetables but herbs, mushrooms, nuts and flowers for salads, garnishes and as a flavouring for stews. By the eighteenth century, pickling had become a popular activity among the gentry, stimulated, I imagine, by excitement about new and improved produce,

and by discovering Asian condiments such as ketchup and piccalilli, which were beginning to make their way to Britain through the growing trade connections with India and the Far East (see page 353). Cookbooks picked up on this, and included plenty of recipes for all sorts of pickled ingredients. Few of these, though, have the pared-down elegance of Charles Carter's lightly pickled lemon salad.

At its heart, pickling is a very simple technique, and in essence my recipe is very similar to Carter's. Like him, I cut up lemons and let them steep in a solution of sugar and vinegar for a few days, although I use water in the pickling liquor rather than wine, as wine tends to alter the flavour too much. Carter's half-and-half mixture of the liquid ingredients seemed a little rough-and-ready, and he gives no indication of how much sugar to use, so I had to play around with ratios of vinegar, sugar and water until I'd got a balance I was happy with. But this was just foot-slogging, the daily grind of any development kitchen: juggling percentages of ingredients in tiny increments, then tasting the results to see what difference it made. Then doing it again. And again. It was laborious, but I knew that as long as I was patient and methodical I'd eventually hit upon what I had in mind. There were other areas, however, where I intended to use modern technology to improve on Carter's original recipe.

For a start, Carter's choice of fruit would have been governed as much by availability as by desirability. We now take it for granted that we can pretty much get whatever ingredient we want, when we want it. By the 1700s, lemons were a lot cheaper and easier to obtain than they had been a few centuries earlier (in the thirteenth century, citrus fruit was so rare in England that, when a Spanish ship with fifteen lemons and seven oranges among its cargo landed in Portsmouth in 1289, Edward I's wife, Queen Eleanor of Castile, snaffled the lot), but Carter would nonetheless have had a limited selection to choose from. I, on the other hand, was able to order what are widely regarded as the best lemons in the world: those from Amalfi, in the Campania region of Italy. You can eat an Amalfi lemon just as you would an orange; even the skin is edible. If a scientist were trying to dream up the perfect pickling lemon, he'd have

difficulty topping the Amalfi. It has a good, thick rind, which is what contains much of the fruit's fragrance, but its pith is far less bitter than most other types of lemon, which results in a lovely balance of fragrance, fruitiness, bitterness and acidity. By precision-slicing Amalfi lemons on a mandolin and adding them to a pickling liquor, I hoped to get a harmonic mixture of sweetness, sourness and aroma.

There was a sophisticated piece of technology that was going to help me with that: the chamber

vacuum sealer used in sous-vide cooking (see page 76).※ If you put a fruit or vegetable in a sous-vide bag and suck out the air, the bag crumples inwards and moulds itself tightly around the foodstuff, exerting pressure upon it. This pressure crushes and compacts the cells, causing the juice they contain to mingle, which concentrates the flavour and heightens the colour. So I sealed the lemon slices and pickling juice in a sous-vide bag and let them steep together. The results were amazing; it added depth and really integrated the flavours.

The restrained, balanced acidity and fragrance of the salad meant it was an ideal partner for almost any ingredient that needs a

※ *It's just possible that Carter was aware of the vacuum pump. The first one was invented by Otto von Guericke in 1654 and the technology was then refined by two of Britain's greatest scientists, Robert Boyle and Robert Hooke. Even so, he could hardly have anticipated its role in cooking, which only really became apparent 10–15 years ago, when a number of chefs around the world, including me, started exploring its potential. I'd like to think, though, that if Carter saw the effect a vacuum-packer has on certain fruit and vegetables, he'd be saying, "I want one of those."*

boost of fresh natural flavour and something to counterbalance its richness. Oily mackerel was, I felt, a natural candidate for this, particularly since it meant I'd have an opportunity to use a couple of wonderful fish techniques I'd perfected: salt-curing and hay-smoking. I first read about smoking in hay in a book of traditional recipes from Burgundy. In the early days at the Fat Duck I used to wet hay, set light to it, then pack the charred remains around a leg of lamb before putting it in a salt crust and baking it, which added a wonderful farmyard flavour to the meat. Later I did something similar with calves' sweetbreads, and served them with chicken roasting juices and cockles. I took the step of adapting the technique to fish while I was researching how to make a fish pie that had a good variety of textures and a nicely distinct set of flavours, rather than the usual nondescript hodgepodge. Following up a hint in Alan Davidson's book *North Atlantic Seafood*, I experimented with packing halibut fillets in hay,

placing them in a squirrel cage trap and putting the whole caboodle on a portable barbecue. It produced great results: because the hay burned up in seconds, it imparted a much more delicate smokiness than a long, slow smoking over wood would have done. (I've got to admit, too, that I'm drawn to the speed and drama of it all. The *whoomph!* as the hay catches and flames billow out is enough to satisfy the pyromaniac lurking inside every chef.) Since then, I've used it to smoke a variety of fish, including mackerel. The process is so quick that the heat of the flames doesn't have time to cook the fish, so the flesh has to be tenderised either by cooking or curing.

Curing seemed to me an appropriate way of treating the fish. Not only would it give it a good firm texture and retain fresh characteristics of the mackerel that would be altered by cooking, but it would also mean that the dish combined three of the oldest forms of preservation: salting, smoking and pickling. There was a pleasing symmetry to it all that I liked.

HAY-SMOKED MACKEREL, LEMON SALAD & GENTLEMAN'S RELISH

Makes 6 portions

Pickled Lemons

350g	Chardonnay vinegar
165g	Golden caster sugar
6	Amalfi lemons

In a saucepan, gently heat 500g water and the vinegar. Add the sugar. Once all the sugar has melted, remove the saucepan from the heat and allow the mixture to cool completely.

In the meantime, slice the lemons widthways to make circular cross-sections, using a mandolin set to a 1.5mm thickness. Carefully ensure all pips are discarded.

Place the cooled pickling juice and lemons in a sous-vide bag. Seal under full pressure and refrigerate. Keep in the fridge for 48 hours before using.

Hay-smoked Mackerel

15g	Coriander seeds
2g	Black peppercorns
35g	White caster sugar
125g	Sea salt flakes
25g	Lemon zest
25g	Lime zest
3	Whole mackerel, filleted and v-boned
500g	Meadow-fresh hay
	Grapeseed oil

Heat a dry pan and toast the coriander seeds and black peppercorns until fragrant. Set aside to cool, then lightly crush with a pestle and mortar.

In a bowl, combine the crushed aromatics, sugar, salt, lemon zest and lime zest. Spread the cure evenly on to a tray.

Trim the mackerel fillets and carefully ensure all pin bones have been removed. Place the 6 mackerel fillets flesh-side down on to the cure. Cover the tray in clingfilm and place it in the fridge for 2 hours 30 minutes. Rinse the fillets under cold water and pat dry.

At the restaurant, we use a smoker, but you can achieve good results using a fish-grilling clamp. Wrap the mackerel in damp muslin. Place a layer of hay in a fish-grilling clamp and place the wrapped mackerel fillets on top in a single layer. Cover the fillets with more hay and close the clamp.

It is best to complete the next part outdoors. Using a blowtorch, ignite the hay, and then place the clamp on a tray and allow the flames to die out. Remove fillets from the muslin.

Once indoors, wipe a non-stick pan with a small amount of grapeseed oil and place over a moderate heat. One at a time, place the mackerel fillets skin-side down into the pan and press the fillets down gently, ensuring even pressure is applied. They need only remain in the hot pan for approximately 10–12 seconds, to allow the skin to break down slightly.

Remove from the heat and portion each fillet into 4 pieces, cutting at an attractive diagonal angle.

Refrigerate until needed.

Pickled Lemon Dressing

100g	Strained, pickled lemon juice reserved from pickled lemons
100g	Extra virgin olive oil

Place the lemon juice in a small bowl. Gradually whisk in the olive oil to emulsify.

Refrigerate until needed.

Lemon Mayonnaise

60g	Pasteurised egg yolk
30g	Dijon mustard
290g	Grapeseed oil
15g	Chardonnay vinegar
4g	Salt
40g	Lemon juice

Combine the egg yolk and mustard and pass the mixture through a sieve into a bowl. Gradually add the oil to the egg mixture, whisking to emulsify. Add the vinegar, salt and lemon juice and mix well.

Refrigerate until needed.

(continued overleaf)

Gentleman's Relish

150g	Peeled and de-germed garlic
1.5kg	Semi-skimmed milk
105g	Rinsed and drained anchovies
15g	Japanese breadcrumbs
85g	Extra virgin olive oil
30g	Lemon juice
90g	Reserved lemon mayonnaise (approximately)

Place the garlic in a small saucepan and add 300g milk and 1 tablespoon water. Bring the mixture slowly to a simmer, then remove from the heat. Pour the mixture into a sieve, discarding the milk. Rinse the garlic under cold water and return to the saucepan.

Repeat this process 3 more times.

Use the remaining 300g semi-skimmed milk to follow the same process as before, but this time allow the milk to continue to simmer gently until it has reduced to one-fifth of its original volume (approximately 65g).

Place the cooked garlic and reduced milk in a Thermomix and blitz on a high setting for approximately 3 minutes. Add the anchovies after 1 minute. It will be necessary to stop the Thermomix every 30 seconds to lift the lid and scrape down the sides of the jug. This will ensure an even and thorough blitzing of the mixture. Add the breadcrumbs and blitz at high speed for 1 more minute.

Reduce the speed setting and remove the plastic lid. Gradually add the olive oil and lemon juice until fully emulsified.

Pass the garlic and anchovy mixture through a fine-mesh sieve and weigh it. Add 30% of its weight in lemon mayonnaise (approximately 90g), and combine well.

Refrigerate until needed.

To Serve

Reserved gentleman's relish
Reserved hay-smoked mackerel pieces
Reserved pickled lemons, drained
Variety of seasonal leaves, including chicory
Reserved pickled lemon dressing

Place a spoonful of gentleman's relish on each of the 6 plates, and, using a palette knife, spread the mixture in a swipe across the plate, to create a beautiful, even layer of sauce.

Arrange 4 pieces of mackerel on each plate at different angles, followed by 3–4 pickled lemon pieces in and around the mackerel.

Place the various leaves in an attractive arrangement around the elements and complete the dish by drizzling with pickled lemon dressing.

BROTH OF LAMB

[1730]

POTTAGE OF LAMB'S HEADS

✽ Take two Lambs Heads, split one, and the other leave whole; cleanse them very well, then make a Hole in the Top of the Lamb's Head; take out the Brains, and set them with the others; then force the Head with a very light Forc'd-meat made of Sweetbread and Marrow, and well seasoned, but not too high; make some Forc'd-meat balls, very small ones; then take half Broth half Gravy, and stove it together with your Forc'd-meat Balls, and scald off some Cabbage Lettice whole; stove up the Lambs Heads in your Broth, and boil off the Appurtenances, and then mince them very fine; then toss them up in Broth, season them a little, and stove them, and at last put to them a little Cream; and then put French Manchet stoved in Gravy in the Bottom of your Dish, fill it up with your Soup, put in your Heads, lay on some quarter'd Lettice, but first put on your Coolio, and garnish with the Brains fry'd in Batter, poach'd Eggs, Slices of Bacon, and Lemon sliced, so serve it hot ✽

Charles Carter, *The Complete Practical Cook* (1730)

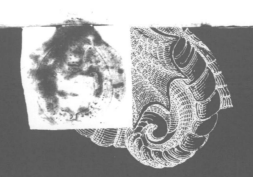

Lamb broth, cabbage, sweetbreads, marrow, poached egg—Charles Carter's recipe had a skilful combination of ingredients that offered a promising foundation for a modern dish for Dinner. Yet, as with so many chefs from previous centuries, he was tantalisingly brief about the parts he presumably considered common knowledge. The cooking liquor in the pottage was a key element, used both to braise the lamb and to provide the soup for the final dish, yet his "half Broth half Gravy" gave little guidance as to its composition. Fortunately, I had a pretty good idea of a cooking liquor that would fit the bill. I used to serve a lamb dish at the Fat Duck that was, in essence, a refined Lancashire hotpot that showcased several lamb preparations: sweetbreads, neck, rack, tongue, jelly, juices. To make the jelly, I pressure-cooked roasted bones, minced lamb shoulder, aromatic vegetables and herbs, then clarified the liquid to produce a consommé with a distinctive flavour: fragrantly sweet and intensely meaty. Ash and I decided to revisit this consommé to see if we could adapt it for Broth of Lamb.

What we came up with derives from two central principles of my cooking. The first is the use of Asian ingredients and techniques to enhance texture and flavour, heighten the sensory aspects of a dish and, in particular, accentuate the savoury umami taste, which can really add depth and complexity. The second is ensuring that the delicate aromatics hold on to all their fresh characteristics and subtle but fragile top notes. Heat is often the enemy in this endeavour: cook leeks for too long, for instance, and you lose some of their lovely fragrance, and get a slightly stewed, cooked-out flavour.

The main Asian ingredient we decided to use was *katsuobushi*: skipjack tuna—also known as bonito—that has been smoked, fermented and dried, then shaved into flakes. Although katsuobushi is still little known and relatively uncommon in the West, in Japan it's a supermarket staple because it's an essential component of *dashi*, the umami-rich stock that forms the basis of miso soup and many other Japanese dishes. Dashi is made by putting sheets of dried *kombu* (giant kelp) in water, which is taken to 60°C/140°F and held there for an hour, after which the kombu is taken out, the pan is taken off the heat and katsuobushi is added for a few seconds, then removed. Despite the brevity of this union, it has a dramatic impact on the dashi, rounding out the flavours and introducing a light smokiness and plenty of umami. So, since katsuobushi added to kombu water gives it an extra dimension, I reasoned that it could work well when added to a lamb stock.

The base of our lamb stock was lamb bones, lamb fat, aromatics and lamb shoulder (which seemed to me better than the head for producing a really tasty liquid). To further intensify its flavour, we chose to use the technique of cold infusion. Infusing is often done using a liquid that is at or near boiling point (your early-morning cuppa is a form of infusion), as this speeds up the process and extracts plenty of flavour. However, it achieves this at the expense of many of the most characterful but volatile molecules, which simply evaporate. The alternative is to submerge the flavourings in a warm or even cold liquid and let their aromas spread and mingle slowly, to produce a gentler infusion. Ash and I began trying out different aromatics that might add character to the stock by means of cold infusion.

Over time, we isolated a set of ingredients that complemented one another and had a decisive impact on the overall flavour, until eventually we had an elegant and effective series of carefully staged infusions. Once the katsuobushi (which needs the stimulus of 80°C/176°F) has done its work, the temperature of the lamb stock is dropped to a moderate 50°C/122°F, and ingredients are added according to how fragile or robust they are, and how much of their flavour needs to be imparted. First parsley and peppercorns, followed by delicate coriander, and, right at the end, rosemary, so you get just a hint of it.

Controlled heat is also the key to another central element of the dish: a celery fluid gel. I wanted celery to provide some of the keen, green, fresh notes in the dish, so we put finely sliced celery in the garnish, along with pickled baby onions, radishes and turnip dice for crunch, texture contrast and sudden bursts of flavour. I also added the micro-herb celery cress for fragrance. But I was keen for that celery note to pervade and complement the broth itself, and a technique that I'd developed at the Fat

Duck called a fluid gel seemed the best way to achieve this because it has great flavour release.

A fluid gel is essentially a refined purée created not by cooking something until it's soft and then blending it, but by juicing the ingredient and using a setting agent to solidify it slightly. The advantages of this are that, since heat hasn't been applied to it, the gel has a very fresh flavour profile, and since no starch-based ingredients have been used to thicken it, it's very clean in the mouth and the flavour comes through undiminished. I had been developing the technique using gellan, a setting agent that resists melting even at relatively high temperatures, making it suitable for dishes with warm ingredients (which would cause setting agents with a low melting point, such as gelatine, to liquefy). If I made a celery fluid gel with gellan, I could place little dollops of it in the bowl into which the lamb broth was to be poured. The two would intermingle but the gel would retain enough of its integrity to provide lovely little pockets of flavour and acidity.

Alongside these garnishes I put sweetbreads, much like the original recipe, although I chose to use veal sweetbreads, which have a luxuriant texture, rather than lamb, which can be dry. And, picking up on another cue from Carter's recipe, I decided that the visual centrepiece of my dish should be a slow-cooked hen's egg—plump, oval and bright white against the brown of the broth, sitting there almost daring you to cut into it. A slow-cooked egg is a real pleasure to eat: the yolk rich, the white delicate, the flavour particularly intense. But it's also a challenge to produce, consistently and in quantity, eggs with not just a runny yolk, but—and this is the hard part—a perfectly set white too. The technical difficulty comes down to the fact that there's no exact science to simmering an egg slowly in water. We tried out hundreds of different temperatures and times, charted the results and came to the conclusion that it was impossible to narrow the process down to one set of numbers that worked consistently. Even once we'd isolated a temperature range that set eggs to the desired consistency (ours was 60–65°C/140–149°F), that still left the question of how long to leave the eggs in for, since even very fresh ones from a reliable supplier (the eggs we use at Dinner are less than 36 hours old) respond differently according to the time of year. The variation isn't massive from day to day, but it is significant, and over a season the time it takes for an egg to be done when cooked at, say, 61°C/142°F, can gradually shift from 45 minutes to nearly 2 hours. So we had to create a system that would take these variables into account.

Thus, each morning at Dinner, part of the misc en-place involves lowering batches of eggs into a water bath set to 61°C/142°F (not too many at a time, as overcrowding will lower the temperature and skew the results). The chef will have noted when the eggs were ready the previous day and begins checking progress from five minutes before that time. So if yesterday's batch was perfectly cooked after 50 minutes, the chef will crack an egg open at 45 minutes to determine if the batch is ready or needs longer and proceed accordingly, cracking a second when it's expected to be ready, and so on. This constant monitoring and painstaking approach means each egg has the perfect set: that beautiful balance between tension and fluidity, so that, at the first touch of the knife, the white gives and gapes, allowing the yolk to ooze smoothly into the intense, umami-rich, deep brown lamb broth, turning it golden.

BROTH OF LAMB

Makes 6 portions

Lamb Stock

280g	White port
1.4kg	Chopped lamb bones
110g	Rendered lamb fat
2.3kg	Minced lamb shoulder
625g	Peeled and finely sliced onions
5g	Star anise
625g	Peeled and finely sliced carrots
140g	Finely sliced celery
190g	Finely sliced cleaned mushrooms
20g	Peeled and finely sliced garlic
950g	Sliced tomatoes
10g	Thyme
20g	Rosemary

Pour the white port into a saucepan over a moderate heat. Flame the mixture with a blowtorch and reduce to 140g.

Preheat the oven to 180°C/350°F.

Spread the lamb bones evenly in a roasting tray and roast them in the oven until golden brown, turning frequently.

In the meantime, heat a thin layer of rendered lamb fat in a large pressure cooker and caramelise the lamb mince in batches. Set aside.

Keep any remaining lamb fat in the pressure cooker and cook the onions and star anise until softened. Add the carrots, celery, mushrooms and garlic and cook for 5 more minutes, stirring regularly.

Add the reduced white port to the pressure cooker, followed by the roasted bones and caramelised mince. Add the juices from deglazing the roasting tray, followed by 3 litres cold water. Bring the stock to the boil, skimming off all scum and impurities.

Add the tomatoes, thyme and rosemary, and stir the mixture one last time before securing the lid of the pressure cooker. Cook for 2 hours.

Allow the pressure cooker to depressurise and the stock to cool slightly before opening the lid. Strain through a fine-mesh sieve, followed by a fine-mesh filter bag. Chill the stock in the fridge overnight.

Remove and discard all the fat from the surface of the chilled stock. Store in the fridge until needed.

Clarified Lamb Consommé

150g	Peeled sand carrots
115g	Button mushrooms, cleaned
15g	Flatleaf parsley
3g	Rosemary
3g	Thyme
350g	Egg white
3 litres	Lamb stock

Place the sand carrots in a food processor and blitz until very finely minced. Remove and set aside in a bowl. Blitz the mushrooms in the same way and add to the carrots. Roughly chop the herbs and add to the fine vegetable mixture.

In a separate bowl, whisk the egg white until soft peaks have formed. Set aside.

Place the lamb stock in a large saucepan and add the vegetable and herb mixture, as well as the egg white. Use a hand blender to blitz the stock until the whole mixture is fully emulsified. Bring the stock to a gentle simmer, stirring regularly to prevent it catching on the bottom of the pan.

As soon as the stock starts to simmer, reduce the heat and make a hole in the raft that will have formed. Allow to simmer for 1 hour, then check the stock for clarity.

Carefully scoop out the coagulated egg and vegetable mixture and discard. Ladle the clear stock out of the saucepan and pass through a fine-mesh filter bag.

Pour the strained, clarified consommé into a clean saucepan and reduce to 1kg over a gentle heat, skimming off all scum and impurities. Pass the clarified consommé through a fine-mesh filter bag and store in the fridge until needed.

Finished Consommé

1kg	Reduced lamb consommé
15g	Bonito flakes
8g	Flatleaf parsley
0.5g	Lightly crushed black peppercorns
20g	Coriander leaves
3g	Rosemary

Place the lamb consommé in a saucepan and heat to 80°C/176°F.

Remove the saucepan from the heat and add the bonito flakes. Allow to infuse for 5 minutes.

Pass the consommé through a fine-mesh filter bag and allow to cool to 50°C/122°F, before adding the parsley and crushed peppercorns. Cover with clingfilm and allow to infuse for 20 minutes.

Add the coriander leaves and infuse for a further 10 minutes. Add the rosemary and infuse for 5 minutes.

Pass the consommé through a fine-mesh sieve, followed by a fine-mesh filter bag, and store in the fridge until needed.

Pickled Onions

115g	Chardonnay vinegar
5g	Salt
5g	Sugar
6–8	Cippolini onions

Preheat the water bath to 85°C/185°F.

In a small saucepan, heat 60g water with the vinegar, salt and sugar until everything has dissolved. Remove from the heat and set aside to cool.

Before peeling the onions, soak them in a small bowl of warm water for 5 minutes. Then, using a paring knife, carefully peel them, removing as little of the root as possible and keeping the point at the top of the onion.

Place the peeled onions and cooled pickling liquid in a small sous-vide bag, ensuring that the onions are lying flat and in a single layer. Seal under full pressure.

Place the sous-vide bag in the water bath to cook for approximately 1 hour, or until the onions are soft all the way through. Plunge the bags in iced water to stop further cooking, then store them in the fridge until required. Pickle for 24 hours before using them.

Slow-cooked Hen's Eggs

6–9	Fresh medium hen's eggs

Preheat a water bath to 61°C/142°F.

Slowly lower the eggs into the water bath and cook for 1 hour, checking on them after 50 minutes, as the cooking time may vary according to the eggs' freshness. Only 6 eggs are required, but it is a good idea to have several extras to test the cooking time.

Once cooked, remove them from the water bath and gently plunge them into an ice bath to stop further cooking.

Store the eggs in the fridge until needed.

Celery Fluid Gel

880g	Celery stalks
45g	Chardonnay vinegar
7g	Golden caster sugar
2g	Salt
5g	Gellan F (low-acyl gellan)

Place the washed celery stalks into a juicer. Pass the juice through a fine-mesh filter bag and set 500g juice aside.

Bring the vinegar and sugar to the boil in a small saucepan, just until the sugar dissolves. Set the mixture aside to cool fully.

Place the celery juice and salt in the Thermomix and bring to 90°C/194°F on a medium setting. Add the gellan F and blitz for 10 seconds at high speed. Lift the lid and scrape down the sides of the jug. Blitz for 1 more minute to ensure the gellan has completely dissolved. Pour the mixture into a large bowl and place the bowl in iced water. Allow to cool completely.

Place the set gel, along with the cooled vinegar and sugar mixture, in a clean Thermomix. Blitz for 1 minute, then lift the lid and scrape down the sides of the jug. Continue to blitz for 1 more minute to incorporate fully.

Scrape the fluid gel into a shallow container and place inside a chamber vacuum sealer. Under full pressure, close the lid and keep a close eye on the gel, stopping the process as soon as the bubbles rise to the top. Repeat this process several more times until the gel no longer bubbles.

Pass the celery gel through a fine-mesh sieve and refrigerate in a piping bag until needed. This fluid gel is best used on the day it is made.

Veal Sweetbreads

180g	Veal sweetbreads
125g	10% herb brine (see page 79)
150g	Plain flour
50g	Egg white, lightly whisked
65g	Japanese breadcrumbs

Preheat the water bath to 65°C/149°F.

Trim off all visible fat from the sweetbreads and rinse well under cold running water. Place the sweetbreads in a sous-vide bag and add the brine. Seal under full pressure and brine the sweetbreads for 2 hours.

Remove the sweetbreads from the sous-vide bags and rinse for 30 minutes under cold running water. Pat the sweetbreads dry and place them in a sous-vide bag, ensuring they are all lying flat and in a single layer. Seal under full pressure.

Cook the sweetbreads in the water bath for 2 hours, then place the bag in iced water. Once the sweetbreads are cool enough to handle, remove from the bag, trim them and cut them into even-sized pieces of 7g each. Set aside.

Place the flour, egg white and Japanese breadcrumbs in 3 separate bowls.

Toss the cooked sweetbreads in the flour and dust off the excess. Place them in the egg white and drain off the excess. Finally, roll them in the breadcrumbs, gently pressing them into the sweetbreads.

Store on kitchen paper in the fridge until needed.

(continued overleaf)

To Serve

6	Reserved slow-cooked hen's eggs
1	Rinsed celery stalk
	Reserved celery fluid gel
120g	Peeled and diced turnips (5mm dice)
7	Baby radishes
6	Reserved pickled onions
	Sea salt flakes
	Cracked black pepper
500g	Grapeseed oil
18	Reserved coated sweetbreads
	Celery cress
620g	Reserved infused lamb consommé
1g	Tarragon
2g	Rosemary
	Sherry vinegar

Preheat a water bath to 55°c/131°F.

Half an hour before plating up, place the eggs in the water bath to reheat gently.

Peel the celery and cut 5cm long pieces into fine julienne strips. Place 7 or 8 strips in the centre of a bowl to make a nest in which the egg will be placed. Pipe 3 small dollops of celery fluid gel in a triangle formation around the nest.

Blanch the diced turnips in boiling water for 10–20 seconds and refresh them immediately in iced water. Drain them.

Taste a radish after rinsing and quartering them; you may want to blanch them in the same way as the turnips. When quartering the radishes, ensure the leaf remains intact on each piece. Quarter the pickled onions. Set the vegetables aside.

First, peel the eggs one by one into a little bowl, then carefully tip them into the centre of each of the 6 bowls, on the celery nest. Season with sea salt flakes and cracked black pepper.

Arrange the diced turnip cubes, radish quarters and pickled onions around the outside of the egg.

Heat a small saucepan of grapeseed oil to 180°c/350°F.

Gently lower the coated sweetbreads into the hot oil and fry until golden.

Remove with a slotted spoon and drain on kitchen paper. Season with sea salt flakes and serve 3 per portion in the bowl surrounding the egg, on top of the vegetable pieces.

Garnish the dish with celery cress and any additional celery strands.

In the meantime, gently heat 620g of the finished consommé and add the tarragon and rosemary to infuse. Gradually add several drops of the sherry vinegar to taste, and, using a tea strainer, divide the consommé into 6 small jugs that hold 100g each. Serve the jugs alongside the serving bowls.

BRAISED CELERY

[1732]

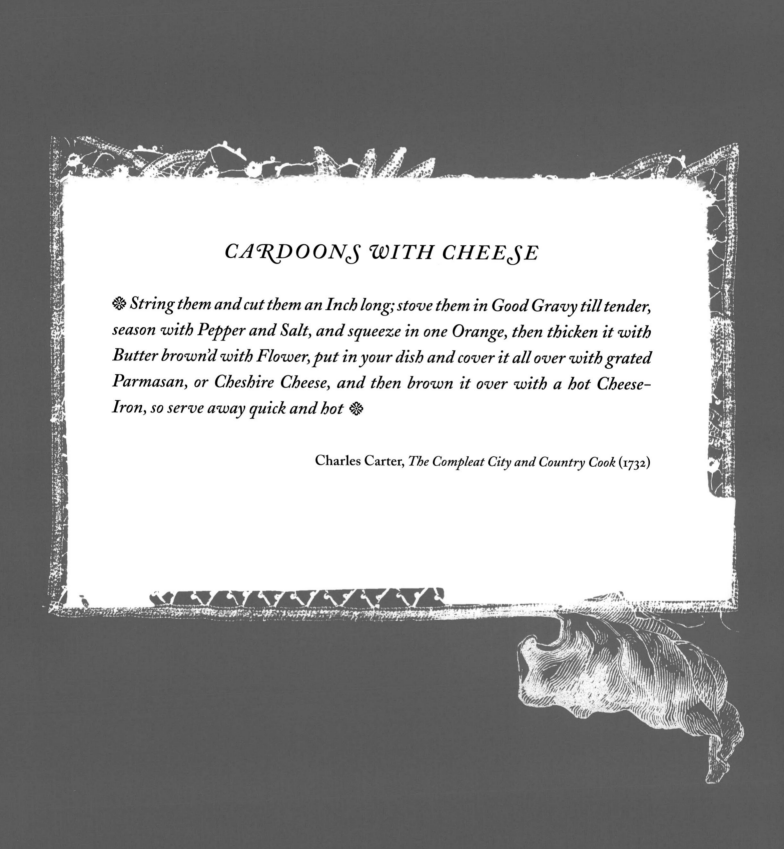

CARDOONS WITH CHEESE

✤ *String them and cut them an Inch long; stove them in Good Gravy till tender, season with Pepper and Salt, and squeeze in one Orange, then thicken it with Butter brown'd with Flower, put in your dish and cover it all over with grated Parmasan, or Cheshire Cheese, and then brown it over with a hot Cheese-Iron, so serve away quick and hot* ✤

Charles Carter, *The Compleat City and Country Cook* (1732)

Three years ago, I visited Fes in Morocco. In the narrow alleyways that thread through the ancient medina, or walled city, I noticed vendors perched by tiny portable trestle tables selling stacks of what looked like jumbo-sized, spiky heads of celery, but were in fact cardoons, a relative of the globe artichoke. Business was brisk and plenty of people were departing with fat bags of the stuff. To an English visitor nowadays it's an unfamiliar sight, but scroll back to the seventeenth century and something similar would have been happening in markets here, too.

Vegetables hadn't been particularly popular in the Middle Ages (at least, for those who had enough money to be choosy; the poor were more concerned about whether, rather than what, they were going to eat). They were disdained by the rich as peasant food, and according to the theory of the humours, which governed most educated people's approach to cuisine (see page 89), many vegetables were likely to induce wind and melancholy—a physical and spiritual double-whammy of unpleasantness that perhaps explains why they appear in relatively few early medieval recipes.

By the sixteenth century, however, this situation had changed. Excitement about new produce from the New World, coupled with enthusiasm for innovative horticultural methods imported from the Low Countries, made vegetables a more enticing prospect to cultivate and to eat. Moreover, the Renaissance Italian style of cuisine, which had by now begun to revolutionise English cooking in much the same way as it had done in the rest of Europe (see page 118), featured vegetables prominently. They became fashionable as a result, and cookbooks included recipes for artichokes, asparagus and cardoons where there were virtually none before.[*] And the French cuisine that succeeded Italian as the dominant creative force in cooking (see page 338) integrated vegetables even further into the culinary canon. In the 1700s, when English chefs began exploring the French notion of putting a cheese topping on dishes, the cardoon was one of the first vegetables that got this treatment— it was usually braised in gravy, covered with Parmesan and browned using a cheese-iron (a long handle with a metal plate at the end, which could be heated in the fire), much like Carter's recipe. By this period, vegetables were no longer shunned, but featured in simply prepared, bona-fide side dishes. In cookbooks, recipes for cardoons topped with cheese might appear alongside boiled or fried versions. But at more or less the same time, the cardoon was already being usurped by a vegetable that, although technically unrelated, looked like its smaller, less prickly cousin: celery.

Wild celery, which was called "smallage" in England, has been common in Europe since ancient times (it's mentioned in the *Odyssey*, where it's known as *selinon)*, but it was bitter and strong-tasting, so English cooks tended to use it mainly as a flavouring or seasoning, or in a medicinal capacity, such as in a pottage designed to purify the blood. To add a milder celery-style flavour to recipes, they originally used lovage instead, or another long-forgotten plant called Alexanders. However, some time in the sixteenth century, the Italians began breeding versions of the plant that quickly

[*] *A number of European artists were similarly inspired. The cardoon features in Caravaggio's "Still Life with Flowers and Fruit" (1601) and Felipe Ramírez's "Still Life with Cardoon, Francolin, Grapes and Irises" (1628), as well as in several extraordinary works by Juan Sánchez Cotán, including "Still Life with Cardoon and Carrots" (c. 1603), which seem almost modern in their austerity.*

supplanted the bitter, wild variety. "Smallage transferred to culture becomes milder and less ungrateful," observed the naturalist John Ray in *Historia Generalis Plantarum* (1686–1704), "whence in Italy and France the leaves and stalks are esteemed as delicacies." In England too, cultivated celery came to be esteemed over rivals such as lovage, Alexanders and cardoons, and eventually took their place completely.

When it comes to providing a satisfying, substantial main course, vegetarians are still not well served by most chefs, who almost inevitably resort to something starch-based. There are a lot of rice, pasta, pulses and potatoes in the vegetarian dishes on British menus. Chefs in previous centuries have generally been equally neglectful of the non-meat eater, particularly in Britain, where, by the 1730s, beef was already so integral to our national identity that the writer Henry Fielding was eulogising it in *The Grub-Street Opera*:

> *When mighty Roast Beef was the*
> *   Englishman's food,*
> *It ennobled our brains and enrich'd*
> *   our blood.*
> *Our soldiers were brave and our*
> *   courtiers were good.*
> *Oh! the Roast Beef of Old England,*
> *And old English Roast Beef!*

I was surprised and pleased, therefore, to come across Charles Carter's recipe for Cardoons with Cheese. This, it seemed to me, offered the basis for a really appetising vegetarian dish for Dinner—fragrant and filling with a nice hit of umami and very little in the way of starch. And right from the start I could see that, for all that I'd be using modern technology such as a sous-vide machine and water bath, in its fundamentals my approach wouldn't be that far from Carter's: the vegetable softened in a flavour-packed braising liquid, then topped with a rich cheese sauce and put under the grill until the surface was gratinated—flecked golden brown and deliciously crispy. These were techniques I had spent a lot of time refining at the Fat Duck. They would no doubt need some adjustments for this dish, but the foundations were already in place.

It eventually became clear, however, that there was one area in which I was going to part company with Carter. I decided against using cardoons. I've cooked with them before— risotto with cardoons and marrow bone was an early recipe at the Fat Duck—and I'd have liked to keep faith with the original ingredient. After all, I like forgotten and dismissed aspects of cooking, neglected cuts of meat such as onglet or skirt, unfashionable kit such as the pressure cooker, and supposedly old-fashioned techniques such as brining and potting. But in the amounts needed at Dinner, they turned out to be unreliable. One batch would be fine, the next stringy and tough, and the flavour could be disappointingly bland. And so, much like the eighteenth-century Brits before me, I forsook the cardoon in favour of celery, which really was, as John Ray observed, a less ungrateful vegetable—light, refined and reliably flavourful. A great British ingredient that's under-used and often undervalued.

Cheese needs a good punch of acidity to balance the richness, and some textural contrast to its smooth fluidity. Gradually, Ash and I assembled a set of ingredients for the garnish that would provide that punch: pickled walnuts and little cubes of apple compressed in the sous-vide machine, then marinated in cider in a sous-vide bag for 24 hours. Along with a dressing of nutty, sweet, acidic walnut vinaigrette, these ingredients would add a crunch and bite and yield to the teeth: the ideal vehicles for flavour encapsulation.

BRAISED CELERY

Makes 6 portions

Walnut Vinaigrette

75g	Grapeseed oil
65g	Walnut oil
50g	Walnut vinegar
40g	Chardonnay vinegar
10g	Wholegrain mustard

Combine the grapeseed oil and walnut oil in a jug.

In a separate bowl, whisk together the walnut and Chardonnay vinegars.

Gradually add the oil mixture to the vinegar mixture while blitzing with a hand blender until fully emulsified. Add the wholegrain mustard and whisk well to incorporate.

Store in the fridge until needed.

Pickled Walnuts

200g	Chardonnay vinegar
10g	Golden caster sugar
5g	Salt
100g	Walnut halves

Combine the vinegar with 50g water, the sugar and salt in a small saucepan and heat until the salt and sugar have dissolved. Set aside to cool completely.

Pour the pickling juice into a sous-vide bag and add the walnuts. Seal the bag and allow the walnuts to pickle in the fridge for at least 24 hours before using.

Compressed Cider Apple Cubes

| 2 | Granny Smith apples |
| 300g | Cider |

Peel, core and quarter the apples, then slice the wedges into 8mm slices.

Place the apple slices and cider in a sous-vide bag, ensuring they are all lying flat and in a single layer. Seal under full pressure.

Pierce the bag and repeat this process.

Place the compressed apple slices and the cider in a new sous-vide bag and seal. Allow the apple slices to pickle in the fridge for at least 24 hours before using them.

Before using the compressed apple slices, remove them from the pickling liquid, drain and cut them into 5mm dice.

Pickled Candy Beetroot

70g	Chardonnay vinegar
4g	Salt
80g	Extra virgin olive oil
3	Candy (Chioggia) beetroots

Gently heat the vinegar in a small saucepan and add the salt, stirring until dissolved. Remove from the heat, add the olive oil and set aside to cool.

Peel the beetroots and use a mandolin to slice them 1mm thick. Use a 5cm-diameter pastry cutter to cut out uniform discs.

Place the beetroot discs and cooled pickling liquid in a sous-vide bag and seal. Allow to pickle in the fridge for 24 hours before using.

Cheese Sauce

180g	Parmesan cheese, diced into 1cm cubes
375g	Vegetable stock (see page 94)
300g	Semi-skimmed milk
10g	Dijon mustard
10g	Tapioca starch powder
70g	Unsalted butter, cubed and at room temperature
80g	Plain flour
125g	Finely grated Gruyère cheese
250g	Double cream
6g	Salt
5g	Sherry vinegar

Line a deep tray with a double layer of clingfilm. Set aside until needed.

Put the Parmesan cubes in a Thermomix and blitz to a fine powder.

Heat the vegetable stock to 90°C/194°F, then add the Parmesan powder. Stir to emulsify, then transfer to a jug to infuse for 20 minutes. Do not stir it again, as you do not want to use the un-melted Parmesan that has settled at the bottom of the jug. Pass this cheese stock through a fine-mesh sieve, followed by a double layer of muslin, and pour into a saucepan. Add the milk, Dijon mustard and tapioca starch powder and blitz with a hand blender. Heat this mixture to 85°C/185°F.

In the meantime, melt the butter in a separate pan. Once the butter has completely melted, add the flour and stir to combine. Cook this roux over a medium heat, stirring continuously until it starts to foam. Gradually add the warm cheese stock mixture, stirring continuously.

Reduce the heat to a gentle setting and cook until all the flour has cooked out. This takes approximately 10–15 minutes.

Add the finely grated Gruyère cheese and stir until it has melted completely.

Add the double cream and stir to emulsify. Use the salt and sherry vinegar to season the sauce and stir to combine well before pouring it into the lined tray. Tap the tray gently to remove any air bubbles.

Cover with clingfilm and place in the fridge until needed.

Braised Celery

18   Celery stalks
500g   Vegetable braising liquid
          (see page 220)

Preheat a water bath to 90°C/194°F.

Snap the celery stalks off at the root and peel the outer skin. Trim them into 14cm long pieces and place them in a sous-vide bag along with the vegetable braising liquid. Ensure they are lying flat and in a single layer.

Cook in the water bath until softened. They should be firm but with no crunch. This should take around 1 hour 30 minutes, depending on the size.

Plunge the bag in iced water to prevent further cooking, and store in the fridge until needed.

To Serve

Reserved braised celery
Reserved cheese sauce
Parmesan cheese
Reserved compressed cider apple cubes
Reserved pickled walnuts, thinly sliced
Reserved pickled candy beetroot
Reserved walnut vinaigrette
Celery cress
Seasonal vegetables or mushrooms, such as baby onions, turnips, morels or ceps

Preheat the oven to the grill setting.

Remove the celery stalks from the sous-vide bags and drain on a tray lined with kitchen paper.

Meanwhile, transfer the set cheese sauce to a piping bag.

Place the celery stalks on a large tray, curved-side up, and pipe the cheese neatly into the grooves. Use a warmed palette knife to smooth over the surface.

Finely grate Parmesan over the celery-cheese stalks to cover them generously. Place under the grill until the cheese colours, like a gratin. Gently remove the celery-cheese pieces and, using a large spatula, place 3 pieces on each plate.

Garnish the dish with compressed apple cubes, sliced pickled walnuts, sliced candy beetroot and a dash of walnut vinaigrette. Top with the celery cress.

The dish can be changed each season to include a variety of vegetables such as pickled baby onions, turnips and seasonal mushrooms sautéed in lemon juice.

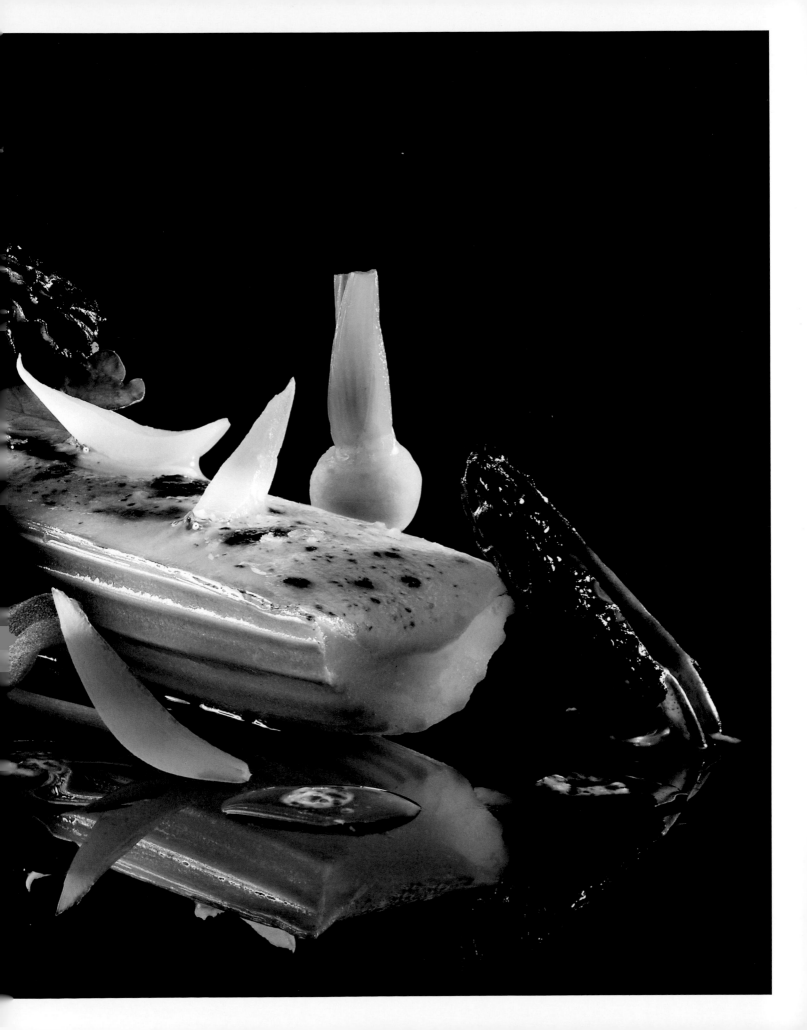

SPICED PIGEON

[1777]

TO BOIL PIGEONS WITH ARTICHOKES

❊ *Take some artichokes, boil them, and take out the bottoms; boil some pigeons, but take care that they are not over-done; while they are boiling, make a ragout of sweet herbs and fresh mushrooms; they must be all hot together, and there must be as many pigeons as artichoke-bottoms; first lay in the dish the artichoke-bottoms; then pour on some of the ragout; then lay a pigeon upon every bottom, shake a very little pepper over the pigeons, and prick their breasts in two or three places with a fork; then shake on a little basket-salt, and squeeze over that some Seville orange, then pour over it the rest of the ragout* ❊

Charlotte Mason, *The Lady's Assistant for Regulating and Supplying her Table* (1777, 3rd edition)

In parliament in the eighteenth century, ministers would call themselves Whig or Tory. These weren't yet parties in the modern sense, more loose collections of like-minded individuals, among which various blocs might jockey for supremacy. Although the court's involvement in government had diminished, the king's consent was still required for any act to be passed, so the rule of the country essentially lay in the hands of whichever group was able to gain the king's trust. During George I's reign (1714–27), these men were bound to come from the Whigs, who had supported the idea of a Hanoverian prince becoming king of England, while many Tories still retained Stuart sympathies.

Getting ahead in Georgian politics required artful manipulation, and the most successful politician of the period was Robert Walpole. Manoeuvred out of the cabinet in 1717 by his rivals, Walpole ensured he remained a political presence by exploiting the rift between George I and his son, the Prince of Wales, who had been banished from the royal residence at St James's Palace. The dismissed prince had set up what was in effect a rival court at Leicester House, giving political aspirants a place where they could debate issues, develop contacts and ingratiate themselves with the future king. Walpole spent hours here, cynically fomenting opposition to the Whigs in the hope that it would force them to give him a government post just to shut him up. The strategy worked: by 1720 he was back in the cabinet, and a year later he was appointed First Lord of the Treasury (effectively making him Prime Minister, although the term wasn't yet used officially), a position that he held for the next twenty-one years, the longest period that any British politician has ever been in charge of government.

While in office, Walpole played the down-to-earth squire, retaining his Norfolk accent, adopting a simple, uncultivated way of speaking and munching apples during parliamentary debates. Word got around that he prioritised letters from his gamekeeper over dealing with dispatches from parliament. It was an image that went down well with the gentry and merchant class, who were generally practical, self-made men who felt little connection with the German king and his court. However, Walpole's public persona was a carefully cultivated act; like many Whig grandees, his personal tastes were as sophisticated and extravagant as those of any courtier. He built the imposing Houghton Hall in Norfolk and decorated it with spectacularly expensive paintings by Rembrandt, Rubens and Poussin. His dining habits became similarly aspirational. Early in his career he had served homely country food, but by 1714 he employed a French cook, Solomon Sollis, and his table was reputedly laden with costly, complicated dishes. This is borne out by an inventory of his house, in which the only cookbook listed is Patrick Lamb's *Royal Cookery*, which was part of the French-inspired, technically complex style of cuisine known as court cookery (see page 218).

Walpole's culinary tastes were, however, out of step with the gentry, who moved away from elaborate French dishes to the extent that, by 1730, the bottom had already dropped out of the market for court cookery books, and those that survived—such as Lamb's and Carter's—did so by radically remodelling themselves along the lines of Mary Kettilby's and E. Smith's more domestic works (see page 261). In part, court cookery fell out of favour because of an increasingly deep-rooted anti-French sentiment prompted by the continual wars with France.

But there was another, equally nationalistic dynamic shaping British cuisine. Through the Act of Union (1707), England had become part of a larger and more diverse entity called Great Britain. Continued military and mercantile success had turned the country into a major international force. Such dramatic and relatively rapid transformations, and the inevitable uncertainty that went with them, pushed people to question the country's core values and what it meant to be British. In some ways, the 1700s can be seen as a testing ground for the answers they came up with. It's no coincidence that the personification of Britain in the form of John Bull first appeared at this time in John Arbuthnot's pamphlet *Law is a Bottom-less Pit* (1712). Satirical artists portrayed Bull as a stout man dressed in a heavy overcoat, waistcoat and riding boots or gaiters—in short, a typical, no-nonsense country squire. Gradually this became a cultural ideal, and the character of British cuisine changed to fit in with it. There was a greater emphasis on indigenous produce, simplicity and thrift. The gentry and merchant class were well aware of the work that had gone into making their money, so they were determined to use it wisely, even when showing off at the dining table. In *The Experienced English House-keeper* (1769), Elizabeth Raffald declares that her aim is "to join economy with neatness and elegance". Increasingly, cookbooks followed this line, paying attention to classic British rustic ingredients such as pigeons, mushrooms and ale.

※

Although it's served up less often nowadays, pigeon was for centuries a central feature of British cuisine. Pegones Rostyd appears on an extant fourteenth-century menu, and one of our oldest cookbooks, *The Forme of Cury*, has a recipe for Peions Ystewed:

Take peiouns and stop hem with garlec ypylled and with gode erbis ihewe, and do hem in an erthen pot; cast therto gode broth and whyte grece, powdour fort, safroun, verious & salt.

In the Middle Ages, having a store of pigeons and doves was an invaluable form of provisioning during the winter months when food was scarce. By the fifteenth century, most manor houses had a dovecote, and household account entries like Dame Alice de Bryene's for 11 May 1413—"one quarter bacon, one capon, two chickens, twenty pigeons"—show that pigeon was eaten on almost every day that meat consumption was permitted (see page 91). Many of these dovecotes were impressive architectural structures: squat stone towers lined from floor to ceiling with internal roosting cavities, or pigeon holes, which could house hundreds of birds. At Ingatestone Hall, the country house of Sir William Petre (who was secretary of state for four Tudor monarchs), records show that 1,080 pigeons were taken from the dovecote between Easter and Michaelmas in 1552. By the end of the following century, England had over 20,000 dovecotes—more than any other country. This was the apogee of pigeon popularity. In the 1700s fewer were kept, possibly because they were now seen as a threat to farming. Previously, landowners had shown little concern about the birds' ability to strip a field bare because it mainly affected common land. However, once they'd grabbed this land for themselves by means of enclosure (see page 260), they became a lot less tolerant of pigeons' consumption of crops.

Despite this, eighteenth-century cookbooks are full of interesting and varied pigeon recipes, from Pickled Pigeon and Stuffed Pigeons Braised in Beer to Potted Pigeons, Pigeon Dumplings and Pigeons in Lettuce. In *The Experienced English House-keeper*, Elizabeth Raffald has a raft of recipes, including the wonderfully named Pigeons Transmogrified, in which the birds are placed in hollowed-out cucumbers with their heads poking out of the ends, garnished with a bunch of barberries in their bills. What attracted me about Charlotte Mason's recipe, however, was its intelligent combination of ingredients. Teaming pigeon with artichoke was a smart piece of cooking—the flavours match one another really well—and they seemed an excellent basis for a dish at Dinner. What I wanted in particular was to pay homage to the era's legacy of classic British country fare. As I read other pigeon recipes of the period, beer stood out as another very typically British ingredient. Beer, artichoke and pigeon: they felt as though they belonged together, the sort of thing John Bull might happily devour at a tavern. Ash and I began looking at ways to combine the three ingredients.

Some of the elements of the dish needed relatively little work. I had already developed techniques for cooking artichokes and pigeons. Part of my approach to cuisine is a set of what might be called foundation preparations or techniques, which can be used in many different dishes: pickled lemons and acidulated onions, for example, feature a lot in my restaurants to add flavour, texture and acidity. For vegetables, I had created an intensely fragrant stock as a medium in which to braise them. I knew it suited artichokes very well, so we put them in a sous-vide bag with some braising liquid,

vacuum-sealed it, and cooked the artichokes until they were tender and had taken on some of the braising liquid's flavours.

The water bath is a superb way of cooking food to a precise level of doneness, but it won't give it any colour, nor any of the deep, strong Maillard-reaction flavours that are the result of a high heat (see page 77). So the next stage in the process was always going to be a quick stint on the *plancha*, or flat-top grill, to get that lovely brown colour and caramelised flavour. In Mason's recipe, she had squeezed in some Seville orange to introduce a little sweetness and acidity, but I thought acidulated onions might serve the same purpose while better complementing the artichoke. Cooking these two together created the kind of robust, rustic flavours we were after, but I also wanted the dish to reflect the elegant economy championed by Elizabeth Raffald—that thriftily ingenious use of ingredients vaunted by cookbooks of the period. We hit upon the notion of re-using the braising liquid from the artichoke's vacuum-pack bag. After sautéing acidulated onions in a pan, then adding the artichokes and browning them too, we poured over some of the braising liquid and let it reduce down to a beautiful glaze. All it then needed was a little seasoning. Mason had asked for "sweet herbs" without being specific, but we were looking for ingredients that reinforced those big, rustic flavours. The combination that worked best was thyme with chopped rocket, which introduced a welcome green, peppery flavour to the dish.

The pigeon breasts were cooked in much the same way: vacuum-packed in a sous-vide bag and cooked in a water bath, then seared swiftly, skin-side down, which gave me the best of both worlds: a soft, succulent texture from the water bath's precise and even temperature, and delicious roast-bird flavours from the quick burst of high heat on the plancha. Mason is very specific about the importance of salt in this dish, so we worked on a spiced salt to season the meat, mixing salt with various combinations of ingredients that suit game until we found a group that had the flavour profile we wanted: peppercorns and allspice; star anise, with its liquorice-like edge; citrusy coriander seeds, and the subtly nutmeggy fragrance of shards of mace. Once on the plate, the pigeon and artichokes looked the part: they had the same enticing golden-brown colour, and the thin stalks of the artichokes meant they resembled nicely seared bone-in chops.

It was the sauce—or more specifically, the beer in it—that caused the most difficulties during development. For the foundation of the sauce, we followed the same Raffald-style principle of economy and made a stock with all the parts of the pigeon that were left once the breasts had been removed. The carcasses were roasted in the oven, and carrots, onions, garlic and button mushrooms were sliced finely (to maximise surface area so that they give up as much of their flavour as possible) and softened in the pan. The bones and meat were then added to the vegetables, and the whole lot was cooked for a couple of hours in a pressure cooker, which locks in lots of flavour and makes it more complex. The liquid was then reduced to boil off some of the water and further intensify the flavour.

These are techniques that have become standard at all my restaurants, and they produced a deliciously rich pigeon stock. Introducing beer to the mix, however, gave us a real headache. We'd gone for an organic ale with a distinct hoppy character that tasted convincingly old-fashioned and traditional. The trouble was that it turned incredibly bitter when reduced. Ash and I experimented with dozens of other ales and got the same result: an unbelievable, mouth-puckering bitterness. (Try heating up a little in a pan and you'll see exactly what I mean.) We explored every method we could think of, but nothing worked. Or, if it did, it compromised the other flavours: cooking the ale out in the stock, for example, drove off the hoppiness. After a frustrating, infuriating week of exploring one technique after another and wasting countless batches of carefully reduced pigeon stock in the process—making this stage of development neither neat nor economical— I was beginning to think we'd have to give up on the idea. And I hate doing that.

I decided we should have one final go at it. Nothing fancy—we just let the ale go flat so that it didn't have too much froth, then added it to the stock right at the end, crossed our fingers, and tasted the result. It worked perfectly, producing exactly the balance of flavour I'd been hoping for. It was a great reminder that it's easy, when cooking, to over-think things. Sometimes, simplest is best.

SPICED PIGEON

Makes 6 portions

Pigeon Stock

2.3kg	Pigeon carcasses (with head, feet and entrails removed)
60g	Plain flour
1.4kg	Chicken wings
140g	Unsalted butter
1.1kg	Peeled and finely sliced carrots
1.1kg	Peeled and finely sliced onions
20g	Peeled and sliced garlic
375g	Sliced cleaned button mushrooms
15g	Thyme
2	Bay leaves

Preheat the oven to 170°C/340°F.

Chop the pigeon carcasses into small pieces, and toss them in flour to ensure they are evenly coated. Spread them out evenly on a roasting tray and roast them in the oven until golden brown, turning frequently. Remove them from the tray and set aside. Drain and reserve the excess fat.

Increase the oven temperature to 190°C/375°F.

Chop the chicken wings into small pieces and toss them in flour to ensure they are evenly coated. Spread them out evenly on a roasting tray and roast them in the oven until golden brown, turning frequently.

Remove them from the tray and set aside. Drain and reserve the excess fat. Deglaze the roasting pan with some cold water and set these juices aside.

Melt the butter in a large pressure cooker and add the carrots and onions. Sweat them without allowing them to colour. Once softened, add the garlic and mushrooms and continue to cook for 5 more minutes, stirring regularly.

Add the roasted pigeon bones and chicken wings, along with the fat and reserved juices from the roasting trays. Pour 4.5 litres cold water into the pressure cooker and bring the stock

to a simmer, skimming off all scum and impurities. Add the thyme and bay leaves and stir one last time before securing the lid of the pressure cooker. Cook for 2 hours.

Allow the pressure cooker to depressurise and the stock to cool slightly before opening the lid. Strain through a fine-mesh sieve, followed by a fine-mesh filter bag, and chill the stock in the fridge overnight.

Remove and discard all the fat from the surface of the chilled stock. Heat in a large saucepan and gently reduce to 10% of the original quantity, to yield approximately 450g reduced pigeon stock. It is important to continue skimming the stock as it reduces.

Once the stock has reduced, pass it through a fine-mesh filter bag and refrigerate until needed.

Brown Butter

250g	Unsalted butter, diced into 2cm cubes

Place the butter cubes in a wide-bottomed pan and gently melt, whisking continuously. After several minutes, the butter will give off a nutty aroma and the solids will turn brown.

Once the butter reaches 190°C/375°F, remove the pan from the heat and allow to cool. Pass the brown butter through a fine-mesh filter bag and refrigerate until needed.

Braised Artichokes

1	Lemon, halved
1g	Citric acid
6	Baby violet artichokes
100g	Vegetable braising liquid (see page 220)

Preheat a water bath to 90°C/194°F.

Place 2 litres cold water, the lemon and citric acid in a large container. Stir and set aside.

Prepare the artichokes one at a time, working as quickly as possible to prevent discolouring by oxidisation. Pull off the main outer leaves until only the tender leaves are exposed. Trim the stem, leaving about 3cm from the base of the artichoke. Using a paring knife, peel down the stem and around the base of the artichoke and neatly trim any leaves from around the sides. Cut the artichokes in half and carefully remove the fibrous inner section. Slice off the top of the artichoke straight and plunge into the acidulated water, ensuring they are fully immersed by using a cartouche on top of the water.

Once the artichokes have all been prepped, place them in a single layer in a sous-vide bag, along with the vegetable braising liquid. Seal the bag under full pressure and place in the water bath to cook until they are soft throughout. This should take about 1 hour.

Keep them in the sous-vide bag, refrigerated, until needed.

(continued overleaf)

Spice Powder

20g	Coriander seeds
2g	Star anise
3	Allspice berries
1g	Black peppercorns
1.5g	Mace blades

Heat a hot, dry pan and toast the spices. Allow to cool.

Place the cooled spices in a Thermomix and blitz on a high setting for 1 minute. Pass this spice powder through a fine-mesh sieve and reserve to make the spice salt.

Spice Salt

80g	Sea salt flakes
10g	Spice powder

Place the sea salt flakes in a Thermomix and add the spice powder. Blitz on a high setting for 1 minute.

Store the spice salt in an airtight container.

Pigeon Sauce

5g	Coriander seeds
1g	Star anise
3g	Black peppercorns
250g	Reserved reduced pigeon stock

Heat a dry pan and toast the coriander seeds and star anise until fragrant. Set aside to cool, then lightly crush using a pestle and mortar. Toast the black peppercorns separately and leave them whole.

In a small saucepan, heat the reduced pigeon stock to 80°C/176°F, then remove from the heat. Add the toasted spices, cover the saucepan with clingfilm and allow to infuse for 20 minutes.

Pass the sauce through a fine-mesh filter bag and chill until needed.

To Serve

12	Squab pigeon breasts
	Reserved braised artichokes and their braising liquid
	Extra virgin olive oil
100g	Low-acid onions (see page 264)
90g	Wild rocket
45g	Thyme leaves
	Salt
	Cracked black pepper
	Reserved pigeon sauce
	Ale, at room temperature and left open to become flat
	Lemon juice
	Reserved brown butter, melted
	Reserved spice salt
	Baby thyme, to garnish

Preheat a water bath to 60°C/140°F. Preheat the oven to 50°C/122°F.

Place the pigeon breasts in sous-vide bags, ensuring they are lying flat in a single layer. Seal under full pressure. Place the sous-vide bags in the water bath and cook until the internal temperature reaches 56°C/133°F. This takes approximately 15–20 minutes.

Rest the pigeon in the warm oven, still in the bags.

In the meantime, remove the cooked artichokes from the sous-vide bags, reserving the vegetable braising liquid. You will need 100g.

Slice the artichokes into quarters and heat a small amount of olive oil in a non-stick pan. Colour the flat sides of the artichokes by searing them until golden, then drain on kitchen paper.

In the same pan, add 100g of the reserved vegetable braising liquid and reduce it slightly. Add the low-acid onions while you finely chop the wild rocket. Heat through gently, then stir in the finely chopped wild rocket and the picked thyme leaves. Season with salt and pepper. Before the mixture reduces completely, add the artichokes and ensure they have warmed through.

Weigh the pigeon sauce and add it to a small saucepan. Heat gently and add 8% of its weight in ale. Taste the sauce and adjust the acidity with a few drops of lemon juice.

Take the pigeon breasts out of the oven and remove them from the sous-vide bags. Drizzle some olive oil into a very hot non-stick pan and add the pigeon breasts skin-side down, colouring the skin until crisp and golden. Apply gentle pressure with a spatula on each breast to ensure even colouring.

Remove the seared breasts from the pan and lightly brush with the melted brown butter. Season both sides with a generous pinch of spice salt and trim the edges. Slice each breast in half at an angle. The ideal serving temperature is 56°C/133°F (medium-rare).

To serve, place a spoonful of the low-acid onion mixture on a small tray lined with kitchen paper to drain off any excess liquid, then spread it out evenly to cover the base of the plate. Place the 4 pigeon pieces on top of the low-acid onions, and arrange the 4 artichoke quarters attractively in between. Spoon over the finished pigeon sauce, garnish with baby thyme leaves and season with salt and cracked black pepper.

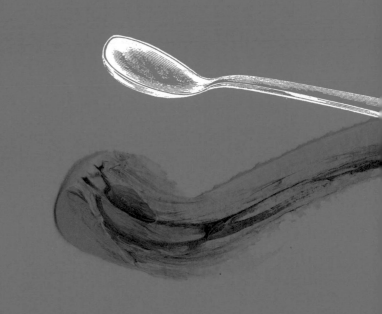

BROWN BREAD ICE CREAM

[1808]

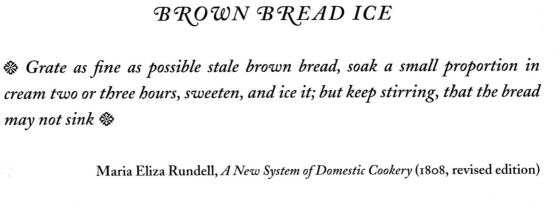

BROWN BREAD ICE

❊ *Grate as fine as possible stale brown bread, soak a small proportion in cream two or three hours, sweeten, and ice it; but keep stirring, that the bread may not sink* ❊

Maria Eliza Rundell, *A New System of Domestic Cookery* (1808, revised edition)

If you add salt to water it reduces its freezing point to below 0°c. Nowadays this is common knowledge, but before 1530, European chefs—and, for that matter, scientists—had no notion of how to artificially freeze a liquid using salt. Without this knowledge they were unable to make ice cream, which needs a temperature below zero in order for the mixture of water and other ingredients to freeze. It's thought that the discovery of the refrigerant properties of salt originated in the East: *Panchatantra*, an Indian collection of fables written in about 200 BC, mentions that water only becomes really cold if it contains salt. The information was at some point picked up by the Arabs, and they introduced it to the West during their occupation of Spain from 711 to 1492. The earliest written account of the principles behind making ice from water and salt is by the Arab physician and historian Ibn Abi Usaybi'a (1203–70) in his *Book of Essential Information on the Classes of Physicians*.

The first European reference to salt in this context is in *Problemata* (1530) by the Italian Marco Antonio Zimara (who's better known for his work on perpetual motion machines). Over the next hundred years it became a talking point among the scientific community, both in Italy and elsewhere, with a number of scientists exploring the cooling properties of various salts and gradually amassing a body of technical detail. The English philosopher Sir Francis Bacon, who is widely considered to be the "father of science" because of his development of a scientific methodology, published several formulae for salt mixtures. (He was later to die as the result of further research into refrigeration: he contracted pneumonia after venturing into the snow to stuff a dead fowl with it in order test its effectiveness as a means of preservation.)

This investigative work continued to develop and expand, particularly after Daniel Fahrenheit invented the mercury thermometer in 1714, and ten years later a temperature scale that was widely adopted, making comparative work easier to perform. But by the 1660s, chefs were already producing water ices and a form of milk-based ice cream. They would have been cruder than their modern-day counterparts—the mixture may well not have been churned, in which case it would have been fairly solid and grainy; and it would be another fifty years or so before eggs were introduced to create a smoother, richer texture—but these creations were seen as magical by diners in the seventeenth and eighteenth centuries.

The first record of ice cream being served in England was in May 1671, at a feast at Windsor for the Order of the Garter, during which King Charles II's table alone was presented with "one plate of white strawberries and one plate of Ice Cream". The next record of its appearance was also at a banquet, in September 1688, to celebrate the recent birth of King James II's son, James Francis Edward. According to the *London Gazette*, "there was served up a very fine dessert, with many great pyramids of dry sweet meats, between which were placed all such Fruits, Ice Creams, and such other varieties as the Season afforded." (The paper's even tone hides the fact that, for most of the country, the birth of a Catholic heir was no cause for celebration. Ultimately, it precipitated the events that led to James fleeing the country and being replaced by William of Orange.)

The first printed English recipe for ice cream is in *Mrs Mary Eales Receipts* (1718), supposedly written by the confectioner to the late Queen Anne, although this is open to debate since women were not employed in the royal palace kitchens. However, the fact that monarchs keep cropping up in connection with ice cream is not surprising, because making it was an expensive business, and iced confections were confined to the tables of the rich until well into the nineteenth century. The principal cost was obtaining and storing the ice in the first place. Refrigerators didn't yet exist; crude versions of the technology began to be developed in the early 1800s, but it wasn't until after World War II that they became standard features in most households. So some form of storage had to be built, and these could be highly technical constructions. One old engraving depicts an outbuilding with double doors opening on to a deep, brick-lined, cone-shaped pit with a drain extending from its base, covered by a wagon wheel to prevent it becoming blocked. The ice to fill such a pit would come from frozen ponds and lakes (necessitating a bevy of estate workers for maintenance and harvesting), or might be imported at great expense from North America, Norway or Greenland, particularly if there had been a mild winter. Despite this, ice cream became a craze among the gentry in the eighteenth century, and there was a competitive adventurousness about the flavours chefs came up with to gratify fashionable Georgian gourmands. Alongside the classics we know and love today, such as caramel, coffee, lemon and pistachio, there were quirkier offerings, such as tea, jasmine, violet, and even Parmesan cheese.

Parmesan ice cream was originally designed to look like a wedge of cheese, complete with a "rind" made of caramelised sugar, and excitement about the culinary possibilities of the new foodstuff resulted in many such counterfeit confections. By the middle of the eighteenth century, pewterers were selling hinged moulds artfully modelled to resemble crayfish, hens, squirrels and truffles, among other things, which could be filled with ice cream, then sealed with a mixture of wax, suet and rosin (a resin from conifers often used by string musicians to give their bow some friction) and placed in a tub of ice and salt until frozen. The practice recalls the medieval passion for making one food imitate another: in the fifteenth century, chefs were taking pains to make meat look like fruit (see page 59); 300 years later, they were still at it, making ice cream look like plums, pears, cherries and apricots. The Victorians took this idea to the limit, turning it into a fabulous piece of culinary showmanship. In his *Encyclopaedia of Practical Cookery*, Theodore Garrett has pictures of ices fashioned into asparagus, flower baskets and cup cakes. Illustrations in books by one of my favourite Victorian cooks, the ice-cream doyenne Mrs Marshall, show pyramids of peaches, a pair of doves nestling among apples and pears, and an overflowing basket of fruit surrounded by lemons, pears and melons garnished with real sprigs of maidenhair fern.

This elaborate Victorian artistry was made possible in part by the rapid pace of the Industrial Revolution in Britain (see page 401). The development and growth of factories enabled the manufacture of increasingly sophisticated equipment. The snowball effect of Victorian technological innovation also led to a mechanisation of the ice-cream-making process. In 1843, the confectioner to the Royal Zoological Gardens, Thomas Masters, invented the first machine capable of freezing and churning at the same time, and then took the classic Victorian approach to promoting it by writing a book with a heavy emphasis on

product placement (although its title, *The Ice Book: Being a Compendious and Concise History of Everything Connected with Ice from its First Introduction into Europe as an Article of Luxury to the Present Time with an Account of the Artificial Manner of Producing Pure and Solid Ice and a Valuable Collection of the Most Approved Recipes for Making Superior Water Ices and Ice Creams at a Few Minutes' Notice*, was hardly a marketing man's dream). Over the next fifty years, such devices became increasingly popular and accessible, as the production-line techniques and growing markets of the British capitalist economy led to cheap goods being produced on a large scale. By the 1880s, Mrs Marshall was selling her own patented version of the hand-cranked machine in her shop on Mortimer Street, London, along with all sorts of other equipment for the ice-cream enthusiast, who by this stage might be not a professional chef, but a member of that burgeoning new class, the bourgeoisie. Ice cream had been democratised.

One other event contributed to the increased popularity and accessibility of ice cream in Britain. In Italy, between 1848 and unification in 1861 (known as *il Risorgimento*: the Resurgence), there was a series of confrontations between nationalists and the forces of the various factions—principally Austria, the Papacy and the Bourbon royal family—that had carved up the country between them. Violence and financial uncertainty forced many Italians to make their way to Britain, where the less skilled made a living in the summer by selling ice cream from mobile stalls on the streets. At first, this new foodstuff was viewed with scepticism. "Ices in the streets!" scoffed a trader interviewed by Henry Mayhew for his survey of social conditions in the capital, *London Labour and the London Poor*. "Aye and there'll be jellies next, and then mock turtle, and then the real ticket, sir… Penny glasses of champagne, I shouldn't wonder." Suspicions about the product were, in fact, well founded. The street

trade was conducted in such an unhygienic manner—prepared in dirty cellars, adulterated with other ingredients and served in poorly washed receptacles—that food poisoning was common. In 1901 a public outcry led to government regulation of the conditions under which commercial ice cream was made and sold. Despite this shaky start, in the end the man on the street succumbed to the same magic that had entranced the Georgian aristocracy a couple of centuries earlier. By the 1930s, Wall's had a fleet of more than 8,000 tricycles selling ice cream across the country.

Brown bread ice cream's popularity in the 1800s is often ascribed to Victorian thrift. It's certainly true that the middle class flourished thanks to money diligently earned rather than inherited, so they made a virtue of careful household management. That's one of the reasons for the nineteenth-century trend for vast cookbooks with instructions on every aspect of domestic economy, such as those by Eliza Acton, Mrs Beeton and the irascible Maria Rundell (her spats with her publisher became so acrimonious that the Lord Chancellor had to intervene), whose recipe was the starting point for mine.

Finding a use for stale bread was no doubt attractive to penny-watching Victorians. But brown bread ice cream first appeared in cookbooks of the Georgian age, a period known for culinary extravagance rather than restraint. (Indeed, the buttoned-up character of the Victorian era is often seen as a reaction against the wilful excesses of Georgian society.) Although brown bread might seem an odd choice of flavouring, it already had a longstanding association with cream.

In his diary entry for 13 July 1665, Samuel Pepys reports that he "dined well, and mighty merry, especially my Lady Slaning and I about eating of creame and brown bread, which she loves as much as I". Patrick Lamb's *Royal Cookery* (1710) has a recipe for Cream Toasts, in which sliced bread is soaked in cream, then fried (perhaps an early form of *pain perdu*). Brown bread ice cream may come from an eagerness to explore the potential of these ingredients in a new type of dessert. Excitement, rather than economy, might well have been the driving force behind its creation.

Maria Rundell's recipe attracted my attention partly because I'd already done some research on the use of bread in historical desserts and found it very interesting. When I was developing a treacle tart for the Hind's Head I visited the Hampton Court kitchens, where food historians Marc Meltonville and Richard Fitch cooked me a Tart of Bread from *The Good Housewife's Handmaid for the Kitchen* (1594). Having combined melted butter, sugar, breadcrumbs and rosewater, they placed the mixture on a pastry base in a heavy pan and cooked it between copper trays of hot coals. The end result had a good flavour and texture, somewhere between a cake and a madeleine, and I banked bread as a historical ingredient to explore further.

But there was also a more modern historical link that triggered my interest in Rundell's dish. My head of creative development, Jocky, and I both had vivid memories of being served brown bread ice cream in the 1980s, when it became a standard part of the pub-grub repertoire for a while. It was basically a frozen dessert, or parfait: brown bread sprinkled with sugar and put under the grill, then mixed with whipped cream and eggs, frozen, and cut into slabs for service. I've always believed that if you experience an emotional association like this you should pursue it. If an ingredient has resonance for me, then it's likely it'll have the same effect on others too. Our perceptions of taste and flavour come not just from what we experience in the mouth and nose; they're also determined by what the brain makes of it all. The emotional associations a dish evokes can actually make it seem even more delicious. A chef would be crazy not to try to tap into that.

There is, however, a technical challenge with using bread to make an ice cream. The presence of gluten can turn the base mix into a texture that is, for me, too gloopy. After trying out many different breads and techniques, we came up with the method of taking a brown sourdough loaf and putting it in a low oven for a while so that it really dried out, which subdued the gluten, then placing the dried bread in milk to infuse overnight. This solved the texture issue, but created a colour issue in its place: the mixture didn't end up brown enough. Colour plays a huge part in our appreciation of food, so if we were going to serve up brown bread ice cream it absolutely had to be a convincing shade of brown. We looked around for something dry but dark that could be added to the milk infusion, and settled for a rye crispbread. We had the colour and base flavour we wanted: the two ingredients complemented one another really well, and the crispbread introduced a slightly different sort of acidity to the mix.

The main requirements for an ice cream base are relatively fixed: some form of fat for structure and smoothness; some form of sugar (such as sucrose, fructose or glucose) or other sweetener such as honey for balance, texture and sweetness; and what are termed "milk solids, non-fat" (in other words, the things in milk and cream apart from fat, such as proteins, minerals, vitamins and lactose) to give it body. The art of ice-cream-making is choosing ingredients and juggling percentages so you fulfil these requirements while getting exactly the texture and flavour you want. For the fat component I chose yoghurt to supply a touch of acidity to cut the richness. For part of the sugar component I used dark brown muscovado sugar to provide colour and a molasses-like characteristic. For other flavourings I looked to the bread-making process itself for inspiration and added some malt extract and yeast. What was particularly exciting was that the mixture captured several tastes at once: not just sweetness and a little bitterness from the muscovado sugar, but also a slight savouriness from the malt extract and a range of acidity from the sourdough bread, crispbread and yoghurt.

Nowadays, modern chefs tend to use ice cream as a garnish, but I wanted to serve this at Dinner as a dessert in its own right. The idea was to have a large spoonful of ice cream on the plate, accompanied by some textural contrasts to its frozen smoothness. Gradually I isolated a set of ingredients that fitted the brief: some salted butter caramel whipped to a very light airiness; an olive oil biscuit; a crumble made from toasted breadcrumbs, oats and crystallised breadcrumbs; some lemon zest and pear for freshness, fruitiness and a touch more acidity; a sprinkle of vanilla salt, which, along with the butter caramel, added saltiness to the range of tastes in the dish, giving it a wonderfully complex flavour profile. To finish it off, picking up on the yeast and malt extract in the ice cream, I made a yeast caramel and piped a zigzagged flourish over the top, an old-style bit of decoration I hoped might take some diners back to pub lunches they'd had in the 1980s.

BROWN BREAD ICE CREAM

Makes 6 portions

Infused Milk

960g   **Brown sourdough bread,
cut into bite-sized cubes**
3kg   **Whole milk**
60g   **Rye crispbreads**

Preheat the oven to 170°C/340°F.

Place the bread cubes in a single layer
on a roasting tray. Allow the bread to
dry out and toast as dark as possible
without burning.

Place the toasted bread pieces and
crispbreads in a Thermomix and blitz
well to make fine crumbs.

Divide the crumbs and milk equally
between two large sous-vide bags and
seal under full pressure. Allow the
mixture to infuse overnight.

Strain the mixture through a fine-mesh
sieve and refrigerate until needed.
It should yield 950g infused milk.

Brown Bread Ice Cream

950g   **Reserved infused milk**
60g   **Skimmed milk powder**
50g   **Malt extract**
95g   **Pasteurised egg yolk**
85g   **Golden caster sugar**
40g   **Dark muscovado sugar**
18g   **Fresh yeast**
78g   **Granular maltodextrin, DE=19**
375g   **Yoghurt**

In a large saucepan, combine the
infused milk, milk powder and malt
extract, and gently heat to 52°C/126°F.

In the meantime, in a separate
container, blitz the egg yolk, sugars,
fresh yeast and maltodextrin together.
Add the yolk mixture to the milk and
whisk, bringing the temperature up to
70°C/158°F. As soon as that temperature
is reached, carefully monitor it to
ensure that the mixture remains at
this temperature for 10 minutes.

Fill a large bowl with iced water and
pour the ice cream base into a large
sous-vide bag, without sealing it.
Carefully place the bag in the iced
water and allow to cool completely.
Add the yoghurt just before churning
the ice cream. Churn, then store in
the freezer in a sealed container.

Olive Oil Biscuits

140g   **Unsalted butter**
125g   **Golden caster sugar**
220g   **Plain flour**
4g   **Salt**
1g   **Vanilla powder**
2g   **Baking powder**
60g   **Egg yolk**
50g   **Extra virgin olive oil**

Using the paddle attachment in a
mixer, cream together the butter and
sugar, then add the flour, salt, vanilla
powder and baking powder. Add the
yolk and olive oil and bring the dough
together. Wrap in clingfilm and allow
to rest in the fridge overnight.

Preheat the oven to 170°C/340°F.

Roll the dough out to 2mm thick
between 2 sheets of baking parchment.
Place the dough on a baking sheet,
peeling away the parchment at the
same time. Place in the oven and bake
until golden brown—approximately
20–25 minutes.

Once removed from the oven, and
while they are still warm, use a 4.5cm-
diameter round cookie cutter to cut
individual biscuits.

Store in a sealed container until needed.

Whipped Caramel

400g   **Whipping cream**
0.8g   **Vanilla powder**
300g   **Glucose**
300g   **White caster sugar**
300g   **Whole milk**
240g   **Unsalted butter, cubed and
at room temperature**
10g   **Salt**

Place the whipping cream and vanilla
powder in a small saucepan and
set aside.

In a separate larger saucepan, over
a moderate heat, allow the glucose,
sugar, milk, butter and salt to melt and
reduce. As soon as it starts taking on
some colour, place the saucepan with
the whipping cream and vanilla powder
over the heat and gently bring to the
boil. Remove from the heat, cover and
set aside.

Continuously whisk the caramel,
allowing it to come to 152°C/306°F.
Depending how long this takes, you
may need to reheat the whipping
cream gently.

Once the caramel has reached
temperature, remove it from the
heat and immediately add the warm
whipping cream in 3 stages, whisking
continuously until completely emulsified.
Return the large saucepan to the heat
and bring the mixture back to the boil.

Pass the caramel through a fine-mesh
sieve into a container and cover with
clingfilm, allowing the film to touch
the surface of the caramel. Set aside
to cool.

Once the caramel has reached room
temperature, place it in a mixer and
whip for 4–5 minutes using the whisk
attachment.

Place the whipped caramel in a piping
bag and store in the fridge until needed.

Yeast Caramel

25g   **Dry instant yeast**
115g **Golden syrup**
115g **Barley malt extract**

Place the yeast in a small bowl, cover with a little water and whisk to combine. Cover with clingfilm and put in a warm place for 4 hours.

Place the golden syrup, barley malt extract and yeast in a small saucepan over a medium heat. Stir continuously with a small spatula until the mixture is a dark golden brown. Take care not to overheat the caramel. It should reach the soft ball stage. The consistency can be checked by removing it from the heat and dropping a very small amount into iced water. It should retain a ball shape but still be relatively soft. The temperature should be 115°C/239°F. Pour this mixture into a bowl and leave to cool.

Scrape off and discard the froth from the top of the caramel. Place the cooled caramel in a piping bag and refrigerate until needed.

Caramelised Breadcrumbs

100g **Sugar**
80g   **Brown bread, roughly cut into small pieces**

Place 90g of the sugar and 80g water in a saucepan and bring to 150°C/300°F. While whisking, add the remaining 10g sugar, along with the breadcrumbs. Pour on to a silicone mat and leave to cool.

Once cooled, blitz well. Sift the crumbs through a perforated tray and discard the fine crumbs. Pick out and discard any large crumbs, so that you are left with uniform medium-sized crumbs.

Set aside in a sealed container until needed.

Toasted Bread Cubes

40g   **Brown bread, diced into 5mm cubes**

Preheat the oven to 180°C/350°F.

Place the bread cubes on a baking tray.

Toast in the oven until evenly browned. Leave to cool and store in a sealed container until needed.

Vanilla Salt

1g   **Vanilla powder**
12g   **Sea salt flakes**

Combine the powder and sea salt flakes and set aside in a sealed container.

To Serve

    Reserved whipped caramel
    Reserved olive oil biscuits
    Reserved caramelised breadcrumbs
    Reserved toasted bread cubes
1   **Pear, peeled and diced into 5mm cubes**
    Grated lemon zest
    Toasted oats
    Reserved vanilla salt
    Reserved brown bread ice cream
    Reserved yeast caramel

Place an 8cm presentation ring in the centre of a plate and pipe the whipped caramel into it to a height of 1cm. Remove the presentation ring and place the olive oil biscuit in the centre of the caramel, pressing down gently.

Place alternating caramelised breadcrumbs, toasted bread cubes, diced pear, lemon zest and toasted oats on the rim of the whipped caramel, surrounding the olive oil biscuit. Sprinkle with the vanilla salt.

Place a rocher of brown bread ice cream on top of a sheet of kitchen paper. Cut a very small opening in the yeast caramel piping bag, and pipe the yeast caramel on top of the ice cream in a zigzag.

Gently place the ice cream on top of the olive oil biscuit and serve immediately.

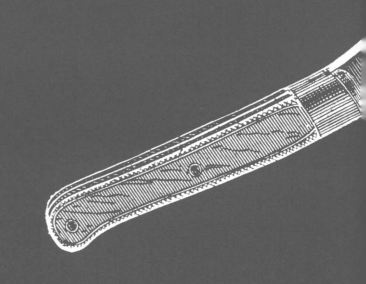

SAUCE ROBERT

[1816]

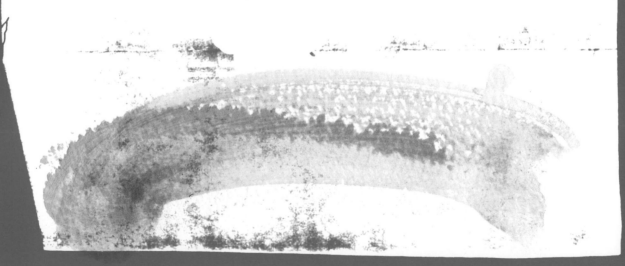

SAUCE ROBERT

 *Après avoir coupé en petits dés trois gros oignons, vous les colorez blonds dans du beurre clarifié, puis vous les égouttez, et les travaillez avec du consommé et deux grandes cuillerées d'espagnole travaillée. La sauce étant réduite à point, vous y mêlez un peu de sucre en poudre, un peu de poivre, un peu de vinaigre et une cuillerée à bouche de moutarde fine* ❀

❀ *Finely dice 3 large onions, then cook them in clarified butter until lightly coloured. Drain and add some consommé and 2 large spoonfuls of espagnole sauce. Once the sauce is fully reduced, add a some granulated sugar, pepper, a little vinegar and a tablespoon of Dijon mustard* ❀

Antonin Carême, *L'art de la cuisine française au dix-neuvième siècle* (1833–44)

It all began with a photograph of a piece of meat. Plump and beautifully marbled with fat like a piece of Wagyu beef, it was the best pork chop I had ever seen. The photo had been taken by Ash and he'd sent it to me with a message that read: *Look at this. Unbelievable!* I could only agree. Already I was thinking, if this tastes as good as it looks, then it has to go on the menu at Dinner.

And it did taste that good. The black-foot pigs from which the chop had come spend a large part of their lives rooting around for acorns in orchards, which gives the meat an amazing rich, nutty flavour. It was unlike any pork I'd had before, and I definitely wanted it on the menu.

The kitchen at Dinner is kitted out with a charcoal oven. It's fearsomely hot—the *whoomph!* of heat when you open the door is like a slap in the face—and it's perfect for giving food a barbecue-like chargrilled character, which was definitely something I wanted for the chop. However, that intense heat meant I had to adopt a slightly different approach to cooking it. In many of my recipes, meat is sealed in a sous-vide bag, heated in a water bath until it reaches the desired internal temperature, then browned briefly to add colour and flavour. Here, though, it was no good fully cooking the pork first, then searing it in the charcoal oven: the oven's extreme heat meant that, by the time the meat was nicely striped, the interior would already be overcooked. Nonetheless, the water bath was essential to the process. The chops couldn't simply be cooked from start to finish in the charcoal oven because by the time the centre had reached the desired temperature, the surface would have charred too much. The way round this was to use the water bath to bring it to the optimal temperature for going into the charcoal oven, rather than actually cooking it: it needed to be warm enough so that the heat would penetrate efficiently in exactly the time it took for the outside to acquire a lovely crust.

Perfecting that crust pushed us to customise the charcoal oven a little. Normally it has a set of metal bars, just like a barbecue grill. These have a wonderful effect on meat, as fat drips on to the charcoal, sending up smoke that flavours the food, but because there's only intermittent contact between flesh and hot metal, you get stripes of browning rather than a proper crust. Our solution was to put a heavy metal sheet on top of one half of the bars. One side of the meat was seared on this for an even crust, then the chop was flipped on to the bars so the other side became nicely striped— the best of both worlds. We ended up with a beautifully cooked, beautifully charred piece of meat. The question now was what garnish to add in order to showcase the splendour of the chop and enhance its flavours. I had an idea for something that might do just that: sauce Robert, which is one of the great sauces of the French classical tradition.

From around 1450 to the end of the sixteenth century, the major force in cuisine was Italian. Chefs including Martino de' Rossi and Bartolomeo Scappi (see page 118) built up a body of techniques and recipes that influenced cooking throughout Europe. Scappi's *Opera dell' arte del cucinare* (1570) has woodcut illustrations of pans, strainers and ranks of kitchen knives for every conceivable purpose— evidence of a well-established and highly developed culinary tradition. At that point you'd have bet money on Italy providing the foundations of classical cuisine, but in the 1600s, Italy lost its dominance and France took its place as the centre of culinary creativity.

Part of the reason for this was geopolitical. Until unification in 1870, Italy was a patchwork of kingdoms, duchies, republics and papal states. During the Renaissance, the energy and excitement of new ideas had provided a consensus of sorts among these antagonistic factions, but once that had run its course, the country's lack of unity limited its influence elsewhere. In the long run, this would lead to a lively and inventive regional cuisine that has given Italy an extremely strong culinary identity. But in the seventeenth century it meant that Italian cooking no longer held sway in Europe. By the 1650s the *Opera* was out of print.

The other reason for French culinary ascendancy was the appearance, in 1651, of *Le Cuisinier françois* by La Varenne. Little is known about the chef, including his real name (La Varenne is a pseudonym, taken from an earlier chef who supposedly not only cooked for the French king Henry IV, but pimped for him too). But *Le Cuisinier françois* finally demonstrates the true culinary potential of the Renaissance principles of harmony and refined simplicity. La Varenne takes the baton from Scappi and really runs with it. A number of the techniques that we now think of as the basics of good cooking, such as slow-simmering tough cuts of meat, flavouring with a bouquet garni, reducing liquids to concentrate flavour or using a roux to thicken a sauce, make their first appearance here. His most famous creation, duxelles of mushrooms (named after the Marquis d'Uxelles, for whom La Varenne worked), is still a classic filling for omelettes and garnish for veal chops. The recipes emphasise natural flavours, a balance of ingredients and delicate presentation. La Varenne wrote with less clarity and precision than Martino or Scappi, and exotic flavourings like musk and ambergris still found a place among his pages, but his book nonetheless represented a real break with the past. *Le Cuisinier françois* marked the end of medieval cuisine and the beginning of French classical cooking.

French chefs picked up on La Varenne's ideas and took them forward with such speed and enthusiasm that within twenty-five years he was already seen as old-fashioned. His work was superseded by other books, notably *Le cuisinier roïal et bourgeois* (1691) by Massialot, *The Modern Cook* (1733) by Lord Chesterfield's chef Vincent La Chapelle (who criticises Massialot but steals many of his recipes), *Les Dons de Comus* (1739) by François Marin and *La Cuisinière bourgeoise* (1746) by Menon. However, what really consolidated the status of French cuisine was the French Revolution.

We think of the restaurant as a pretty well-established part of our culture, but it's actually a relatively modern phenomenon. When they first opened in the 1760s, restaurants were simply places to get a restorative (or *restaurant*) bowl of soup. Eating out was done in taverns, inns and cafés that generally served basic fare designed to fuel people on the go, much in the manner of a motorway service station. Fine dining took place at court or in the residences of the wealthy, who would have their own private chef. Between 1789 and 1799, the French Revolution tore this privileged set-up apart. As noble families either fled the country or lost their heads, many chefs suddenly found themselves out of a job, and looked to restaurants for employment. However, working in a restaurant is a very different prospect from catering for a private individual. Chefs had to develop an extensive repertoire in a short space of time, and many of them turned for inspiration to the works of Antonin Carême.

In 1793, when he was just ten years old, Carême was abandoned by his impoverished family and found work as a kitchen boy in a Paris chophouse. Five years later he began an apprenticeship with the pâtissier Sylvain Bailly on the rue Vivienne, a move that fitted perfectly with his talents. Carême later declared: "I believe architecture to be the first among the arts, and the principal branch of architecture is confectionery." He undoubtedly had an architect's eye for detail, precision and visual showmanship, and it was this that took him to the top of his profession. Admittedly, he was also fortunate to be working at a time when service was done *à la française*, in other words with all the dishes served at the same time, a style of presentation that emphasised decorative display and led to the pâtissier becoming the star of the kitchen. By 1804, Carême had his own shop on rue de la Paix and a thriving freelance business creating extravagant edible temples, harps, lyres, pagodas and gondolas made of spun sugar, pastry, meringue, marzipan and icing for grand Parisian dinners. His real leap into the limelight, though, was becoming the principal chef working for Charles Maurice de Talleyrand-Périgord, the Foreign Minister under Napoleon Bonaparte.

In the early part of Napoleon's rule, Talleyrand was the government's foremost political strategist for international relations. Napoleon ordered him to "receive the diplomatic corps brilliantly so that foreigners will want to visit you", and also wanted "an invitation to be a recompense for ambassadors of sovereigns with whom I am happy". Carême was a key part of that recompense, producing grand banquets at the Foreign Office in Hôtel Galliffet and at Talleyrand's country estate, Château Valençay, many of which are recorded in Carême's 1822 book, *Le Maître d'Hôtel Français*. He worked on the wedding banquet of Napoleon's brother, Jerome, and made the cake for Napoleon's wedding to Marie-Louise of Austria in 1810. At a ball thrown for Napoleon on the eve of his departure to campaign in Germany, Carême created thirty impossibly tall *suédoises* (cold desserts made of fruit cooked in syrup, arranged in layers in a mould and covered with jelly flavoured with fruit, wine or liqueur). They were, according to Carême at least (he was an energetic self-promoter), the talk of the city.

The partnership of Talleyrand and Carême petered out in 1814 when the Russian troops entered Paris. Talleyrand and the diplomats who had been Carême's main guests moved to Austria to haggle over European borders at the Congress of Vienna. Carême still had work over the next two years, devising meals for Tsar Alexander I and the restored French monarchy —for a ball at which Louis XVIII was guest of honour he created giant military trophies in sugar and mastic as table centrepieces—and he was informally invited to return with the Tsar to St Petersburg. But in the end he chose a more surprising course: accepting a post in the household of the Prince of Wales. In 1816 the world's greatest chef came to Britain to cook for the future King George IV.

Although George wouldn't become king until 1820, he had effectively been ruling the country as Prince Regent since 1810, when George III had relapsed into porphyria-induced madness to spend his last decade sightless and wandering confusedly around Windsor Castle in his dressing gown. Despite this, the man the British people called "Farmer George" was

generally held in high regard. His son, on the other hand, was considered decadent, indulgent and uncouth—the rogering roisterer of the *Blackadder* television series.

There was some truth to this. George conducted a series of clumsy and all-too public affairs and married disastrously twice (his first words upon seeing his second wife were "I am not well, pray get me a glass of brandy"). His debts were gargantuan, and so was his appetite. Prodigious consumption of food and drink swelled him to more than twenty stone and earned him the nickname The Prince of Whales. Naturally, he provided fantastic visual material for satirists. In *High Life Below Stairs!* (1819), the caricaturist Isaac Robert Cruikshank portrays the Prince Regent as a mutton-chop-whiskered, big-bellied buffoon wedged in his chair, with one foot on the dining table and the other snagged in the tablecloth, knocking over crockery and spilling goblets of wine while waving a fork in the air. But George also had a reputation as a wit and good conversationalist. The Duke of Wellington often clashed with the king, yet even he had to admit George was "devilish entertaining" and "a most magnificent patron of the arts". Unlike the previous three Georges, who had few cultural interests, George IV appreciated Jane Austen and Sir Walter Scott, took an interest in science, commissioned works of art by Gainsborough, Romney, Stubbs and Canova, and commissioned John Nash to build Brighton Pavilion and re-model Buckingham Palace.

George was also a great connoisseur of French food, and lured Carême to Britain with the offer of £2,000 per annum (the equivalent of about £120,000 in today's money, and at least double what some of the highest-ranking officials in the royal household were getting) and the opportunity to work in one of the best kitchens in the world. The Brighton Pavilion had, according to the *Brighton Ambulator*, "every modern improvement to facilitate the process of the culinary art", including clockwork roasting spits, lead-lined ice bins, a water tower and a large steam-table that could keep forty dishes warm at the same time. With these innovations and an enormous budget (monthly expenditure on meat alone was upwards of £500, around £30,000 in today's money), Carême created spectacular banquets with dozens of dishes, from celery soup, perch in Hollandaise sauce and vol-au-vents (which he invented) to chicken à la reine, turbot in a prawn sauce, apple pudding with rum and vanilla soufflé, not forgetting his trademark sugar constructions of Italian pavilions, Swiss hermitages and giant meringues.

Despite all this, Carême stayed with George IV for barely a year, driven away by a combination of homesickness, the dismal British weather and his employer's appalling gluttony. (In the left-hand corner of *High Life Below Stairs!* Carême is pictured with a grin of dismay on his face and his palms spread out before him, as though pleading with gorging George for moderation.) After an even briefer and equally disappointing stint working for Tsar Alexander I, he returned to Paris to work for Baron de Rothschild and to compose his encyclopaedic *L'Art de la cuisine français au dix-neuvième siècle*, which was published in five volumes from 1833 onwards, with the last two completed by one of Carême's students after his death in 1833.

L'Art de la cuisine is the first great bible of French classical cuisine because it seeks to bring order to the processes involved in cooking and recognise its fundamental principles. One of Carême's most significant initiatives was to group sauces into families, and show how espagnole, velouté, allemande and béchamel, the four "mother" sauces, could be used to create an infinite variety of *petites sauces*, including sauce Robert. Although Carême wasn't the inventor of the sauce—a version of it, called Barbe Robert, appears as early as the fifteenth century in one of my favourite historical cookbooks, the *Vivendier*—he's the one who gave it a place in the classical tradition.

A classic sauce, a classic cut: using sauce Robert to garnish my black-foot pork chop seemed a suitable tribute to one of the founders of *haute cuisine*, and a nice acknowledgement of an extraordinary moment in time when the greatest chef in the world was working in Britain.

In general, pork-based sauces have a distinctive flavour that makes them less versatile than sauces with beef or chicken as their foundation. But as the garnish for a cut of pork, I thought, sauce Robert would be perfect. Its base of highly concentrated pork stock would add intensity and depth to the flavour of the meat, and the other core ingredients—gently softened onions for a touch of sweetness, some typical bouquet garni herbs for fragrance and the mustard that gives the sauce its kick of acidity— would all complement the meat beautifully.

Although sauce Robert has a long history, its ingredients and techniques aren't fixed and immutable. In *The Lady's Assistant for Regulating and Supplying her Table* (1777), Charlotte Mason presented a very pared-down version, in which diced onions and bacon are browned, then cooked gently in veal gravy until tender and finally vinegar and mustard are added. In *Larousse Gastronomique*, the sauce is thickened with flour and white wine is used. So, while I kept an eye on Carême's recipe as I developed my own, I wasn't about to follow it to the letter. To achieve the effects he wanted, Carême used a set of ingredients that, if you followed his method for making Sauce Espagnole, was lengthy and elaborate. I intended to simplify the process and get a very precise balance and depth of flavour.

One of the keys to this was a piece of equipment that Carême didn't have access to: the pressure cooker. I've been using, and trying to popularise the use of, the pressure cooker pretty much ever since the Fat Duck first opened in 1995. As far as I'm concerned, it's the chef's secret weapon for making a really intense, full-flavoured stock. The reason for this is down to the physics that determines the boiling point. Liquid boils when it has sufficient energy (from heat) to "push up" with greater force than atmospheric force is "pushing down". At that stage, molecules begin to escape in the form of steam. At sea level, where atmospheric pressure is at its greatest, water boils when it reaches 100°C/212°F. High up, where the air is thinner, the molecules require less energy in order to break free and therefore need less heat. On top of Mount Everest, water boils at 72°C/162°F.

The pressure cooker is well named. The pressure it exerts is greater than atmospheric pressure at sea level, and consequently any liquid it contains has to push harder to escape, and needs a lot of energy in order to do so: the temperature inside a pressure cooker can reach around 120°C/250°F before coming to the boil. This increased heat confers particular benefits. The higher temperature increases the extraction of flavour from the ingredients by kick-starting the Maillard reactions that add complexity (see page 77).

So, while the foundation of my sauce Robert would, like Carême's, be a highly reduced meat stock, I planned to put all the ingredients in the pressure cooker first, to capture and intensify the flavours as much as possible. Moreover, since the centrepiece of this dish was a pork chop, I wanted the stock to derive its flavour from pig, rather than the partridge, veal and cured ham that Carême used in his espagnole sauce base. However, pork stock needs care. Use too many bones in it, and it ends up dull and muddy. Pork meat will give the stock flavour, but doesn't provide much in the way of gelatine, so it has too thin a texture unless you reduce it, by which time that flavour can be unpleasantly, overpoweringly strong. My strategy, therefore, was to add pigs' ears to the stock as well, which not only have robust, porky flavour, but also provide plenty of gelatine, resulting in a thick texture and delicious mouthfeel. Pigs' ears have their own drawbacks and can make the stock somehow flat, so creating a stock that has just the right depth, strength and texture is a real balancing act. Eventually, though, I created a stock using three parts of the pig: bones, ears and shoulder.

Once the big-flavoured foundations were laid, the finishing of the sauce was simple. Carême's requires little more than three steps: softening onions, adding and reducing the base stock, and adding the final flavourings of vinegar and mustard. Here, my recipe is more complicated because I saw this stage as an opportunity to deepen the flavours further, and introduce some fresh, clean, aromatic notes. Achieving this was a question of introducing the top notes of the dish while holding on to their volatile aromas and making the flavours work together. So, once the shallots and garlic had been lightly caramelised and the Alsace bacon fried until golden brown to give a smoky bacon flavour, the cooking process was essentially a gentle and carefully staged infusion, which is one of the best methods for retaining the freshness and distinctiveness of the ingredients and avoiding a "cooked-out" characteristic. The flavours of the meat, onions and garlic were allowed to meld with the stock, followed by a very brief infusion of thyme and sage, the punchy aroma of which can give a real boost to meaty flavours. Alongside a rich, fragrant mushroom spelt risotto, they create a sauce robust enough to stand up to the perfect pork chop.

BLACK-FOOT PORK CHOP
WITH SAUCE ROBERT

Makes 6 portions

Pork Stock

2kg	Pork bones
6	Pigs' ears, rinsed and trimmed
100g	Extra virgin olive oil
125g	Unsalted butter
2kg	Pork shoulder, diced
800g	Peeled and finely sliced onions
600g	Peeled and finely sliced carrots
20g	Peeled and sliced garlic
15g	Thyme

Preheat the oven to 170°C/340°F.

Spread out the pork bones evenly on a roasting tray and roast them until golden brown, turning frequently. Deglaze the roasting pan, reserve the juices and set aside.

In the meantime, slice the pigs' ears into strips and heat half the olive oil and half the butter in a large pressure cooker. Once the butter starts to foam, fry the diced pork shoulder and pigs' ears in batches until golden brown. Remove from the pan and set aside.

Add the remaining olive oil and butter to the pan, followed by the onions and carrots. Sweat until softened, then add the garlic and cook for 5 minutes. Add the roasted bones, caramelised pork shoulder and pigs' ears to the pressure cooker, followed by 4 litres cold water.

Bring the stock to a simmer, skimming off all impurities. Add the thyme and stir again before securing the lid of the pressure cooker. Cook for 2 hours.

Allow the pressure cooker to depressurise and the stock to cool slightly before opening the lid. Pass the stock through a fine-mesh sieve, followed by a fine-mesh filter bag, then refrigerate overnight.

Remove the fat from the surface of the stock, place in a pot and reduce it to 15% of the original amount (approximately 625g), skimming off all impurities.

Refrigerate until needed.

Sauce Robert

40g	Unsalted butter
50g	Finely sliced shallots
1g	Peeled and sliced garlic
40g	Finely diced Alsace bacon
400g	Reserved reduced pork stock
1g	Thyme
2g	Sage
15g	Wholegrain mustard
	Lemon juice

Heat half the butter in a small saucepan. Add the sliced shallots and gently caramelise, then add the garlic and cook until lightly caramelised. Remove the garlic and shallots from the saucepan and set aside.

Add the remaining butter and lightly fry the Alsace bacon until light golden brown. Set aside.

In a clean saucepan, heat the reduced pork stock to 80°C/176°F. Remove from the heat and add the caramelised shallots, garlic and Alsace bacon. Cover the saucepan with clingfilm and leave to infuse for 20 minutes.

Add the thyme and sage and infuse for 5 more minutes. Pass the mixture through a fine-mesh sieve, followed by a fine-mesh filter bag. Add the wholegrain mustard and lemon juice and whisk to emulsify.

Refrigerate until needed.

Smoked Ham Hock

1	Ham hock
250g	Diced Alsace bacon (5mm cubes)
100g	Peeled and diced onions
100g	Peeled and diced carrots
80g	Rinsed and sliced leeks
80g	Rinsed and sliced celery
10g	Peeled and sliced garlic
5g	Thyme
1	Bay leaf
10g	Flatleaf parsley
1g	Black peppercorns
30g	Wood smoking chips

Preheat a water bath to 88°C/190°F.

Rinse the ham hock under cold running water for 3 hours, then remove and set aside.

Place the ham hock, Alsace bacon, vegetables, herbs, peppercorns and 1.5kg cold water in a large sous-vide bag. Seal the bag under full pressure and place in the water bath for 7 hours.

Remove the sous-vide bag from the water bath and plunge into iced water. Once cooled, remove the meat from the bone, discarding all fat and sinew.

Soak the wood smoking chips for 10 minutes, then drain. Place the chips and a tray of ice directly underneath the wire shelf of a smoke box. Divide the ham hock into equal-size portions and place them on the wire shelf. Using a blowtorch, light the smoking chips and close the smoke box lid. Allow the chips to smoke for 2–3 hours. Check and relight if necessary every 20–30 minutes. The size of the chips will determine how long the smoking process will take; check the flavour when you check on the chips.

Dice the ham hock into 8mm cubes and refrigerate until needed.

Roast Chicken Stock

6kg	Chopped chicken wings
25g	Thyme
20g	Rosemary
3	Bay leaves

Preheat the oven to 190°C/375°F.

Spread out the chicken wing pieces evenly on a roasting tray and roast them until golden brown, turning frequently. You may need to do this in batches, as overcrowding the tray will cause the chicken to steam.

Deglaze the roasting trays with water and place the roasted wings, along with the juices, in a large pressure cooker with 4.8 litres cold water. Bring to the boil, skimming off all scum and impurities.

Add the thyme, rosemary and bay leaves, and stir the mixture one last time before securing the lid of the pressure cooker. Cook for 2 hours.

Allow the pressure cooker to depressurise and the stock to cool slightly before opening the lid. Strain the stock through a fine-mesh sieve, followed by a fine-mesh filter bag. Chill the stock in the fridge overnight.

Remove and discard all the fat from the surface of the stock. Heat the stock in a large saucepan and gently reduce to 300g. It is important to continue skimming the stock as it reduces.

Once the stock has reduced, pass it through a fine-mesh filter bag and refrigerate until needed.

Cream Sauce Base

75g	Madeira
300g	Double cream
300g	Reserved reduced chicken stock
50g	Unsalted butter, cubed and at room temperature
80g	Peeled and finely sliced shallots
5g	Peeled and sliced garlic
80g	Washed and finely sliced leeks
20g	Finely grated Parmesan
2g	Lemon juice

Pour the Madeira into a small saucepan over a moderate heat. Reduce to 15g.

Place the double cream in a second saucepan and bring to the boil. Turn the heat down to moderate and allow the cream to thicken and reduce to 190g. It will colour as this happens.

In a third saucepan, gently heat the chicken stock to 80°C/176°F.

Combine the reduced Madeira, reduced cream and the reduced chicken stock, and whisk to emulsify. Set aside.

In a separate, clean pan, gently melt half the butter and add the sliced shallots. After 5 minutes, add the sliced garlic and cook until lightly caramelised. Remove the caramelised shallots and garlic from the pan and set aside.

Melt the remaining butter in the same pan, add the leeks and cook until lightly caramelised. Remove the caramelised leeks from the pan and set aside.

Return the cream sauce to the heat and bring to 85°C/185°F, before adding the cooked shallots, garlic and leeks. Add the grated Parmesan and stir well to combine.

Remove the sauce from the heat and blitz in a Thermomix for 30 seconds at high speed at 80°C/176°F, until fully incorporated. You may need to stop halfway to scrape down the sides of the jug.

Pass the cream sauce base through a fine-mesh sieve and return the strained sauce to a clean pan. Gently heat to 85°C/185°F, stirring continuously. Add the lemon juice and stir to incorporate. Pass the

cream sauce base a second time through a fine-mesh sieve and store in the fridge until needed.

Dashi

6g	Kombu
5g	Bonito flakes

Place 300g water in a saucepan and add the kombu. Heat to 60°C/140°F and maintain that temperature for 1 hour.

Discard the kombu and keep the water at 60°C/140°F. Stir in the bonito flakes and allow to infuse for 3 minutes.

Pass the dashi through a fine-mesh sieve, followed by a fine-mesh filter bag, and refrigerate until needed.

Mushroom Purée

65g	Unsalted butter, cubed and at room temperature
65g	Peeled and finely sliced shallots
150g	Finely sliced cleaned shiitake mushroom caps
100g	Finely sliced cleaned button mushrooms
20g	Mirin
250g	Reserved dashi
30g	White soy sauce

Heat a deep-based pan and gently melt the butter. Add the sliced shallots and cook until lightly caramelised. Add the sliced shiitake and button mushrooms and cook until lightly caramelised.

Add the mirin and simmer gently until the mushrooms are coated in the shiny sauce. Add the dashi and simmer gently until the entire mixture reduces to approximately 320g.

Remove from the heat and add the white soy sauce. Place the mixture in a deep container and blitz to a very smooth purée using a hand blender.

Pass the purée through a fine-mesh sieve and store in the fridge until needed. Ensure the surface of the purée is covered with clingfilm so it does not form a skin.

(continued overleaf)

Spelt Sauce

220g **Reserved cream sauce base**
130g **Reserved mushroom purée**
5g **White soy sauce**
5g **Sherry vinegar**
1g **Salt**

Gently melt the cream sauce base before removing it from the heat and combining it with the mushroom purée in a small bowl. Add the white soy sauce, sherry vinegar and salt and thoroughly combine. Refrigerate until needed.

Cooked Spelt

230g **Vegetable stock (see page 94), plus additional if necessary**
40g **Extra virgin olive oil**
150g **Pearled spelt**

In a saucepan, heat the vegetable stock and 230g water to 90°C/194°F.

In the meantime, in a separate, deep-based pan, heat the olive oil and lightly toast the pearled spelt until nutty and light brown in colour. Add the hot stock and cook over a moderate heat, stirring regularly.

Once the liquid has been absorbed almost completely, and the spelt has softened in texture, remove the pan from the heat. Refrigerate until needed.

Finished Spelt

15g **Extra virgin olive oil**
90g **Diced large close-cap mushrooms (8mm dice)**
240g **Reserved spelt sauce**
270g **Reserved cooked spelt**
150g **Reserved diced ham hock**
12 **Quartered pickled onions (see page 291)**
Vegetable stock, if needed
Sherry vinegar
Salt and pepper

Heat the olive oil in a sauté pan and cook the diced mushrooms over a high heat until soft and fragrant.

Remove the mushrooms from the oil and drain on a small tray lined with kitchen paper. Set aside.

In a separate large, deep pan, gently heat the spelt sauce. Add the cooked spelt and stir to incorporate. Cook for approximately 2 minutes, stirring continuously. You may need a small amount of vegetable stock to bring the spelt together.

Add the diced ham hock and quartered pickled onions. Stir to combine. Just before serving, add the cooked mushrooms and adjust the acidity with a few drops of sherry vinegar. Season with salt and pepper.

To Serve

6 **Ibérico black-foot pork chops, 260–280g each**
Olive oil
Sea salt flakes
Brown butter, melted (see page 315)
Cracked black pepper
Reserved finished spelt
500g **Grapeseed oil**
50g **Dehydrated pork crackling pieces**
Lardo, shaved finely and cut into 9cm squares
380g **Reserved sauce Robert**

Preheat a water bath to 60°C/140°F. Preheat the oven to 60°C/140°F.

Neatly French trim the pork chops, place them in sous-vide bags and seal under full pressure. Place in the water bath for 5 minutes.

Remove the chops from the bag, rub olive oil over them and season with salt.

At the restaurant, a Josper charcoal oven is used to give the chops a smoky char-grill flavour. A similar effect can be achieved at home with a barbecue or griddle pan.

Heat a cast-iron griddle, if using, and sear both sides of the chops to make a golden crust. Alternatively, place them on a griddle over hot coals on the barbecue. Transfer to a preheated oven, resting on scrunched-up pieces of kitchen foil in a tray so that they do not touch the bottom. Using a probe thermometer, monitor the internal temperature of the chops while they are resting.

Once the ideal serving temperature of 56°C/133°F is reached, remove the chops from the oven. Brush them with brown butter and season with sea salt flakes and cracked black pepper. Put them on serving plates and place a spoonful of the cooked spelt next to them.

Meanwhile, heat the grapeseed oil and deep fry the dehydrated pork crackling pieces until puffed and golden. Remove with a slotted spoon and drain on kitchen paper.

Place a layer of thin lardo on top of the spelt and cover with the pork crackling pieces. Spoon the sauce Robert over and around the dish and serve.

CUCUMBER KETCHUP

[1826]

CUCUMBER CATSUP

❄ *Take large old cucumbers and pare them, cut them in slices, and break them to a mash, which must be sprinkled with salt and covered with a cloth. Keep in all the seeds. Next day, set the vessel aslant to drain off the juice, and do this till no more can be obtained. Strain it, and boil it up with a seasoning of white pepper, sliced ginger, black pepper, sliced shalot, and a little horse radish. When cold, pick out the shalot and horse radish, and bottle the catsup, which is an excellent preparation for flavouring sauces for boiled fowls, dishes of veal, rabbits, or the more insipid meats* ❄

Mrs Margaret Dods, *The Cook and Housewife's Manual* (1826)

The appendix of *The Cook and Housewife's Manual* contains various instructions on how to clean furniture and clothes made of calico (an Indian unbleached cotton originally made in Calicut, which gave the fabric its name). "Rice-water is now very much used," observes Mrs Dods. "Boil a pound of rice in five quarts of water, and when cool enough, wash in this, using the rice for soap."

The fact that late-Georgian housewives might welcome advice on how to clean traditional Indian fabrics is an indication of just how much commerce and consumerism had changed by the early nineteenth century. England had been building up a network of outposts, plantations and factories in China, India and the West Indies since the 1600s, and merchants now traded on a global scale, importing exotic goods such as gingham, silk, muslin and porcelain, which were snapped up by a landed gentry keen to show off their wealth and status.

Exotic foodstuffs were equally sought after. One of the original incentives for eastern trade was to find a reliable source for the spices, such as pepper, mace and nutmeg, that were still an essential part of cooking in Tudor and early Stuart England. Later, tea from China (it wasn't cultivated on a large scale in India until the 1820s) became so popular that by 1700 England was importing more than 45,000 kilograms of the stuff annually. The ever-increasing number of merchants, clerks, soldiers and sailors who spent time in the East meant there was a curiosity about Asian dishes back home, and a market for them too. The first printed cookbook to include Indian recipes was Hannah Glasse's *The Art of Cookery Made Plain and Easy* (1747), which offers instructions for several types of pilau. In *The Lady's Assistant for Regulating and Supplying her Table* (1777), Charlotte Mason has a recipe for Curree of Chickens, and over the next half-century or so the Indian style of cooking became sufficiently integrated into British life that Thackeray could use curry as the catalyst for a comic scene in *Vanity Fair* (1847–8). When the heroine, Becky Sharp, goes to dinner at the house of Joseph Sedley, who normally works in India but is at home recuperating from a liver complaint, she is determined to show enthusiasm for all things Indian in order to snare a suitor. She therefore expresses great interest in the curry on the table, and Joseph's father—being "a coarse man, from the Stock Exchange, where they love all sorts of practical jokes"—encourages her to try it. Pretending pleasure while "suffering tortures with the cayenne pepper", she is then offered a chilli. Understandably expecting something cooling, given the name, she eats it and ends up calling desperately for water, much to her own chagrin and the men's amusement.

The interest in Asian cuisine led to a demand for the condiments that supplied its characteristic flavours. Jars of pickle, chutney and soy were brought back by traders, and British cooks were soon trying to copy them. (The change in climate and resources often led to them being substantially altered, however. In India and China, for example, pickles and sauces could be left to ferment under the hot sun; in Britain, vinegar had to be added to achieve the same effect. Piccalilli developed from trying to give a fiery kick to cauliflower using mustard instead of chilli.) This is also how ketchup first reached British shores. The word derives from *kê-tsiap*, a Chinese dialect word meaning "brine of pickled fish". Gradually, however, it became a catch-all term for a variety of soy-based condiments and fermented fish sauces. Sailors on merchant vessels in the Indian Ocean and South China Sea came across ketchup (or catchup or catsup), picked up on the fact that it kept for a long time, and started taking barrels of it on board to spice up the monotonous ocean-going diet of bully beef and tack biscuits. Hannah Glasse's recipe for catchup acknowledges its maritime provenance: in a chapter entitled For Captains of Ships, she gives instructions "To make Catchup to keep twenty years".

Most of the sailors who brought ketchup back to Britain worked for the East India Company, a private organisation engaged in Asian trade that has had an enormous influence on the British diet and culinary history. Towards the end of the sixteenth century, hemmed in by a Portuguese-Spanish alliance that barred access to their stocks of spices, and envious of profitable Dutch trade in Indonesia, English merchants petitioned Queen Elizabeth I for permission to set up a trading company. A Royal Charter was granted in 1600, and the following year The

Company of Merchants of London trading into the East Indies (or the East India Company, as it was more commonly known) sent four ships to Sumatra under the command of James Lancaster. The trip's success was modest: although Lancaster returned in September 1603 with holds full of peppercorns, James I (who had become king upon Elizabeth's death in March of that year) had also acquired a large quantity of the spice and the subsequent glut halved market prices. Nonetheless, it was deemed successful enough to justify further voyages. During the seventeenth century, the Company continued to explore Asia, developing trade links with Sumatra, Java, Yemen, Siam, Japan, China and India, which would become the country in which the Company was most heavily involved. The history of the East India Company is inextricably entwined with the history of India.

The realities of maritime trade meant it was a risky business for merchant and sailor alike. Shipwreck was a constant possibility. Scurvy meant the body count was often terrifyingly high. On the first voyage, a quarter of the crew were dead by the time they reached the Cape of Good Hope. By the time the second voyage (in 1604) reached Table Bay, they were, in the words of their commander, "a swarme of lame and weake diseased cripples". The Company representatives (or "factors"), who were deposited on foreign shores to set up factories and secure trading concessions, were no less likely to succumb to malaria, dysentery, typhoid or cholera. Luck and chance played their part in the Company's growth—the establishment in 1639 of an outpost in Madras (now Chennai), which later became a major trading centre and proved to be of great strategic importance, was due to the local Company agent having a mistress in nearby San Thomé. But, one way or another, it prospered.

After the Civil War, the Restoration of Charles II further advantaged the Company. Both had similar views on finance and foreign affairs, mistrusted the Dutch and preferred to deal with the Catholic powers where possible. It was Charles who rented Bombay (Mumbai), which he had received as part of his wedding dowry, to the Company. It would become their second major trading centre, at times eclipsing even Madras. Equally significantly, it was owned by England, and had the Union Flag flying above it. The East India Company had, in effect, made its first colonial acquisition, and was obliged for the first time to practise civilian administration and government on Indian soil. It set a precedent of sorts for the future.

Two years later, after a disagreement with the Nawab of Bengal over customs duties had led to a series of battles that culminated in a stand-off at Hijili island on the Rasulpur River, the Company set up a factory close to the island in Calcutta (Kolkata), which was to become its third major trading centre. Having established a strategic triangle of Bombay in the north-west, Madras in the south-east, and Calcutta in the north-east (which meant that, in a military crisis, they could move on all sides), the Company was now supremely well set up to conduct business. By the early 1700s, they were sending ten ships a year to India, and another five or so to China, Persia and Sumatra, and £500,000 per annum (about £100 million in today's money) was being divided between the 2,000 or so stockholders. The Company was generating wealth and jobs on a vast scale, and had become firmly entwined not just with the English economy, but also with the state and society. It was an ambiguous relationship that would ultimately push the Company towards territorial control of India.

Although business grew unimpeded in the first half of the eighteenth century, the secure foundations for trade were becoming increasingly fragile. After the death in 1707 of its last great emperor, Aurangzeb, the Muslim Moghul Empire gradually lost overall control, as rival groups, in particular the Hindu Marathas, took over parts of the country. This alone would have disrupted the Company's business, forcing local representatives to renegotiate the advantageous trade concessions they had built up over years, but there was soon a far greater disruption in the form of the French. France had been slow to spot the commercial potential of the East, but in 1719 it set up its own Compagnie des Indes and, under the guidance of the clever, energetic Marquis of Dupleix, quickly established itself as the second biggest trader in the region after Britain. Throughout most of the century, the two countries were at war, engaging in a series of conflicts that were ultimately about securing superpower status by amassing as much territory and influence as possible, while at the same time limiting or reducing the opposition's land and leverage. India became part of this game of power politics, with skirmishes and sieges in Madras, Tiruvadi, Trichonopoly and Arcot, and attempts by both sides to put puppet rulers in charge of large parts of the country.

Not surprisingly, European interference in Indian politics caused dismay among local rulers. The Nawab of Bengal, Siraj ud-Daula, stormed Calcutta in the summer of 1756 and imprisoned 146 of its defenders in Fort William's detention cell, an 18 x 15-foot semi-basement that wasn't designed for such numbers. Many were either crushed to death or perished from dehydration or heat exhaustion. According to the account of one of the prisoners, John

Zephaniah Holwell, only twenty-three survived overnight incarceration in the "Black Hole of Calcutta", and the name has since become synonymous with any kind of hell on earth. Robert Clive (who became known as Clive of India) regained Calcutta in February 1757 and defeated Siraj's army three months later. The victory was seen as a confirmation of superior British military might, and the Company was emboldened to pursue its interests even more vigorously on the back of it. By the 1790s it had more than 150,000 troops in the subcontinent.

By this point, the East India Company was no longer just a business venture. The Company's governors had always insisted that commerce, not conquest, was their aim, but some of its operatives decided that protecting those business interests necessitated a quasi-imperial agenda. Clive secretly sent a letter to Pitt the Elder (who had headed the government during the Seven Years War and was a well-known advocate of British expansionism) suggesting that India "may possibly be an object too extensive for a mercantile company" and wondering "whether the execution of a design that may hereafter be still carried to greater lengths, be worthy of the government's taking it in hand". Ultimately, the government came round to Clive's way of thinking. It passed a Charter Act in 1813 that removed the Company's monopoly on trade in India (and another in 1833 revoking its monopoly in China and elsewhere). After the Indian uprising of 1857, a mutiny by Indian troops who worked for the Company, it decided to take over the governance of the country. A year later, the Government of India Act created the British Raj, which ruled over the country until its partition into India and Pakistan in 1947.

Inspired by the influx of condiments from India and China, British cooks began making ketchup, mainly with mushrooms, presumably because a tradition of using mushrooms in pickles had existed since the late Middle Ages, so it made good culinary sense for cooks to try them out in a condiment that appeared broadly similar to a pickle. Soon, however, cookery books were full of all kinds of ketchups: walnut, oyster, anchovy (which was probably the nearest to the Asian original in terms of flavour profile), beer, mussel, elderberry, cucumber. The enthusiasm for the new condiment is an indicator of a shift in attitudes towards cooking. In the Middle Ages, and even in the Tudor and Stuart periods, pickling and other forms of preservation were valued mostly as a way of providing food and variety during the lean winter months, and each autumn the lady of the manor house would organise a lot of salting, smoking, drying and pickling. By the eighteenth century, however, pickles and ketchups were prized as home-bottled sauces that could be used to flavour melted butter, finish a stew or garnish cooked meat or cold cuts. They were, in effect, some of the first examples of convenience food. In *The Experienced English Housekeeper* (1769), for example, Elizabeth Raffald treats lemon pickle and walnut catchup as storecupboard staples, and directs the reader to add them to many of her sauces and braising liquors.

Raffald also sold both products in her Manchester shop, and by the middle of the next century, as the Industrial Revolution took hold, mass-produced condiments became commonplace. The flamboyant celebrity chef Alexis Soyer (see page 372) made a deal with Edmund Crosse and Thomas Blackwell to market a range that included Sultana's Sauce and Soyer's Relish ("an entirely new and economical condiment, adapted for all kinds of viands, which, by those who have tasted, has been pronounced *perfect*").

To many people, the idea of ketchup made with cucumber, or indeed anything other than tomato, seems strange. But in fact, tomato is the interloper here. After all, it's a New World fruit that arrived in Europe only in the sixteenth century, and even then it took a while to gain acceptance, featuring in Italian kitchens for the first time at the close of the seventeenth century, and in British ones towards the end of the eighteenth.

It was probably American industrialisation that helped the tomato become the primary ingredient for ketchup. After the Civil War (1861–5), during which many soldiers were, apparently, introduced to tinned goods for the first time and liked the convenience, the canning and bottling industry in the States expanded enormously. One of the beneficiaries of this growth was tomato ketchup: tomato factories began making it from the trimmings, discards and other leftovers from the canning process. By the 1890s there were many commercial brands on the shelves, from Thurber's Baldwin Tomato Catsup, to Curtice Brothers' Imperial Tomato Ketchup, to the Joseph Campbell Preserve Company's Beefsteak Tomato Ketchup, confidently billed as "A Revelation to Lovers of this Popular Condiment". At this stage, other types of ketchup were still being sold, but the economics of the tomato industry meant it was always likely to win out over other ingredients. Tomato ketchup was easy and cost-effective to make as a by-product of canning, and as a result production soared and the price plummeted. In 1870, a quart of Baldwin ketchup cost $2.50; by the turn of the century it was down to ten cents. Cheap and aggressively marketed by companies intent on maintaining profit, tomato ketchup became increasingly popular at the expense of other versions. In Britain, it took a while for the tomato to take over—in the early part of the twentieth century, ketchup was still thought of as primarily mushroom-based, with tomato coming a poor third to walnut—but eventually here, too, tomato usurped the other ingredients.

I'm always curious about forgotten and dismissed aspects of cooking, so the story of mushroom ketchup intrigued me, and I began developing my own. The end result was a great garnish, packed with concentrated savoury umami taste that really boosted meaty flavours and made a fantastic accompaniment for, say, a chargrilled steak. It confirmed to me that ketchup had a lot of untapped potential, so when I came across Dods's recipe, I read it with interest. It promised something fresh and sharp with a beautiful green colour. The clincher for me, though, was that cucumber is somehow quintessentially English, conjuring a pastoral fantasy of country houses, Pimm's and high tea. Cucumber sandwiches were going to be served to Lady Bracknell in *The Importance of Being Earnest*, before Algernon Moncrieff scoffed the lot. One of the key considerations in my approach to cooking is context—a dish's deliciousness comes not just from the balance of flavours, but also from the emotional associations it evokes for the diner. So I liked the idea of tapping into that sense of Englishness; it seemed appropriate for a historic British menu, and could work well in a recipe showcasing some of the produce Britain is famous for. I think that, even at this early stage, I already had in mind a seafood dish. We have suppliers in Devon and the Outer Hebrides who provide the Fat Duck with the most fantastic scallops, and it struck me that cucumber ketchup might be a perfect match for them, so long as I could get the right harmony of textures, flavours and contrasts.

The traditional way of making ketchup is to simmer the ingredients slowly until they've reduced to a jammy mass. Doing this to a cucumber, though, would simply drive off the freshness and dull its lovely colour. I wanted to keep both, so I needed a different approach, one that avoided using too much heat, which would soon give the cucumber a cooked-out characteristic. The solution was to make a fluid gel using the setting agent gellan gum (rather than gelatine, which would melt in the warmth of the scallops; see page 289). By juicing the cucumber and blitzing it in a blender to loosen it, the only heat involved would be a very brief warming to 90°C/194°F to let the gellan do its work.

The cucumber juice for the fluid gel was made from the skin and outer part of the flesh. Once that was trimmed off, I was left with a neat, green cuboid. I began looking at ways to use the rest of the cucumber in the dish, and gradually I built up a number of components that complemented one another. More strips of flesh were sliced off the cucumber with a mandolin, ready to be diced and added to the fluid gel to add texture. But here, too, I employed a very modern technique to really concentrate that flavour: the chamber vacuum sealer. Vacuum-packing is an essential part of the sous-vide method, in which food is sealed into a bag from which the air has been removed (see page 76). Usually this is in preparation for cooking in a water bath, but the chamber vacuum sealer can be used as a tool in its own right. Repeatedly vacuum-sealing fruit or vegetables, for example, turns out to be a very effective way to firm up their texture and concentrate the colour and flavour. Cucumber responds particularly well to the process; as the cell walls are sundered and compacted, the texture becomes denser and the juice from the cells mixes freely to make it fuller in flavour. The cucumber becomes more intensely itself.

Having cut strips from the cucumber with the mandolin, I was left with the heart with its rows of little seeds. This I also compressed, then seared it to provide a nice contrast of warm and cold. By now the dish was developing its own logic and integrity, and the finishing touches more or less suggested themselves. Drawing on the classic oyster–cucumber pairing, I garnished it with borage leaves, which have a hint of oyster in their flavour. Since the elements of the dish were extremely clean and unfatty, I wanted to add a bit of richness to bring it all together, so the final touch was a butter emulsion mixed with bergamot juice, which has acidity to balance the richness, and also a floral characteristic reminiscent of Earl Grey tea, whose distinctive flavour comes from the fruit. It was a nice addition of traditional Englishness, and a sidelong reference to one of the East India Company's primary imports.

ROAST SCALLOPS WITH CUCUMBER KETCHUP

Makes 6 portions

Cucumber Elements

5   Large cucumbers

Cut the cucumbers into 8cm lengths. Square them off by trimming them into perfect rectangles, reserving any offcuts in a large bowl.

Using a mandolin set to 5mm, slice the cucumbers around the heart. Place the cucumber sheets in a sous-vide bag, ensuring they are lying flat. Place the perfectly squared-off rectangular hearts in a single layer, in a second sous-vide bag.

Seal both bags under full pressure. Pierce small holes in both bags and repeat the process. Place the cucumber hearts in the fridge until needed.

Take out the cucumber sheets, trim off any cucumber skin, and dice the compressed flesh into 5mm cubes. Set aside in the fridge until needed.

Juice all the cucumber offcuts and pass through a fine-mesh filter bag. Set the juice aside in the fridge until needed.

Cucumber Fluid Gel

135g	**Chardonnay vinegar**
35g	**Sugar**
850g	**Reserved cucumber juice**
8g	**Salt**
9g	**Gellan F (low-acyl gellan)**

Combine the vinegar and sugar in a small saucepan. Bring to the boil, then remove from the heat and set aside to cool.

Place the cucumber juice and salt in the Thermomix and bring to 90°c/194°f on a medium setting. Add the gellan F and blitz for 10 seconds at high speed. Lift the lid and scrape down the sides of the jug. Continue to blitz for 1 more minute to ensure the gellan has completely dissolved. Pour the mixture into a large

bowl and place the bowl in iced water. Allow to cool completely.

Place the set gel, along with the cooled vinegar and sugar mixture, in a clean Thermomix. Blitz for 1 minute, lift the lid and scrape down the sides of the jug. Continue to blitz for 1 more minute to incorporate fully.

Scrape the fluid gel into a shallow container and place in a chamber vacuum sealer. Under full pressure, close the lid and keep a close eye on the gel, stopping the process as soon as the bubbles rise to the top. Repeat this process several more times until the gel no longer bubbles. Pass through a fine-mesh sieve and refrigerate until needed.

Pickled Shallots

50g	**Chardonnay vinegar**
2g	**White caster sugar**
2g	**Salt**
100g	**Very finely diced shallots**

Heat the vinegar, 25g water, sugar and salt in a small saucepan until dissolved. Remove and leave to cool completely.

Place the shallots in a fine-mesh sieve under cold running water for 30 seconds. Drain well and add to the cooled vinegar mixture. Store in the fridge until needed.

Cucumber Ketchup

600g	**Reserved cucumber gel**
210g	**Reserved compressed cucumber dice**
25g	**Reserved pickled shallots**
4g	**Dill**

Place all the ingredients except the dill into a bowl and stir to combine. Finely chop the dill and stir it in. Store in the fridge until needed.

Butter Emulsion

200g   Unsalted butter, cubed and at room temperature

Gently heat 80g water in a saucepan and gradually add the butter, whisking continuously to emulsify. Once emulsified, blitz the mixture with a hand blender to incorporate fully.

To Serve

6	**Reserved cucumber hearts**
20g	**Extra virgin olive oil**
24	**Large cleaned scallops**
	Salt
100g	**Reserved butter emulsion**
100g	**Trimmed and blanched purple-sprouting broccoli**
	Bergamot juice
	Reserved cucumber ketchup
	Borage leaves and flowers
	Sea salt flakes

Slice the compressed cucumber hearts on the diagonal into 2 equal pieces.

Heat the olive oil in a non-stick pan and sear the cucumber hearts until caramelised. Sear the scallops for 1 minute until lightly browned, then turn over for 10 seconds to heat through the other side. Season with salt.

In a separate saucepan, heat the butter emulsion and gently warm through the purple-sprouting broccoli. Drain the broccoli and set aside. Season with salt. Add a dash of bergamot juice to the warm emulsion to taste.

Spoon the cucumber ketchup on to a plate and arrange the scallops, cucumber hearts and broccoli on the plate. Drizzle a little of the emulsion over the scallops and around the dish, and season the scallop with sea salt flakes. Garnish with borage leaves and flowers.

SAUCE REFORM

[1846]

NO. 35 SAUCE A LA REFORM

❊ Cut up two middling-sized onions into thin slices and put them into a stewpan with two sprigs of parsley, two of thyme, two bay-leaves, two ounces of lean uncooked ham, half a clove of garlic, half a blade of mace, and an ounce of fresh butter; stir them ten minutes over a sharp fire, then add two tablespoons of Tarragon vinegar, and one of Chili vinegar, boil it one minute; then add a pint of brown sauce (No. 1), or sauce Espagnole (No. 2), three tablespoons of preserved tomates, and eight of consommé (No. 134); place it over the fire until boiling, then put it at the corner, let it simmer ten minutes, skim it well, then place it again over the fire, keeping it stirred, and reduce until it adheres to the back of a spoon; then add a good tablespoonful of red currant jelly, and half do. of chopped mushrooms; season a little more if required with pepper and salt; stir it until the jelly is melted, then pass it through a tammie into another stewpan. When ready to serve, make it hot, and add the white of a hard-boiled egg cut into strips half an inch long, and thick in proportion, four white blanched mushrooms, one gherkin, two green Indian pickles, and half an ounce of cooked ham, or tongue, all cut in strips like the white of egg; do not let it boil afterwards. This sauce must be poured over whatever it is served with ❊

NO. 698 COTELETTES DE MOUTON A LA REFORM

❊ *Chop a quarter of a pound of lean cooked ham very fine, and mix it with the same quantity of bread-crumbs, then have ten very nice cotelettes, lay them flat on your table, season lightly with pepper and salt, egg over with a paste-brush, and throw them into the ham and bread-crumbs, then beat them lightly with a knife, put ten spoonfuls of oil in a sauté-pan, place it over the fire, and when quite hot lay in the cotelettes, fry nearly ten minutes (over a moderate fire) of a light brown colour; to ascertain when done press your knife upon the thick part, if quite done it will feel rather firm; possibly they may not all be done at one time, so take out those that are ready first and lay them on a cloth till the others are done; as they require to be cooked with the gravy in them, dress upon a thin border of mashed potatoes in a crown, with the bones pointing outwards, sauce over with a pint of the sauce reform (No. 35), and serve. If for a large dinner you may possibly be obliged to cook the cotelettes half an hour before, in which case they must be very underdone, and laid in a clean sauté-pan with two or three spoonfuls of thin glaze; keep them in the hot closet, moistening them occasionally with the glaze (with a paste-brush) until ready to serve; the same remark applies to every description of cotelettes* ❊

Alexis Soyer, *The Gastronomic Regenerator* (1846)

When George IV died in 1830, Britain was already in turmoil. The economy was suffering a downturn and there had been a series of violent protests and destruction of machinery by agricultural workers unhappy with labour conditions, low wages and the loss of jobs due to the mechanisation of farming. They became known as the Swing Riots because letters outlining the protestors' grievances were often signed "Captain Swing", the fictitious figurehead of the movement.

Social dissatisfaction had been incubating since the 1790s. The example of the French Revolution had emboldened ordinary people to seek change. Radical groups such as the London Corresponding Society had started demanding universal suffrage. In his *Rights of Man* (1791) Thomas Paine called for equality and an end to social privilege based on birth and property, for which he was tried *in absentia* and convicted of seditious libel—an extreme response that shows just how threatened and insecure the government felt. Many people either feared or anticipated that the revolution would spill out across the Channel.

That it didn't is probably largely due to the French First Republic's declaration of war in 1793. Apart from a brief peace settlement from March 1802 to May 1803, Britain was permanently at war with France (led at first by the French revolutionary government, then by Napoleon Bonaparte) until victory at the Battle of Waterloo in 1815. The threat of invasion by the French presented a more tangible and immediate threat than social injustice, and united the country in a common purpose.

Such a respite was bound to be temporary. Social divisions by now penetrated so deeply that it was only a matter of time before things started to fall apart. The end of the war led to mass unemployment: 300,000 soldiers and sailors were let go. The government passed the highly unpopular Corn Laws (1815), which were designed to protect British farmers from foreign competition, but ended up lining the pockets of landowners and stifling free trade. The economy worsened, exacerbated by a series of bad harvests, prompting petitions and open-air demonstrations once again demanding universal suffrage, parliamentary reform, lower taxation and relief from poverty. The government acted in as panicky and aggressive a manner as it had in the 1790s. The most infamous example was a rally in 1819 at St Peter's Field in Manchester: cavalry charged the crowd, killing at least eleven people and wounding more than 400. Emphasising just how low the government had fallen since the victory of 1815, people called it "The Peterloo Massacre".

It was clear to politicians of all stripes that something had to be done. In 1830, with George IV dead, working-class radicalism gathering momentum and a general election in the offing, the scene was set for an overhaul of the political system. The Duke of Wellington, the hero of Waterloo and leader of an essentially Tory government since 1828, was unable to form a workable administration, so the new King William IV had no choice but to offer his Whig counterpart Earl Grey the chance to head government. He accepted, but only on the condition that he would be allowed to carry out parliamentary reform. For the next two years a Reform Bill ricocheted around Westminster being amended and rejected until it was finally accepted in 1832.

Historians often see the bill as simply an attempt by the governing elite to maintain its grip on power. By giving the right to vote to

small-scale property owners, they could divide and rule. The newly enfranchised middle classes no longer had common cause with the working class, and without their support, the working class had a lot less political muscle. However, self-preservation wasn't the only motive behind the Reform Act. Among the Whigs there were many politicians with a genuine concern about social injustice and recognition of the need for change. Some increasingly felt they had to earn the respect of the people in whose name they governed, and act in a way that justified the privileges that came with power. This was the beginning of the sense of civic duty and philanthropism that became defining characteristics of Victorian society. It was the beginning, too, of Liberalism, as the Whigs became increasingly divided. The party infighting that had attended the Reform Bill's stormy passage through parliament made it clear to a number of prominent, pro-reform Whigs that they no longer had much in common with their colleagues, and the time had come to strengthen their own position within the party. To this end, in 1836 Edward Ellice, Sir William Molesworth, Joseph Parkes and E.J. Stanley established a gentlemen's club.

To modern eyes, traditional clubs often appear to be anachronistic bastions of privilege and sexism, so this might seem an odd approach to radical politics. But in the nineteenth century, clubs were a vital part of political debate and identity. They had grown out of the taverns and coffee houses, which since the late 1600s had provided an alternative location for a bit of gossip and schmoozing for the smart and socially ambitious. Towards the end of the eighteenth century, certain places had become the traditional meeting point for particular political groupings: White's (or White's Chocolate House, as it was then known) established itself as the informal headquarters of the Tory party, while Brooks's was the Whig stronghold. In May 1836, liberals among the Whig party rented a narrow house at 104 Pall Mall, and in order to show exactly where their political sympathies lay, they named it the Reform Club after the bill they had fought so hard for. The place became a centre of debate for Liberals and reformers, and developed an impressive list of members over the years, including Asquith, Gladstone, Churchill and Lloyd George (both of whom resigned when their friend Baron de Forest was blackballed), Lord Palmerston, Isambard Kingdom Brunel, Henry James, W.M. Thackeray, E.M. Forster, the renowned horticulturalist and pineapple-cultivator Joseph Paxton, and H.G. Wells.* But the club is perhaps equally famous for employing one of the greatest chefs in British culinary history: Alexis Soyer.

…and Phileas Fogg, the hero of Jules Verne's Around the World in Eighty Days (1873). Fogg is in the reading room of the Reform Club when he solemnly bets twenty thousand pounds that he can "make the tour of the world in eighty days or less".

---

† *The typical classical French hierarchy in a kitchen runs like this: the chef-de-cuisine is the head chef, with overall responsibility for every section of the kitchen. He and his assistant, the sous-chef, manage a number of chefs-de-partie: rôtisseur, poissonier, pâtissier, saucier, garde-manger (responsible for larders, produce and preparation of raw ingredients, among other things) and entremetier (responsible for making soups and cooking vegetables and egg and pasta dishes), who each head up a particular section and have commis-chefs (ranked first, second, third, and so on, according to skill and length of service) working under them. The sous-chef is usually one of the chefs-de-partie. So far, so orderly. But the challenge of keeping staff happy often results in the invention of new posts. Between the chef-de-cuisine and sous-chef there may be a senior sous-chef, and between the sous-chef and chefs-de-partie there may be a junior sous-chef. Below the chefs-de-partie but above the commis-chefs there may be a demi chef-de-partie.*

Soyer was a talented Frenchman who had already made a name for himself in Paris, first at the famous Rignon restaurant and then at Maison Douix, where he became *chef-de-cuisine*† when he was only seventeen. However, Soyer was highly ambitious, and public unrest in the city, coupled with complications in his private life (his lover had fallen pregnant) threatened to slow his progress to the top. In 1831 he chose to follow in his eldest brother's footsteps and come to Britain to find work as a private chef to a noble family. By 1836 he was employed by Archibald Kennedy, Marquess of Ailsa, who had been a vigorous proponent of the Reform Bill and was, therefore, a prime mover in the establishment of the Reform Club. As the club's popularity grew, it was decided that it needed to offer decent dining facilities. Soyer, sensing rightly that this was the perfect stage for his particular talents, pushed his employer to put him up for the job. In 1837, at the age of twenty-seven, he became the club's head chef.

Soyer had an eye for detail, a sophisticated palate and a flair for theatrical presentation, all of which made him especially adept at the vast banquets so beloved by the Victorians. Over the next thirteen years he created a series of spectacular dinners that often made the newspapers. One of the most famous was given in 1846 in honour of Ibrahim Pasha, the son of the ruler of Egypt. Among the dozens of dishes served were veal broth garnished with blanched cockscombs; poached turbot in a sauce made of lobster roes; lamb served with veal quenelles, stewed cucumbers and asparagus purée; hares in redcurrant sauce, and, of course, Soyer's signature dish: Mutton Cutlets Reform. The meal finished with a convincing 2½-foot-high representation of a pyramid made of meringue

and pineapple cream, accompanied by an edible framed portrait of the Pasha himself, made with jelly, eau-de-vie and gold leaf. "The impression grows on us that the man of his age is neither Sir Robert Peel, nor Lord John Russell, nor even Ibrahim Pasha, but Alexis Soyer," the *Globe* newspaper breathlessly reported. That same year, he created a menu of twenty-six dishes for a private dinner at the Reform, in which the highlight was an outrageously costly champagne- and truffle-stewed crayfish.

Soyer was clearly a creative chef, but what I find really inspiring about him is that his curiosity and inventiveness extended well beyond cuisine. He took a keen interest in science and technology, and was constantly looking for ways to apply both to the kitchen, inventing nifty gadgets—a mechanical oven-timer, a tendon separator, a plug strainer, even a prototype pressure cooker—as well as a number of domestic ranges and stoves. Soyer seemed to have a genuine knack for finding practical mechanical solutions to culinary problems. His most significant invention was a portable army stove that was so adaptable and economical in its use of fuel that it revolutionised military kitchens. ❋

Soyer's first real opportunity to tinker with kitchen design and technology came in 1838, when the Reform Club's founders decided to demolish, rebuild and enlarge the Pall Mall premises. During the three-year refit that followed, Soyer consulted extensively with the architect, Charles Barry, to produce the ultimate user-friendly, state-of-the-art kitchen.

❋ *The stove remained standard army issue until the Falklands War, when the majority were lost when the supply vessel* Atlantic Conveyor *was hit by an Exocet missile. Soyer is still toasted every year in the officers' mess in Aldershot at the Annual Dinner for Army Food Service Officers.*

The end result had steam-driven dumb waiters, slate-lined larders, self-cooling fish slabs for seafood preparation and every possible cooking device, from massive ranges and charcoal grills to soufflé ovens, bains-marie, hotplates and even gas stoves (an innovation that wouldn't reach the domestic market for another fifty years; in this, Soyer was lucky that Pall Mall was the first London street to be lit by gas lamps, so he had a ready supply of fuel). When the club reopened its doors on 24 April 1841, its kitchens were widely regarded as the best in Europe. "The gastronomic art, certainly, never before had so many scientific appliances at its disposal," declared the *London Gourmet*, and a guided tour of the kitchen became *de rigueur* among the fashionable set. Soyer once claimed that, during one ten-month stretch, he received 15,000 visitors.

In 1846, however, Soyer's relationship with the club soured. He, along with the butler and kitchen clerk, was accused of falsifying the butcher's bill and pocketing the difference. Soyer resigned in protest, and although the accusation was never proven and he was soon—albeit ungraciously—reinstated, he remained resentful about how he had been treated and left for good four years later. At first glance it seems bizarre that the club would get rid of one of its best assets. There is, perhaps, a clue to their behaviour in that boast of 15,000 visitors. Soyer was viewed by some as getting above his station and eclipsing the club's other activities. This was not the Alexis Soyer Show, and there were committee members who resented that fact that the chef behaved as if it was. I think, though, that Soyer's fall from grace has more to do with overextending himself. By the mid-1840s he was busy developing a range of sauces for Crosse & Blackwell, marketing a miniature spirit stove called Soyer's Magic

Stove and overseeing the compilation of his first cookery book, *The Gastronomic Regenerator*. His talent and ambition had perhaps led him to push too far, on too many fronts, and he lost sight of the attention to detail that got him to the top in the first place.

By 1846, then, when Soyer was accused of theft, there were already rumblings of complaint about the conduct of the Reform Club's chef, brilliant though he was. "The beef was tough and the potatoes were sent out cold," reports one member. "The veal cutlets supplied for dinner were not fit to be eaten," says another. Four years later, the Annual General Meeting minuted its "dissatisfaction with the management of the Coffee Room and the attention of the cook to the comfort of the members", and Soyer resigned for the second and final time.

It's not hard to see why Soyer was disliked and mistrusted in some quarters. He was, without a doubt, a shameless attention-seeker and social climber, and an opportunist who had few qualms about passing off others' ideas as his own. He was French and a dandy, both things that were viewed with suspicion by many English people. He wore diamond rings, gold-braided waistcoats, yellow gloves and highly colourful clothes cut in a sort of zigzag shape that apparently gave him an oddly lopsided appearance. (Even his top hat, cane handle and cigar case were slanted.) The staid Victorians, with their exaggerated concern for propriety, must have been puzzled at what to make of him, and he was "frequently disparaged as a Charlatan", according to one friend, the journalist George Augustus Sala. I suspect there were a number of club members who praised Soyer to his face but lampooned him once they were ensconced with their cronies behind the closed doors of the reading room.

At the same time, this figure of fun worked hard throughout his life at finding ways to prevent the poor going hungry, acting as an unpaid consultant to hospitals and poorhouses, and thinking up and publicising dozens of practical measures to deal with the appalling potato famine in Ireland, which killed about a million people between 1845 and 1852. During the Crimean War (1853–6), he travelled to Scutari and the Crimean peninsula (again unpaid, and facing the very real threat of death, not just from Russian guns, but also from malnutrition or cholera) to overhaul the army's hospital catering procedures, saving countless lives in the process. Both of these are remarkable achievements, and you can't help feeling that, had Soyer been slightly more sober in his dress and deportment, he might now be as celebrated as Auguste Escoffier, another Frenchman who came to London and revolutionised cuisine.

❋

Some recipes begin with sudden flashes of inspiration, or from the excitement of discovering a new ingredient—a eureka moment. But cuisine is at least as much a craft as it is an art, and just as many wonderful recipes come from trying to find solutions to the practical considerations of running a restaurant, such as bringing the right balance of dishes to a menu.

At the Hind's Head, we had gradually been changing the character of the dishes we served, keeping the food recognisably pub-style rather than restaurant-style, but edging the menu towards something more traditionally British and refined. Alongside beautifully cooked classics such as oxtail and kidney pudding, pork belly and steak and chips, we'd been

hoping to introduce some less well known elements of historical cuisine. To that end, I had been looking through old cookbooks, and sauce Reform caught my eye. Old recipes, even as late as the eighteenth century, can be tantalisingly brief and unspecific. By contrast, Soyer's recipe was a model of professionalism, laid out in stages with precise amounts and timings, and careful descriptions of preparation and consistency. Like most chefs, I'd heard of sauce Reform, but I'd not come across it before, or actually made it, so it was a real thrill to read what Soyer had originally written. The recipe

seemed workable and I liked the look of the ingredients; they would produce something approaching a sweet-and-sour sauce that could make a great garnish for lamb, or, even better, veal, which not only suited such a sauce very well, but also allowed me to deliver a belated riposte to the member whose complaint about veal "not fit to be eaten" helped ensure Soyer's exit from the Reform Club.

With all the ingredients going into the same pot and then being passed through a "tammie" (a fine-mesh sieve), Soyer's sauce would have ended up quite stewed and mushy. This may have been exactly how his clients liked it— clubs have a reputation as a haven for super-annuated schoolboys with a taste for stodgy food that reminds them comfortingly of school dinners—but I felt we could make something fresher, lighter and more suited to the modern palate. The key was to prepare the base elements of the sauce separately, and combine them only at the end, just before service, in order to hold on to the distinct character of each set of ingredients and prevent the flavours all blurring into one (a bit like when, as a kid, you rolled different strands of Plasticine together until eventually all the bright primary colours disappeared and you were left with a drab, khaki-coloured lump). This would also give greater control over the exact balance of sweetness and acidity in the sauce. The presence of redcurrant jelly among the ingredients encouraged me further down this route, as it's an essential ingredient in Cumberland Sauce, which is often prepared in separate stages to manage the balance of tastes and flavours.

The shallots are sweated with garlic and wine, then allowed to cool before ox tongue, lemon juice and capers are added. The gutsier base notes of red wine, beef stock, orange juice (an addition that came from looking at Cumberland sauce recipes) and vinegar are simmered, reduced and infused as a separate process. For service, the two liquids are warmed together briefly, and the finishing touches are added. In Soyer's recipe, even some of the more delicate flavourings are added at early stages in the cooking process. Like a lot of chefs, then and now, he put his parsley in right at the beginning, subjecting it to lengthy cooking that would have killed off its freshness. (As a rule of thumb, any herb that you can eat raw is too delicate to stand up to much heat, so parsley stalks can go in early but not the leaves. In general, at my restaurants, herbs are added only when a pan comes off the heat.) In my version of the sauce, therefore, many of the touches of texture and delicate, aromatic top notes are added right at the end for maximum impact: Worcestershire sauce for umami and depth of flavour, sherry vinegar for acidity, those pieces of egg white for texture, and fresh chives, chervil, tarragon and parsley for fragrance and freshness. The end result uses virtually all of Soyer's ingredients but is, in many ways, different from the original—a reformed Reform sauce, if you like.

VEAL CHOP WITH SAUCE REFORM

Makes 6 portions

7% Veal Brine

140g Salt
15g Thyme
2 Garlic cloves, peeled

Place 2kg water and the salt in a saucepan and bring to the boil, then remove from the heat. Make a secure muslin parcel of the thyme and garlic cloves and place it in the saucepan once it has been removed from the heat.

Allow the brine to cool. Once completely cool, remove and discard the muslin parcel.

Refrigerate the brine until needed.

Brining the Veal

2kg 7% veal brine
6 Veal chops
120g Smoked duck fat (see page 182)

Place the brine and veal chops in a large sous-vide bag and seal. Allow the veal chops to brine for 2 hours.

Remove the chops from the sous-vide bag, discard the brine and rinse the chops for 10 minutes under cold running water. Pat dry and place the chops in individual sous-vide bags, with 20g smoked duck fat in each bag, and seal under full pressure.

Refrigerate until needed.

Beurre Noisette

350g Unsalted butter, cubed and at room temperature
10g Peeled and finely diced garlic
5g Thyme
5g Rosemary

Melt the butter in a saucepan and bring it to 180°c/350°F.

Remove from the heat and allow to cool. Once the butter has cooled to 110°c/230°F, add the garlic, thyme and rosemary and allow to infuse overnight.

Melt the butter in a saucepan over a gentle heat. Pass the melted butter through a double layer of muslin cloth and refrigerate until needed.

Beef Stock

1.6kg Chopped beef bones
1.2kg Sectioned oxtail or calf's tail, in 2.5cm pieces
100g Rendered beef fat
1.2kg Diced, lean beef shin
900g Peeled and finely sliced onions
10g Star anise
900g Peeled and finely sliced carrots
240g Sliced cleaned button mushrooms
30g Peeled and finely sliced garlic
15g Thyme
2 Bay leaves
50g Flatleaf parsley

Preheat the oven to 180°c/350°F.

Spread out the beef bones and sectioned oxtail evenly in a roasting tray and roast in the oven until they are golden brown, turning frequently.

In the meantime, heat a thin layer of rendered beef fat in a large pressure cooker and brown the lean, diced shin in batches. Set aside.

Add the remaining beef fat to the pressure cooker and cook the onions and star anise until lightly caramelised. Add the carrots, mushrooms and sliced garlic and cook for 5 more minutes, stirring regularly.

Add the roasted bones and browned meat to the pressure cooker. Pour in 4.8 litres cold water and bring the stock up to the boil, skimming off all scum and impurities.

Add the thyme and bay leaves, and stir the mixture one last time before securing the lid of the pressure cooker. Cook for 2 hours.

Allow the pressure cooker to depressurise and the stock to cool slightly before opening the lid. Strain the stock through a fine-mesh sieve and add the parsley to infuse for 10 minutes. Pass through a fine-mesh filter bag and chill in the fridge overnight.

Remove and discard all the fat from the surface of the chilled stock.

Heat the stock in a large saucepan and gently reduce to 15% of the original quantity, to yield approximately 725g reduced beef stock. It is important to continue skimming the stock as it reduces.

Once the stock has reduced, pass it through a fine-mesh filter bag and refrigerate until needed.

(continued overleaf)

Ox Tongue

145g	Salt
8g	Curing salt
1	Ox tongue

Preheat a water bath to 65°c/149°F.

Combine 1 litre water, the salt and curing salt in a container and use a hand blender to combine it well. Store the brine in the fridge while preparing the tongue.

Wash the tongue well and scrape off any dirt. Trim off the front part of the tongue (it will not be used).

Cut a rectangle from the centre of the tongue by trimming off corners. Divide that piece again into quarters.

Place the 4 pieces of tongue along with 1 litre of the brine in a sous-vide bag and seal. Cook the tongue in the water bath for 48 hours.

Once the tongue pieces are cooked, plunge the bag in an ice bath. Allow to cool completely before removing the pieces from the brine and dicing them into 1.5cm cubes. Store in the fridge until needed.

Sauce Elements

15g	Extra virgin olive oil
250g	Peeled and finely diced shallots
15g	Peeled and finely diced garlic
250g	White wine
75g	Lilliput capers
55g	Lemon juice
100g	Reserved ox tongue dice
	Salt and pepper

Heat the olive oil and sweat the shallots and garlic until soft. Do not allow them to colour.

Add the wine and allow it to reduce to a syrup. Remove from the heat and allow it to cool completely.

Once the mixture has cooled, add the capers, lemon juice and diced ox tongue. Season with salt and pepper and store in the fridge until needed.

Sauce Base

150g	Red wine
50g	Orange juice
50g	Red wine vinegar
500g	Reserved reduced beef stock
1	Bay leaf
1	Clove
1	Blade mace
2	Crushed juniper berries
1g	Thyme
10g	Redcurrant jelly
20g	Lemon peel

Place the red wine, orange juice and red wine vinegar in a saucepan and reduce by half over a gentle-to-moderate heat.

Add the reduced beef stock, bay leaf, clove, mace, juniper berries and thyme. Bring to a simmer. Whisk in the redcurrant jelly and simmer for 5 more minutes. Remove from the heat and allow the sauce to stand for 10 minutes to infuse further.

Pass the sauce through a fine-mesh sieve and set aside.

In the meantime, blanch the lemon peel in boiling water for approximately 2 minutes, and then refresh in a bowl of iced water. Drain the peel and finely slice it into julienne strips. Add them to the sauce base and store in the fridge until needed.

Veal Chops

6	Veal chops

Preheat a water bath to 60°c/140°F.

Place the 6 bags of veal chops in the water bath for 35 minutes, or until the internal temperature reaches 52°c/126°F.

Remove them from the water bath and allow to rest for 10 minutes.

To Serve

6	Reserved veal chops
300g	Melted reserved beurre noisette
1g	Chervil
1g	Tarragon
1g	Chives
3g	Flatleaf parsley
90g	Reserved sauce elements
270g	Reserved sauce base
1	Hard-boiled egg white, finely chopped
	Sherry vinegar
	Worcestershire sauce
10g	Extra virgin olive oil
	Smoked sea salt flakes

After the chops have been removed from the water bath and have rested for 10 minutes, remove them from their bags.

At the restaurant, we grill the chops over an open-flame grill. At home, you could cook them on the barbecue or use a griddle pan, turning the chops every 10–15 seconds, brushing them with melted beurre noisette each time.

Remove the chops from the grill once their temperature reaches 58°c/136°F, which is the ideal serving temperature. Allow to rest for 5 minutes before serving.

In the meantime, finely chop the chervil, tarragon and chives and set aside. Do the same with the flatleaf parsley.

Over a gentle heat, add the sauce elements to a saucepan, followed by the sauce base. Gently warm through, then add the egg, aromatic herbs and parsley just before removing from the heat.

Finish with sherry vinegar, Worcestershire sauce and olive oil to taste. Season with smoked salt. Serve the sauce Reform in a small jug alongside the veal.

TIPSY CAKE

[1858]

TIPSY CAKE

❊ Take a stale sponge-cake of full size, pierce it with holes making them with a knitting-pin. Pour over by degrees with a spoon half a pint of raisin-wine and a wine glass of brandy mixed. When this quantity is soaked up, which will require the wine to be ladled up from the bottom, stick it thickly over with blanched almonds cut in points or spikes. Just before it goes to table pour over it a thick custard, or whipped cream. Seven or eight sponge biscuits may be boiled up and done in the same way, or, by way of variety, the cake may be sliced with preserve spread between each layer, and then finish as above ❊

PINE-APPLE CREAM

❊ Infuse some foreign pine-apple cut in slices (or the rind only will do) in boiling cream, and proceed as is usual for other fruit creams.

Rub a lump or two of sugar on the peel of a lemon, then sprinkle the juice of half a lemon on the sugar and leave it for a time to melt (a table-spoonful of sugar is enough if the preserve is very sweet). Then mix the jam or jelly with the above; and lastly, add a pint of good cream by degrees to the whole, and whip it steadily till thick; sometimes this will be in five or ten minutes. Cease whipping as soon as it is thick enough. Some cooks add a spoonful of brandy ❊

J.H. Walsh, *The English Cookery Book* (1858)

Amid the seventeenth-century splendour of Ham House by the River Thames in Richmond, there hangs a painting by Hendrick Danckerts from about 1670 entitled *Rose, the Royal Gardener, presenting to Charles II the first pine-apple grown in England*. In the far distance of the picture is a stately mansion, from which extends a long path, flanked on either side by neatly geometric green strips of formal garden. In the foreground a bewigged man on bended knee proffers a somewhat scrawny-looking fruit to the king, who gazes out of the picture at us, one hand on his hip, the other extended ambiguously in the gardener's direction. The painting used to be taken at face value as evidence of when the pineapple was first cultivated in this country, but it turns out to be less reliable than originally thought. There is no written record of this epic event, nor of pineapples being grown in England at the time. The grand house in the background has never been successfully identified. Even the title is potentially misleading, since it was given to the picture only in the 1780s, when the writer Horace Walpole acquired it. The painting is a fiction, a piece of theatre designed in part to show the king in the company of a rising star.

Like the green turtle (see page 402), the pineapple was a product of England's newly acquired colonies in the West Indies. Teaming the so-called king of fruits with the king was a deliberate reminder of his dominion over the islands and his active endorsement of trade there, which was steadily improving English prosperity. A similar kind of symbolic politics had been at play when Charles II was first presented with the fruit on 9 August 1661. A few days earlier, the Privy Council had begun debating a petition calling for a minimum price on sugar; if it was approved, a number of English plantation owners in Barbados stood to benefit financially. The well-timed presentation of a Barbadian pineapple was, therefore, probably intended to sweeten the deal. It aimed to keep the West Indies uppermost in the king's mind, so that the petition would receive due attention. And it worked: ten days later Charles wrote a letter in favour of the petitioners.

The presentation of the pineapple at court is mentioned in John Evelyn's *Diary*, kept between 1641 and 1706, which is one of the best records we have of the Stuart age, and is invaluable to anyone interested in cuisine because Evelyn was not just a diligent diarist, but also a keen gardener and talented cook. (His book on salads, *Acetaria*, is a classic of its time, and his manuscript collection of recipes, now in the British Museum, shows great culinary intelligence.) Evelyn's diary entry is characteristically matter-of-fact: "I first saw the famous Queen-pine brought from Barbados presented to his Majestie", but it marks the beginning of what was to become an English obsession with the fruit, particularly after the Dutch developed a method of growing pineapples from the crown or suckers in the 1680s (rather than simply ripening an already-growing plant, which is probably what John Rose, the royal gardener, did). By 1720, this knowledge had made its way to England. The earliest record of cultivation from scratch of a British pineapple is a painting by Theodore Netscher (now in the Fitzwilliam Museum in Cambridge), which shows a plump, spiky specimen that seems almost to float above an abundance of thick green leaves spreading out in every direction. By now there's no need for a mansion in the background, nor a monarch to give his blessing: the pineapple is a suitable subject in its own right. A Latin inscription at the base of the painting reads: "To the perpetual memory of Matthew Decker, Baronet, and

Theodore Netscher, Gentleman. This pineapple deemed worthy of the Royal table, grew at Richmond at the cost of the former, and still seems to grow by the art of the latter."

At the time, the difficulty involved in growing a pineapple in Europe was enormous. The plants need temperatures above 16°c/61°F, and need not only warm air, but also warm soil and high humidity in order to survive. In the inhospitable European climate, they could be grown only in a pit called a hotbed, or in a special type of hothouse known as a stove. These were highly technical affairs. The hotbeds of Decker's gardener, Henry Telende, were brick-lined pits filled with rubble and hot dung, which was the traditional method of providing a constant source of warmth from the heat that was generated as the dung fermented. One of Telende's innovations was to fill the rest of the pit with tanner's bark: ground oak bark that fermented like dung, but held on to its heat much longer than manure—and smelled a lot less offensive! (This technique was already in use in the Netherlands, but had never before been practised in England.) Throughout the summer, pineapple suckers or crowns were plunged in the hotbed. In October they were transferred to a hothouse or stove of equally elaborate construction—under-floor heating, glazed coverings and ingenious arrangements of flues and chimneys—and the thermometer was regularly and anxiously scrutinised until spring, when the plants would be returned to the hotbeds. And so the process would continue for the 2–3 years it took to produce fruit. Over the next century or so, there were a number of technological advances in the process, such as roller blinds and overlapping panes in place of leaded glass, but the basic approach remained time-consuming and complicated.

The expense involved in all of this was colossal. It has been estimated that, taking into consideration the investment needed to build and stock a pinery, and the slow maturation of the fruit, the cultivation of each one cost the equivalent of £5,000. But that was only part of the attraction. The home-grown pineapple had become the ultimate luxury—a sign that you were seriously rich and ran a very orderly estate. Soon, every ambitious aristocrat was at it. By the 1770s, the botanist Richard Weston reported in *Tracts on Practical Agriculture and Gardening*, "no garden is now thought to be complete, without a stove for raising of pine-apples".

Given the Victorians' zeal for feats of engineering on a grand scale, it will come as no surprise that they too were attracted to the challenge of producing the fruit. During George Stephenson's semi-retirement, the "Father of Railways" and inventor of the *Rocket* locomotive devoted his time to constructing a large pine house and pit at his home in Staffordshire, with the aim of growing pineapples "as big as pumpkins" to compete in agricultural shows. At this stage, cultivation of the fruit was still a rich man's game—Stephenson's main rival was the legendary Victorian gardener Joseph Paxton, who tended Chatsworth, the grand estate of the Duke of Devonshire—but all that was about to change.

In 1845, the same year that Stephenson embarked on his project, the Glass Tax was abolished. Since 1745, with a couple of price hikes in the 70s and 80s, there had been tax on glass based on the weight of materials used, which made glasshouse construction extremely expensive. Repeal of the act followed soon after two other technological developments that, combined with less expensive glass, put hothouse cultivation within reach of the middle

Veue et perspectiue

class: heating by means of hot-water pipes and the development of a form of sheet glass, which allowed for much bigger panes to be made. Once the Glass Tax was abolished, glasshouses could be made bigger and more efficient. Though hothouse cultivation was certainly not cheap, it was now within the compass of more than just the nobility, and those that could afford to took up the challenge. Horticultural competitions of the sort Stephenson had taken part in proliferated, with people vying to produce specimens of enormous size.

Ironically, it was also developments in technology that finished off the home-grown pineapple. In 1864, orange groves in the Azores succumbed to disease and the plantation owners started producing pineapples instead. The Azores were much nearer to Britain than the West Indies, and by using modern steamships for transportation, the fruit could be brought over in just a few days. Within twenty years, they were the principal exporter of the fruit to Britain. Freshness had always been the edge that the home-grown pineapple had over its tropical rivals, but once this was removed it could no longer compete, particularly since the beneficial climate and conditions on islands like the Azores meant pineapples could easily be produced on an industrial scale, making them far cheaper. As they became common, pineapples came to seem commonplace. The fruit lost the sense of wonder that had once surrounded it. As if to confirm this, Netscher's portrait of the very first pineapple ever to be grown in Britain now hangs in an awkward space high above a doorway in the Fitzwilliam Museum, largely ignored by visitors as they pass by.

When it appears in print as a series of precisely described steps, a recipe always looks as though there was an inexorable logic behind its creation. Sometimes recipe development really is like that: you have a clear mental picture of the dish and a reasonable idea of the techniques that might accomplish it. Often, though, development is a more haphazard business, especially at the beginning. It's like piecing together an old jigsaw that you've found in a shoebox—there's no picture to guide you, nor any guarantee that you'll have all the pieces in order to complete the puzzle. All you can do is work on whatever separate bits make sense, in the hope that a moment of inspiration will eventually bring them all together. Tipsy Cake was one of these recipes. It grew out of John Henry Walsh's 1858 recipe, a rotisserie and something served up at Fat Duck staff lunches, though at the start I had no notion that these things might belong together. And at that point, pineapple, which eventually became the showpiece of the dish, wasn't part of my thinking at all.

Tipsy Cake was a popular nineteenth-century dessert that appears in many Victorian cookbooks, including Mrs Beeton's *Book of Household Management*, where it's illustrated by an engraving of an ornate, two-handled, twist-stemmed cake dish surmounted by a cloud-shaped mound of the stuff. Clearly related to trifle (in *Modern Cookery For Private Families*, Eliza Acton even offers Brandy Trifle as an alternative name for Tipsy Cake), it was essentially a method of using up leftover or stale sponge cake by lacing it with alcohol and smothering it with cream. To my mind, it must have fulfilled much the same function that tiramisu did at British dinner parties in the 1980s: classy pedigree, easy to assemble and full of enough cream and alcohol that it could hardly fail to be a crowd-pleaser, no matter what your skills in the kitchen.

Naturally, it was the dish's wonderful name that first caught my eye, conjuring up the surreal image of a drunken dessert. (It had had the same effect on chefs in the past, resulting in a number of variant inebriates such as tipsy lairds, tipsy parsons, tipsy squires and even tipsy hedgehogs, bristling with flaked almonds for spines.) I was sure the name would be an intriguing prospect on Dinner's menu, and the basic ingredients offered a good base for a dish, so long as I could bring some refinement to it.

The first spark of inspiration, however, came from something that wasn't refined at all. For staff meals one of the chefs started making monkey bread, which is a breakfast pastry made from segments of dough topped with butter, sugar and cinnamon to give it a caramelised flavour as it bakes in the oven. Monkey bread has been around in America since at least the 1970s, but it was new to me. I really liked the crisp, caramelised crust and it set me thinking that this might be a good template for Tipsy Cake. The little cluster of balls of dough looked appealing, and that crust provided not just depth of flavour, but also a great texture contrast.

The staff-lunch monkey bread was made with focaccia dough, but I looked at many different types of bread and eventually settled on brioche, which I've used before for a variety of dishes, from a simple *pain perdu* (sweet eggy bread) to the "toast" that accompanies my nitro-poached egg-and-bacon ice cream. Its high egg and butter content gives brioche dough a soft crumb, and a richness that makes it a superb vehicle for caramelisation. It also gives it a lovely, flaky, golden-brown crust, which was just what I was looking for, and gradually I developed a technique for accentuating the crisp, caramelised texture: dipping frozen balls of dough in melted butter and golden caster sugar, then putting them in their little cast-iron cooking pots and allowing them to prove for several hours. As the dough expands the sugar coating crazes a little like a crackle glaze, enhancing the flakiness.

It was important, too, to keep the alcohol in check. Walsh's half pint of raisin wine (made from dried grapes to produce a concentrated, viscous and intensely sweet wine) and glass of brandy might have softened up an old sponge nicely, but it would have packed quite a punch, overshadowing the rest of the dish. Wine can be a fantastic enhancer of flavour, adding depth and complexity, so I wanted to keep it in the recipe, particularly since I knew that the wine-making method in the Sauternais region of France (which depends on careful management of "noble rot", or the fungus *Botrytis cinerea* that dries out the grapes) produces what is in effect the ultimate raisin wine, Sauternes, which is sweet with touches of caramelised fruit, and toasted or even floral notes. It seemed ideal. But although this was a "tipsy" cake, I didn't want it to have a huge hit of booze, so instead of soaking the brioche in alcohol at the start, I chose to add periodic doses of a sugar, cream, Sauternes and brandy mixture during the cooking process. This gave me the control and subtlety of flavour I was looking for; and a quick final brush with brandy just before serving added the right amount of freshness and intensity. I had a dish that was ready to go on the menu, but still I had no thought of pineapple in connection with it. However, in Dinner's kitchen I also had an amazing clockwork spit-roasting device, which eventually brought the two together.

Even when the plans for Dinner were at the drawing-board stage, I had been determined that the place should have a rotisserie, not least as a homage to a time when the English were considered masters of the art of roasting by the rest of Europe. The designer Adam Tihany created a beautiful piece of equipment that somehow managed to look modern and traditional at the same time: heavy wrought-iron loops revolving patiently before a stainless steel grate, powered by a gigantic watch mechanism encased in glass. The rotisserie looked spectacular and I put it centre stage in the kitchen.

The problem was that I wasn't sure, at first, how best to make use of it. Roasting meat was the obvious option—a cut of beef perhaps, since the French nicknamed us *les rosbifs* ❋ in deference to our skill at the spit, but it wasn't very practical because spit-roasting doesn't allow the chef as much control as other cooking methods. This was less of a problem for the medieval cook because all the guests at the banquet would be eating at the same time. In a modern restaurant, with a stream of orders throughout service, it would be hard to spit-roast meat to a high standard, and even harder do so with the kind of consistency that's essential to a good restaurant.

I had already begun wondering whether my best bet would be to finish a small bird such as quail on the spit to crisp up the skin when I remembered a visit I'd made to the food

historian Ivan Day, at which he'd served up a dessert of pineapple larded with vanilla sticks. It was roasted on an old-fashioned rotisserie constructed so that weighted ropes turned the spit. How this had failed to come to mind before I don't know, particularly since I'd actually taken Adam Tihany to see Ivan's spit before he began work on his own, but as soon as I thought of it, I knew I'd found what I was looking for. A row of whole pineapples, slowly twisting in mid-air, presented a surreal picture that was far more eye-catching and original than a cut of meat. Once I starting thinking along these lines, it wasn't long before I realised that pineapple might be a perfect accompaniment for Tipsy Cake. When John Evelyn first tasted the fruit, he described it almost as if it were a wine: "it has yet a grateful acidity, but tastes more of the Quince and Melon", and the intense sweetness of a ripe pineapple can indeed be intoxicating. I could see how it might complement the Sauternes in the cake, and how roasting the fruit would give it a slightly caramelised flavour that would sit beautifully with the brioche, especially if the fruit was basted with something to emphasise the caramel flavour and provide a welcome balance to the sweetness of the dish.

So that's how Tipsy Cake is served: with a strip of rich, sticky, golden-coloured pineapple as a decorative, delicious garnish. And customers, it seems, are as captivated by the vision of pineapples on a spit as I was. It has become a talking point and an iconic image for the restaurant. I like to think that, in its own small way, it gives the pineapple back a little of the sense of spectacle it once had.

❋ *Later, as the quality of British produce and cooking declined and the Brits became an international byword for bad food,* les rosbifs *turned into an insult aimed at the poverty of our cuisine. From the late 1980s, as British cooking began its spectacular resurrection, this reputation was increasingly outdated, but not everyone got the message. In 2005, as the IOC was choosing the host city for 2012 Olympics, the French President, Jacques Chirac, said of Britain: "You can't trust people who cook as badly as that. After Finland it's the country with the worst food." The next day, Paris unexpectedly lost out to London by 54 votes to 50, and many in France believed Chirac's comment had cost them the Games.*

TIPSY CAKE

Makes 6 portions

Brioche Balls

8.5g	Fresh yeast
65g	Whole milk
310g	Whole egg
535g	Soft (T45) flour
15g	Salt
60g	White caster sugar
335g	Unsalted butter, cubed and at room temperature

Place the fresh yeast, whole milk and 250g of the egg in a small bowl and stir to dissolve the yeast.

Place the flour, salt and sugar in the bowl of a mixer. Add the egg mixture to the flour and mix at slow speed using the dough hook.

Increase to moderate speed for 10 minutes, then check to see how much the gluten has developed. This can be done by stopping the machine, pinching off a small piece of dough and stretching it between your fingers to look at its elasticity. It should stretch significantly to a thin, transparent window, without snapping. If this is not the case, continue to mix at moderate speed for 5 more minutes. Continue to do this until you are satisfied that the gluten has developed.

Reduce the speed of the machine and add the remaining 60g egg. Allow to combine, then gradually add the soft butter cubes, continuing to mix until all the butter has been incorporated.

Switch the machine off and place the dough in a large container that has been lined with clingfilm. Cover with clingfilm and allow the dough to rest overnight in the fridge.

Remove the dough and roll it out to a thickness of 1.6cm. Cut the dough into 2cm long pieces and return to the fridge for 30 minutes.

Cut the dough into small square pieces that weigh approximately 12g each (you need 30 for this recipe, and any leftovers can be frozen). Place them on a tray and return them to the fridge.

With plenty of flour on your hands, roll each piece of dough into a ball, using the work surface and the palm of your hand to help shape it. Place the balls crease-side down on a tray and transfer them immediately to the freezer. It is important to work speedily and in batches of 10, so that the balls are taken from the fridge, shaped and placed in the freezer as quickly as possible.

The brioche balls can be made well ahead of time and stored in the freezer.

Cooking Cream

75g	Demerara sugar
75g	Golden caster sugar
40g	Sauternes
65g	Brandy
1	Vanilla pod, seeds only
500g	Whipping cream

Place the sugars, alcohols and vanilla seeds in a deep-sided container and blend for 5 minutes using a hand blender.

Add the cream no more than 2 hours before serving, and stir to combine. Seal and refrigerate until needed.

Smoking Syrup

125g	White caster sugar
	Fine oak smoking chips

Place 125g water and the sugar in a small saucepan and bring to the boil. Remove from the heat and allow to cool to room temperature.

Place the cooled syrup in a container to make a layer no more than 5mm deep. Wrap the container in clingfilm and pierce 2 small holes in it. Keep the clingfilm nearby.

Put ½ teaspoon smoking chips in a smoking gun, insert the nozzle into one of the holes and light the gun, allowing the smoke to fill the container. After 15 seconds it should be filled with smoke. Remove the nozzle and wrap the container completely in clingfilm. Leave to smoke for 5 minutes.

Remove the clingfilm, stir the syrup well and repeat the process once more with fresh chips. Set aside in the fridge.

Pineapple Caramel

375g	White caster sugar
95g	Unsalted butter, cubed and at room temperature
4g	Salt
170g	Apple juice

Place a large, deep pan over a medium heat and add a thin layer of sugar. As the sugar starts to melt and colour, swirl the pan gently and add another layer of sugar. Do not stir the melting sugar, as it may seize and form crystals. Do this until all the sugar has melted and is a dark golden copper colour.

Reduce the heat and add the butter in stages, whisking well to emulsify. Remove from the heat and add the salt. Gradually add the apple juice, stirring regularly until the mixture is well combined.

Return the pan to the heat and bring to the boil. Remove from the heat and allow to cool.

Refrigerate until needed.

(continued overleaf)

Roasted Pineapple

| 1 | Pineapple |
| | Reserved pineapple caramel |

Preheat the oven to 200°C/400°F on the full grill setting. Remove the skin from the pineapple and slice it into 6 long pieces from top to bottom. They should be approximately 4.5cm wide and 3cm deep, and as long as the height of the pineapple. Trim all 6 pieces until they look similar in shape.

In the meantime, gently heat the pineapple caramel and set aside.

Make small diagonal incisions on each pineapple piece. Brush each piece with the caramel and sear in a large non-stick pan over a fairly high heat to caramelise the presentation side.

Place the pineapple pieces, incision-side up, on a roasting tray. Brush the pieces with the caramel and place in the oven for 2 minutes. Baste the pieces regularly with the caramel until they have grilled to a deep golden colour. Take care not to overcook them; they should still be slightly firm.

Remove from the oven and set aside.

Tipsy Cake

750g	Unsalted butter, melted
750g	Golden caster sugar
30	Reserved frozen brioche balls
	Reserved cooking cream
	Reserved roasted pineapple
	Brandy, for brushing
	Reserved smoking syrup
1	Lime

Place the melted butter in a large bowl. Ensure that it is completely melted, but not hot. Place the sugar in a separate large bowl.

Take 5 frozen brioche balls at a time and dip them briefly in the melted butter, then coat them completely in the sugar. Place the coated brioche balls seam-side down in a mini cast-iron pot. The seam side will be evident as it will be slightly flatter. Do the same with 5 more pots. You may need additional sugar.

Cover the cast-iron pots with clingfilm and put in a warm place (20–24°C/68–75°F) to allow the brioche to prove. This should take approximately 4 hours. The environment should not be so warm that the sugar melts. The brioche will double in size and cracks will appear where the sugar crust splits.

At Dinner, the Tipsy Cakes are transferred to a deck oven halfway through baking, so that they are exposed to the all-important solid bottom heat, which caramelises the cooking cream. At home a similar effect can be achieved using a pizza stone.

Once you are satisfied that the brioche has proved well, preheat the oven to 180°C/350°F and place a pizza stone inside one side of the oven to heat up.

Once the oven has preheated, remove the clingfilm from the cast-iron pots and place all 6 cast-iron pots in the oven, next to the pizza stone. Bake for 15 minutes.

Carefully and quickly remove the pots from the oven, and, using a knife, make small incisions between the brioche pieces where they have joined. Ladle 25g cooking cream into the centre of each brioche pot and return to the oven immediately—but this time place the pots on the hot pizza stone.

After 5 minutes, open the oven and ladle 15g cooking cream into the centre of each brioche pot. Close the oven door and cook for 5 more minutes. Repeat this process one last time, using 15g cooking cream. After the final 5 minutes, carefully remove the pots from the oven.

To serve, brush a very small amount of brandy on top of the brioche and place on a suitable serving dish, such as a wooden board. Brush a little of smoking syrup on each pineapple piece, followed by a squeeze of lime juice, and place one alongside each pot.

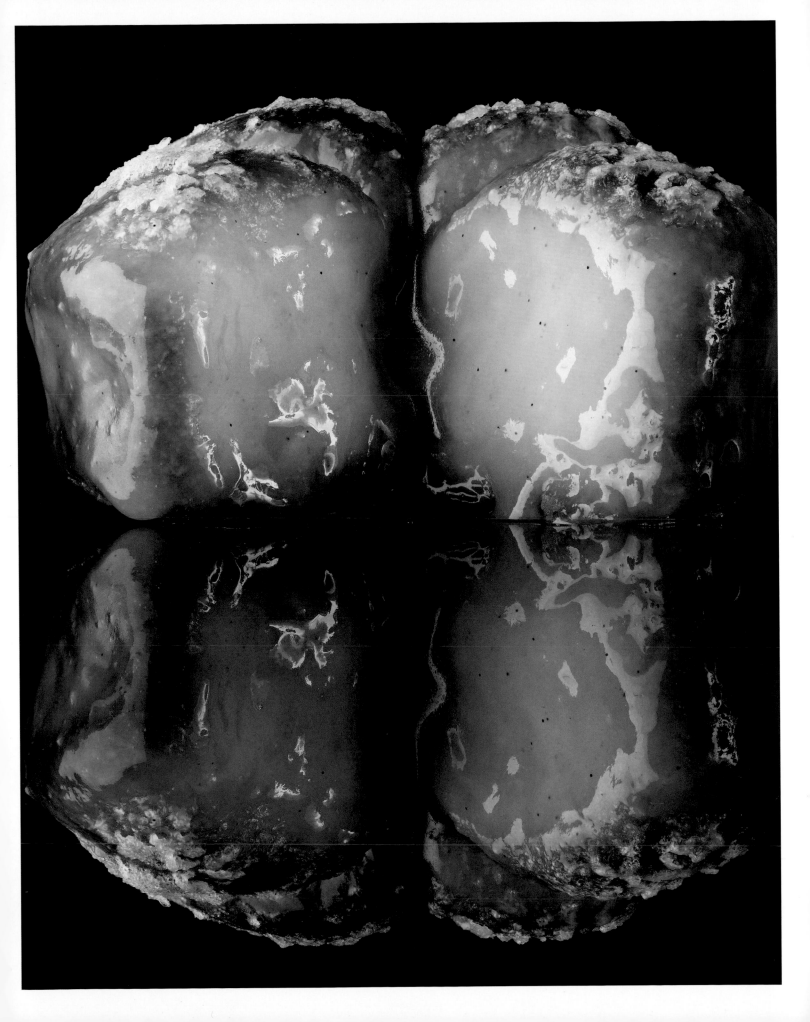

MOCK TURTLE SOUP

[1892]

MOCK-TURTLE SOUP

❋ Peel three onions, scrape and wash two good-sized carrots, peel and wash a turnip, wash and trim a head of celery, and then cut all these vegetables into slices; fry them in ½lb of butter till they are a nice pale brown. Put 2lb. of leg of veal and 2lb. of leg of beef into a saucepan with 1 pint of cold water, fit the lid on tightly, and let it stand at the side of the fire for an hour, keeping it just warm enough to draw the gravy from the meat; then put it into a larger saucepan or pot, add to it the fried vegetables, a bunch of parsley, a bunch of sweet herbs, a bit of garlic the size of a pea, three leaves of sage, a blade of mace, four cloves, half-a-dozen peppercorns, 1 teaspoonful of salt, 1 table-spoonful of white sugar, ½lb. of lean ham (mild), half a calf's head nicely prepared and with the skin left on, and 4qts. of cold water. Put this over the fire, let it boil up quickly, and skim well. The half head should be laid in the pot skin upwards. When the liquor is well skimmed, add 1 teacupful of Marsala, and keep the soup simmering, not boiling, for two hours, taking off the scum as it rises. Take out the half head, remove the bones, and trim off any rough pieces; return bones and trimmings to the soup, and let them simmer for four hours, continuing to remove all scum as it rises. Put the meat from the head between two dishes, laying a heavy weight on the top one to press the meat well, and leave it there till cold. Mix 5 table-spoonfuls of flour with ¼ lb. of fresh butter, brown it slightly in the oven, then mix it with 1 saltspoonful of salt, nearly 1 saltspoonful of white pepper, 1 or 2 grains of cayenne, and 1 table-spoonful of flour of mustard; stir this into the soup, together with 1 teaspoonful of anchovy sauce and 1 dessert-spoonful of soy. When the soup has simmered for four hours after the head has been taken out, let it boil for fifteen minutes, and then strain it through a fine sieve. Cut the meat of the head into pieces about ¾ in. square, put it into the strained soup, return it to the fire, add the strained juice of a lemon, simmer for twenty minutes, add 2 wineglassfuls of brown sherry, pour the soup into the tureen, and serve immediately. Serve with cayenne and cut lemons ❋

Theodore Francis Garrett, *The Encyclopaedia of Practical Cookery* (1892)

Between 1800 and 1900, British society changed more rapidly and radically than at any time in its history. In the first half of the century the population rose by 73 per cent, at the astonishing rate of two million a decade. People migrated to the towns and cities in droves, searching for work and opportunities. Between 1801 and 1831, the boom towns of the Industrial Revolution, such as Manchester and Birmingham, more than doubled in size. In 1800, only a quarter of the population lived in towns and cities; by 1881 more than 80 per cent were urban dwellers, and had adopted very different ways of living—and, of course, eating.

Much of the important groundwork for this transformation had taken place more than a hundred years earlier, on the back of colonial acquisitions in North America and the West Indies. The trade in tobacco and, in particular, sugar, made Britain rich, led to the expansion of the fleet and encouraged the development of the kind of business networks and technology that would capitalise on and increase that prosperity. Inventions like the flying shuttle, spinning jenny and power loom revolutionised textile manufacture. James Watt's improvements to the steam engine enhanced the power and efficiency of factories. Henry Cort's innovations of the 1780s significantly improved the process of making iron. Production of coal, which fuelled the Industrial Revolution, and iron, which provided one of its principal raw materials, increased massively. Coal output doubled between 1750 and 1800, and quadrupled by 1845. Production of the basic form of iron known as pig iron (which could then be fashioned into other forms, such as wrought iron) quadrupled between 1740 and 1788, and would do so again over the next twenty years.

By 1848 Britain's production would be greater than that of the rest of the world put together.

Of course, this expanded production would have counted for little had there not been a similarly energetic development of the means to distribute it all. From the 1770s an extensive network of canals was built for transportation. The advances in construction made by Thomas Telford and John McAdam (whose method of making roadways is still essentially the one used today) transformed British roads, allowing horses to carry far more weight at a much greater speed. In the 1750s six companies operated the Manchester–London route, which took four days. By 1816 the journey had been cut by half and 200 companies were doing it. Once the railways were set up in the 1830s (this too was conducted at an astonishing pace: 10,000 miles of track were laid in little more than a decade), Britain could produce and supply goods to domestic and foreign markets more efficiently than any other country in the world. Money could be made on a big scale. It led to what Disraeli memorably described as "a convulsion of prosperity" in Victorian England.

Increased wealth created a classic capitalist set-up. The rise of industry and factories and the accumulation of wealth required lawyers, bankers, engineers, architects and clerks to support, organise and administer it. The surge in demand and production of goods led to a huge increase in the number of shops (a number of familiar chains and brands, such as Boots and Lipton, were founded in the late nineteenth century) and also of shopkeepers, who rose in number by 54 per cent between 1850 and 1870. The middle class was on the rise.

Ambitious, but perhaps not entirely confident of their place in the hierarchy (they had been granted the right to vote only when the

Great Reform Act was passed, amid riots, resignations and much opposition, in 1832), the middle classes devoted a lot of their wealth and leisure time to showing just how well-off they were. Top hats became extravagantly tall, dresses more voluminous. The number of domestic servants in employment increased from 900,000 in 1851 to nearly a million and a half a mere twenty years later, presumably in the belief that employing a member of the working class proved that you had risen above them. Naturally, food was also press-ganged into this one-upmanship, just as it had been ever since medieval kings started throwing banquets featuring peacocks and pricy saffron on the menu. A decent income, coupled with the increase in the number of shops, meant that the middle classes could actually choose what they ate, and their choices were often governed more by status-seeking than by taste and flavour. And, as the welter of contemporary books on domestic etiquette show, the dining table was now a showcase not just for food, but for all manner of knick-knacks purchased to demonstrate the hosts' good taste: candelabra, cruet sets, decanters, fancily folded napkins and vases full of carefully arranged flowers would vie for attention amid the fine china dinner plates.

One of the gastronomic status symbols of the age was the turtle, or, more specifically, the green turtle (*Chelonia mydas*), prized as much for its lovely, rich, green-coloured fat as for its delicious flesh. The animal came, appropriately enough, from the waters around the Caribbean islands that had provided much of Britain's wealth in the first place: Barbados, Jamaica, Bermuda, St Kitts, Antigua and Montserrat. The earliest recipe appeared in Richard Bradley's *The Country Housewife and Lady Director, Part II* (1732). Bradley was the first

Professor of Botany at Cambridge University, and so, as you might expect, he had a well-developed taste for the exotica of the natural world and ready access to them. (It's said he was the first person to bring a crocodile to the country, keeping it in the grounds of his house in Essex.) But in fact, turtle dishes quickly made it to the mainstream of cuisine. One of the best barometers of the tastes of the times is Hannah Glasse's *The Art of Cookery Made Plain and Easy*, which stayed in print for more than a century and was regularly revised to take in new culinary developments. There were no turtle recipes in the first edition of 1747, but by 1751 the fourth edition had instructions on how "To dress a Turtle the West India Way". In the 1760s, six pounds of turtle meat at the Shakespeare's Head tavern in Covent Garden would set you back £1 1s, which was about half a craftsman's weekly wage. Despite, or perhaps because of, being very expensive, turtle soup became a craze that lasted well into the Victorian age. In the 1880s Britain was still importing about 15,000 turtles a year.

This transportation was difficult—during the voyage the animals were kept in large water tanks—and brutal for the turtles themselves. They tended to pine in captivity, eat little and lose weight. In order to prevent them from escaping, they would usually be placed on their backs, although the *Encyclopaedia of Practical Cookery* talks of turtles lying "about the deck to which they are frequently nailed through the forefins". Such practices might seem to us monstrous and inexplicable, but until William Wilberforce pushed through the Slave Trade Act of 1807, at the same time that turtles were being brought from the West Indies to grace Georgian tables, West Africans were being captured and transported to the West Indies in almost equally inhumane conditions, to furnish the labour force that made produce of the islands so profitable.

The turtles weighed anything from 60 to 200 pounds or more, and manhandling and preparing them for cooking wasn't easy. In the 1750s, *The Gentleman's Magazine* reported that the King's Arms tavern in Pall Mall had had to remove the oven door in order to admit a 350-pound specimen. And there's a remarkable 1874 drawing by the French artist Jules-Descartes Férat, entitled *La Décapitation d'une Tortue de Mer*, which shows a stone-flagged kitchen with a turtle suspended from the ceiling by a chain attached to its tail. A group of chefs in white hats and long white aprons watch as one of their number springs towards the turtle, sword raised high above his head, like an unsaddled cavalryman determined to go down fighting. Even the instructions in an 1870s edition of *Mrs Beeton's Book of Household Management* make her sound like a Jack the Ripper of the kitchen, blithely advising the cook to cut off the head a day in advance, to lean heavily on the shell with a knife while cutting it off all around, and to angle the knife towards the bones "for fear of touching the gall, which may sometimes escape the eye". Originally, all this surgical butchery went into creating a single course made up of a variety of dishes that used each bit of the animal, rather like Peking duck on a grand scale. The belly would be boiled and the back baked, and these would be positioned at the top and bottom of the table. The fins and guts were stewed in rich sauces and placed at the corners. A tureen of turtle soup provided the centrepiece. Over time, however, the popularity of the soup eclipsed other dishes, and in many nineteenth-century cookbooks the only turtle recipe is the one for soup. However, the association of turtle with a measure of ritual and formality remained, and for the Victorians it became the ultimate public symbol of having pushed the boat out. "Some hundreds of tureens of turtle soup are served annually at the Lord Mayor's dinner in Guildhall," Mrs Beeton observes in a footnote to her recipe. The turtle was so linked with the pomp and circumstance of civic ceremony that in a satirical lithograph of the 1830s, *Fatal Effects of Gluttony, A Lord Mayor's Day night mare*, portly Lord Mayor John Key is in bed in a nightshirt and nightcap surrounded by the huge number and variety of animals he has indulged in at dinner—lobster, turkey, sturgeon, venison, duck and other game birds—but centre stage is the turtle that slumps reproachfully on his chest.

Since the soup was so celebrated, it will come as no surprise that a mock version very quickly appeared for those who couldn't cope with the cost or the complexity of making the real thing. Mock turtle soup made its first appearance in the 1758 edition of Glasse's *The Art of Cookery Made Plain and Easy*, using a calf's head in place of turtle meat. There was debate about the effectiveness of the technique: "imitation is the sincerest flattery," wrote Theodore Francis Garrett, "but there is a great deal of difference between dishes made of real turtle and those concocted to resemble it as nearly as possible". And some recipes were clearly less skilful than others: in *London Labour and the London Poor*, Henry Mayhew reports a street-seller saying: "I once had some cheap mock in an eating-house and it tasted like stewed tripe with a little glue" (which, given the many outrageous and even dangerous cases of food adulteration in Victorian times, may not have been far from the truth). Nonetheless, mock turtle soup became extremely popular in its own right, to the extent that, by the beginning of the nineteenth century, this British dish had been taken up by the French too. "Mock turtle soup… has had Parisian tongues wagging for several years," noted the famous gastronome Grimod de la Reynière in his *Almanach des gourmands*. He considered the soup a novelty, enjoyed by his countrymen simply because it was so highly prized elsewhere. Yet by the end of the century, *Potage de fausse tortue au claire* was a staple of French brasseries.

❁

The starting point for this Fat Duck recipe was an old cookbook. Bound in tattered red leather with gilt lettering, volume two (N–Z) of Theodore Francis Garrett's *Encyclopaedia of Practical Cookery: a Complete Dictionary of All Pertaining to the Art of Cookery and Table Service* (1892) is thicker than a telephone directory. With Victorian thoroughness, its entries march purposefully through the alphabet from Nantes Cake to Yellow Garnish for Soup à la Prince Ferdinand, accompanied by dainty engravings of oak celery stands and "egg snow (moulded)".

Browsing the thick, smooth, time-darkened pages, my eye was caught by one of Garrett's recipes for mock turtle soup. It made an impact for several reasons. There was a tug of nostalgia: seeing the name triggered memories of the mock turtle soup that was sold in cans when I was a kid growing up in London in the 1970s. There was a touch of pride, too: it has always irked me that we Brits are constantly knocked for our cuisine, so I liked the idea of a British dish that had made it into the classic French repertoire. The soup's biggest attraction, however, was that it reminded me of *Alice's Adventures in Wonderland*.

Carroll's book has always had a strong hold over me. I love its surreal humour and the way that, no matter how bizarre the situation she finds herself in, Alice tries to deal with it in a rational, logical manner—such as the time when the miniaturised Alice, while swimming in a pool of her own tears, encounters a mouse and carefully considers how best to address it, first trying formal English and, when that fails, basic French, on the grounds that it might have come to England with the Normans. (During recipe development I often feel as though I've tumbled down the White Rabbit's hole into some other world, where pressing questions such as how best to create sand you can actually eat, or what meat you'd like to find inside a fruit, seem entirely logical.) So the fact that one of Carroll's most memorable characters is a tearful Mock Turtle who teaches Alice the lobster quadrille and sings "Beautiful Soup" was a powerful incentive to try out the dish.

Soup is a great vehicle for creativity and already I could see plenty of ways that, using modern technology and knowhow, I could enhance Garrett's recipe. I've developed several methods for intensifying stock, like browning onions with star anise to really boost the meaty flavours, and using a pressure cooker to hold on to as much flavour as possible (see page 342), and these techniques could easily be introduced to a mock turtle recipe. And I could replace the calf's head with other cuts, such as oxtail and beef shin, and bones to give a greater depth and complexity of flavour. But these were just improvements to the recipe; I still needed to find a direction for the development of the dish.

I went back to *Alice* for inspiration, leafing past the White Rabbit—"oh my ears and whiskers, how late it's getting!"—and the hookah-smoking caterpillar; past the Duchess and the Cheshire Cat; past the Mad Hatter and the March Hare taking tea, until I reached

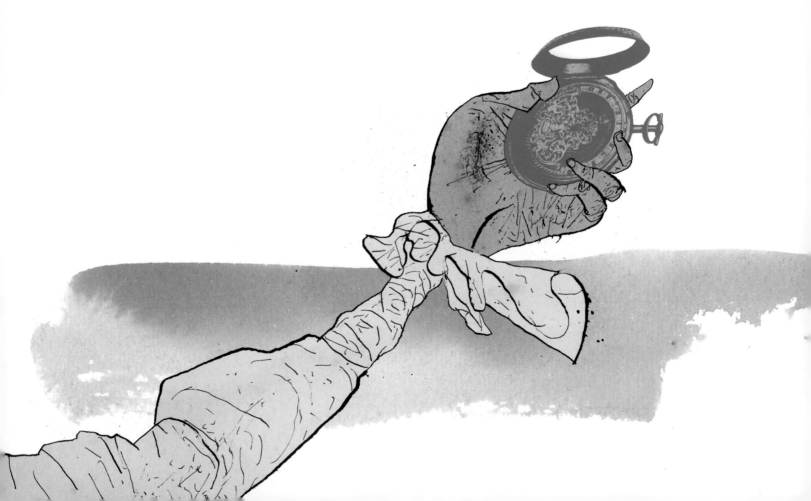

chapter 9. And there it was, staring at me from Tenniel's classic illustration of the Mock Turtle.

I'd read the book many times. I'd seen the drawing many times. But it was only now that it dawned on me exactly what I was looking at, and it was a revelation. The head that stuck out of that turtle shell was a calf's head. The back flippers were in fact hooves, and a calf's tail dangled behind. It wasn't a turtle, but a mock turtle. Tenniel's fantasy creature cleverly alluded to the ingredients of the soup, so why couldn't I reverse the process and create a soup that alluded to features of Carroll's story?

It's always an exciting moment in recipe development when you find the little key that opens the door. More often than not, once you've found that, the rest seems to evolve almost of its own accord. So it was with my mock turtle soup recipe. I realised that I could deepen the flavour of the soup, and make a playful reference to Carroll's contemptuous caterpillar sitting on his mushroom, by combining the meat stock with mushroom stock and mushroom ketchup. And I saw a way of using the classical technique known as a royale (a moulded savoury custard) to create some

Carroll-style whimsy. By moulding the royale into an ovoid, then topping it with a small blob of swede gel, I could make what looked like an egg with the yolk on the outside—precisely the sort of topsy-turvy egg a mock turtle might hatch from. (I could even garnish it with matchstick-sized enoki mushrooms to remind the diner again of the caterpillar and his perch, and also to give a sense of the strange shifts in scale and perspective that beset Alice as she grows bigger or smaller.)

There was room, too, for some nods to the original recipe. Traditionally, one of the key flavourings for mock turtle soup was Marsala or, more commonly, Madeira, which goes very well with mushrooms (try using it instead of wine in a mushroom risotto, for example), so I added it to my mushroom stock. And alongside the mock turtle egg I nestled tiny cubes of ox tongue, which would give a little of the fatty richness of actual turtle soup, and provide a reminder that a meaty body part gave the mock version much of its character.

The key detail from *Alice* that brought all the dish's elements into harmony, however, was the Mad Hatter's watch, which is discussed at the tea party (it appears to tell the days of the month rather than the time of day) and then gloomily dipped in a cup of tea by the March Hare. I had already created a dish at the Fat Duck in which scented water was poured over a stock cube wrapped in gold leaf. I realised I could adapt this and take it on a stage by fashioning the stock cube into a fob watch.

In order to pack as much flavour as possible into a such a small amount of stock, however, I had make sure it was extremely concentrated. The traditional method for doing this is

reducing it: boiling the stock so that much of the water evaporates, leaving a thick, deeply flavourful syrup. The problem with this is that as the heat drives off the water it also cooks the stock, kick-starting reactions between the flavour molecules that alter the stock's character. If I wanted to retain the clarity and freshness of the ingredients, an alternative technique had to be found. I was faced with a question that could have come straight from the pages of *Alice*: how could I reduce a liquid using cold instead of heat? The solution involved some of the most cutting-edge technology and methodology that I use in the kitchen.

Some of the water could be removed by ice-filtering the stock. This technique is perfect for making a crystal-clear consommé because it traps impurities in a kind of gelatine mesh, but a side benefit is that the gelatine traps a certain amount of water too, which would help concentrate the stock. To drive off a lot of the rest of the water, I employed another heat-free process: a centrifugal juicer. Take the ice-filtered stock, refreeze it, break it up with a rolling pin, put it in a centrifugal juicer and hit the button and it spins, separating the contents into granite-like shards of ice and a translucent golden-brown liquid.

The final piece of technology was the Rocket—not Stephenson's steam engine that revolutionised locomotion in 1829, thereby accelerating Victorian industrial supremacy, but a vacuum centrifuge with that name. With its strobe and purple flashing lights, the Rocket

mesmerised my development chefs, who took any and every opportunity to use it. Putting my double-reduced stock in the Rocket needed no excuse, however. It's designed to boil off water at an extremely low temperature: the presence of a vacuum means there's no pressure "pressing down" on the liquid, so far less energy in the form of heat is required to cause the liquid to "push up" and evaporate. The end result is an extremely concentrated liquid (it's a great way to maximise the flavours of fresh fruit juice, for example), and the minimal heat means no reactive flavours are introduced. Here, I used the Rocket to create an incredibly intense syrup, which, instead of freeze-drying (which produces a powder so thirsty for moisture that it tends to suck it from the air, spoiling its gold-leaf covering as it does so), I combined with gelatine and placed in specially designed fob-watch moulds. Tease a tea-bag-style string into the top with a little paper tab printed with the words *Mad Hatter's Tea*, let it set, pop it out of the mould, wrap it carefully in gold leaf and you've got a convincing facsimile of a pocket watch.

Originally, the dish was served in bowls containing an ox-tongue and lardo terrine, garnished with little cubes of pickled turnip (another nod to an ingredient in Garrett's recipe), truffle and cucumber, along with micro-parsley. Beside each table setting a bookmark was placed, which was printed with relevant passages from *Alice's Adventures in Wonderland*, a brief history of mock turtle soup, and Tenniel's wonderful illustrations of the turtle and the tea party as a memento of Mad-Hatter madness for diners to take home with them. The waiters would bring the watches to the table in a presentation case, from which could be heard the sound of ticking. Each diner took a watch from the case, put it in a teacup containing hot water, turning the water into a gold-flecked brown liquid that could then be poured around the contents of the bowl.

It was a beautiful dish, but there was an aspect of its presentation that nagged at me: you normally pour into a teacup, not from it. The illogic was inelegant, and eventually I simply had to sit down and take another look at the components and the logistics to see if I could improve them.

I came up with the notion of a capacious glass cup, the sort of thing you'd get a jumbo-sized latte in, teamed with a specially designed glass teapot. The garnishes—egg, meat, truffle, pickled veg, tiny mushrooms—are placed in the cup; the teapot containing the hot water fits neatly on top of the cup, and the whole apparatus is brought to the table. When the waiter offers each diner a fob watch, they place it in the teapot, swirl it around to produce the gold-flecked broth, which they then pour into the cup. Now the dish followed a logic. Diners were given a teaspoon to eat with (either right- or left-handed, as a nod to Tweedledum and Tweedledee), but they were also free to drink

the last remnants straight from the cup. The dish really had turned into a tea party!

Of course, you can't have a tea party without nibbles, so it seemed essential that we serve some sort of sandwich alongside, preferably triangular and neatly trimmed. And as it happened, I knew of something with a Mad Hatterish strangeness that would fit suitably with the topsy-turvyness of the rest of the dish – the toast sandwich. Popularised by Mrs Beeton in her *Book of Household Management* (which was published in 1861, just four years before *Alice*), the toast sandwich appeared alongside beef-tea, egg wine and calf's foot broth in her chapter on food "very tempting to the appetite of an invalid".❖ Its very name made people do a double-take and, as such, it seemed exactly what the Mad Hatter might serve up, which made it the perfect foundation for an accompaniment to my mock turtle soup. Mrs Beeton gave the option of adding "a little pulled meat, or very fine slices of cold meat", but I had other ideas for making this an all-out Victorian extravaganza. I had read somewhere that a couple of Queen Victoria's favourite fillings were bone marrow and anchovies, so I took these as my starting point and gradually built up a layered sandwich with a number of complementary flavours and textures: egg yolk mustard, egg white mayonnaise, sliced truffle, cucumber (of course), home-made tomato ketchup. What added to the madness of it all was that, although I tried out many different sorts of bread, the only one that really worked was the mass-produced fluffy stuff because that gave the best texture contrast with the toast. So surrounding all these costly, top-quality ingredients (sometimes we also put a dollop of sustainable caviar on top of the mock-turtle egg because the Victorians were, at the time, the world's foremost consumers of the stuff) you have the least artisanal bread imaginable. Lewis Carroll would, I suspect, have treasured the juxtaposition.

Naturally, the "Queen Victoria Toast Sandwich", as it became known, needed a suitable piece of tableware for serving. I commissioned a tiered cake-stand with a difference. The tiers themselves were all set at slightly different angles, recalling that cartoon vision of plates stacked high until teetering impossibly. Each upright column separating one tier from the next was fashioned in the flared shape of a top hat. And in the uppermost one we tucked a feather and a piece of card marked "In this style 10/6"—a final reminder of the Mad Hatter and the tea party that had helped inspire the dish.

❖ *In November 2011, a couple of years after I started working on a toast sandwich, the Royal Society of Chemistry tried to revive Mrs Beeton's original, presenting it not as a food for invalids, but as the cheapest nutritious lunch available, and therefore ideal for a time of economic hardship. The RSC calculated that a piece of toast, seasoned and sandwiched by two slices of buttered bread, cost 7.5p, and offered £200 to the person who found a cheaper alternative. They were inundated with replies, of which about a hundred actually did turn out less expensive. The declared winner was an oatcake flavoured with peanut butter and beef dripping, which came in at 7p.*

MAD HATTER'S TEA PARTY
MOCK TURTLE SOUP

Makes 6 portions

Mock Turtle Soup at the Fat Duck

At the Fat Duck we use two types of centrifuge to reduce the stock to a syrup, which allows the stock to reduce without the application of heat. Here I have suggested an alternative to reduce your consommé more easily at home.

To make our gold consommé watches, we add bronze leaf gelatine to this concentrated stock syrup, along with a 10-year-old Madeira. The mixture is dispensed into the watch moulds and refrigerated until set. Once set, the watches are gently covered with gold leaf and refrigerated until service. The watch is lowered into 40g hot water and then dissolves, creating an aromatic and richly flavoured consommé.

Infused Beef Stock

1.35kg	Beef bones
400g	Sectioned oxtail
50g	Grapeseed oil
1.35g	Diced lean beef shin
650g	Peeled and finely sliced onions
5g	Lightly crushed star anise
650g	Peeled and finely sliced carrots
470g	Syrah red wine
300g	Cherry tomatoes, quartered

Preheat the oven to 180°C/350°F.

Combine the beef bones and oxtail in an even layer on a roasting tray and roast in the oven until golden brown, turning frequently.

Heat the grapeseed oil in a large pressure cooker and sear the diced shin in batches, until deep golden brown.

Remove the last of the browned shin, add the onions and star anise and allow the onions to caramelise. Once caramelised, add the carrots and continue to cook, stirring regularly until both are evenly coloured. Add the red wine and reduce to two-thirds of the original volume.

Add the roasted beef bones and oxtail and browned shin, followed by 2.4 litres cold water. Bring to the boil, skimming off all scum and impurities as necessary. Secure the lid of the pressure cooker and cook for 2 hours.

Allow the pressure cooker to depressurise and the stock to cool slightly before opening the lid. Pass through a fine-mesh sieve and refrigerate overnight.

Remove the fat from the surface of the stock and allow to come to room temperature. For the next step the stock should be cool, but not gelled.

Whisk together the stock and cherry tomatoes and allow the flavours to infuse for 20 minutes. Strain the infused beef stock through a fine-mesh sieve and refrigerate until needed. It should yield 2.5kg.

Mushroom Stock

280g	10-year-old Madeira
140g	Unsalted butter, cubed and at room temperature
1kg	Button mushrooms, cleaned
10g	Thyme
4g	Black peppercorns

Place the Madeira in a saucepan over a moderate heat, flame the alcohol and reduce to a syrup. Set aside.

Melt half the butter in a large pressure cooker and add half the mushrooms. Cook over a medium heat until well caramelised, then remove the caramelised mushrooms and set aside. Deglaze the pressure cooker with a dash of water; pour out and reserve this water.

Repeat this process with the second half of butter and the remaining mushrooms.

Make a secure muslin parcel with the thyme and black peppercorns and add to the pressure cooker along with the caramelised mushrooms, deglazing liquid, Madeira syrup and 2.1 litres cold water. Secure the lid of the pressure cooker and cook on full pressure for 30 minutes.

Allow the lid of the pressure cooker to depressurise and the stock to cool slightly before opening and strain through a fine-mesh sieve. Allow to cool and remove the fat that accumulates on the surface.

Transfer the strained stock to a large, clean saucepan and bring to the boil. Reduce to 700g, then allow to cool. Refrigerate until needed.

Clear Consommé

2.5kg	Reserved infused beef stock
700g	Reserved reduced mushroom stock
25g	Mushroom ketchup
420g	Lustau Solera Sherry
335g	White soy sauce

Combine all the ingredients and divide into 4 large sous-vide bags. Place all the bags in the freezer until frozen solid.

Place 2 perforated trays over deep containers and cover each tray with a fine-mesh filter bag or double layer of muslin. Empty the contents of each frozen bag on to the prepared trays.

Allow the stock to defrost and ice-filter in the fridge (approximately 2–3 days).

Once the stock has completely defrosted, discard the natural gelatine and impurities that have collected in the bag, and reserve the clear consommé that has filtered. It should yield approximately 2.6kg clear consommé.

(continued overleaf)

Mock Turtle Consommé

| 2.6kg | Reserved clear consommé |
| 60g | 10-year-old Madeira |

Place the consommé in a large saucepan and reduce to 1.75kg over a gentle heat. Remove the saucepan from the heat and stir in the Madeira.

This recipe yields more consommé than required for 6 portions, but it freezes well.

Mock Turtle Eggs

The Yolk

400g	Swede juice
6–8	Drops red food colouring
2.5g	Salt
20g	Chardonnay vinegar
0.9g	LT-100 (high-acyl gellan)

Gently heat a clean, dry sauce dispenser in a warm oven and ensure the tray of egg moulds is at hand. The egg moulds we use are plastic hemispherical chocolate moulds measuring 2.7cm deep and 3cm in diameter.

Pass the swede juice through a fine-mesh sieve. Add the red food colouring and mix to combine well. Place the coloured swede juice, salt and vinegar in a Thermomix and bring up to 90°c/194°F at low speed.

Add the LT-100 to the Thermomix and continue to blitz on a medium setting for 2 more minutes. Stop the Thermomix halfway through to scrape down the sides of the jug.

Immediately pour into the warmed sauce dispenser and dispense very small amounts into each egg mould. A drop with a diameter of 1cm will suffice.

Allow the mock egg yolk to set in the moulds for 10 minutes before dispensing the white.

The White

380g	Turnip juice
110g	Double cream
4g	Salt
10g	Fish sauce

0.8g	LT-100 (high-acyl gellan)
0.2g	Gellan F (low-acyl gellan)
0.8g	Guar gum

Gently heat a clean, dry sauce dispenser in a warm oven.

Pass the turnip juice through a fine-mesh sieve and add to a Thermomix along with the double cream, salt and fish sauce. Bring up to 90°c/194°F at low speed. Add the LT-100, gellan F and guar gum and continue to blitz on a medium setting for 2 more minutes.

Immediately pour into the warmed sauce dispenser and dispense the egg white on to the set yolks to fill the moulds. Place in the fridge to set.

Carefully unmould when ready to assemble and serve yolk-side up.

Pickled Turnip and Cucumber

200g	Chardonnay vinegar
4g	Salt
2g	Sugar
1	Peeled turnip, diced into 5cm cubes
1	Peeled cucumber, sliced into 5mm slices

Combine the vinegar, salt and sugar in a small saucepan and heat until the salt and sugar have dissolved. Divide the pickling juice between 2 bowls and set aside until needed.

Add the diced turnip to the first bowl of pickle juice and allow to pickle for 15 minutes. Drain and set aside.

Place the sliced cucumber in a sous-vide bag, ensuring it is lying flat and in a single layer. Seal the bag in a chamber vacuum sealer under full pressure. Pierce the bag several times and repeat the process twice more.

Remove the compressed cucumber slices and dice into 5mm cubes. Add to the second bowl of pickling liquid and allow to pickle for 15 minutes. Remove, drain and set aside.

The turnip and cucumber should be pickled no more than 30 minutes before serving.

Toast Sandwich

Gastrique

150g	Lustau Solera sherry
50g	Sherry vinegar
75g	White caster sugar
100g	Oloroso sherry

Place all the ingredients in a small saucepan and gently simmer over a medium heat until 79° Brix.

Remove from the heat and allow to cool. Scoop off the foamed head and pour the syrup into a squeezable dispensing bottle or piping bag until ready to assemble the sandwich.

Tomato Ketchup

2.5kg	Tinned plum tomatoes in juice
150g	Peeled and chopped onions
5g	Peeled garlic
1g	Ground ginger
0.4g	Five-spice powder
	Cayenne pepper
20g	Dijon mustard
1g	Salt
30g	Icing sugar

Place the tomatoes and all juices into a saucepan and bring to the boil. Cover with a cartouche and reduce the heat to a simmer. Allow the mixture to simmer for 10 minutes before removing from the heat and gently passing through a sieve. Gently pass the mixture through a second fine-mesh sieve, but do not crush the tomato seeds or skins, as this may cause bitterness.

Return the passed tomato juice to a clean saucepan and add the remaining ingredients, including a pinch of cayenne pepper, except the icing sugar. Bring to a rapid simmer and allow the mixture to reduce by half.

Remove the mixture from the heat and pass through a fine-mesh sieve. Return the mixture to a clean saucepan once again and add the sugar. Reduce to the consistency of ketchup (yielding approximately 210g), and remove from the heat. Allow to cool completely and refrigerate until needed. The ketchup can be frozen in batches.

Bone Marrow Salad

50g	**Rendered bone marrow (see page 79)**
2g	**Sherry vinegar**
2g	**Smoked anchovies**
2g	**Salted capers**
2g	**Chives**
2g	**Flatleaf parsley**
5g	**Peeled shallots**

Bring the rendered bone marrow to room temperature and use a small whisk to whip it to a light, creamy consistency. Add the sherry vinegar and mix to combine well.

Finely brunoise all the elements and gently combine with the bone marrow.

Mayonnaise Base

1	**Egg**
30g	**Pasteurised egg yolk**
10g	**Pasteurised egg white**
17g	**Dijon mustard**
25g	**Sherry vinegar**
350g	**Grapeseed oil**

Place the egg in a small saucepan of cold water over a high heat. Remove the egg after 5 minutes and plunge into iced water.

Combine this part-cooked egg, the pasteurised egg yolk, pasteurised egg white and Dijon mustard in a small bowl. Add half the sherry vinegar. Combine well, then transfer to a deep-sided container.

Process with a hand blender, gradually add the grapeseed oil until fully emulsified. Add the remaining sherry vinegar to loosen it slightly. You will need 250g.

Egg White Mayonnaise

14g	**Chives**
250g	**Reserved mayonnaise base**
300g	**Hard-boiled egg white, diced into 3mm cubes**
	Truffle oil
	Sherry vinegar
	Salt

Finely chop the chives and fold them into the mayonnaise along with the diced egg white. Season with the truffle oil, sherry vinegar and salt. This recipe yields much more mayonnaise than is required for the sandwiches, but it is delicious and can be stored in the fridge for use on other dishes.

Egg Yolk Mustard

65g	**Hard-boiled egg yolk (approximately 4 eggs)**
65g	**Sweet mustard (preferably Savora)**

Pass the hard-boiled egg yolk through a fine-mesh sieve into a small bowl and add the mustard, combining well. Pass again through a clean fine-mesh sieve and refrigerate until needed.

Assembling the Sandwich

6	**Fresh white bread slices**
3	**Well-toasted white bread slices**
	Reserved egg mayonnaise
1	**Whole black truffle, finely sliced**
	Reserved gastrique
	Reserved egg yolk mustard
2	**Peeled and cored cucumbers, finely sliced lengthways**
	Reserved tomato ketchup
	Reserved bone marrow salad

Remove the crusts from the bread and the toast. Use a small heavy tray or large metal spatula to flatten the toast pieces into super-thin slices.

Spread the egg mayonnaise evenly on 3 of the slices of bread. Top with the finely sliced black truffle and carefully squeeze the gastrique in a zigzag on top of the truffle.

Thinly spread the egg yolk mustard on the remaining 3 slices of bread, and evenly place the cucumber slices on top. Trim off any overlapping cucumber.

Carefully spread a thin layer of tomato ketchup on one side of the toast, and place the toast ketchup-side down on to the bread slices with the egg mayonnaise, truffle and gastrique.

Spread the bone marrow salad on top of the toast and place the bread slices containing the egg yolk mustard cucumber-side down on to the toast.

Ensure the slices are lined up neatly and trim any edges if necessary.

Slice the 3 sandwiches into quarters diagonally, with each sandwich yielding 4 neat, triangular sections. Allow 2 portions per person.

Elements in the Mock Turtle Soup Bowl

6	**Reserved mock turtle eggs**
	Brined and cooked ox tongue (see page 378), diced into 5mm cubes
	Whole black truffle, diced into 5mm cubes
	Reserved pickled turnip and cucumber
	Golden enoki mushrooms
	Black mustard seeds
	Micro-parsley

When ready to serve, carefully remove the mock turtle eggs from their moulds and place each egg in the centre of a small bowl. Arrange alternating cubes of ox tongue, black truffle, cucumber and turnips in a circular fashion surrounding the egg. Top the egg with the enoki mushrooms and several mustard seeds and garnish with micro-parsley.

To Serve

12	**Reserved toast sandwiches**
6	**Dressed soup bowls**
330g	**Reserved warm consommé**

All the elements should be served at the same time. The warm broth should be poured into the dressed soup bowl, in which the mock turtle egg nestles between the diced elements.

The sandwiches are served alongside the soup to complete the tea party.

THE MOCK TURTLE'S STORY

Turtle soup reached the height of its popularity in 19th century Britain but because turtle meat was prohibitively expensive and difficult to import, an alternative 'mock' turtle soup was developed using calves' head and feet. This is why the Mock Turtle in *Alice in Wonderland* has the body and shell of a turtle and the head, tail and feet of a calf.

GLOSSARY

Brix
A scale, measured in degrees, that gives the amount of sucrose dissolved in water. It is measured by a refractometer, and represents the sucrose as a percentage of the total. For example, 100g of a 25° Brix simple syrup contains 25g sucrose dissolved in 75g water.

Charcoal powder
A commercially available, natural, non-toxic, tasteless and odourless product often used for medicinal purposes. Also known as activated charcoal or carbon.

Curing salt
Usually a mixture of table salt and sodium nitrate, used in food preservation to preserve the colour of meat and prevent spoilage by bacteria.

Freeze-dried strawberry powder
A powder made from pure strawberries, used as a flavouring and colouring. Available from specialist suppliers.

Freeze-dried yoghurt pieces
Yoghurt that has been freeze-dried into small, crispy pieces, used for their intense flavour and texture. Available from specialist suppliers.

Gellan
A multi-functional hydrocolloid that can be used as a stabiliser, a gelling agent and as a way of altering texture and creating suspensions. It is often used in preparations that must be heated to high temperatures that gelatine would not withstand. It comes in low-acyl (gellan F) and high-acyl (gellan LT-100) forms, which have different but sometimes complementary applications. Gellan F melts at a higher temperature than gellan LT-100, and is more sensitive to the mineral content of a liquid during dissolution.

Isomalt
A type of sweetening agent made from beet sugar, which can be used to make tuiles and sugar glasses. It is related to sucrose but has a less sweet taste, and does not absorb as much moisture.

Kabosu
A citrus fruit, related to the yuzu, which is used in Japanese cooking.

Malic acid
The principal acid in apples, which also occurs in other fruits. It can trigger a high saliva response and thus augment the impression of juiciness.

Maltodextrin
A type of saccharide that can replace sugar and is available in several forms. It can be used to create body and texture, and to prevent crystallisation. It is available as granules or a fine powder, with a dextrose equivalent ranging from two to twenty.

Pacojet
A machine that can shave a block of ice to a very fine powder and is used to make ultra-smooth purées.

Pectin jaune
A food agent used as a texture and gelling agent. It can be used in high-sugar preparations with fruits. Unlike Pectin NH, it is not thermo-reversible.

Pectin NH
A form of low-methoxyl pectin that can be used to set gels with low acidity and low levels of dissolved solids. It is thermo-reversible.

Sodium caseinate
A protein naturally found in milk, in which the calcium ions have been replaced by sodium. It is widely used in the dairy industry for its ability to absorb water and fats, as well as its foaming and emulsifying properties.

Sodium citrate
The sodium salt of citric acid, a sequestrant (stabilising food agent) that can reduce calcium ions and lower calcium levels. It is also widely used as a food agent for flavour and as a preservative, as well as a stabiliser for emulsified fats.

Soy lecithin
A complex mixture of phospholipids that have emulsifying properties, which is derived from soya beans. It can be used to make liquid chocolate more tolerant of water, or to improve the foaming of water-based sauces.

Spray-dried apple
Vacuum-dried apple juice granules that are used to add flavour. Available from specialist suppliers.

Thermomix
A machine that can blend or process a foodstuff while heating it, which is invaluable when making fluid gels.

Transglutaminase
An enzyme that catalyses a bond between lysine and glutamine, two amino acids that can be found in proteins, and makes them adhere. It can be used for binding and sticking together proteins.

RECIPE GUIDELINES

✤

❧ Before embarking on a recipe, it's a good idea to read through it a couple of times and visualise what's involved, as some of the processes are complicated or take more than a day to prepare.

❧ Precision is vital to this style of cooking. To reproduce the recipes accurately, use the best-quality ingredients you can find and monitor heat with an oven thermometer and digital probe. For some of the dishes you will need a very precise set of digital scales. All the recipes have been carefully tested, so when the instructions call for a very specific amount, such as 0.7g, it's because such exactitude is necessary to get the best results, and a variation of as little as 0.1g will make a difference.

❧ Unless otherwise indicated, dishes serve six people. In order for ingredients to be mixed, blended or processed effectively, it has sometimes been necessary to direct the cook to make a larger quantity than needed for the recipe. With some of these preparations—stocks, for example—the excess can be frozen in batches. With others, such as fluid gels or mayonnaise, you'll need to use a little culinary ingenuity and think of other dishes in which you might use the surplus. Make sure you keep in mind the shelf-life of the ingredients involved—most items should be refrigerated and used within 2–3 days.

❧ In general, in ingredients lists, the amount requested is the weight after coring, peeling, trimming and so on. With thyme and rosemary, unless otherwise stated, the amount refers to sprigs, not picked leaves. Whenever possible, chop the herbs just before adding them in order to retain maximum freshness. With liquids, the amount requested is the weight after it has been strained of pips and pulp, if necessary.

❧ To make the stocks according to the recipe instructions, you will need a 12-litre pressure cooker. Always let the pressure cooker depressurise before opening the lid; it's safer that way, and ensures that you hold on to many aromas that would otherwise be lost.

❧ When bringing a mixture up to temperature in a Thermomix (particularly when dissolving gelling agents), it's best to double check the temperature using a digital probe.

❧ Unless otherwise stated, eggs are large and free range, salt is table salt and pepper is freshly ground black pepper. In recipes that call for commercially produced purées or essential oils, buy the best quality products you can find. Some of the dishes require specialist ingredients and equipment, but everything used in the recipes is available online.

BIBLIOGRAPHY

Detailed here are the books I found most valuable during the writing of this book. The first section lists the sources of the historical recipes that inspired me. In general I consulted editions in the British Library, but all of these books can be obtained from online bookshops. Many of them can also be viewed online either at www.gutenberg.org or www.hearthcook.com.

The second section lists the books I used to gain a better understanding of the context of particular periods. These range from broad accounts of British history and biographies of celebrated chefs to entertaining pieces on the pig, the pineapple and Pepys at table. If you're looking to learn more about British culinary history, they offer a great starting point.

Primary Sources

Anon., *The Forme of Cury*, 1390

Thomas Austin (ed.), *Two Fifteenth-century Cookery-Books: Harleian MS 279 & Harleian MS 4016*, 1888

Antonin Carême, *L'art de la cuisine française au dix-neuvième siècle*, 1833–44

Charles Carter, *The Complete Practical Cook*, 1730

Charles Carter, *The Compleat City and Country Cook*, 1732

Mrs Margaret Dods, *The Cook and Housewife's Manual*, 1826

Theodore Francis Garrett, *The Encyclopaedia of Practical Cookery*, 1892

Mary Kettilby, *A Collection of Above Three Hundred Receipts In Cookery, Physick and Surgery*, 1714

Patrick Lamb, *Royal Cookery* (3rd edition), 1726

W.M., *The Queen's Closet Opened* (4th edition), 1658

Charlotte Mason, *The Lady's Assistant for Regulating and Supplying her Table* (3rd edition), 1777

Robert May, *The Accomplisht Cook*, 1660

John Nott, *The Cook's and Confectioner's Dictionary*, 1723

William Rabisha, *The Whole Body of Cookery Dissected*, 1661

Maria Eliza Rundell, *A New System of Domestic Cookery* (revised edition), 1808

Alexis Soyer, *The Gastronomic Regenerator*, 1846

E. Smith, *The Compleat Housewife*, 1727

A.W., *A Book of Cookrye*, 1591

J. H. Walsh, *The English Cookery Book*, 1858

Hannah Wolley, *The Queen-like Closet or Rich Cabinet*, 1670

Secondary Sources

Ken Albala, *Eating Right in the Renaissance*, University of California Press, 2002

Fran Beauman, *The Pineapple: King of Fruits*, Chatto & Windus, 2005

Maggie Black, *The Medieval Cookbook*, British Museum Press, 2012

Maggie Black, Jane Renfrew, Jennifer Stead and Peter Brears, *Food & Cooking in Britain*, English Heritage, 1985

Peter Brears, *Tudor Cookery: Recipes & History*, English Heritage, 2003

Asa Briggs, *A Social History of England*, Penguin, 1985

Susan Campbell, *A History of Kitchen Gardening*, Frances Lincoln, 2005

Lizzie Collingham, *Curry: A Tale of Cooks and Conquerors*, Vintage, 2006

Kate Colquhoun, *Taste: The Story of Britain through its Cooking*, Bloomsbury, 2007

Ruth Cowen, *Relish: The Extraordinary Life of Alexis Soyer, Victorian Celebrity Chef*, Phoenix, 2007

Andrew Dalby, *Dangerous Tastes: The Story of Spices*, British Museum Press, 2000

Alan Davidson, *The Oxford Companion to Food*, Oxford University Press, 1991

Ivan Day, *Ice Cream*, Shire Publications, 2011

George Dodd, *The Food of London: A Sketch of the Chief Varieties, Sources of Supply and Machinery of Distribution of the Food for a Community of Two Millions and a Half*, London, 1856

Christopher Driver and Michelle Berriedale-Johnson, *Pepys at Table: Seventeenth Century Recipes for the Modern Cook*, Bell & Hyman, 1984

J. C. Drummond and Anne Wilbraham, *The Englishman's Food: Five Centuries of English Diet*, Pimlico, 1991

John Evelyn, *Acetaria: A Discourse of Sallets*, Dodo Press, 2007

Rachael Field, *Irons in the Fire: A History of Cooking Equipment*, Crowood, 1984

Paul Freedman, *Food: The History of Taste*, Thames & Hudson, 2007

Hannah Glasse, *First Catch Your Hare: The Art of Cookery Made Plain and Easy (1747)*, Prospect Books, 2005

Jane Grigson, *English Food*, Penguin, 1992

Miles Hadfield, *A History of British Gardening*, Penguin, 1985

Bridget Ann Henish, *Fast and Feast: Food in Medieval Society*, Pennsylvania State University Press, 1976

Christopher Hibbert, *The Story of England*, Phaidon Press, 1992

Christopher Hibbert, *The English: A Social History 1066–1945*, HarperCollins, 1994

Constance B. Hieatt, *An Ordinance of Pottage*, Prospect Books, 1988

Constance B. Hieatt and Sharon Butler (eds), *Curye on Inglisch: English Culinary Manuscripts of the Fourteenth Century*, Oxford University Press, 1985

Ronald Hutton, *The Stations of the Sun: A History of the Ritual Year in Britain*, Oxford University Press, 1996

John Keay, *The Honourable Company: A History of the English East India Company*, HarperCollins, 1991

Ian Kelly, *Cooking for Kings: The Life of Antonin Carême, the First Celebrity Chef*, Short Books, 2003

Gilly Lehmann, *The British Housewife: Cookery Books, Cooking and Society in Eighteenth-century Britain*, Prospect Books, 2003

Harold McGee, *On Food & Cooking: An Encyclopaedia of Kitchen Science, History and Culture*, Hodder & Stoughton, 2004

Stephen Mennell, *All Manners of Food: Eating and Taste in England and France from the Middle Ages to the Present*, Basil Blackwell, 1985

Kenneth O. Morgan (ed.), *The Oxford Illustrated History of Britain*, Oxford University Press, 1984

Sara Paston-Williams, *The Art of Dining: A History of Cooking & Eating*, The National Trust, 1993

Peter Ross, *The Curious Cookbook*, Mark Batty Publisher, 2012

Colin Spencer, *British Food: An Extraordinary Thousand Years of History*, Grub Street, 2002

Roy Strong, *The Story of Britain: A People's History*, Pimlico, 1998

Roy Strong, *Feast: A History of Grand Eating*, Jonathan Cape, 2002

Reay Tannahill, *Food in History*, Three Rivers Press, 1988

Robin Weir and Caroline Liddell, *Ices: The Definitive Guide*, Grub Street, 1995

Anne Willan, *Great Cooks and their Recipes: From Taillevent to Escoffier*, Pavilion, 1995

Anne Willan, *The Cookbook Library*, University of California Press, 2012

C. Anne Wilson, *Food & Drink in Britain: From the Stone Age to the 19th Century*, Academy Chicago Publishers, 1991

C. Anne Wilson (ed.), *'The Appetite and the Eye': Visual Aspects of Food and its Presentation within their Historical Context*, Edinburgh University Press, 1991

C. Anne Wilson (ed.), *Waste Not, Want Not: Food Preservation from Early Times to the Present Day*, Edinburgh University Press, 1991

C. Anne Wilson (ed.), *Luncheon, Nuncheon and other Meals: Eating with the Victorians*, Leeds, 1992

C. Anne Wilson (ed.), *'Liquid Nourishment': Potable Foods and Stimulating Drinks: 5th Symposium on Food History*, Edinburgh University Press, 1993

Julian Wiseman, *A History of the British Pig*, Duckworth, 1986

ACKNOWLEDGEMENTS

First, I'd like to thank the food historians Marc Meltonville, Richard Fitch and Ivan Day, who have been incredibly generous with their time and expertise. Their enthusiasm for, and commitment to, culinary history underpin this book, though any mistakes or misapprehensions in the text are of course entirely my own.

Next, I'd like to thank my agent, Zoë Waldie at Rogers, Coleridge & White, for setting up and safeguarding this project; and my amazing team at Bloomsbury for dedicatedly turning my words and ideas into the best book they could possibly be. Richard Atkinson and Natalie Hunt had the vision and sensitivity to steer everything in the right direction; Peter Dawson created a beautiful book design with the able assistance of Louise Evans, and Marina Asenjo did a spectacular number on the production. I have to acknowledge the terrific job of copyediting and overseeing the text done by Laura Gladwin; the gimlet-eyed proof-reading of Sarah Barlow; the intelligent indexing of Hilary Bird, and the behind-the-scenes contributions of Xa Shaw Stewart, and of Rachel Calder of the Sayle Literary Agency.

I have to mention of the work of my historical researcher, Polly Russell, who haunted the British Library on my behalf, piecing together information from old books and manuscripts and dealing skilfully with whatever arcane requests I sent in her direction. Every project has one person without whom it would never have happened. For this book, Polly's the one. I also have to give a special mention to my co-writer, Pascal Cariss. There was a huge amount of information that had to go in this book, from research in libraries and reference books, from meetings and collaborations with historians, and from the technical side of recipe development. Pascal somehow succeeded in bringing all this information together to produce what I think is a magnificent read. He has an incredible knack for making the complicated understandable without dumbing down the detail. Over the years he has been continually bombarded by my brain-dumping and has managed to decipher all of it—no easy task! His patience, enthusiasm and perseverance never cease to amaze me.

The visual side was, from the start, a crucial part of the concept. I've been fortunate enough to have the most gifted and creative team working on this that you could possibly imagine. Every time Romas Foord showed me one of his photographs for the old recipes, I was blown away by its beauty and its cleverness. Part of this is down to the stylist, Polly Webb-Wilson, who seemed entirely unfazed by requests for anything from a pig's head to an eighteenth-century armoire, and always came up with the goods. As for Dave McKean's fabulous illustrations— what can I say? The man is a genius. Once I knew he was on board, I was sure this book would be lifted to another level, and he's exceeded my expectations!

At the Fat Duck, dozens of people have been involved in this project. I'd like to single out Monya Kilian Palmer for not only taking responsibility for the day-to-day management of the book (the very definition of a thankless task), but also turning the historic recipes into real food on a plate. Thanks must also go to Claire Gibbs, Melissa Lyons and, in particular, Fiona Moore for keeping the whole show on the road; and to my PA, Deborah Chalcroft, for organising my time. At the heart of this book, of course, are the modern recipes, and they wouldn't have come to fruition without the extraordinary imagination, resourcefulness and determination of my head chef at the Fat Duck, Jonny Lake; my head pastry chef at the Fat Duck, Hideko Kawa; my head chef at the Hind's Head, Kevin Love; my head pastry chef at Dinner, Daniel Svensson; and, above all, my head chef at Dinner, Ashley Palmer-Watts, who not only helped develop many of the recipes, but also did an absolutely brilliant job of masterminding the modern recipe photography as well. I have to acknowledge, too, the skill, support and inventiveness of James "Jocky" Petrie, Otto Romer, Tom Allen, Dale Osborne, Jonny Glass, Allan Herrick, Evan Moore, Deiniol Pritchard and Neil Snowball, who worked tirelessly on recipe development, photo shoots and more. Thank you all.

INDEX

In memory of Jorge and Maggie –
two truly great men and truly great chefs who lit up
everything they touched and inspired everyone they met.

First published in Great Britain and the United States in 2013

This edition published in 2014

Text copyright © 2013 Cape Press Ltd.
Written in cooperation with Pascal Cariss

Photography © 2013 Romas Foord
Illustrations © 2013 Dave McKean

50 Bedford Square, London WC1B 3DP
1385 Broadway, New York, NY 10018
387 George Street, Sydney, NSW 2000

Bloomsbury is a trademark of Bloomsbury Publishing Plc.

Bloomsbury Publishing, London, New Delhi, New York
and Sydney

A CIP catalogue record for this book is available from
the British Library.

Library of Congress Cataloging-in-Publication Data
has been applied for.

ISBN: 978 1 4088 5757 1

10 9 8 7 6 5 4 3 2 1

Design: Peter Dawson, Grade Design
Artwork: Dave McKean
Photography: Romas Foord
Props styling: Polly Webb Wilson
Index: Hilary Bird
Historical researcher: Polly Russell

Printed and bound in South China

All papers used by Bloomsbury Publishing are natural, recyclable
products made from wood grown in well-managed forests.
The manufacturing processes conform to the environmental
regulations of the country of origin.

www.bloomsbury.com/hestonblumenthal
www.bloomsburyusa.com

The text for this book is set in Adobe Caslon.

Note on the coat of arms: After being appointed OBE in 2006, Heston Blumenthal became eligible for a coat of arms. A design was duly developed that incorporates references to his life and symbols of the five senses: hands for touch, lyres for sound, an apple for taste, a magnifying glass for sight (and scientific examination), and lavender for smell and to recall the moment when he was inspired to become a chef, dining in the lavender-scented gardens of a restaurant in the South of France. The duck alludes to his restaurant, and the three roses allude both to the heraldic Tudor rose of England and to the fact that the Fat Duck has gained three Michelin stars.